T5-AXT-229

Publisher
David P. Ewing

Associate Publisher
Tim Huddleston

Acquisitions Editor
Brad Koch

Managing Editor
Cheri Robinson

Developmental Editor
B. Rustin Gesner

Production Editor
Peter Kuhns

Editors
Lisa D. Wagner
Nora Loechel

Acquisitions Assistant
Geneil Breeze

Editorial Secretary
Karen Opal

Technical Editor
Kurt Hampe

Book Design and Production
Scott Cook, Christine Cook, Tim Groeling, Carrie Keesling,
Joe Ramon, Kelli Widdifield, Allan Wimmer

Proofreaders
Terri Edwards, Carla Hall-Batton,
Suzanne Tully, Julie Walker

Indexed by
Loren Malloy, Tina Trettin

ABOUT THE AUTHOR

Frank Conner is the coordinator of the CAD/CAM/CNC program at Grand Rapids Junior College where he is an Applied Technology Specialist and Instructor. Mr. Conner was chairperson of the committee that developed the *AutoCAD Certified Operator's Examination* and also is a private consultant to the CAD/CAM industry. He attended Southwestern Michigan College, Grand Valley State University, and received his master's degree from Norwich University. Mr. Conner is listed in *Who's Who in the Computer Industry* and *Who's Who in Education*; he is a founding member of the Society of Manufacturing Engineers Local Executive Committee, and is the chair of the Forest Hills Public Schools Advisory Board on Technology and Programming. Mr. Conner has authored four books on AutoSketch and has developed several training manuals relating to the CAD/CAM/CNC industry.

THE
AUTOCAD®
TUTOR

Frank Conner

New Riders Publishing, Carmel, Indiana

The AutoCAD Tutor

By Frank Conner

Published by:
New Riders Publishing
11711 N. College Ave., Suite 140
Carmel, IN 46032 USA

Copyright©1992 by New Riders Publishing

Printed in the United States of America 1 2 3 4 5 6 7 8 9 0

Frank, Conner, 1959-

AutoCAD Tutor / Frank Conner.
   p. cm.
Includes index.
ISBN 1-56205-081-8 : $29.95
   1. Computer graphics. 2. AutoCAD (Computer file) I. Title
T385.C654 1992
620'.0042'02855369—dc20
   92-28884

CIP

ACKNOWLEDGMENTS

Special thanks to the many dedicated individuals who gave extraordinary efforts to developing and editing *The AutoCAD Tutor*.

To begin, thanks to Tim Huddleston and Rusty Gesner. Tim and Rusty assisted me in developing the direction and format that became the final book. In addition, Tim gave helpful assistance in the final edit of the book.

Special thanks to Tim Huddleston (again) and Rob Tidrow, who contributed to the first edition.

No author can complete a book without an excellent editing staff. Peter Kuhns, Nora Loechel, and Lisa D. Wagner have done an outstanding job. Thanks to them for putting in many hours to develop the final product in front of you.

In addition, special thanks to Kurt Hampe, the technical editor for *The AutoCAD Tutor*.

Thanks to Geniel Breeze who coordinated the stages of author development and ensured that all Federal Express packages from New Riders reached me and that my packages reached the appropriate staff at New Riders.

I thank my wife, Raenell. Because of our time constraint to meet the new school year, she did not see me many evenings and weekends. I thank Reanell for both her support and understanding.

I know that we have developed an outstanding product that fills a strong void in the AutoCAD learning environment. I hope this book adds to your success as an AutoCAD user and prepares you for a long and successful career.

TRADEMARK ACKNOWLEDGMENTS

WARNING AND DISCLAIMER

This book is designed to provide information about the AutoCAD computer program. Every effort has been made to make this book as complete and accurate as possible, but no warranty or fitness is implied.

The information is provided on an "as is" basis. The author and New Riders Publishing shall have neither liability nor responsibility to any person or entity with respect to any loss or damages arising from the information contained in this book or from the use of the disks or programs that may accompany it.

TABLE OF CONTENTS

3 Creating Your First AutoCAD Drawing 43

4 Drawing a Gasket 71

6 Drawing a Gear 149

7 Creating an Electrical Schematic Diagram 207

INTRODUCING THE AUTOCAD TUTOR

AutoCAD is the most popular computer-aided drafting (CAD) program in the world today. Hundreds of thousands of people use AutoCAD in their daily work; many use AutoCAD as the primary tool of their profession. As a drawing program, AutoCAD enables you to draw with amazing speed and accuracy, and to create drawings that are very simple or extremely complicated. You can use AutoCAD to draw a plain two-dimensional box or to create a three-dimensional model of a space station. AutoCAD enables you to draw the head of a pin at its actual size, or to draw the solar system in full scale. In short, if you can imagine an object, you can draw it in AutoCAD.

AutoCAD, however, can be used for more than just drawing. The program has found a home in hundreds of different applications—from basic design and drafting work, to architectural and engineering design, to geographic and geologic mapping, to computer-aided manufacturing and machining. New applications surface nearly every month for the program, and developers have created hundreds of add-in programs to customize AutoCAD for many specific and unique uses.

AutoCAD's versatility results from its tremendous power and flexibility. This flexibility means that very few AutoCAD users work with the program in exactly the same way. Nevertheless, the beauty of AutoCAD is that basically all AutoCAD users work with the same set of concepts and commands. After you master a handful of commands and concepts, you can be productive with AutoCAD. You then can customize the program in many ways to make your work easier.

New users are easily intimidated by AutoCAD's size and power. Remember, however, that AutoCAD is a drawing program at heart. As you work through this book's exercises, you will find that using AutoCAD is no great mystery. The program is easy to learn, and soon you will discover that you, too, can use AutoCAD to draw practically anything you can imagine.

How To Use this Book

The AutoCAD Tutor is designed to teach you how to use AutoCAD, and to show you how the program can be used by drafters and designers in a variety of drawing disciplines. When you successfully complete all the exercises in this workbook, you too will be a productive AutoCAD user. In addition, you will be prepared to pass the AutoCAD Certification Examination. To help you achieve these goals, this workbook offers a series of self-guided tutorials that can be used in a classroom environment under an instructor's supervision or as a self-teaching aid.

First-time users of a computer program learn more rapidly when they are able to see and experience the way commands are applied. That is why this book introduces AutoCAD concepts and commands by showing you how to use them in real-world applications. The book simulates the contents of the AutoCAD screen to help you see what is happening when you enter commands, choose options, and create drawings. This format minimizes the fear and frustration associated with using a software package as powerful as AutoCAD.

AutoCAD is such a large program that this book teaches you only the most useful commands—those that give you a general knowledge of the program. Although The AutoCAD Tutor does not teach all the AutoCAD commands or introduce every drawing technique, it does provide a foundation of basic information that you can use to become a productive AutoCAD user. When you become productive, you can expand your skills by learning about AutoCAD's more advanced functions, such as customizing menus and AutoLISP programming.

The AutoCAD Tutor is based on proven training techniques that have been applied for years in classroom situations. Take as much time as you need to work through each lesson and review difficult operations until you understand the concept or command being introduced. Many factors affect the speed at which you can do the exercises, such as the speed of your computer and your knowledge of computers and operating systems. Typically, a lesson should take about two hours to complete. This assumes that you are taking the time to learn each new concept, not just duplicate the keystrokes. Do not get discouraged if you need more than two hours to complete a lesson. Everyone learns at a different pace, and the time required to complete an exercise has no bearing on how well you eventually will use AutoCAD.

You can use this tutor as a learning tool for self instruction, classroom instruction, and industry training. Regardless of the learning environment, you should be ready to take the AutoCAD Certified Examination when you master all of the concepts in this book. If you pass the exam, you will be certified as an entry-level AutoCAD operator. Even if you do not take the exam, you probably will apply these skills in a business environment. If you do take the exam and pass it, however, you will have an official certification that verifies your newly attained AutoCAD skills.

LEARNING AUTOCAD THROUGH SELF INSTRUCTION

By using the workbook along with the AutoCAD program documentation, you can teach yourself to be an entry-level AutoCAD operator. The AutoCAD Tutor is designed to be used as a self-guided teaching tool—you can sit at your own computer and learn AutoCAD at your own pace. The text and exercises provide enough conceptual information and hands-on practice to develop quickly a working knowledge of AutoCAD. You can think of the text's explanations of commands and concepts as your teacher. The book's exercises act as a lab for practicing AutoCAD commands until you are comfortable with them.

LEARNING AUTOCAD IN A CLASSROOM ENVIRONMENT

In a classroom setting, this workbook acts as an application tool that supplements lectures and assigned readings and practice sessions. After your instructor introduces the concepts covered in a lesson, you should use the workbook to expand your understanding by actually using the commands in an exercise. If you are new to AutoCAD, you will master the program more thoroughly if you can see how a command is applied instead of simply hearing or reading about it.

LEARNING AUTOCAD IN AN INDUSTRY TRAINING ENVIRONMENT

In the fast-paced world of industry training, neither trainers nor trainees have time to fall behind. If you are using this book as part of an industry training course, you will learn to use AutoCAD in an intensive, hands-on environment. The *AutoCAD Student Workbook* provides the trainer with a logical format that introduces commands and concepts in an ordered manner. By using a guided tutorial, trainees can stay on task and work at the same pace. Further, this book helps document your learning process. It can be taken back to the office or home and used as a tool for continued practice and learning.

PREPARING FOR THE AUTOCAD CERTIFIED OPERATOR EXAMINATION

The *AutoCAD Certification Examination* is a national test that determines whether AutoCAD users have achieved the level of expertise they need to perform as entry-level AutoCAD operators. This workbook uses the same kinds of drawing exercises used in the test. To prepare for the examination, you should go through each of the exercises and make sure that you understand each command before moving on to the next lesson.

To pass the examination, you must have a complete understanding of AutoCAD's inquiry commands, as well as a sound mastery of the two-dimensional drawing and editing commands. *Inquiry commands* give you information on the drawing database (these commands are introduced in the second half of the workbook).

The first-level examination does not require you to draw in three dimensions, but by finishing lessons one through twelve, you will add 3D drawing to your repertoire of AutoCAD skills. These final lessons continue to build on your 2D drafting skills and your knowledge of commands. If your goal is to pass the *AutoCAD Certification Examination*, do not neglect the lessons on 3D. Although most AutoCAD drafters do not utilize the program's 3D capabilities, a knowledge of 3D increases your understanding of AutoCAD and of drafting and design. Further, your employer will place a higher value on your abilities if you possess 3D drafting skills.

ASSUMPTIONS ABOUT THE READER

The AutoCAD Tutor is designed to teach basic AutoCAD skills. When you are finished with the workbook, you should be able to perform any basic two-dimensional and some three-dimensional drafting tasks. This text, however, does not teach drawing or drafting techniques, nor does it teach the use a computer or a computer operating system.

The text assumes, therefore, that you have some training or experience in drafting or design. You should be familiar with basic drafting concepts and terms, and should understand the fundamentals of two-dimensional geometry. You do not need to be an expert in any of these areas to complete the workbook successfully or to become a certified AutoCAD user. If you do have such skills, however, you will find this book's exercises much easier to complete and understand.

The text also assumes that you have a basic working knowledge of computers and computer operating systems. AutoCAD is designed for a variety of hardware platforms and several different operating systems. For this reason, the text cannot discuss the "computer-specific" aspects of AutoCAD use. You do not need to be an expert in computers to use AutoCAD successfully, and no computer programming experience is required at all. You do, however, need to know how to turn on your computer, how to use floppy and hard disk drives, and how to perform certain tasks at the operating-system level. You should understand how directories and files work, for example, and you should know how to copy, delete, and rename files. If you are unfamiliar with computers, you need to learn about them before you attempt to learn AutoCAD.

HARDWARE REQUIREMENTS

As mentioned earlier, AutoCAD can run on a variety of hardware setups and under a number of different operating systems. For space reasons, this book cannot address AutoCAD's use on all types of systems. The text, therefore, assumes that you have a DOS-based computer system with the following components:

- An 80386- or 80486-based central processing unit with a math coprocessor and a hard disk drive

- A keyboard

- A pointing device, such as a mouse or a digitizing pad with a puck or a stylus

- A VGA color monitor

If your system differs from the one described here, you first need to make sure that it will support the AutoCAD program. If you are using a computer that is part of a classroom or industrial training environment, then it should run AutoCAD. Check with your instructor to make sure AutoCAD runs on your machine and familiarize yourself with the machine if you have not used it before.

If you are using your home or office computer, you may not be able to run AutoCAD. Check with your computer dealer to make sure the machine supports AutoCAD.

This book also assumes that AutoCAD already is loaded on your computer, and that the required peripheral devices (such as a mouse) also are installed. This book does not teach you how to install AutoCAD on a computer or how to configure a computer to work with AutoCAD. If you are using a computer that is part of a classroom or industrial training environment, then AutoCAD already should be loaded on the computer, and all the required devices should be hooked up. If you are using your home or office computer, see your Autodesk dealer for help with installing the program and configuring your machine.

CONVENTIONS USED IN THIS BOOK

This workbook uses a variety of typographical conventions to make your learning experience easier. These conventions follow the command structure employed by AutoCAD. Throughout the book, special type-faces represent AutoCAD's on-screen prompts and messages, and indicate the input you should type in response to those prompts and messages.

AutoCAD Prompts

AutoCAD continually displays prompts that ask you for information. In this book, all prompts appear in a special typeface, such as `Command:` or `From point:` to simulate their appearance on-screen. By following the prompts, you will understand what response is required by AutoCAD. Further, by matching the book's prompts with those appearing on-screen, you ensure that you are performing the correct operation for an exercise.

User Input

As an AutoCAD user, you must input information at the AutoCAD prompts. Occasionally, you type the information at the computer's keyboard; other times you use your pointing device to input the information. AutoCAD is both a menu- and prompt-driven system. You can use your pointing device to select commands from an on-screen menu, a pull-down menu, or a tablet overlay, or you can type the command. Unless specified otherwise, all menu selection is from the pull-down menus at the top of the drawing editor.

AutoCAD's menu system presents commands in a logical manner that you should have no trouble mastering. Commands that add new geometry to the drawing, for example, are located under the Draw menu—commands that edit geometry are found under the Modify menus. You learn about the menus in the workbook's early lessons. When an exercise instructs you to select a command or option from a menu, the instructions appear in *italic* type.

When the book shows you what to type, the required input appears in a bold special typeface. Examples are **LINE** or **@5<315**. Here, **LINE** is a command, and **@5<315** is input you would type in response to a prompt.

Entity Selection

You need to use your pointing device frequently in the exercises to select or pick parts of the drawing on-screen. When an exercise instructs you to select an entity or pick a location on-screen, the instructions appear in *italic* type. To pick entities or screen locations, use the pointing device to move the crosshair cursor or pickbox until it is on the correct item or location. Then press or click on the pointing device's pick button.

COMMAND SEQUENCES

Most of the exercises in this workbook are divided into separate, easy-to-follow steps. Each step is numbered, and many steps feature a command sequence to help you understand what is happening on the AutoCAD screen. A command sequence represents the AutoCAD prompts and tells you exactly what you should do in response to each prompt. Command sequences are divided into two columns: the first column features the AutoCAD prompts, and includes the responses you should make to the prompts; and the second column briefly explains what happens when you make the recommended response. The following command sequence shows you how these columns appear in an exercise:

Command: **LINE** ↵	Starts the LINE command
From point: **4,4** ↵	Starts the new line at the absolute coordinate 4,4
To point: **6,8** ↵	Ends the line at the absolute coordinate 6,8
To point: ↵	Ends the LINE command

Be sure to watch the command sequences closely as you work through each exercise. They help you ensure that you are at the right place in AutoCAD, and that you get the right results from the exercise.

BOXED INFORMATION

In each lesson, you will find special information that appears in boxes. Each lesson begins with a list of the objectives you should try to achieve in that lesson's exercises. Immediately following is another box, which lists the commands, subcommands, or system variables that are introduced in the lesson. This box shows you each command's proper name, and provides a quick explanation of the command's function.

Each lesson features a boxed list of tasks you need to complete to perform the exercise successfully. Use this list as a checklist to ensure that you complete all the steps before you go on to the next exercise.

From time to time, the text offers special information that stands apart from the current discussion or exercise. This type of information appears in a box under the heading "Note." Even though this special information may not help you in completing each exercise, it increases your understanding of the concept or command you are studying in the exercise.

Many AutoCAD commands feature options that enable you to use the commands in certain ways. When a lesson introduces a command that has a significant number of options, the options are listed in a special box, under the heading "Options." You can use this box as a reference when you are using the command and need to know an option's function.

TERMINOLOGY

The AutoCAD Student Workbook uses a specific terminology to instruct the reader to perform certain functions. These terms and definitions are as follows:

- ↵. Press the Enter key.

- Ⓐ, Ⓑ, Ⓒ, ... Bubble points are specific areas or lines in an AutoCAD figure that help to guide you through the creation of the lesson's drawing. Bubble points that appear in figures are referenced in the exercises.

- **Choose.** Invoke or select a menu or dialog box item. Use the input device to perform this function—highlight the item or place an arrow on the dialog box button and press the input device button.

- **Enter.** Type the specified text and press the Enter key. For example, *Enter* **RED** means to type the word **RED** at the appropriate prompt or in a dialog box.

- **Pick.** Move the pointer or crosshairs to a location on-screen and press the input device button.

- **Select.** To select an object, place the pick box on an entity and press the input device button.

- **Issue.** Enter a command name or choose it from the menu.

USING *THE AUTOCAD TUTOR DISK*

An optional disk is available with *The AutoCAD Tutor* that includes files of the finished drawings from each lesson. The disk also contains drawing files that you need to use for some of the review questions at the end of each lesson. One file is used in Lesson 9 to reduce the amount of drawing needed in the lesson. The completed lesson drawings are to be used as a reference—use them to see how the drawing should look on-screen.

To use the disk, you either can copy it onto your hard drive or use it directly from the floppy disk drive. If you use the files from a floppy disk drive, start AutoCAD then place *The AutoCAD Tutor Disk* in your computer's floppy disk drive. From within AutoCAD, choose File, then Open. Choose drive A (or B, depending on the configuration of your floppy disk drive), then the file, then OK.

If you want to work from the hard drive, copy *The AutoCAD Tutor Disk* drawing files into the desired directory of your hard disk drive. From within the drawing editor, Choose File,Open, the file name, then OK.

When the drawing appears on-screen, you can use it to complete the review questions or as a guide to creating your own drawings. When you are finished with the drawing, simply choose File,Save. To exit AutoCAD, choose File,Exit AutoCAD. You learn more about ending a drawing session in Lesson 2.

The AutoCAD Tutor Disk is intended to be a reference tool to help you learn drawing and editing tools in AutoCAD. For this reason, the drawings are coded so that the student cannot copy them and turn them in to an instructor as finished drawings. The coding, however, does not alter the looks of the drawing or affect AutoCAD in any way.

OTHER LEARNING RESOURCES

As you work through this book, you may find that some commands are not as easy to understand as others. Because this tutor does not go into great detail about AutoCAD commands and concepts, you should look to other resources for more information about the program. The first such resource is the *AutoCAD Reference Manual*, which is included in the AutoCAD program documentation. Although it is not a teaching tool, the manual does provide good documentation on all of AutoCAD's commands, subcommands, and system variables, and it features examples that show you how most of them can be used. Also included in the AutoCAD package is the *AutoCAD Tutorial*, which is helpful in introducing the AutoCAD drawing environment.

You also should investigate commercially available AutoCAD books, which examine the program in greater detail than this workbook. New Riders Publishing offers several general tutorial and reference books on AutoCAD, including *Inside AutoCAD Release 12*, and the *AutoCAD Reference Guide*. You can find these and other New Riders books at your local bookstore.

Another source of AutoCAD knowledge is an Authorized AutoCAD Training Center (ATC). These accredited educational institutions provide industry training and are certified by Autodesk, Inc., the maker of AutoCAD, as meeting a high level of educational quality. These training centers are required by contract to provide intensive short-term training for the professional environment. To find the ATC nearest you, contact your local AutoCAD dealer.

GETTING STARTED WITH AutoCAD

OVERVIEW

AutoCAD is the most popular CAD software in use today. One of the main reasons for AutoCAD's popularity is its user interface. The *user interface* connects the user with the software. AutoCAD's user interface, the Drawing Editor, is an electronic drafting table, where you use AutoCAD's commands to create and edit images and models.

AutoCAD users spend most of their time entering commands and creating geometry in the Drawing Editor. The Drawing Editor also enables the user to define new drawings, perform file management tasks, and print drawings. Although each of these additional functions complement AutoCAD, the real key to mastering the program is a solid understanding of AutoCAD's commands. A *command* is the method through which you communicate with AutoCAD. A command specifies that some action take place, such as a line drawn or a circle erased. The Drawing Editor would not function without the commands. The commands control what happens inside AutoCAD and enable you to perform a multitude of tasks, from drawing simple lines and arcs to editing complex drawings and creating three-dimensional models.

In addition to the drawing and editing commands, AutoCAD features aids and supplemental commands that help you use the software more effectively. These commands enable you to do such things as setting a grid for drawing lines and cleaning up the screen after a circle is erased. Such special commands enhance the programs' productivity and ease of use, and add functionality to the software.

AutoCAD enables you to input commands in a variety of ways. Many experienced AutoCAD users believe that the best way to input commands is to type them at the Command: prompt. This method of command entry is the most complete, because it requires you to respond to all of AutoCAD's prompts and messages, and that you be familiar with the commands. If you are not familiar with the commands or if you just do not like to type, you can use your computer's pointing device to select commands from the screen menu, the pull-down menus, or from a digitizer tablet overlay. Using the pull-down menus often accesses a dialog box that performs the same function as typing an AutoCAD command but with an easier, visual, point-and-pick method. Although this lesson focuses on typed input, you learn several methods of command input in subsequent lessons. As you become more familiar with the program, you can decide which method (or combination of methods) works best for you.

TOPICS COVERED IN THIS LESSON

In this lesson, you learn to do the following:

- Navigate the Drawing Editor
- Create simple entities
- Erase geometry
- Set up drawing aids
- Create a complete drawing
- End a drawing session

COMMANDS COVERED IN THIS LESSON

This lesson teaches you how to use the following AutoCAD commands:

- **CIRCLE.** Draws circles
- **COORDS (System variable).** Controls coordinate display at the top of the screen
- **ERASE.** Deletes entities from the drawing
- **GRID.** Displays a rectangular array of reference dots at user-defined increments
- **LINE.** Draws straight line segments
- **QSAVE (QUICK SAVE).** Saves the drawing without prompting for a file name
- **REDRAW.** Cleans up the current viewpoint by redrawing the screen
- **SAVE.** Saves the drawing file and returns to the Drawing Editor
- **SAVE AS.** Saves the drawing to disk with a specified name
- **SNAP.** Restricts the crosshairs' movement to a specified increment
- **TEXT.** Places user-defined text in the drawing

AutoCAD is a very powerful software package, comprising many simple and advanced commands. As you learn to use the software, however, you should not be overwhelmed by its extensiveness. Despite its size and complexity, remember that AutoCAD is basically a drawing tool. You can become productive with AutoCAD very quickly, and can learn the program at your own pace. This lesson shows you how easily you can get started using AutoCAD. The following exercises introduce the program's user interface by showing you how to navigate the Drawing Editor and how to draw simple figures.

Your goal in this lesson is to learn how to use the Drawing Editor to create the drawing shown in figure 2.1.

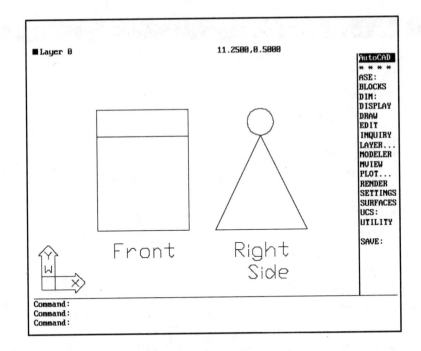

EXERCISE 1: NAVIGATING THE MAIN MENU AND DRAWING EDITOR

A few preliminary steps are necessary before you start drawing in AutoCAD. To begin a new drawing, you first must start AutoCAD. AutoCAD can be configured for many different *hardware platforms* (IBM-compatible computers, Macintosh computers, Sun workstations, and others) and *operating systems* (such as MS-DOS, Macintosh, and UNIX), so this book cannot instruct you on how to start the software on your specific system. Refer to your installation manual or ask the person who installed the software on your computer. To start AutoCAD on a DOS-based IBM PC, for example, simply type **ACAD** at the DOS prompt. On the other hand, if you have a Macintosh or AutoCAD for Windows, you might double-click on the AutoCAD icon. Regardless of your hardware platform or operating system, once you start AutoCAD, the Drawing Editor appears on-screen.

STARTING A NEW DRAWING

Step 1.0: Using the appropriate DOS command or process, start AutoCAD and access the Drawing Editor:

Start AutoCAD   Displays the Drawing Editor

LEARNING ABOUT THE DRAWING EDITOR

All the AutoCAD functions required to develop your drawings are performed inside the Drawing Editor. The AutoCAD Drawing Editor is made up of the following five areas (see figs. 2.2 and 2.3):

- **Status Line.** The status line runs across the top of the screen and displays the name of the current layer, snap and grid settings, and coordinate information.

- **Screen Menu.** This menu runs down the right edge of the AutoCAD Drawing Editor screen. Use the pointing device to select any command from the screen menu.

- **Command Prompt.** The prompt area is the location where AutoCAD displays command names as you type them or select them from a menu. AutoCAD also uses the prompt area to display messages and lists of options. You should constantly monitor the prompt area.

- **Pull-down Menu Bar.** When you move the crosshairs into the status line, the status line changes into the pull-down menu bar. The menu bar displays the names of AutoCAD's pull-down menus. Many of AutoCAD's commands are accessed from the pull-down menus.

- **Drawing Area.** This area is AutoCAD's "electronic drafting table," where you create and view your drawings. The crosshairs' cursor appears in the drawing area.

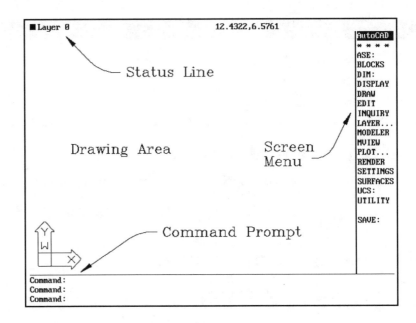

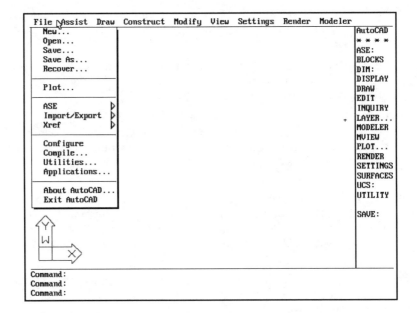

WORKING IN THE DRAWING EDITOR

Now that you are in the Drawing Editor, you should see the crosshairs' cursor somewhere on-screen. The *cursor* displays the position of the input devise on-screen. By moving the input device, the cursor moves correspondingly. Take a few moments to practice moving the cursor and getting used to the Drawing Editor and its parts.

Step 2.0: Move your input device, which can be a mouse, puck, or stylus. If the computer does not have a pointing device, you can use the keyboard's arrow keys to control the crosshairs' movement.

Step 2.1: When you move the pointing device or press the arrow keys, the crosshairs should move. Spend a few seconds simply moving the pointing device around. Notice how its motion corresponds to the cursor's on-screen movements.

Step 3.0: Familiarize yourself with the screen menu. Move the crosshairs to the screen's right edge so that the cursor moves into the screen menu. When you do this, a line of text becomes highlighted, informing you that this command or menu is selected if you press your pointing device's pick button.

Step 3.1: Move the highlight up and down by moving the pointing device. Do not select a command yet; you can issue commands later.

NOTE

AutoCAD supports many different pointing devices (which also are called *input devices*). A *pointing device* may be a mouse, a stylus, or a puck. A mouse may have one, two, three, or more buttons. A *stylus* is a device that looks like a pen and connects directly to your computer or works with a digitizing tablet. A *puck* is like a mouse, but usually has four or more buttons. A puck is almost always used with a digitizing tablet.

All these input devices feature a *pick button*, which is the button you press (or "click") when you want to select a command from an AutoCAD menu or pick a specific point on the Drawing Editor screen. The button you press depends on the type of device you have. If you use a two-button mouse, you usually use the left button as the pick button; if you use a puck, the top button is generally the pick button.

Step 4.0: Familiarize yourself with AutoCAD's pull-down menus by moving the cursor up into the status line. The status line disappears and is replaced by the pull-down menu bar, which displays the names of AutoCAD's nine pull-down menus.

Step 4.1: Notice that the crosshairs turn into a small arrow. Move the arrow to the right and left by moving your pointing device. When the arrow touches a pull-down menu's name, the name is highlighted.

Step 5.0: Practice pulling down a few menus. First, move the arrow to the Draw pull-down menu name. Then click the pointing device's pick button. The Draw menu drops down from the menu bar (see fig. 2.4). The menu contains several commands that enable you to draw entities, create dimensions, and perform other tasks. Move the arrow up and down along the menu, and notice that each command name is highlighted when the arrow touches it. You can activate any of the commands by placing the highlight on its name and clicking your pointing device's pick button. In addition, some commands have a right arrow to the right of the command. Choosing this command displays a second menu with additional commands or options. This option display method is called a *cascading menu.* For now, however, do not click on any of the command names. Go back up to the menu bar and pull down each of the nine menus. Look at the menus and get acquainted with the lists of commands they contain.

Figure 2.4:

The Draw pull-down menu with the Line command highlighted.

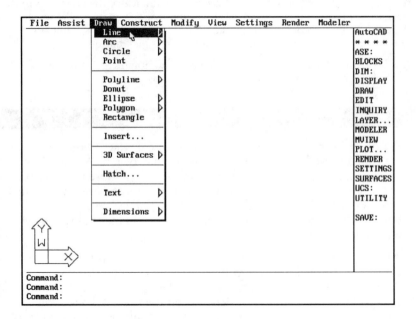

Naming Conventions

Now that you are familiar with the Drawing Editor, you are ready to name this new drawing. When you specify a name for a new drawing, AutoCAD uses the name for the drawing's data file, which is stored on disk. Because the drawing's name is used as the file name, the name must conform to the DOS file-naming conventions. This means the name can be no more than eight characters long. The file name can include any letter of the alphabet or any number, and also can include the following non-alphabetic characters:

    $ # & @ ! ( ) - { } ' _ ~ ^ `

File names (and, therefore, AutoCAD drawing names) cannot contain the following characters:

    + = / [ ] " ; : , ? * \ < > |

Further, drawing names cannot contain blank spaces or periods.

DOS file names generally end with a three-character extension. AutoCAD automatically adds the extension DWG to drawing file names.

For more information on DOS, see *Maximizing MS-DOS 5*, by New Riders Publishing.

Naming the New Drawing

Use the File pull-down menu and the New command to name the drawing. The name is specified by entering it in an input box in the New File Name input box.

Step 6.0: Under the pull-down menu, choose File, then New. This command enables you to name a new drawing. A dialog box appears in which you must select to save or discard the present drawing or cancel the command.

Step 6.1: Click on **D**iscard Changes to exit this drawing without saving. The Create New Drawing dialog box appears as seen in figure 2.5. Notice that a vertical line, which represents the cursor, is flashing in the New Drawing Name input box. This action tells you that this box is the default. A *default* is the value AutoCAD uses unless another is specified.

Step 6.2: Type **LESSON2** in the New **D**rawing Name dialog box and press Enter. As with any default box, to input information simply type the name and press Enter. (In dialog boxes that are not the default, you need to choose the input box with the pointer to make the box active for input.) The dialog box disappears and the drawing is saved with the name LESSON2.

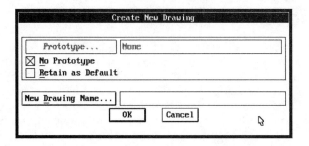

EXERCISE 2: CREATING SIMPLE ENTITIES

In this exercise, you create entities (or geometry) to add to your new drawing. *Entities* are the objects you draw in AutoCAD. Entities can be simple objects, such as lines, circles, and arcs, or sophisticated objects, such as quadratic curves and spheres. Drawings are built by creating entities and positioning them in relation to one another.

To become familiar with the way the Drawing Editor works, use AutoCAD's LINE command to create a few lines. Although the LINE command is the most basic of all of the drawing commands, LINE is the foundation for almost every drawing created in AutoCAD. To create a line, simply define the line's start point and end point. To see how the LINE command works, create the simple shape shown in figure 2.6.

TASK TO BE COMPLETED IN THIS EXERCISE
• Draw a polygon

The figure in this exercise consists of four straight lines. You create the lines by specifying starting and ending points for each line. You need only to specify the points; AutoCAD actually creates each line by drawing it between the points. In this exercise, you specify the points by "picking" them on-screen with your pointing device. This means that your drawing might not match the one in figure 2.6. The purpose of this exercise is to further familiarize you with the Drawing Editor, not to help you create perfect geometry. (That comes later!)

Step 1.0: Start the LINE command by entering it at the **Command:** prompt:

Command: LINE ↵   Starts the LINE command

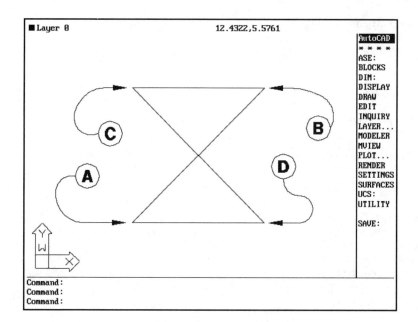

Step 1.1: AutoCAD prompts you for the starting point of the first line (**point** A in fig. 2.6). To pick point A, move the crosshairs to the lower left corner of the drawing area. When the crosshairs are in the same position as A, press your pointing device's pick button:

`From point:` *Pick a point at* Ⓐ   Specifies the line's
                                               starting point

NOTE

If you move the input device after picking a point, you can see that AutoCAD creates a "ghosted" line between the selected point and the center of the crosshairs. This action is called *rubberbanding,* and the ghosted line is called a *rubberband line.* This line shows you where the line appears when you pick the next point. Rubberbanding is helpful when you are creating inexact geometry, or when you want to see how a line looks before you actually draw it.

After the line is created, notice that AutoCAD continues to display the `To point:` prompt. AutoCAD assumes that you want to draw more than one line when you are using the LINE command, and that each line's ending point acts as the starting point for the next line. Because the LINE command works in this manner, you can draw multisided figures by issuing LINE once, and then creating all the connected lines in the entity.

Step 1.2: AutoCAD prompts you for the line's ending point (point B in fig. 2.6). Use your pointing device to pick the ending point:

To point: *Pick a point at* Ⓑ *in*   Specifies the line's
the Drawing Editor   ending point,
                                          creating the first
                                          diagonal line

Step 1.3: Continuing with the LINE command, draw the next two lines in the figure:

To point: *Pick* Ⓒ *(see fig. 2.6)*   Specifies the ending
                                          point of the second line

To point: *Pick* Ⓓ *(see fig. 2.6)*   Specifies the ending
                                          point of the third line

Step 1.4: The hourglass figure is now nearly complete. All you need to do is create the fourth line, which forms the bottom of the shape and closes the figure. Complete the drawing by using the LINE command's Close option. The Close option draws a line between the last point you picked and the first point you picked after you issued the LINE command. To issue the Close option, type CLOSE at the prompt or select it from the on-screen menu:

To point: CLOSE ↵   Draws a line from
                                 Ⓓ to Ⓐ,
                                 closing the figure

This completes the object shown in figure 2.6. Now that you have drawn some geometry, you can do some editing.

EXERCISE 3: ERASING GEOMETRY

AutoCAD's editing commands are truly the most powerful part of the software. These commands help trim your drawing time, as well as enable you to modify existing entities in many sophisticated ways. Like the drawing commands, editing commands can be either simple or complex.

One of the most commonly used editing commands is the ERASE command. The ERASE command removes one or more whole entities (such as lines, circles, and arcs) from the drawing.

For this exercise, erase the entire drawing you just created. When you invoke the ERASE command, you must select the object or objects to erase. The crosshair cursor disappears and is replaced by a box cursor, called a *pickbox*. To select an object, simply use your pointing device to move the pickbox onto the object and click the pick button. AutoCAD highlights the selected object, but does not erase it. If you want to select more than one object, use the pickbox and continue selecting. AutoCAD highlights all of the objects you select. When you have selected all the objects you want to erase, press Enter. AutoCAD then erases the objects from the drawing and the ERASE command ends.

TASK TO BE COMPLETED IN THIS EXERCISE

- Erase the entire object drawn in Exercise 2

USING THE **ERASE** COMMAND

Now practice using ERASE by erasing the object, one line at a time. First, select and erase one line; then issue the ERASE command again and get rid of the remaining lines.

Step 1.0: Invoke the ERASE command:

Command: **ERASE** ↵	Starts the ERASE command

Step 1.1: Use the pickbox to select the line between A and B (see fig. 2.7):

Select objects: *Pick the line between* Ⓐ *and* Ⓑ	Selects line AB
1 found	Displays the number of entities selected for editing

Step 1.2: Erase the objects by pressing Enter to end the selection set:

Select objects: ↵	Erases the line and ends the ERASE command

Step 2.0: Reissue the ERASE command; use the pickbox to highlight the remaining three lines. After you select all the lines, press Enter to erase them:

Command: **ERASE** ↵	Starts the ERASE command
Select objects: *Pick the line between* Ⓑ *and* Ⓒ	Selects line BC
1 found	
Select objects: *Pick the line between* Ⓒ *and* Ⓓ	Selects line CD
1 found	
Select objects: *Pick the line between* Ⓓ *and* Ⓐ	Selects line DA
1 found	

Figure 2.7:

Line AB high-lighted during the ERASE command.

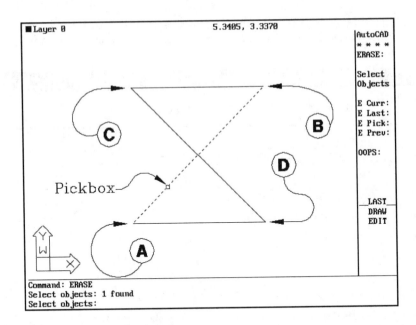

Step 2.1: Now that all the lines are selected, erase them and end the ERASE command by pressing Enter:

`Select objects: ↵`　　　　　　Ends object
selection, erases
the selected lines,
and exits from the
ERASE command

Whenever you are using an AutoCAD command (such as ERASE) that enables you to select multiple objects, press Enter to tell AutoCAD when you have selected all the desired objects. When you press Enter at a `Select objects:` prompt, AutoCAD stops prompting you to continue selecting objects and then performs the desired task (such as erasing, copying, or moving) on the selected objects. When AutoCAD completes its operation on the objects, the command ends and the `Command:` prompt reappears.

Sometimes you may issue a command and then realize that you really do not want to use it. For example, you may issue the ERASE command

and then decide that you do not want to erase anything. AutoCAD is very forgiving when you make such a mistake. Simply press Ctrl-C to end a command before it executes. This means that you should type **C** while holding down the Ctrl key. This is AutoCAD's cancel sequence. When you use Ctrl-C, AutoCAD aborts the current command and returns to the `Command:` prompt.

CLEANING UP THE SCREEN

You should now have a blank screen except for several small marks, called *blips*. These blips are not part of the drawing, but indicate the locations where you selected points in the drawing area. To remove these blips, use the REDRAW command. The REDRAW command redraws the drawing, cleans the screen, and removes any drawing marks such as blips.

Step 3.0: Use REDRAW now to clear the blips off the screen:

`Command:` **REDRAW** ↵   Removes blips from
                                  the screen

EXERCISE 4: SETTING UP DRAWING AIDS

One of the primary reasons for AutoCAD's popularity is the accuracy with which it enables you to create drawings. You can achieve a high degree of accuracy by typing in exact coordinates for the points used in your drawings. (This technique is covered in later lessons.) AutoCAD also has on-screen drawing aids that simplify the drawing process and help you create accurate drawings. Several of these commands are covered in this exercise.

The SNAP command is one of AutoCAD's drawing aids. The SNAP command defines the smallest increment that AutoCAD recognizes when you move the crosshairs. This command enables you to select exact points easily in the Drawing Editor. In this exercise you learn how to control AutoCAD's SNAP settings.

This exercise also shows you how to turn on and modify the Drawing Editor's on-screen grid. The *grid* is an array of dots that you can turn on and off. The dots act like the intersections of the horizontal and vertical lines in graph paper, and help you judge distances in the drawing and positioning of objects.

This exercise closes by teaching you how to control the display of coordinates on the screen.

SETTING THE SNAP INCREMENT

By moving your pointing device, you can position crosshairs anywhere on-screen. Their response is smooth but inexact. Sometimes, however, you need the crosshairs' movement to be precise. For example, you want the crosshairs to travel in exact increments rather than roll smoothly across the screen and rest in a general position. You can alter the crosshairs' movement by changing the increment by which it moves. This increment, called the *snap*, is controlled by the SNAP command. When you alter the SNAP setting, you maintain accuracy as you work on drawing components that require precise measurements.

Change the SNAP setting by using the SNAP command or the Drawing Aides dialog box. The SNAP command also turns the snap action on and off. When snap is off, the cursor moves smoothly; when snap is on, the cursor "jumps" according to the increment of motion you have defined. You can set the snap increment any time while you are drawing. Use SNAP now to change the snap increment.

Step 1.0: Issue the SNAP command:

`Command: SNAP ↵`   Starts the SNAP command

Step 1.1: After you invoke the SNAP command, AutoCAD prompts you for the increment size. The default value is 1 unit. For the drawing you are about to create, set the increment to .25 units, as follows:

`Snap spacing or ON/OFF/Aspect/`   Sets the snap
`Rotate/Style<1.0000>: .25 ↵`   increment to .25 units

You have set the crosshairs' increment of motion at .25 units. Use your pointing device to move the crosshairs and see how they "jump" to the new increment. Also notice that AutoCAD displays Snap within the status line at the upper left corner of the screen.

NOTE

Do not get SNAP confused with OSNAP, which is used in the next chapter. SNAP and OSNAP are two different commands.

TURNING ON THE GRID

The SNAP command assists you in physically positioning the crosshairs. AutoCAD's GRID command helps you visually place the crosshairs. The GRID command places an array of dots on-screen. These dots are not part of the drawing, nor are they geometry. Rather, the dots serve as a visual reference while you create entities in AutoCAD. You can use the GRID command to turn the grid on and off, and to set the amount of space between the dots (this is called the *grid size*).

Step 2.0: Use the GRID command to set the grid size:

Command: **GRID** ↵   Starts the GRID
                                           command

Step 2.1: After you invoke the GRID command, AutoCAD prompts you for the size of the grid. The default value is 0. For this exercise, make the grid size .5 units, to space the dots 1/2 unit apart from each other, both horizontally and vertically:

Grid spacing(X) or ON/OFF/Snap/   Creates a .5-unit
Aspect <0.0000>: .5 ↵   grid on-screen

Notice the grid on your screen. This grid serves as a visual reference when you draw, in much the same way as the lines on a piece of graph paper. Like SNAP, GRID helps you control the accuracy of your drawing. Grids are especially helpful when you want to draw or position entities with your eye alone instead of using exact coordinates.

CHANGING COORDINATE DISPLAY

AutoCAD offers another drawing aid to help you create geometry. The COORDS system variable helps you determine where your crosshairs are located in relation to the coordinate system. (AutoCAD's coordinate system is explained in greater detail in Lesson 3.) In the upper right corner of the screen, AutoCAD displays the location of the cursor, according to its current relation to the X and Y axes. When COORDS is turned off, AutoCAD updates the coordinates display only when you press your pointing device's pick button. When COORDS is on, AutoCAD updates the coordinate display as the cursor moves across the screen. This constantly updating display is very helpful if you are trying to put the crosshairs at a specific coordinate in the drawing.

Step 3.0: For the following exercise, you need to change the coordinate display to length and angle:

Command: *Press F6 twice*   Toggles COORDS to
                                           length and angle
                                           (polar coordinates)

```
<Coords off>
<Coords on>
```
Specifies that
COORDS is turned
off then on, and that
the coordinate
display is updated
as the cursor moves
around the screen

EXERCISE 5: CREATING A COMPLETE DRAWING

Now that you have defined the drawing aids for the drawing in this exercise, you can use the commands to create the object shown in figure 2.8.

Figure 2.8:

The drawing that you create in this exercise.

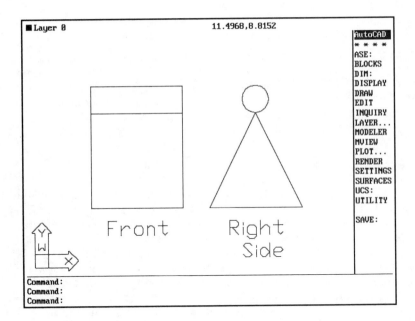

DRAWING THE LARGE RECTANGLE

To start the drawing, use the LINE command to create a 3.5 unit-by-3.5-unit rectangle. The standard decimal units in AutoCAD can be any real world unit that you need. This means that the 3.5 unit-by-3.5-unit rectangle can be any size, such as 3.5 inches by 3.5 inches, or even 3.5 miles by 3.5 miles. This is because AutoCAD draws in full scale. (The concept of full-scale drawing is discussed in detail in Lesson 3.)

Tasks To Be Completed in this Exercise

- Draw a large rectangle
- Draw a small rectangle
- Draw a three-sided polygon
- Draw a circle
- Add text to the drawing

To create the rectangle, first use the LINE command to select the starting point of the first line. After you select the starting point, AutoCAD prompts you for the line's ending point. Move the crosshairs to the right and watch the coordinate prompt in the status line. Notice that the prompt indicates the length of the line and the angle at which you are drawing it, rather than the X,Y coordinate location of the cursor.

Step 1.0: To start the rectangle, use the LINE command to select the first point of the first line, as follows:

Command: **LINE** ↵	Starts the LINE command
From point: *Pick a point at* Ⓐ *(see fig. 2.9)*	Selects the starting point of the first line

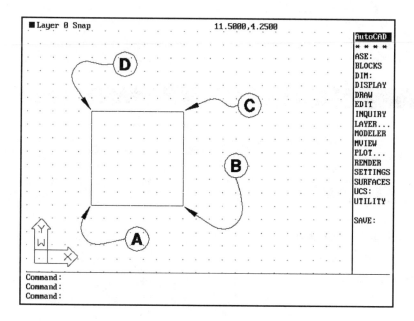

Figure 2.9:

The 3.5 unit-by-3.5-unit rectangle with the end points labeled.

Step 1.1: Next, AutoCAD displays the `To point:` prompt to prompt you for the line's end point. Point B is 3.5 units to the right of the starting point. To locate this exact location, move the crosshairs to the right until the coordinate prompt displays `3.5000<0`, and then click the pointing device's pick button. You also can find the exact location of point B by counting the number of grid points and calculating the 3.5 value, remembering that the grid is set to .5 units:

`To point:` *Pick a point 3.5 units*   Picks the
to the right   second point

NOTE

Remember, if you make a mistake while you are creating entities, issue the **U** command. This command undoes the last command executed and removes the last entity created, such as a line. You then continue from the previous point. UNDO can be used to undo commands as far back as you need to go.

Step 1.2: When you create a line, AutoCAD rubberbands a ghosted line from the crosshairs to the line's end point to help you create the next line. Create the second line by using the pointing device to move the cursor directly up from point B, and press the pick button when the status line displays `3.5000<90`:

`To point:` *Pick a point 3.5 units up*   Picks the third point

Step 1.3: To define the third line, move the cursor directly to the left from point B, and press the pick button when the status line displays `3.5000<180`:

`To point:` *Pick a point 3.5 units*   Picks the forth point
to the left

NOTE

You can complete the rectangle in one of two ways. You can draw a line from point D to point A, or you can use the LINE command's Close option. When you use the LINE command to create multiple lines that are joined end-to-end, the Close option closes the entity by drawing a line from the last specified end point to the first line's starting point.

Step 1.4: Use the LINE command's Close option to complete the rectangle:

`To point:` **Close** ⏎   Closes the rectangle
                              by drawing a line
                              from Ⓓ to Ⓐ
                              and ends the LINE
                              command

The 3.5 unit-by-3.5 unit rectangle is now complete.

DRAWING THE SMALL RECTANGLE

Now you need to draw the second, smaller rectangle, which sits on top of the large rectangle you just created. The new rectangle measures 3.5 units wide by 1 unit tall. You draw the small rectangle in much the same way you drew the large one. For the new object, however, you need to draw only three lines because the large rectangle's top line also serves as the small rectangle's bottom line.

Because you are drawing only three sides of the small rectangle, if you try to use the Close option to create the line from point C to point D, unexpected results occur. AutoCAD closes the entity by drawing a line from point C back to point A. If you used the Close option, use Undo to erase the incorrect lines, and try again as described in steps 2.0-2.3.

Step 2.0: Issue the LINE command. The first thing you need to do is put the crosshair cursor on point A (see fig. 2.10) and use that point as the first line's starting point. Because you have SNAP and GRID turned on, you can easily move the cursor to point A. Create the first line now:

Command: **LINE** ↵   Starts the LINE command

From point: *Pick* (A) *(see fig. 2.10)*   Specifies the
                                                  starting point of
                                                  the first line

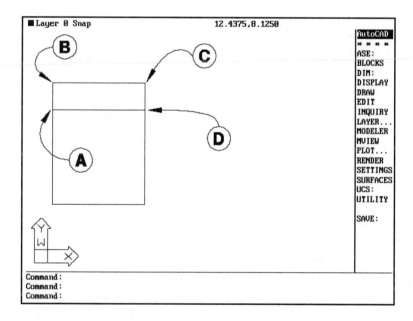

Figure 2.10:

The completed front view.

Step 2.1: Specify the first line's ending point at one unit above the starting point:

To point: *Move the cursor up one full unit* (*when the status line reads* **1.0000<90**) *and click the pick button*

Defines **Ⓑ** and draws the first line of the small rectangle

Step 2.2: Continue with the LINE command. As you did when you drew the large rectangle, use your pointing device to draw the next two lines (from point B to point C, and then from C to D). Use the grid and the coordinate display to help you pick the next points accurately:

To point: *Pick* Ⓒ *(see fig. 2.10)*

Creates the top line of the small rectangle

To point: *Pick* Ⓓ *(see fig. 2.10)*

Creates the third line and closes the small rectangle

Step 2.3: AutoCAD assumes that you want to continue drawing lines and continues displaying the To point: prompt. You now can end the LINE command:

To point: ↵

Ends the LINE command

The front view of the drawing is now complete.

DRAWING A THREE-SIDED POLYGON

You now are ready to complete the drawing by adding the right-side view. To draw this object, you must create a three-sided polygon and a circle. You can easily draw the triangle the same way you drew the large rectangle: by using the LINE command and the Close option. Use the CIRCLE command to create the circle. When you create the triangle, calculate the first line's starting point as it relates to the object you have already created.

Step 3.0: Start the line two grid points to the right of the large rectangle's lower right corner at point A (see fig. 2.11):

Command: **LINE** ↵

Starts the LINE command

From point: *Pick* Ⓐ *(see fig. 2.11)*

Specifies the first point of the triangle's first line

Step 3.1: You need to specify point B to finish the first line of the triangle, but you also need to calculate its location. Simply put, B lies halfway between points A and C, horizontally. Point B also lies on the same row of grid marks as the large rectangle's top line. Because the triangle's line AC is 3.5 units long, you can move 1.75 units to the right of point A, and then go up 3.5 units to find point B:

To point: *Pick* Ⓑ *(see fig. 2.11)*   Draws line AB

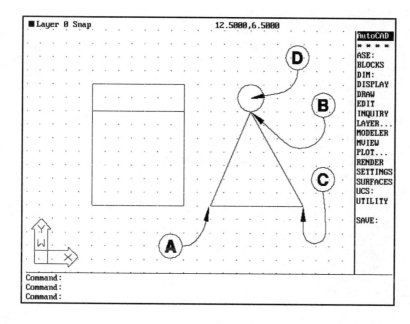

Step 3.2: Continuing with the LINE command, pick point C. You can pick C by reversing the process you used to pick point B:

To point: *Pick* Ⓒ *(see fig. 2.11)*   Draws line BC

Step 3.3: Finish the three-sided polygon by using the LINE command's Close option to connect points A and C:

To point: **C** ↵   Closes the three-sided polygon and ends the LINE command

The triangle is now complete, and you are ready to top it off with a small circle, as was shown in figure 2.11.

Drawing the Circle

Now you are going to learn another AutoCAD command: CIRCLE. CIRCLE is the second-most commonly used drawing command, after LINE. The CIRCLE command creates a circle. After selecting CIRCLE, use the defaults and options to select the type of circle you want.

The CIRCLE command has the following options:

- **Radius.** Creates a circle defined by its center point and the radius you specify

- **Diameter.** Creates a circle defined by its center point in the drawing and the diameter you specify

- **3P (three-point).** Creates a circle defined by specifying three points, through which the circle's circumference passes

- **2P (two-point).** Creates a circle defined by specifying two end points of a diameter chord

- **TTR (tangent, tangent, radius).** Creates a circle defined by specifying two objects to which the circle is tangent, as well as its radius

To add the circle to the drawing, use the CIRCLE command. You must define the circle's center point and enter the radius.

Step 4.0: Issue the CIRCLE command:

```
Command: CIRCLE ↵
```
Starts the CIRCLE command

Step 4.1: Continuing with the CIRCLE command, specify the circle's center point (point D in fig. 2.11). The circle has a radius of .5 units and lies directly above the top point of the triangle (point B). The center point therefore lies .5 units above B. After locating your cursor on point B of the triangle, move the cursor directly up by .5 units (one dot above B). Then pick the point:

```
3P/2P/TTR/<Centerpoint>: Pick a point
at Ⓓ (see fig. 2.11)
```
Defines the circle's center

Step 4.2: To create the circle, indicate the circle's radius. Because AutoCAD knows where the circle's center is, the program simply constructs the circle based on the radius and center point. Specify the circle's radius:

```
Diameter/<Radius>: .5 ↵
```
Creates a circle with a radius of .5 units

In this exercise, you use the circle's radius because AutoCAD assumes by default that you want to base the circle on a radius. (The default value in AutoCAD is always in brackets, such as <Radius>.) If you wanted to specify the circle's diameter instead, you would Enter **D** (for Diameter) at the Diameter/<Radius>: prompt. Another prompt then appears, asking you to specify the circle's radius. In this case, the circle's diameter is one unit.

ADDING TEXT TO THE DRAWING

You now have created all of the basic entities and are ready to add the text to the drawing. To add the text to the drawing, use the TEXT command.

The TEXT command enables you to add a text string, such as the word "Front," to your drawing. Like many AutoCAD commands, the TEXT command has several options.

OPTIONS

The following are the first-level options for the TEXT command. Many commands contain various levels of options. As you become a more advanced user of AutoCAD, experiment with the levels beyond the context of this book, which covers only first-level, or beginning level options. All of these options are accessed by selecting the first level option; additional options are then displayed. From here, you select additional options as required:

- **Justify.** Sets the way text is positioned in relation to the justification. Enables you to insert text that is center justified on a certain point, right-justified in relation to a point, or fit to a specified length.

- **Style.** Sets the new text style to the previously defined styles that you specify.

- **Start point.** As the default, Start point sets the starting point for left-justified text to the point you specify.

To add text to your drawing, you first must invoke the TEXT command. The TEXT command enables you to place a string of text anywhere within the drawing. The command features many options (far too many to cover here) that can size, rotate, and angle the text so that you can achieve just the right look for your drawing. AutoCAD also features many built-in styles of text. You can select the style of text you want with TEXT command. You can combine several styles of text in a drawing, and customize the angle and rotation of each text entry. For this exercise, however, you simply add the word "Front" to the drawing, so that it is horizontal and centered under the rectangle.

Step 5.0: Issue the TEXT command:

Command: **TEXT** ⏎   Starts the TEXT command

Step 5.1: Specify that you want the text string to be centered horizontally on a certain point:

```
Justify/Style/<Start point>: C ↵
```
Specifies that the text is centered on the start point

Step 5.2: Pick the center point (point A in fig. 2.12). The point is centered horizontally under the large rectangle's bottom line. You know that the line is 3.5 units long, so find the center point of the line and move the cursor directly down one full unit (two grid marks). Then click the pointing device's pick button to specify that point as the center point:

```
Center point: Pick Ⓑ (see fig. 2.12)
```
Identifies the point on which the text is to be centered

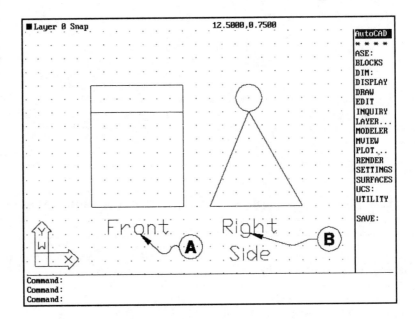

Figure 2.12:

The finished drawing with text.

Step 5.3: AutoCAD now prompts you to specify the text's appearance. First, specify the text's height, in units. By default, AutoCAD makes the text .2 units tall, but that is too small for this drawing. Specify the text as .5 units tall:

```
Height <0.2000>: .5 ↵
```
Defines text height of .5 units

Step 5.4: Specify a rotation angle for the text. By default, AutoCAD displays text at a rotation angle of 0, which means that text appears horizontally in the drawing. You can rotate the text so that it runs vertically, upside-down, or at any other angle. For this exercise, however, the text should be horizontal. Accept the default setting of 0 degrees rotation for the new text:

```
Rotation angle <0>: ↵
```
Accepts the default
rotation angle of 0
degrees, causing
text to appear
horizontally across
the screen

Step 5.5: AutoCAD now prompts you to type in the text that is added to the
drawing. When you type the text, it appears in the prompt area rather than in
the drawing. If you make a mistake while typing the text, use the Backspace key
to correct your error. When the text is right, press Enter, and AutoCAD adds
the text to the drawing at the specified height and rotation angle:

```
Text: Front ↵
```
Specifies the text
string to be added
to the drawing

ADDING A SECOND TEXT STRING

Now add two lines of text under the image on the right side of the
screen. Because this image is the right-side view of the image on the left,
add the word "Right Side" underneath it, as was shown in figure 2.12.
Notice, however, that this text string is in two lines. You repeat the
preceding steps when you add the word "Right" to the drawing, but you
take a short-cut when adding multiple lines of text.

Step 6.0: Begin by following the preceding steps (6.1-6.5) to add the text **Right**
under the image on the right.

Step 6.1: When you invoke the **TEXT** command a second time, the last text
string—in this case, the word "Right"—is selected. Simply by pressing Enter,
you place the new text directly below the existing text. The new line also takes
on the same parameters (such as justification, height, and rotation angle) as the
last text string. Use this method to add the word "Side" under the word "Right."

CLEANING UP THE DRAWING

Now that you have finished your drawing, you need to clean up the
screen, which might be cluttered with blip marks. To remove them from
the screen so as to better see your drawing, use the REDRAW command.
When you invoke the REDRAW command, the screen clears briefly.
Then the drawing is redrawn without the blips. To help you view your
drawing, you also can turn off SNAP and GRID.

First, redraw the screen.

Step 7.0: Issue the REDRAW command:

```
Command: REDRAW ↵
```
Removes blips from
the screen

Step 8.0: Now that the drawing is finished, you do not need to restrict the cursor movement. Press F9 to turn off SNAP. Similarly, you do not need to use the GRID setting any more. Use F7 to turn off the grid.

EXERCISE 6: ENDING THE DRAWING SESSION

You now are ready to leave the Drawing Editor. Not only do you want to leave the Drawing Editor, but also you need to save your drawing to disk so that you can use it later. If you simply quit the drawing now, your work is lost.

TASKS TO BE COMPLETED IN THIS EXERCISE

- Save the completed drawing
- Exit from the Drawing Editor and AutoCAD

SAVING THE COMPLETED DRAWING

While you are working inside AutoCAD, your drawing is held in temporary memory or *file space*. If a power outage occurs or your system breakdowns, everything you have drawn up to that point is lost. You can store your drawing on disk, however, by using the SAVE command. Use the SAVE command during a drawing session to protects your work. By saving the drawing periodically throughout the session, you ensure the drawing is intact up to the last time you saved. Get into the habit of saving a drawing at least once every 15 minutes. You can use the SAVE command or QSAVE command. The QSAVE command saves your drawing without displaying a dialog box.

Step 1.0: Issue the SAVE command to save the LESSON2 drawing to disk:

Command: *Under the pull-down menu*   Saves the drawing to disk
choose File, *then choose* Save

EXITING FROM THE DRAWING EDITOR

When you are finished working on a drawing, exit from the Drawing Editor. If you have not made any changes since the last save, AutoCAD ends. If you have not saved any changes to the drawing, you are prompted with a dialog box to save, discard, or cancel the quit.

Step 2.0: Exit AutoCAD:

Command: *Under the pull-down menu, choose* File, *then* Exit AutoCAD	Saves the drawing to disk and exits AutoCAD

You have successfully created your first AutoCAD drawing. Now you are ready to move on to more sophisticated and challenging problems.

SUMMARY

AutoCAD's user interface is one of the software's main features. The user interface comprises the Main Menu and the Drawing Editor. These areas link you with the software, enabling you to access AutoCAD commands to create and to edit geometry. AutoCAD's basic drawing and editing commands enable you to create complex drawings quickly from simple entities, such as lines and circles. AutoCAD's text-entry capabilities enable you to enhance any drawing by adding text strings, which can be styled in many ways.

IN THIS LESSON, YOU LEARNED TO DO THE FOLLOWING:

- Navigate the Main Menu and Drawing Editor
- Create simple entities
- Erase geometry
- Set up drawing aids
- Create a complete drawing
- End a drawing session

By creating the drawing in this lesson, you learned to start a new drawing from the Main Menu and access the Drawing Editor. Inside the Drawing Editor, you used basic drawing and editing commands to create a drawing. In the next lesson, you learn to do a full drawing setup, then create a drawing based on CAD drawing standards.

REVIEW

1. Start a new drawing and name it **REVIEW1**.
2. Set **SNAP** to .5 units.

3. Set **GRID** to 1 unit.

4. Using the **LINE** command, draw a 4-unit horizontal line.

5. Using the **LINE** command, draw two vertical lines from the end points of the last line, 2 units straight up.

6. Using the **CIRCLE** command, draw two circles on the top end points of the two vertical lines with a radius of **.5**.

7. Inside the three lines, use the **TEXT** command to create center text with a height of **.25** and a rotation of **0**. Use your first name as the text string.

8. Create a second text string directly below the last text string that is your last name.

9. Using the **ERASE** command, remove both circles.

10. Clean up the screen by using the **REDRAW** command.

CREATING YOUR FIRST AutoCAD DRAWING

OVERVIEW

The primary function of AutoCAD is to enable the drafter to create accurate, full-scale drawings that can be applied to many disciplines. In AutoCAD drafting, "accurate" describes a drawing that not only is visually correct, but that also uses a mathematically-precise database. The mathematical database contains the information AutoCAD uses to define the geometry that makes up a drawing's parts, including the end points of lines, centers of arcs, and the radii of circles. When you create a drawing in AutoCAD, the end points of rectangles meet, the exact centers of arcs are positioned correctly, and the radii are specified and calculated internally to 14 decimal places. In other words, AutoCAD drawings are accurate.

To develop such accurate geometry, AutoCAD utilizes the Cartesian coordinate system of geometry definition. This coordinate system is based on X, Y, and Z axes. The X axis is horizontal, and generally lies across the bottom of the screen. The Y axis is vertical, and usually runs up and down the left edge of the screen. The Z axis is perpendicular to the X,Y plane, and projects through the screen toward the user. By specifying points in relation to the X, Y, and Z axes, you create the desired geometry. Further, once the geometry is created, AutoCAD gives you tools to locate exact points, such as end points or centers. This adds to your ability to create an accurate database of drawings. You will learn more about coordinates and the X and Y axes later in this lesson. The Z axis is used in three-dimensional drawing, and is introduced later in this book.

Regardless of a drawing's dimensional size, AutoCAD develops the geometry at full scale. Suppose, for example, that you are drawing a house. If a wall is 72'-1/2" long, you enter **72'-1/2"** into AutoCAD. That is, you do not scale the drawing as you might in manual drafting. The only time you need to scale an AutoCAD drawing is when you plot or print the drawing.

AutoCAD is more than just a drafting package. Much of the information in AutoCAD's database can be used in many different drawings or shared with other software packages. You might, for example, develop libraries of architectural symbols that you can insert into different drawings over several years. The drawing database also can be used to develop Computer Numeric Controlled (CNC) tool paths to cut a part on an automated machine tool. AutoCAD's high degree of accuracy and its use of full scale are necessary because of its versatility.

AutoCAD enables you to set up the drawing environment differently for each new drawing. This means that you have the freedom to specify the type of units to be used, the size of the drawing area, and the manner in which angles are displayed. By setting up AutoCAD for each drawing, you can tailor the program to fit your discipline, as well as to meet your individual drafting needs. This lesson's first exercise shows you how to set up the drawing environment and introduces the options AutoCAD displays during the setup process.

This lesson also discusses AutoCAD's layer system, which works in much the same way as the clear plastic drawing sheets used in overlay drafting. AutoCAD's layers, however, are much more flexible and useful than their plastic counterparts. By placing geometry on different layers, you can assign characteristics, such as color and linetype, to geometry by layers. Layers also enable you to isolate specific parts of a drawing for plotting or tool path development.

As you learned in the previous lesson, to begin your new drawing you must first start AutoCAD. After AutoCAD is started, you then must name the new drawing. To do so, choose File, then New and discard changes to the present drawing. Enter **LESSON3** in the New Drawing Name edit box and press Enter.

You are now ready to begin this lesson's exercises. When you have completed this lesson, you should have a drawing like the one shown in figure 3.1.

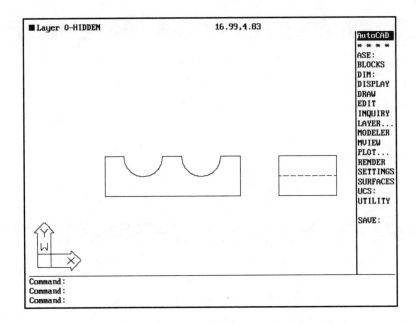

EXERCISE 1: SETTING UP THE DRAWING

AutoCAD is used in a variety of disciplines, ranging from tool-and-die manufacturing to architecture. To accommodate the needs of the many drafting disciplines in which it is used, AutoCAD provides a completely customizable drawing environment. Before you begin an AutoCAD drawing session, you must first define the drawing area so that it suits your requirements. This involves setting the type of units used to create and dimension the drawing, the size of the drawing area, and the layers upon which to draw.

TASKS TO BE COMPLETED IN THIS EXERCISE

The lessons in this chapter show you how to do the following tasks:

- Specify the drawing units
- Specify the system of angle measurement
- Define the drawing area's limits
- Zoom to display the drawing limits
- Define the drawing's layers

SPECIFYING THE DRAWING UNITS

The UNITS command is the first command used in setting up the drawing. The UNITS command controls the input and display of coordinates, angles, and distances in the Drawing Editor.

When you invoke the UNITS command, the Drawing Editor graphic screen changes to the text screen. AutoCAD displays a series of menus and examples from which you select the desired values.

Step 1.0: Start the UNITS command by typing the command's name at the AutoCAD prompt:

```
Command: UNITS ↵
```
Starts the UNITS command

Step 1.1: Specify the type of units (or format of measurement). In this case, use decimal units:

```
Report formats:  (Examples)


  1. Scientific   1.55E'01
  2. Decimal      15.50
  3. Engineering  1'-3.50"
  4. Architectural 1'-3 1/2"
  5. Fractional    15 1/2
```

With the exception of Engineering and Architectural formats, these formats can be used with any basic unit of measurement. For example, Decimal mode is perfect for metric units as well as decimal English units:

```
Enter choice, 1 to 5 <2>: ↵
```
Specifies the default decimal units

Step 1.2: Now that you have specified the type of units you want to use, AutoCAD needs to know how many decimal places to use when calculating and displaying units. Set the units to two decimal places, which is enough for this exercise:

```
Number of digits to right
of decimal point
(0 to 8) <4>: 2 ↵
```
Sets the number of decimal places to two

Specifying the System of Angle Measurement

Step 1.3: Now that you have defined the coordinate information, you need to define the system by which AutoCAD measures and displays angles:

```
Systems of angle measure:    (Examples)
  1. Decimal degrees        45.0000
  2. Degrees/minutes/seconds  45d0'0"
  3. Grads              50.0000
  4. Radians            0.7854r
  5. Surveyor's units     N 45d0'0" E

Enter choice, 1 to 5 <1>: ↵
```
Accepts the default of 1 (decimal degrees)

Step 1.4: Specify the number of fractional places for the angular units, as follows:

```
Number of fractional places
for display of angles (0 to 8)
<0>: ↵
```
Accepts the default of zero fractional places

NOTE

AutoCAD enables you to select the direction of angle zero. This setting affects the creation of geometry and the use of polar coordinates. By default, AutoCAD assumes that all angles start at 0 degrees, and that 0 degrees is at the 3 o'clock position. This means that when AutoCAD measures the number of degrees in an angle, it starts measuring from a line that lies in the 3 o'clock direction from the angle's vertex.

Step 1.5: Specify the direction of angle 0:

```
Direction for angle 0:
  East  3 o'clock = 0
  North 12 o'clock = 90
  West  9 o'clock = 180
  South 6 o'clock = 270

Enter direction for angle 0
<0>: ↵
```
Accepts the default setting for angle 0, which is East 3 o'clock.

Step 1.6: The final selection in the UNITS command determines the direction in which angles are measured, starting from angle 0. Because angles are measured counterclockwise in most drafting applications, accept the default response (No) to the prompt:

```
Do you want angles measured          Accepts the default
clockwise? <N> ⏎                      of counterclockwise
                                      angles
```

The units are now defined for the drawing. A text screen, however, still appears on your monitor.

Step 2.0: To toggle back to the graphics screen, press F1 at the `Command:` prompt. F1 toggles between graphics mode and text mode:

DEFINING THE DRAWING AREA'S LIMITS

Now that you have defined the drawing units, you must define the drawing area. The LIMITS command performs this function by defining the drawing's boundaries and the placement of the grid. The LIMITS command also assists in magnifying the drawing, and is used to control the placement of geometry in the drawing.

Step 3.0: Issue the LIMITS command by entering LIMITS or choose Settings, then Limits:

```
Command: LIMITS ⏎                     Starts the LIMITS
                                      command
```

Step 3.1: Enter the absolute coordinate of the lower left corner of the drawing area:

```
Reset Model space limits:            Accepts the default
ON/OFF/<Lower left corner>           and specifies
<0.00,0.00>: ⏎                       0.00,0.00 as the
                                     lower left corner of
                                     the drawing area
```

Step 3.2: At the following prompt, define the upper right corner of the screen to an area large enough to accommodate the drawing. Set the drawing's upper right corner at X=17 and Y=11 to specify a drawing area equal to a B-size sheet of paper:

```
Upper right corner <12.00,9.00>:     Sets the upper right
17,11 ⏎                              corner of the drawing
                                     at X=17, Y=11
```

Zooming To Display the Drawing Limits

The new drawing area does not show up on the screen when you change only the limits. You must use the ZOOM command to change the magnification or area to be viewed in the drawing. As drawings become larger and more detailed, you will use the ZOOM command frequently.

OPTIONS

The ZOOM command has the following options:

- **All.** Displays the entire drawing to its limits or drawing extents, whichever is larger
- **Center.** Enables you to pick a center point and a unit height or magnification
- **Dynamic.** Presents a resizable box that you can move around the screen, to select the desired zoom area dynamically
- **Extents.** Maximizes the drawing geometry to fit the screen
- **Left.** Enables you to pick a lower left corner and a unit of height or magnification
- **Previous.** Restores a previous Zoom, Pan, View, or Dview
- **Vmax.** Zooms out as far as possible without forcing AutoCAD to regenerate the image
- **Window.** Enables you to place an on-screen window around the area in which you want to zoom
- **Scale.** Enables you to specify a zoom factor that is a multiplier of the limits
- **Scale(X/XP).** Enables you to specify a zoom factor that is a multiplier of the present zoom magnification

As with many commands, ZOOM can be entered at the keyboard or chosen from the menu.

Step 4.0: Issue the ZOOM command:

Command: **ZOOM** ↵   Starts the ZOOM
                                                        command

Step 4.1: Enter All so that you can view the entire drawing (to its limits) on-screen, as follows:

```
All/Center/Dynamic/Extent/Left/      Specifies the All
Previous/Vmax/Window/<Scale          option and zooms
(X/XP)>: A ↵                         out to display the
                                     entire drawing area
```

Although you see very little happen on-screen, AutoCAD adjusts the drawing area to the 17x11 area that you defined when you used the LIMITS command. If you did not use the ZOOM command, you would not be able to view the entities that you create outside the 17,11 area you have created.

LAYERS IN A DRAWING

To finish setting up a new drawing, you must define the drawing's layers. As mentioned earlier, AutoCAD layers are much like the transparent sheets many designers and drafters use in overlay drafting. The sheets enable the drafter to draw several different components of a drawing by placing each component on a separate transparent sheet. The drafter then can overlay the sheets to see their relationships. By using the transparent overlays, the drafter does not have to draw all the components on the same sheet. AutoCAD layers work in much the same way, but as you will learn, they are much more powerful and flexible than ordinary transparent drawing sheets.

You use the LAYER command to separate functional areas within the drawing, such as object lines, text, dimensions, and title blocks. Layers can be controlled with the LAYER command typed at the command prompt or through the Layer Control dialog box. This lesson begins with the LAYER command and then introduces the Layer Control dialog box later in the chapter.

OPTIONS

The LAYER command has the following options:

- **?.** Displays a list of all the drawing's layers and their settings
- **Make.** Creates a new layer and makes it current
- **Set.** Selects a predefined layer as the current drawing layer
- **New.** Creates a new layer, but does not make it current
- **ON.** Makes a layer visible on-screen or during a plot
- **OFF.** Makes a layer invisible on-screen or during a plot

---

- **Color.** Assigns a color to a layer
- **Ltype.** Assigns a linetype to a layer
- **Freeze.** Makes a layer invisible and causes it to be omitted from the drawing-regeneration process
- **Thaw.** Reverses the Freeze option
- **Lock.** Enables a layer to be seen on screen, but the layer cannot be modified
- **Unlock.** Reverses the Lock option

DEFINING THE DRAWING'S LAYERS

You now use the LAYER command to define the three layers for this drawing. After they are created you assign their linetype and color characteristics. After you have established the layers to be used in your drawing, you need to make one of those layers the current layer. The current layer is the active layer; that is, the layer on which you are currently drawing. You can use the LAYER command's Set option to make any layer current at any time (as long as the desired layer is not frozen), but only one layer can be current at a time.

Step 5.0: Issue the LAYER command:

```
Command: LAYER ↵
```
Starts the LAYER command

Step 5.1: Specify the the New option to create new layers in the drawing:

```
?/Make/Set/New/ON/OFF/ Color/
Ltype/Freeze/Thaw/LOck/Unlock:
N ↵
```
Specifies the option to create one or more new layers

Step 5.2: Create three new layers with the names OBJECT, DIM, and O-HIDDEN. You can create multiple layers at one time by separating their names with commas:

```
New layer name(s):
OBJECT,DIM,O-HIDDEN ↵
```
Creates and names three new layers

Step 5.3: Invoke the Ltype option and assign a Hidden line linetype to the layer named O-HIDDEN, as follows:

```
?/Make/Set/New/ON/OFF/ Color/
Ltype/Freeze/Thaw/LOck/
Unlock: LT ↵
```
Specifies the Linetype option

```
Linetype (or ?) <CONTINUOUS>:        Specifies the hidden
Hidden ⏎                              linetype
Layer name (s) for linetype          Assigns the hidden
HIDDEN <0>: O-HIDDEN ⏎               linetype to the
                                      layer O-HIDDEN
```

Step 5.4: Invoke the Color option and assign a color to the layer named DIM, as follows:

```
?/Make/Set/New/ON/OFF/ Color/        Selects the Color
Ltype/Freeze/Thaw/LOck/              option
Unlock:C ⏎
Color: Red ⏎                         Specifies red as the
                                      layer color
Layer name(s) for color 1            Assigns red to the
(red) <0>: DIM ⏎                    layer DIM
```

Step 5.5: Invoke the Set option and make the layer named OBJECT the current layer, as follows:

```
?/Make/Set/New/ON/OFF/ Color/        Selects the Set
Ltype/Freeze/Thaw/LOck/              option
Unlock:S ⏎
New current layer <0>: OBJECT ⏎     Makes OBJECT the
                                      current layer
```

Step 5.6: Exit from the LAYER command by pressing Enter without typing an option word:

```
?/Make/Set/New/ON/OFF/ Color/        Ends the LAYER
Ltype/Freeze/Thaw/LOck/Unlock⏎      command
```

Now that your screen and drawing area are set up, you can begin creating your drawing.

EXERCISE 2: CREATING THE DRAWING

In this exercise, you use AutoCAD's drawing commands to create the geometry previously shown in figure 3.1. You begin the drawing by drawing the rectangle shown in figure 3.2 as a closed polygon. A *closed polygon* is a multisided object with all end points connected. As you work through the following steps, you will create the rectangle by drawing several lines, and then remove two lines to form definition points for two arcs, which will be added to the drawing later.

Figure 3.2:

The 7-unit-by-2-unit rectangle.

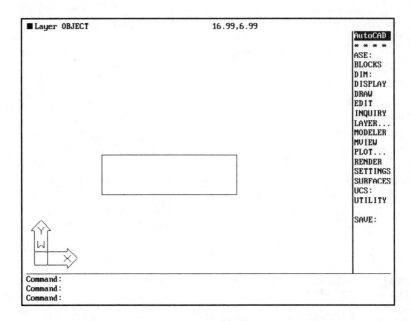

TASKS TO BE COMPLETED IN THIS EXERCISE

- Draw the rectangle
- Erase portions of the rectangle
- Redraw the screen

DRAWING WITH THE ABSOLUTE COORDINATES

In this exercise, you use AutoCAD's LINE command to create a series of lines, which form a rectangle. In Lesson 2, you used the LINE command to create lines, and you picked points on the screen by using your pointing device. Pointing devices are handy if you need to pick points and locate geometry randomly. If you need to draw with precision, however, you should specify points by telling AutoCAD exactly where to place them, based on their relationships to one another and to AutoCAD's X and Y axes.

If you have ever studied geometry, you may remember that 2D geometry can be drawn on a plane, which is divided into quadrants. The plane is separated into quadrants by two lines, called "axes." The horizontal axis is called the X axis; the vertical axis is called the Y axis. The two axes intersect at one point, which is called the origin. Each axis can be divided into an infinite number of equal units, which can be used as a guide, much like the yard lines on a football field. Units are counted starting at the origin, which has a value of 0 in both the X and Y directions (see fig. 3.3).

When you use absolute coordinates to pick a two-dimensional point in AutoCAD, you specify the point in the X,Y format. In this format, the X value represents the point's position along the X axis, and the Y value represents the point's position along the Y axis. Absolute coordinates are defined by their distance from the origin, which is the point 0,0. You specify absolute coordinates by typing their X and Y values at the keyboard.

Suppose that you specified the absolute coordinates 3,2, 7,7, and 13,4. Figure 3.4 shows you where these points would appear in relation to the X and Y axes.

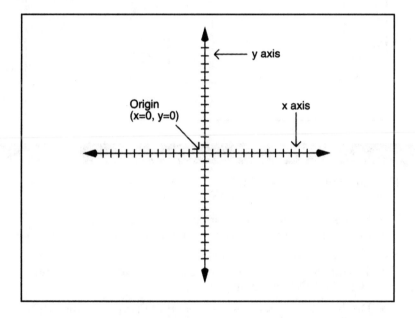

Figure 3.3:

The X and Y axes, as used in AutoCAD, with the origin indicated.

Notice that all these points have positive values. You also can specify points that have a negative X value, a negative Y value, or both. AutoCAD places such points according to their relationship to the origin.

The best way to see how AutoCAD works with coordinates is to practice using them in a drawing. Use absolute coordinates to create the rectangle.

Drawing the Rectangle

To draw the lines that define the rectangle, enter **LINE** to start the command. You also can select Line from the Draw pull-down menu. If you do, you can select which type of line from four options.

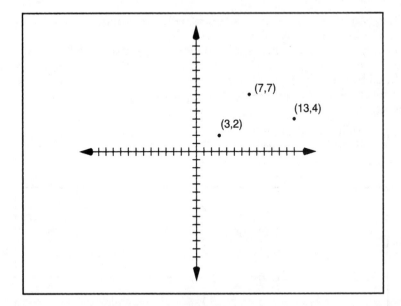

The Line command issued from the Draw pull-down menu is customized to develop the following type of lines:

- **Segments.** Specifies the creation of continuous lines that begin the starting point of a new line from the end point of the last line

- **1 Segment.** Specifies the creation of one line segment and exits the LINE command

- **Double Lines.** Specifies the creation of two sets of lines, one parallel to another

- **Sketch.** Specifies the creation of a free-hand sketch comprised of short line segments

To develop the rectangle, draw eight lines using absolute coordinates. A line seven units long will be the bottom of the rectangle, two lines of two units each make up the side, and three of the lines are one-unit lines that define the rectangle. The remaining two lines pass through the area defined by the arcs. After you draw the lines, go back and erase the two extra lines so that you can create the arcs.

Step 1.0: Issue the LINE command and choose the Segments menu option:

`Command:` *Choose* Draw, *then* Line, *then* Segments	Starts the LINE command

Step 1.1: Specify the absolute point for the starting point of the line:

`Line from point: 4,4 ↵`	Starts the line at the absolute coordinate 4,4

Step 1.2: Specify the absolute point for the ending point of the line:

`To point: 11,4 ↵`	Ends the line at the absolute coordinate of 11,4

NOTE

If you type **LINE** at the command prompt or select Line and then Segments from the Draw pull-down menu, AutoCAD assumes you want to create more than one line. As a result, it *rubberbands* the cursor, which means AutoCAD trails a segment between the last point and the cursor. Rubberbanding helps you visualize where the next point will be placed. If you make a mistake, choose the UNDO command from the screen menu. This removes the last line and enables you to continue drawing your lines.

Step 1.3: Continuing with the LINE command, draw the second line of the rectangle:

`To point: 11,6 ↵`	Draws the rectangle's second line

Step 1.4: Continuing with the LINE command, draw the remaining lines for the rectangle:

`To point: 10,6 ↵`	Draws the first short line
`To point: 8,6 ↵`	Draws the second short line

To point: **7,6** ↵	Draws the third short line
To point: **5,6** ↵	Draws the fourth short line
To point: **4,6** ↵	Draws the fifth short line

Step 1.5: Finish the polygon and end the LINE command. The easiest way to do this is by using the LINE command's Close option. This option finishes the object by connecting the last specified end point with the first point you specified when you issued the LINE command:

| To point: **C** ↵ | Closes the polygon and ends the LINE command |

You now have the outline of the first object, as you saw in figure 3.2.

ERASING PORTIONS OF THE RECTANGLE

To complete the object, you need to add the two arcs. Before you add the arcs, however, you must erase the two lines that cross over the area where the arcs belong (see fig. 3.5).

Figure 3.5:

The rectangle with two lines removed.

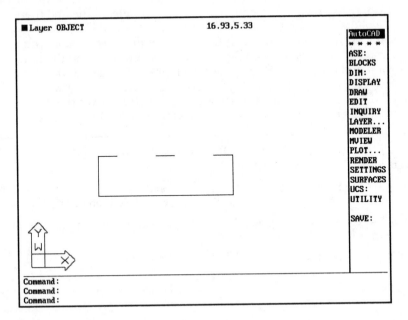

To remove these objects, you first must use the ERASE command. When you issue the ERASE command at the `Command:` prompt, the crosshair cursor disappears and is replaced by a small box called a *pickbox*. You can use your pointing device to move the pickbox around the screen. Position the pickbox on the entity you want to erase, and then click the pointing device's pick button (the left button if you use a mouse). When you select an entity, it is highlighted on-screen. You can use the pickbox to select several entities, and then erase them all at one time by pressing Enter.

You can also issue the ERASE command by selecting it from the Modify pull-down menu. When you select Erase from the menu, you must select one of four options.

OPTIONS

The Erase command issued from the Modify pull-down menu includes the following options:

- **Select.** Enables you to select more than one entity. Press Enter to erase the selected entities.

- **Single.** Selects and erases one entity.

- **Last.** Selects and erases the last entity added to the drawing.

- **Oops.** Returns (un-erases) the last group of erased entities to the drawing.

Step 2.0: Issue the ERASE command and select the two lines to be removed from the drawing. When both lines are highlighted, press Enter to erase them:

`Command:` *Choose* Modify, *then* Erase, *then* Select	Starts the ERASE command
`Select objects:` *Pick the line at* Ⓐ *(see fig. 3.6)*	Selects the first line to be erased
`1 found`	
`Select objects:` *Pick the line at* Ⓑ *(see fig. 3.6)*	Selects the second line to be erased
`1 found`	
`Select objects:` ↵	Erases the lines and ends the ERASE command

Figure 3.6:

*The rectangle with
the two short lines
highlighted.*

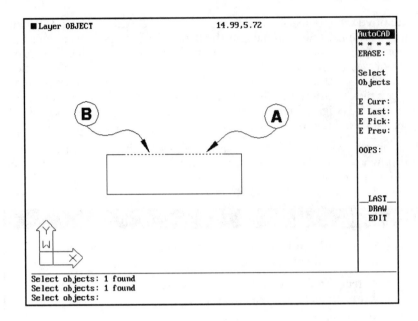

REDRAWING THE SCREEN

When you select an object using commands such as ERASE, selection
marks, or blips, are left on-screen. These blips are used to identify the
location of points picked on the screen. To remove these marks, use the
REDRAW command. The REDRAW command cleans up the screen by
removing any drawing marks.

Step 3.0: Use the REDRAW command to clean up the screen:

Command: **REDRAW** ⏎   Redraws the screen

Your rectangle now should resemble the one in figure 3.5.

EXERCISE 3: CREATING ARCS

In this exercise, you continue to develop the drawing by creating two
arcs (see fig. 3.7). To create the arcs, use the ARC command. AutoCAD
provides several options for creating arcs. Some methods are simple;
others are quite complex. The method you choose depends on the
requirements of your drawing. In this exercise, you create one arc simply
by specifying a series of coordinates. To create the second arc, you use a

special tool called an object snap override. Although object snaps can be difficult to understand, they are extremely accurate and powerful drawing tools. When you learn to use object snaps, you will want to use them whenever possible because they take much of the guesswork out of drawing.

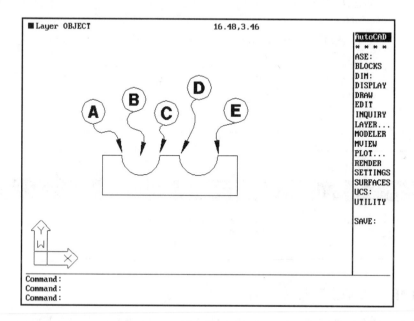

Figure 3.7:

The rectangle with arcs and labeled arc-definition points.

AutoCAD
* * * *
ASE:
BLOCKS
DIM:
DISPLAY
DRAW
EDIT
INQUIRY
LAYER...
MODELER
MVIEW
PLOT...
RENDER
SETTINGS
SURFACES
UCS:
UTILITY

SAVE:

Command:
Command:
Command:

OPTIONS

The ARC command creates an arc based on the following options:

- **3-point.** Pick three points on the circumference of the arc. The first and last points are the end points of the arc.

- **S,C,E.** Pick the starting point, center point, and ending point.

- **S,C,A.** Pick the starting point, center point, and included angle.

- **S,C,L.** Pick the starting point, center point, and length of chord.

- **S,E,A.** Pick the starting point, ending point, and included angle.

- **S,E,R.** Pick the starting point, ending point, and the radius.

- **S,E,D.** Pick the starting point, ending point, and tangent direction.
- **C,S,E.** Pick the center point, starting point, and ending point.
- **C,S,A.** Pick the center point, starting point, and included angle.
- **C,S,L.** Pick the center point, starting point, and length of chord.
- **CONTIN.** Select an end point for an arc that continues tangent to the last arc.

TASKS TO BE COMPLETED IN THIS EXERCISE

- Draw an arc by specifying absolute coordinates
- Draw an arc by using an object snap override

DRAWING THE FIRST ARC

To draw an arc, you must calculate the coordinates for the arc. You know that point A in figure 3.5 is the end point of the first short line that was drawn earlier. From this, you can calculate the remaining absolute coordinates for the arc.

Step 1.0: Issue the ARC command:

Command: **ARC** ↵	Starts the ARC command

Step 1.1: Enter the starting point:

Center/<Start point>: **5,6** ↵	Defines a point at Ⓐ (see fig. 3.7)

Step 1.2: Specify the Center Arc option:

Center/End/<Second point>: **C** ↵	Selects the ARC command's Center option

Step 1.3: Enter the arc center point:

Center: **6,6** ↵

Defines the center of the arc at Ⓑ (see fig. 3.7)

Step 1.4: Enter the arc end point:

Angle/Length of chord/<End point>: **7,6** ↵

Defines the arc's ending point at Ⓒ (see fig. 3.7)

Your first arc is now complete.

Drawing the Second Arc

Now you can create the second arc as was shown in figure 3.7. The first arc was drawn using absolute coordinates. Although absolute coordinates guarantee accuracy, occasionally you may not know which coordinates to use when you have to specify a point in AutoCAD. As you already have seen, however, the pointing device and crosshair cursor are not precise enough when you need to specify extremely accurate points. This is especially true when you want one entity—such as an arc—to attach to the end point of another entity that already has been drawn, such as the lines in the rectangle. Fortunately, AutoCAD features a set of tools that enable you to draw accurately even when you do not know which absolute coordinates to use. These tools are called object snaps.

Understanding Object Snaps

Object snaps enable you to "snap" a point on the object you are currently drawing to a point on another object. Suppose, for example, that you want to draw an arc that starts at the end of an existing line. You want to use the line's end point as the arc's starting point, but you do not know the exact coordinates for the end point. How can you place the arc's starting point so that it lies exactly on the line's end point? If you do not know the point's coordinates, you cannot type them. You can try to "eyeball" the point by using your pointing device and the crosshair cursor, but chances are that you will not be able to place the arc's starting point exactly on the line's end point.

NOTE

Even if you eyeball attaching the arc to the line and it looks as if the two are touching, AutoCAD may not consider the line and the arc to be attached.

Such situations are the perfect time to use an object snap. When you activate an object snap, the crosshair cursor changes to include a large box, which you can use to select any point precisely. You simply position the box so that it surrounds the desired point or touches a portion of the entity to which you want to snap. You then click your pointing device's pick button and AutoCAD automatically finds the point. In the case of the arc and line, you simply position the pickbox over the end of the line and click your pointing device's pick button; AutoCAD zeroes in on the line's end point and makes it the starting point for the new arc.

You can activate AutoCAD's object snaps by holding down the Shift key and pressing button two or three on the input device or by choosing Object Snap from the Assist pull-down menu. When you do, AutoCAD presents a list of options.

OPTIONS

Object Snap options include:

- **ENDpoint.** Selects the end point of an arc or line segment
- **CENter.** Selects the center of an arc or circle
- **INTersection.** Selects the intersection of two objects that cross
- **TANgent.** Selects a tangent point on a circle or arc
- **QUAdrant.** Selects a point directly on the sides, top, or bottom of a circle or arc
- **NEArest.** Select a point on an object close to where the object is picked
- **NODe.** Selects a point entity
- **PERpendicular.** Selects a point perpendicular to a linear object
- **INSertion.** Selects the insertion point of text or blocks
- **MIDpoint.** Selects the midpoint of a line or arc

You also can use object snaps from within other drawing commands when you need to specify attachment points. If you do not want to select an object snap from a menu, you can simply type the first three letters of the snap's name. After the object snap type is specified, the *Aperture Box* appears at the intersection of the cross hairs. To pick a point with object snaps, place the aperture box on the entity near the desired point and press the pick button.

You will use object snaps in other lessons. Although you may find them difficult to understand right now, you will find them a valuable drawing aid after you master their use.

Using an Object Snap To Draw the Second Arc

Now you can draw the next arc. You start by issuing the ARC command, and then you use the ENDpoint object snap to connect the arc's ends to the two lines at the top of the rectangle (point D and point E in fig. 3.7).

Step 2.0: Issue the ARC command:

Command: **ARC** ↵	Starts the ARC command

Step 2.1: Issue object snap ENDpoint by entering END within the ARC command prompt:

Center/<Start point>: **END** ↵	Activates the ENDpoint object snap

Step 2.2: Pick the starting point of the arc by placing the aperture box near the desired point and pressing the pick button:

of *Use the aperture box to select* ⒹD (see fig. 3.7)	Specifies the arc's starting point

Step 2.3: Continuing with the ARC command's next prompt, you can specify the arc's second point, center point, or the ending point. Specify the End option and use the object snap again to snap the arc to the other point at the top of the rectangle:

Center/End/<Second point>: **E** ↵	Selects the ARC command's End option
End point: **END** ↵	Activates the ENDpoint object snap
of *Use the pickbox to select* ⒺE (see fig. 3.7)	Specifies the arc's ending point

Step 2.4: Continuing with the ARC command's next prompt, you can set the arc's direction, radius, center point, or the included angle. The included angle is the angle around which the arc must curve. If you had a 90-degree angle, for example, the arc would curve for 90 degrees or 1/4 of a full circle. Set your arc's included angle at 180 degrees:

Angle/Direction/Radius <Center point>: **A** ↵	Selects the ARC command's Angle option
Included angle: **180** ↵	Creates an arc that covers 180 degrees

This finishes both arcs. You now are ready to create the drawing's second entity.

EXERCISE 4: DRAWING THE RIGHT-SIDE VIEW

Now you can create the object on the right side of the drawing (see fig. 3.8). This object represents the view of the first object's right side. The object consists of a simple box, but also contains a new linetype.

Figure 3.8:

The drawing with the finished right-side entity.

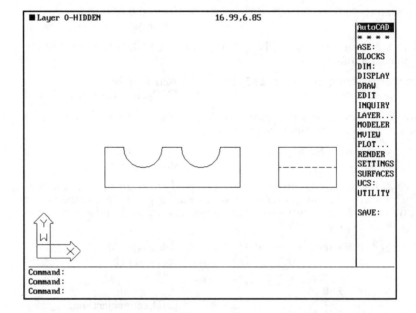

TASKS TO BE COMPLETED IN THIS EXERCISE

- Draw a box
- Change layers
- Create a hidden line

DRAWING THE BOX

The box is easy to draw. It is a 3-unit-by-2-unit rectangle, which you can create with the LINE command.

Step 1.0: Use the LINE command to create the box:

Command: **LINE** ↵	Starts the LINE command
From point: **13,4** ↵	Specifies the coordinate for the lower left corner of the rectangle
To point: **16,4** ↵	Specifies the lower right corner of the rectangle
To point: **16,6** ↵	Specifies the upper right corner of the rectangle
To point: **13,6** ↵	Sets the upper left corner of the rectangle
To point: **C** ↵	Closes the polygon and ends the LINE command

You now have created the object outline and are ready to add the hidden line in the middle of the rectangle. Before you do, however, you need to set a new current layer.

USING A DIALOG BOX TO CHANGE THE CURRENT LAYER

Earlier in this chapter you created a layer, O-HIDDEN, which uses the hidden line linetype. Your next drawing task is to draw a hidden line within the box you just created. First, however, you need to make O-HIDDEN the current layer.

Layers can be manipulated by entering the LAYER command at the Command: prompt or you can use the Layer Control dialog box. The Layer Control dialog box is shown in figure 3.9. The Layer Control dialog box displays the current layers in the drawing and their settings. To use the dialog box, you highlight the layer (or layers) to modify and then pick the button that performs the desired funtion. Some buttons will display a second dialog box, from which you must select the desired settings. To create a new layer, enter the name in the input box and pick the **N**ew button. When you finish setting the layers, select OK to exit the dialog box.

Figure 3.9:

*Layer Control
dialog box.*

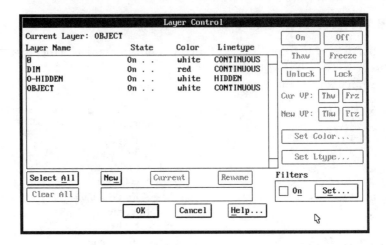

Step 2.0: Use the Layer Control dialog box to make O-HIDDEN the current layer:

Command: *Choose* Settings, *then*
Layer Control

Displays the Layer
Control dialog box

Select O-HIDDEN *by placing the arrow
on the line that displays O-HIDDEN
and pressing the pick button*

Selects the layer to
modify

Choose **C**urrent *by placing the arrow on
the dialog box button and pressing the
pick button on the input device or by
pressing Alt-C and then pressing Enter*

Sets the selected
layer as current

Choose OK *to exit the Layer Control
dialog box*

Closes the Layer
Control dialog box
and accepts the changes

The word **O-HIDDEN** should appear in the upper left corner of the screen
to confirm that it now is the current drawing layer.

CREATING THE HIDDEN LINE

Now you can draw the hidden line one unit up from the lower left
corner of the rectangle.

Step 3.0: Use the LINE command to draw the hidden line:

Command: **LINE** ↵

Starts the LINE
command

From point: **13,5** ↵	Starts the line one unit up from the lower left corner of the rectangle
To point: **16,5** ↵	Ends the line three units to the right of the starting point
To point:↵	Ends the LINE command

Your completed drawing now should resemble the illustration previously shown in figure 3.8.

ENDING THE DRAWING SESSION

As you learned in Lesson 2, when you are finished working on a drawing, you can save the drawing to disk and exit from AutoCAD, as follows:

Command: *Choose* File, *then choose* Save	Saves the drawing to disk
Command: *Choose* File, *then* Exit AutoCAD	Saves the drawing to disk and exits AutoCAD

SUMMARY

A CAD operator must be able to create accurate, full-scale drawings. To do so, you as a drafter first must set up the drawing environment. The Cartesian coordinate system enables you to specify the definition points of the entities in the drawing. As geometry is created, you can control the appearance of objects by separating them on different layers.

IN THIS LESSON, YOU LEARNED TO DO THE FOLLOWING:

- Set up the drawing environment
- Use absolute coordinates and object snaps
- Draw on different layers
- Draw arcs
- Set different linetypes

In addition, you focused on setting up a drawing and creating accurate geometry. In the next lesson, you learn more about coordinate input, develop geometry by using editing commands, and add dimensions to a drawing.

REVIEW

1. Use the **LINE** command to draw a four unit horizontal line.

2. Use the **LINE** command to draw a 3-unit-by-4-unit rectangle.

3. Use the **LINE** command and the INTersection object snap to draw a diagonal line between the corners of the rectangle created in question two.

4. Use the **ARC** command and the MIDpoint object snap to create an arc that uses the end points of the diagonal line in question three as its end points and uses the midpoint of the diagonal line in question three as its center.

5. Use the **LINE** and **LAYER** commands to create one blue line and one red line with a hidden line linetype.

6. Set up a drawing that uses decimal units and is accurate to three places to the right of the decimal.

7. Use **LIMITS** to create a drawing area for the drawing in question five at 75x50 units.

8. Use the **LINE** command to draw a border around the drawing in question six.

9. Create an arc that is a half circle.

10. Use **UNDO** to remove the arc in question nine.

DRAWING A GASKET

OVERVIEW

In the last two lessons, you learned enough AutoCAD basics to create simple drawings, find your way through the program's menu system, navigate the Drawing Editor, and save your drawing files. While this basic knowledge is an important first step in your mastery of AutoCAD, it can take you only so far. After you get beyond the basics, you find that AutoCAD offers hundreds of more advanced drawing and editing tools, which can help you create practically any drawing you can imagine. This lesson introduces some of AutoCAD's most important and frequently used advanced features.

As you learned in the last lesson, AutoCAD uses the Cartesian coordinate system to create geometry. When you select points, AutoCAD uses them to create geometry along the X, Y, and Z axes. Lesson 3 explained that absolute coordinates enable you to create extremely precise drawings. Absolute coordinates are difficult to use, however—especially in complex drawings. They require thorough knowledge of the drawing's units and the X-, Y-, and Z-coordinate locations of entities in the drawing. When you draw with absolute coordinates, you might have trouble drawing entities in relation to one another unless you know absolute-coordinate locations for each entity.

Luckily, AutoCAD also enables you to use relative coordinates. When you use *relative coordinates*, you pick points according to their relationship to previously picked points or existing entities. Relative coordinates free you from the need to know entities' absolute coordinates. This lesson shows you how to draw by using relative coordinates.

You have already used basic drawing commands, such as LINE and CIRCLE, and simple editing commands, such as ERASE. AutoCAD features many other drawing and editing commands that let you create highly complicated entities. The advanced drawing commands enable you to create polygons, ellipses, and lines of varying thicknesses. These commands simplify the creation of complex entities because you simply tell the program your specifications for the entity. AutoCAD then draws the entity for you.

AutoCAD also features advanced editing commands that simplify the creation of complicated geometry. In fact, experienced AutoCAD drafters create more geometry by using the editing commands than by using the drawing commands (with the exception of LINE and CIRCLE). The editing commands enable you to modify or duplicate existing geometry to create new geometry and help you develop more accurate drawings. You learn a number of powerful drawing and editing commands in this lesson.

The final subject covered in this lesson is the addition of dimension information to your drawing. Dimensions play a vitally important role in drawings in many drafting disciplines. Dimensions give the drawing's audience critical information about the drawing's subject, such as the length, width, and angle of lines. AutoCAD's dimensioning capabilities are one of the program's most powerful features. AutoCAD can add dimension information of all types to any drawing, almost automatically, freeing you from calculating line lengths, angles, radii, or scale. The program quickly adds extension lines, dimension lines, text, and arrows at the size you specify. By simply selecting locations on the drawing, you can instruct AutoCAD to develop the correct dimension information automatically.

TOPICS COVERED IN THIS LESSON

In this lesson, you learn to perform the following operations:

- Create a drawing of a gasket
- Create an array
- Add center marks to the drawing's arcs
- Change the display and copy an object
- Add linear dimensions to the drawing
- Add dimensions to a polygon

This lesson teaches you how to use the following AutoCAD commands:

- **ARRAY.** Makes multiple copies of entities
- **CHAMFER.** Connects two lines with a new line segment
- **COPY.** Copies objects
- **Dim ALIGNED.** Draws dimension lines so that they are parallel to the extension line origin points or to a selected entity
- **Dim CENTER.** Constructs a dimensioning center mark or center lines for circles and arcs
- **Dim CONTINUE.** Enables you to use the previous dimension as a reference for the next dimension
- **Dim HORIZONTAL.** Draws the dimension line horizontally
- **Dim RADIUS.** Dimensions the radius of circles and arcs
- **Dim VERTICAL.** Draws the dimension line vertically
- **FILLET.** Enables you to create an arc between any two lines, polylines, circles, or arcs
- **POLYGON.** Draws a regular 2D polygon with as many as 1024 sides

SETTING UP THE DRAWING

As you learned in Lesson 3, you must set up the drawing environment before you actually begin drawing. In this lesson, however, you use dialog boxes to set up the drawing. You also make some minor changes in the setup for this drawing.

Step 1.0: Start AutoCAD, then name the new drawing. (Choose File, then New.) Discard changes to the present drawing and enter **LESSON4** in the New Drawing Name input box and press Enter.

Step 2.0: Issue the **LIMITS** command; make the lower left corner 0,0 and the upper right corner 17,11, as you did in Lesson 3.

Step 3.0: Issue the **ZOOM** command with the All option to see the new drawing limits.

In this drawing you use the same unit settings as in Lesson 3; however, you set them using the Units Control dialog box. This dialog box performs the same function as the UNITS command.

Step 4.0: Issue the Units Control dialog box:

Command: *Choose* Settings, *then* Units Control

Step 4.1: Select the unit settings and choose OK to close the dialog box:

Choose the down arrow *under* **P**recision	Displays the available settings for decimal place accuracy
Choose 0.00	Sets the decimal place accuracy
Choose OK	Exits the Units Control dialog box and saves the settings

This lesson's drawing uses different layers than the Lesson 3 drawing used. After you set up the drawing units, use the Layer Control dialog box to create this drawing's layers. For this lesson, you need to create only two new layers: DIM and OBJECT.

Step 5.0: Use the Layer Control dialog box to set up the drawing layers:

Command: *Choose* Settings, *then* Layer Control	Displays the Layer Control dialog box

Step 5.1: Define the two new layers.

Enter **DIM** *in the new layer input box and choose* Ne**w**	Creates a new layer named DIM
Enter **OBJECT** *in the new layer input box and choose* Ne**w**	Creates a new layer named OBJECT

Step 5.2: Assign the color red to the layer DIM:

Choose the layer DIM, *then* **S**et Color, *then a red color square, then* OK

Step 5.3: Set the current drawing layer:

Choose the layer DIM	Deselects the layer
Choose the layer OBJECT	Selects the layer
Choose **C**urrent, *then* OK	Sets OBJECT as the current layer and exits the layer control dialog box

Now that your drawing environment is set up, you can begin creating the LESSON4 drawing. After you complete this lesson, you have a fully dimensioned drawing of a gasket, like the one shown in figure 4.1.

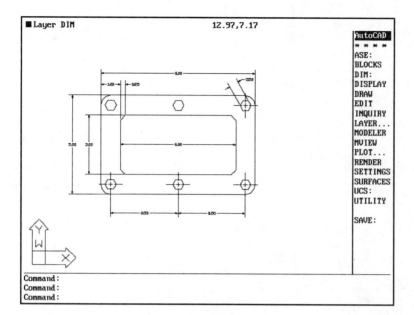

Figure 4.1:

The completed gasket drawing.

EXERCISE 1: CREATING THE GASKET DRAWING

In this exercise, you use AutoCAD's drawing commands to create the geometry shown in figure 4.2. The following steps show you how to create two rectangles, one inside the other, to form the gasket's inner and outer lines. The outer rectangle measures 7 units by 5 units; the inner rectangle is 5 units by 3 units. After you draw the two rectangles, you use two new editing commands to round the corners of the outer rectangle and chamfer the inner rectangle's four corners.

TASKS TO BE COMPLETED IN THIS EXERCISE

- Draw the rectangles
- Round the corners of the outer rectangle
- Add chamfers to the inner rectangle

Figure 4.2:

The rectangles that form the basis of the gasket drawing.

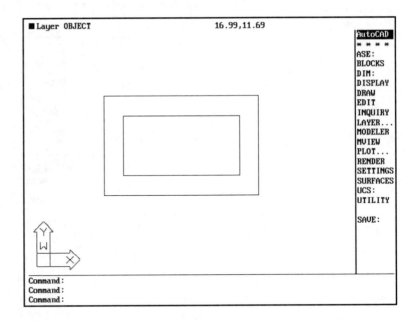

DRAWING THE RECTANGLES

Use the LINE command to draw the two rectangles. As you work through the following steps, you begin the first line using absolute coordinates, as you learned in the last lesson. You then use relative coordinates to create the other lines. You specify relative coordinates by their distance in the X and Y directions from the last point you selected.

Relative coordinates take basically the same format as absolute coordinates (two numbers separated by a comma), but the resemblance ends there. When you enter relative coordinates, use the @ symbol as a prefix to tell AutoCAD to position the following point in relation to the last point drawn. In the following steps, for example, you draw the first point at the absolute coordinates 4,4. For the next point, you enter the relative coordinates @8,0 to specify a point that lies 8 units in the X direction from the first point, and 0 units in the Y direction from the first point.

When you use relative coordinates, positive numbers tell AutoCAD to move in the positive X or Y direction. In the X direction, a positive number tells AutoCAD to move to the right; a negative number moves to the left. In the Y direction, a positive number moves up; a negative number moves down.

Step 1.0: Issue the LINE command and begin drawing the outer rectangle:

Command: **LINE** ↵   Starts the LINE command

```
From point: 4,4 ↵          Begins the line at
(see fig. 4.3)             the absolute
                           coordinate 4,4
```

Step 1.1: Continuing with the LINE command, use relative coordinates to specify the X and Y distance from the last point. Use the @ symbol before the values to indicate relative rather than absolute coordinates:

```
To point: @8,0 ↵          Draws an 8-unit
(see fig. 4.3)             horizontal line to
                           the right

To point: @0,5 ↵          Draws a 5-unit
(see fig. 4.3)             vertical line
                           straight up from
                           the previously
                           specified point

To point: @-8,0 ↵         Draws an 8-unit
(see fig. 4.3)             vertical line to the
                           left from the
                           previously specified
                           point
```

Step 1.2: Close the polygon and end the LINE command:

```
To point: C ↵
```

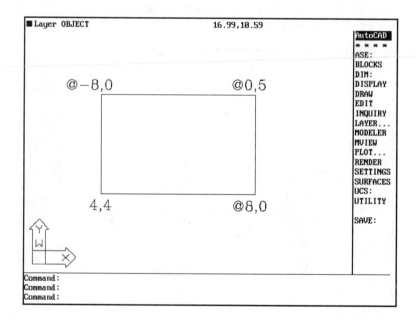

Figure 4.3:
The outer rectangle with coordinates indicated.

Now you are ready to create the inner rectangle.

Step 2.0: Issue the LINE command again, using relative coordinates to draw the inner rectangle:

Command: **LINE** ↵	Starts the LINE command
From point: **5,5** ↵	Begins the line 1 unit above and 1 unit to the right of the original starting point
To point: **@6,0** ↵	Draws a 6-unit line to the right
To point: **@0,3** ↵	Draws a 3-unit line straight up
To point: **@-6,0** ↵	Draws a 6-unit line to the left

Step 2.1: Close the polygon and end the LINE command:

To point: **C** ↵

ROUNDING THE OUTER RECTANGLE'S CORNERS

Now that you have the two rectangles, you need to round the outer rectangle's four corners as shown in figure 4.4. To round the corners, use the FILLET command. The FILLET command rounds off the intersection of two nonparallel lines by placing an arc between them. The arc's size is based on a radius, which you specify. After you invoke the FILLET command, the cursor changes to a pickbox on-screen. To pick the lines that you want filleted, place the pickbox on the lines and click the pointing device's pick button.

Figure 4.4:

The labeled rectangle with filleted corners.

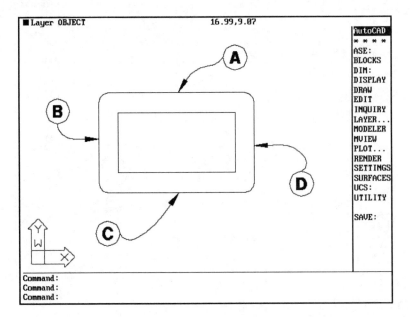

Step 3.0: Issue the FILLET command or choose Contruct, then Fillet:

Command: **FILLET** ↵   Starts the FILLET command

Step 3.1: Select the Radius option to allow for specification of the fillet arc radius:

Polyline/Radius<Select first   Selects the Radius option
>: **R** ↵   object

Step 3.2: Enter the fillet arc radius:

Enter fillet radius <0.00>: **.5** ↵   Sets the fillet arc's radius at .5 units

Now that you have defined the arc's radius, you need only to issue the FILLET command and pick the lines to be filleted.

Step 4.0: To add the fillet to the first corner, invoke the FILLET command again and pick the points where you want the fillet to occur:

Command: **FILLET** ↵   Starts the FILLET command

Polyline/Radius/<Select first   Selects the first
object>:*Pick line A (see fig. 4.4)*   line to fillet

Select second object: Selects the second
Pick line B (see fig.4.4)   line to fillet, creates the
                                       filleted corner between
                                       lines A and B,
                                       and ends the
                                       FILLET command

Step 5.0: Issue the FILLET command and fillet the second corner:

Command: **FILLET** ↵   Starts the FILLET command

Polyline/Radius/<Select first   Selects the first
object>:*Pick line B (see fig. 4.4)*   line to fillet

Select second object: Selects the second
Pick line C (see fig. 4.3)   line to fillet,
                                       creates the filleted
                                       corner, and ends
                                       FILLET command

Step 6.0: Issue the FILLET command and fillet the third corner:

Command: **FILLET** ↵   Starts the FILLET command

Polyline/Radius/<Select first   Selects the first
object>:*Pick line C (see fig. 4.4)*   line to fillet

Select second object: Selects the second
Pick line D (see fig. 4.4)   line to fillet, creates
                                       the filleted corner,
                                       and ends the
                                       FILLET command

Step 7.0: Issue the FILLET command and fillet the last corner:

Command: **FILLET** ↵	Starts the FILLET command
<Select first object>: *Pick line D (see fig. 4.4)*	Selects the first line to fillet
Select second object: *Pick line A (see fig. 4.4)*	Selects the second line to fillet, creates the filleted corner, and ends the FILLET command

The outer rectangle's corners are now rounded. Next, you can chamfer the inner rectangle's corners.

ADDING CHAMFERS TO THE INNER RECTANGLE

To bevel the corners of the inner rectangle, you use the CHAMFER command. CHAMFER places a diagonal line between any two nonparallel lines (see fig. 4.5). AutoCAD chamfers lines by trimming or extending the lines and then connecting them using an angled line segment.

Figure 4.5:

The inner rectangle, with chamfered corners.

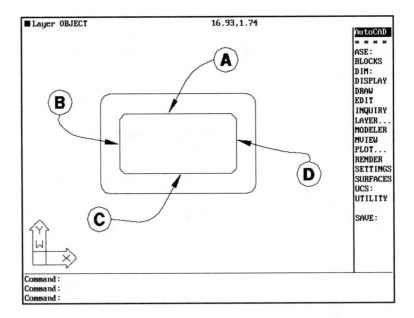

As you did for the FILLET command, you need to define the parameters to be used by the CHAMFER command. CHAMFER performs its function by trimming back the two specified lines and adding a diagonal line, which is measured as a distance from the intersection of the two lines.

Step 8.0: Issue the CHAMFER command or choose Contruct, then Chamfer:

`Command: ` **`CHAMFER`** `⏎`   Starts the CHAMFER command

Step 8.1: Select the Distance option to allow for specification of the chamfer distance from the entity intersection:

`Polyline/Distances/<Select first line>: ` **`D`** `⏎`

Step 8.2: Enter the first and second chamfer distance:

`Enter first chamfer distance`   Sets the value of
`<0.00>:.25`⏎   the first distance
                                        at .25 units

Enter second chamfer distance <0.25>: ⏎   Accepts the first
                                           chamfer distance as
                                           the default value
                                           for the second
                                           chamfer

Step 9.0: Issue the CHAMFER command again and chamfer the inner rectangle's corners:

`Command: ` **`CHAMFER`** `⏎`   Starts the CHAMFER
                                        command

`Polyline/Distances/<Select first`   Selects the first
`line>: ` *Pick line A (see fig. 4.5)*   line to chamfer

`Select second line:`   Selects the second
Pick line B (see fig. 4.5)   line to chamfer,
                                        creates the
                                        chamfered corner
                                        between lines A
                                        and B, and ends the
                                        CHAMFER command

Step 10.0: Repeat the **CHAMFER** command to chamfer the rectangle's remaining corners, as you did when you used the FILLET command earlier.

Step 11.0: Finally, use the **REDRAW** command to clean up the screen, as you did in Lesson 3. Your rectangles now resemble the ones shown in figure 4.5.

EXERCISE 2: CREATING AN ARRAY

In this exercise, you continue to develop the drawing by adding the six-sided polygon shown in the drawing's upper left corner in figure 4.6. You create this geometry by using the POLYGON command. A *polygon* is a single entity that has three or more sides. The rectangle you created earlier in this lesson, for example, is a four-sided polygon.

Figure 4.6:

The gasket drawing with one polygon in the upper left corner.

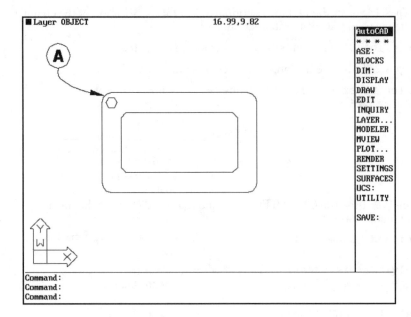

After you create the polygon, you use one of AutoCAD's special editing commands: ARRAY. The ARRAY command makes multiple copies of an entity and arranges the copies in a pattern you specify.

TASKS TO BE COMPLETED IN THIS EXERCISE

- Draw a polygon
- Create an array of polygons around the gasket

DRAWING THE POLYGON

After you invoke the POLYGON command, AutoCAD enables you to specify the number of sides you want the polygon to have. You can specify from three to 1024 sides.

AutoCAD creates a polygon by drawing on an imaginary circle whose radius you specify. You can tell AutoCAD to create the polygon around the outside of this circle (circumscribed) or inside the circle (inscribed). For this example, use the Circumscribed option.

Step 1.0: Issue the POLYGON command and choose the Circumscribed option:

`Command:` *Choose* Draw, *then* Polygon, *then* Circumscribed	Starts the POLYGON command with the circumscribed option

Step 1.1: Enter the number of sides:

`Number of sides <4>:` **`6`** ↵	Specifies a six-sided polygon

Step 1.2: Issue the object snap Center:

`Edge/<Center of polygon>:` **`CEN`** ↵	Activates the object snap Center option to locate the polygon's center

Step 1.3: Use object snap Center to place the polygon's center on the center of an existing arc (see fig. 4.6):

`of` *Use the pickbox to select arc A (see fig. 4.6)*	Specifies the arc center to be used as the center for the polygon

Step 1.4: Specify the radius of the imaginary circle:

`Radius of circle:` **`.25`** ↵

AutoCAD draws the six-sided polygon.

CREATING AN ARRAY OF POLYGONS

As figure 4.7 shows, this drawing requires six polygons. You can use the ARRAY command to create multiple copies of an entity and place the copies in a rectangular or cirucular pattern. For this drawing, you need only to pick the last object drawn (the six-sided polygon) and array it in a rectangular pattern.

Step 2.0: Invoke the ARRAY command or choose Construct, then Array. For this drawing, you need to make five copies of the polygon:

`Command:` **`ARRAY`** ↵	Starts the ARRAY command

Figure 4.7:

The drawing with six polygons.

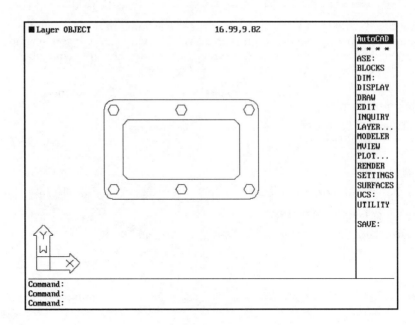

Step 2.1: Specify the object you want to copy:

Select objects: **L** ↵   Selects the last object drawn as the object to array

1 found   Specifies the number of objects selected

Step 2.2: To end the selection process, press Enter at the Select objects: prompt:

Select objects: ↵

Step 2.3: Specify the manner in which you want to copy the six-sided polygons:

Rectangular or Polar array   Creates a rectangular
(R/P) <R>: **R** ↵   array based on columns
                                       and rows, spaced at distances
                                       you specify

Step 2.4: Specify the number of rows and columns:

Number of rows (—) <1>: **2** ↵   Specifies 2 as the number of horizontal rows to be created

Number of columns (|||) <1>: **3** ↵   Specifies 3 as the number of vertical columns to be created

Step 2.5: Enter the distance between rows and columns:

`Unit cell or distance between` `rows (—):-4 ↵`	Specifies a distance of four units between the rows; the negative value places the new objects beneath the original
`Distance between columns (| | |):` `3.5 ↵`	Specifies a distance of units between the columns; the positive value places the new objects to the right of the original

This step finishes the geometry. AutoCAD also can arrange multiple copies of an entity in a *polar*, or circular, array. You create a polar array in an upcoming lesson. For now, however, your drawing resembles figure 4.7, and you now are ready to add dimensioning.

EXERCISE 3: MODIFYING AUTOCAD's DIMENSION VARIABLES

You can dimension any drawing you create in AutoCAD. *Dimensioning* enables the drawing's audience to see critical information about the drawing, including lengths, widths, and angles. AutoCAD has two dimensioning commands, DIM and DIM1, which have several options that assist you in adding dimension information to a drawing.

Before you add dimensions to the drawing, you need to make the DIM layer current. The DIM layer is the layer upon which the dimensions are placed. Make it a practice to place all dimensions on their own layer so that you can turn off the dimension layer and view the rest of the drawing more easily.

Step 1.0: Use the Layer Control dialog box to make O-HIDDEN the current layer:

Command: *Choose* Settings, *then* Layer Control	Displays the Layer Control dialog box
Select DIM, *then choose* **C**urrent, *then* OK	Selects the layer to modify, sets the selected layer as current, and closes the Layer Control dialog box

SWITCHING AutoCAD TO DIMENSIONING MODE

AutoCAD's two dimensioning commands, DIM and DIM1, enable you to add dimension information to a drawing. After you issue the DIM command, AutoCAD switches into dimensioning mode. In this mode, the Command: prompt changes to Dim: and AutoCAD accepts only certain commands. These commands are called *dimensioning subcommands*. This lesson introduces several dimensioning subcommands. After you use the DIM command, AutoCAD remains in dimensioning mode until you type **Exit** or press Ctrl-C at the Dim: prompt. AutoCAD then returns to normal drawing mode and the Command: prompt reappears.

Like DIM, the DIM1 command switches AutoCAD into dimensioning mode. When you use DIM1, however, AutoCAD remains in dimensioning mode for only one dimensioning subcommand. After the subcommand is complete, AutoCAD returns to normal drawing mode.

Step 1.0: Issue the DIM command to switch AutoCAD into dimensioning mode so that you can set up the dimension settings:

Command: **DIM** ↵

CHANGING DIMENSION SETTINGS

Before you dimension the drawing, you must set up the dimension settings, which are called dimension variables, for the drawing. *Dimension variables* control the appearance of dimensions in the drawing. AutoCAD features many dimension variables, each of which controls one aspect of your dimensions' appearance.

The first setting you need to change affects the size of the text that appears in dimensions.

Step 2.0: Issue the DIMTXT variable to specify the dimension text's size:

Dim: **DIMTXT** ↵	Issues DIMTXT to specify a new value
Current value <0.18> New value: **.125** ↵	Sets dimension text size at .125 units

AutoCAD assumes that you want dimension lines to have an arrowhead at each end. You can put other shapes at the ends of dimension lines, but for now, use arrowheads. You need to tell AutoCAD how large you want the arrowheads to be.

Step 3.0: Issue the DIMASZ variable to specify the size of the dimension arrowheads:

`Dim: `**`DIMASZ`**` ↵`	Issues the variable that controls the size of dimension arrowheads
`Current value <0.18>` `New value: `**`.125`**` ↵`	Sets dimension arrowhead size at .125 units

When you dimension a circle or an arc, the program places a mark at the center of the object. The mark normally is a small cross. You can make the center mark large or small. For this example, specify a center mark whose lines extend from the object's center to just beyond its circumference. (You see what these marks look like later in this lesson.)

Step 4.0: Issue the DIMCEN variable to specify the size of the mark used to indicate the center of circles and arcs:

`Dim: `**`DIMCEN`**` ↵`	Specifies the variable that controls the size of the center mark used in dimensioning circles and arcs
`Current value <0.09>` `New value: `**`-.1`**	Specifies the size of the center mark

The negative value specifies that center lines are created that extend beyond the object's circumference. A positive value gives you only a center mark.

EXERCISE 4: ADDING CENTER MARKS TO THE ARCS

Now you learn to use a dimensioning subcommand. In this short exercise, you use the CENter dimensioning subcommand to place a center mark in three of the drawing's corners, which are made of arcs. Because the polygons are centered on those arcs, the arcs' center marks serve as the center marks for three of the polygons, as well. After you create the center marks, take AutoCAD out of dimensioning mode so that you can prepare the drawing for further editing.

- Add center marks to three of the drawing's arcs
- Return AutoCAD to the normal drawing mode

Step 1.0: Issue the CENter subcommand to place center marks on the lower left arc of the outer rectangle (the arcs are the filleted outer corners):

Dim: **CEN** ↵   Places a center mark
                                                     in a circle or an arc

Select arc or circle: Places the center
Use the pickbox to select   mark in the
the lower left corner of   selected arc and
the outer rectangle   ends the CENter
                                                     subcommand

Step 2.0: Repeat this step to put center marks in the lower right and upper right arcs. You need to issue the CENter subcommand each time. After you are done, your drawing resembles figure 4.8.

Figure 4.8:

The drawing with center marks for three of the outer arcs.

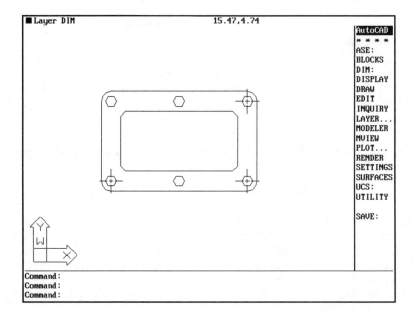

Taking AutoCAD out of Dimensioning Mode

You need to reorient the drawing before you continue your dimensioning work. For now, return AutoCAD to normal drawing mode.

Step 3.0: Press Ctrl-C to end the DIM command:

`Dim:` Ctrl-C

Exercise 5: Changing the Display and Copying an Object

Now that you have marked the centers of three of the corner polygons, you need to mark the bottom, center polygon. Remember, however, that the center marks you just created were based on the corner arcs, not the polygons themselves. Because the bottom, center polygon is not located in an arc, you cannot use the CENter dimensioning subcommand to place a center mark in it. Instead, you can copy the center mark from another polygon and place the copy inside the unmarked polygon. The copy is easier to make, however, if you first zoom in on the effected part of the drawing.

Tasks To Be Completed in this Exercise

- Use ZOOM to change your view of the drawing
- Copy a center mark from one polygon to another
- Set a running object snap override

Using Zoom To Change the View

As you have seen in other lessons, the ZOOM command lets you focus on a specific part of the drawing. By magnifying the gasket's lower left corner, you can more easily edit its entities.

Step 1.0: Issue the ZOOM command so that you can zoom in on the lower left corner of the drawing:

`Command: ZOOM ↵`   Starts the ZOOM command

Step 1.1: AutoCAD gives you the option of zooming into a specific area of the drawing, which you select by enclosing in a window. To specify the zoom area—in this case, the drawing's lower left corner—select the ZOOM command's Window option, then use your pointing device to pick two corners of the window:

`All/Center/Dynamic/Extents/Left/`
`Previous/Vmax/Window/<Scale`
`(X/XP)>: W↵`
	Selects the Window
	option

`First corner:` *Pick the window's first* *corner at* Ⓐ *(see fig. 4.9)*	Defines the upper right corner of the zoom window

Step 1.2: As you move the input device, a window is created on-screen. Move the cursor down and to the left to locate the opposite corner of the window. After the window is the desired size, press your pointing device's pick button:

`Other corner:` *Pick the window's* *cond corner at* Ⓑ *(see fig. 4.9)*	Defines the lowere left corner of the zoom window

When you pick the second corner, AutoCAD zooms into the area defined by the window. After zooming, your screen resembles figure 4.10.

Figure 4.9:

Creating the zoom window.

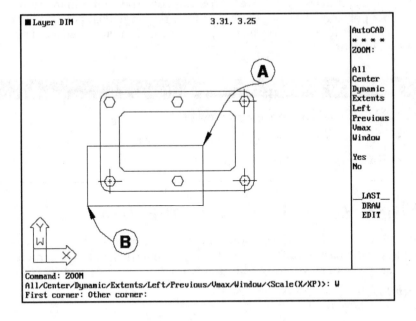

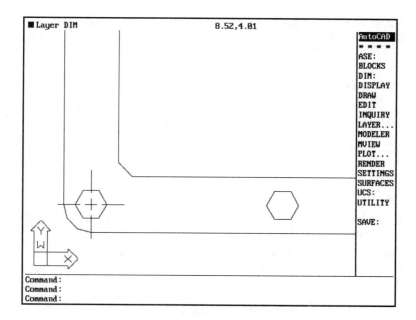

Copying a Center Mark

You now need to create a duplicate of an existing center mark. Use the COPY command to perform this operation. To copy an entity, select the objects to copy, then press Enter. AutoCAD then prompts you for information about the copying procedure. You need to specify the location from which you want to copy the entities, and the location for the copy.

OPTIONS

The COPY command gives you the following options:

- **Base point.** Specifies the point from which you want to copy

- **Displacement.** Specifies the relative distance to copy the object from the original

- **Multiple.** Enables you to make multiple copies of the selected object or objects

The default is Base point or Displacement.

Step 2.0: Issue the COPY command to duplicate an existing entity:

Command: **COPY** ⏎   Starts the COPY command

Step 2.1: To pick the entities you want copied, move the pickbox onto the entities and press the input device button. As you select each entity to be copied, AutoCAD highlights the entity on-screen. The program also tells you the number of objects you selected and the number it found:

`Select objects:` *Pick the six lines*   Selects the entities
that create the center mark of the arc   to be copied
in the lower left corner

`1 found`   Appears six times as you select the
     individual lines

Step 2.2: After you select the entities to be copied, you must end the selection process:

`Select objects:` ⏎

Step 2.3: Use your pointing device to pick the base point of the center marker (the point from which you want to copy the selected objects):

`<Base point or displacement>/`   Specifies the point
`Multiple:` *Pick a point near the center*   from which to copy
of the original center mark   the entities

Step 2.4: Specify where to place the copy using relative coordinates:

`Second point of displacement:`   Copies objects 3.5 units directly to
`@3.5,0`   the right of the basepoint

Now that you have finished copying the objects, you can return to the original zoom factor.

Step 3.0: To zoom out to the original view, issue the **ZOOM** command again, and select the Previous option.

Your drawing resembles figure 4.11.

SETTING A RUNNING OBJECT SNAP

You now can resume dimensioning the drawing. To assist you in selecting several end points, however, create a running object snap. In Lesson 3, you learned how object snaps help you find exact points in a drawing. By using the OSNAP command or the Running Object Snap dialog box, you then can choose one or more object snap settings before you use a drawing or editing command. You do not have to repeatedly specify the desired object snap override during the command.

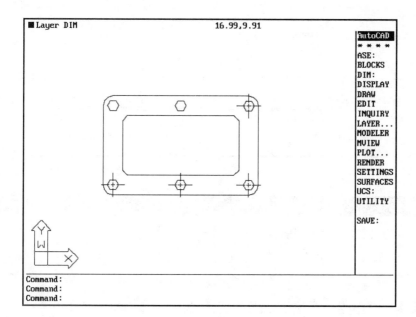

```
■Layer DIM                16.99,9.91                    AutoCAD
                                                       * * * *
                                                       ASE:
                                                       BLOCKS
                                                       DIM:
                                                       DISPLAY
                                                       DRAW
                                                       EDIT
                                                       INQUIRY
                                                       LAYER...
                                                       MODELER
                                                       MVIEW
                                                       PLOT...
                                                       RENDER
                                                       SETTINGS
                                                       SURFACES
                                                       UCS:
                                                       UTILITY

                                                       SAVE:


  Command:
  Command:
  Command:
```

Figure 4.11:
The drawing with the copied center marker.

Step 4.0: Open the Running Object Snap dialog box and define ENDpoint as the default selection option:

Command: *Choose* Settings, *then* Object Snap	Defines ENDpoint as the default
Choose the box to the left of ENDpoint, then OK	selection option

EXERCISE 6: ADDING LINEAR DIMENSIONS TO THE DRAWING

You now are ready to continue adding dimensions to the drawing. This time you use linear dimensions. Just as the name implies, a linear dimension shows the distance between two points. Linear dimensions are defined by the orientation of their dimension line; some linear dimensions lie horizontally, and others lie vertically. This exercise shows you how to use the HORizontal and VERtical dimensioning subcommands to create linear dimensions.

You use dimensions throughout this workbook and in your daily AutoCAD work. You need to know a few terms associated with linear dimensions. Figure 4.12 illustrates the most important terms.

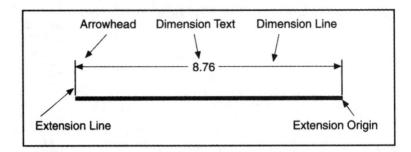

- Add horizontal linear dimensions to the drawing
- Add vertical linear dimensions to the drawing

CREATING HORIZONTAL LINEAR DIMENSIONS

Before you can resume dimensioning, you must return AutoCAD to dimensioning mode.

Step 1.0: At the `Command:` prompt, type **DIM**. When the `Dim:` prompt appears, AutoCAD is ready to accept dimensioning subcommands.

Begin your linear dimensioning work by adding the dimension for the gasket's overall horizontal length. This horizontal dimension goes across the top of the drawing.

Step 2.0: Begin horizontal dimensioning by issuing the HORizontal dimensioning subcommand:

`Dim:` **HOR** ↵

Step 2.1: AutoCAD prompts for information for the first dimension. Pick the two points at which the extension lines are located. These points lie at either end of the gasket, to indicate its total length.

`First extension line origin or`
`RETURN to select:` *Use the pickbox to select the top of the outer triangle's left vertical line*

Specifies the origin
for the dimension

`Second extension line origin:`
Pick the the top of the outer triangle's right vertical line

Specifies the location
of the second
extension line

Step 2.2: Pick a point to position the dimension line. The dimension line (the line that has the dimension text) lies between the extension lines:

`Dimension line location`   Specifies a point
`(Text/Angle):` *Pick a point above the top*   for the dimension
horizontal line of the outer rectangle   line to pass through

Step 2.3: Accept the default dimension text by pressing Enter:

`Dimension text <8.00>:` ↵   Accepts the default dimension text
     of 8.00, indicating that the gasket
     has an overall length of eight units

AutoCAD calculates the dimension (the gasket's total length) and then adds the dimension to the drawing. Your drawing now resembles figure 4.13.

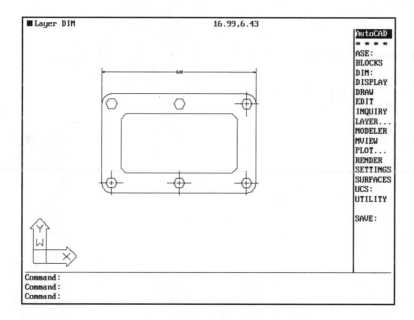

Figure 4.13:

A horizontal linear dimension that shows the gasket's total length.

NOTE

You can type replacement text for the dimension, but this practice is not recommendted. As you create accurate geometry, the DIM command is the final check that your object is drawn correctly. Your drawing should be dimensioned exactly as the drawing shown in the figures. If the dimension text is incorrect at the prompt, finish the dimension, use UNDO to remove it, and then redimension the object. If it still is incorrect, go back to the geometry and fix the error in the drawing.

Continue adding dimensions to the top of the drawing, to show the width of some of the gasket's parts.

Step 3.0: Reissue the HORizontal subcommand and create a dimension that shows the width of gasket's left panel:

Dim: **HOR** ↵   Starts the HORizontal
                                                           subcommand

First extension line origin or   Specifies the origin
RETURN to select: *Use the pickbox*   for the dimension
to select the top of the outer triangle's
left vertical line

Second extension line origin: Specifies the location
Pick the the top of the outer triangle's   of the second
right vertical line   extension line

Dimension line location   Specifies the
(Text/Angle): *Pick a point above the gasket*   location of the
                                       dimension line

Dimension text <1.00>: ↵   Accepts the default text for
                                       the dimension

Your drawing now resembles figure 4.14.

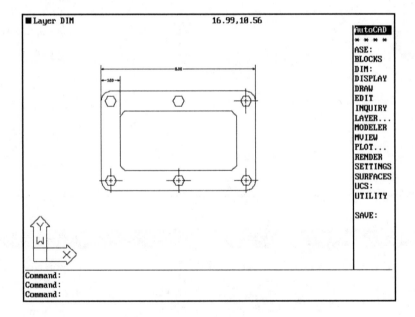

Figure 4.14:

The second dimension.

You now can use another dimensioning subcommand. The CONtinue subcommand enables you to use the last dimension as a reference for the next dimension. You can use CONtinue to show the chamfer's horizontal length, which lies between the left vertical line and the top line of the inner rectangle.

Step 4.0: Issue the CONtinue subcommand to use the last extension line drawn as the starting point for the new dimension:

Dim: **CON** ↵

Step 4.1: AutoCAD uses the second extension line of the previous horizontal dimension as the first extension line of the dimension you are currently drawing. You need only to specify the second origin line for the current dimension:

Second extension line origin
or RETURN to select: *Pick the top*
line of the inner rectangle
Specifies the second
extension line's
location

Dimension text <0.25>: ↵
Accepts the default dimension
text of .25 units

The CONtinue subcommand aligns the current dimension line with the previous dimension line. Your drawing now resembles figure 4.15.

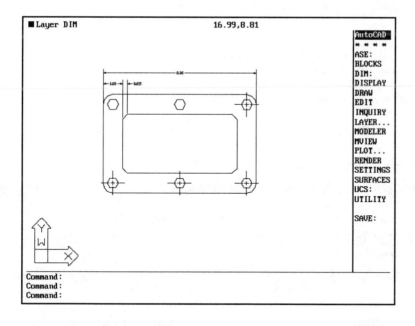

Figure 4.15:

The new dimension, created with the CONtinue subcommand.

Next, use a horizontal linear dimension to show the distance between the polygons' center points at the bottom of the drawing.

Step 5.0: Issue the HORizontal subcommand and continue dimensioning the drawing:

```
Dim: HOR ↵
```
Starts the HORizontal subcommand

```
First extension line origin
or RETURN to select:
```
Pick the bottom line of the polygon's center mark in the drawing's lower left corner (see the 3.50 dimension in figure 4.16)

Specifies the dimension's origin

```
Second extension line origin:
```
Pick the bottom line of the middle polygon's center mark

Specifies the second extension line's location

```
Dimension line location
(Text/Angle): Pick a point about
one unit below the gasket
```

Selects a point for the dimension line to pass through

```
Dimension text <3.50>: ↵
```
Accepts the default text for the dimension

Step 6.0: Use CONTinue to add a dimension between the middle and lower right polygons, beginning from the second extension line of the dimension you just drew:

```
Dim: CON ↵
```
Starts the CONtinue subcommand

```
Second extension line origin
or RETURN to select:
```
Pick the bottom line of the polygon's center mark in the drawing's lower right corner

Specifies the second extension line's location

```
Dimension text <3.50>: ↵
```
Accepts the default text for the dimension

Your drawing now resembles figure 4.16.

You now can add a horizontal dimension to the middle of the drawing to show the length of the gasket's interior hole. However, to avoid having extension lines and objects overlap, suppress the extension line.

Step 7.0: Issue the dimension variables DIMSE1 and DIMSE2 and suppress the dimension extension lines:

```
Dim: DIMSE1 ↵
```
Starts dimension variable DIMSE1

```
Current Value <off> New
value: ON ↵
```
Surpresses first extension line

```
Dim: DIMSE2 ↵
```
Starts dimension variable DIMSE2

```
Current Value <off> New
value: ON ↵
```
Suppresses seconds extension line

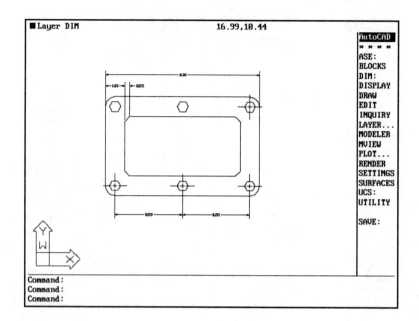

Step 8.0: Issue the HORizontal subcommand and dimension the length of the gasket's interior hole:

Dim: **HOR**   Starts the HORizontal
                                                                    subcommand

First extension line origin   Specifies the
or RETURN to select: *Pick the*   dimension's origin
left vertical line of the inner rectangle

Second extension line origin: Specifies the second
Pick the right vertical line of the   extension line's
inner rectangle   location

Dimension line location   Selects a point for
(Text/Angle): *Pick a point*   the dimension line
in the center of the gasket's interior hole   to pass through

Dimension text <6.00>: ↵   Accepts the default
                                                              text for the dimension

Your drawing now resembles figure 4.17. Because you are finished with the interior dimensions, set DIMSE1 and DIMSE2 back to off.

Step 9.0: Enter **DIMSE1** and enter **OFF**

Step 10.0: Enter **DIMSE2** and enter **OFF**.

Figure 4.17:

Dimensioning the length of the gasket's interior hole.

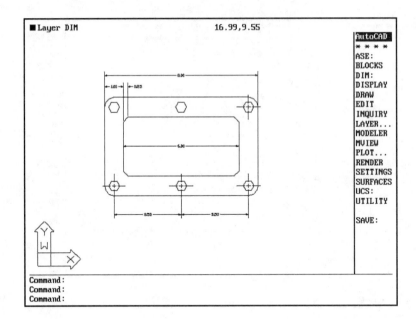

ADDING VERTICAL LINEAR DIMENSIONS TO THE DRAWING

You now can add vertical linear dimensions to the drawing. Use the VERtical dimension command. The VERtical subcommand is similar to the HORizontal subcommand because you select the location of the extension and dimension lines, then approve the dimension text.

Begin by creating a vertical linear dimension on the drawing's left side, to show the gasket's total height.

Step 11.0: Issue the VERtical subcommand and position the dimension:

`Dim: VER ↵`	Starts the VERtical subcommand
`First extension line origin or RETURN to select:` *Pick the left end of the gasket's top horizontal line*	Specifies the dimension's origin
`Second extension line origin:` *Pick the left end of the gasket's bottom horizontal line*	Specifies the second extension line's location
`Dimension line location (Text/Angle):` *Pick a point to the left of the gasket*	Selects a point for the dimension line to pass through
`Dimension text <5.00>: ↵`	Accepts the default text for the dimension

Your drawing now resembles figure 4.18.

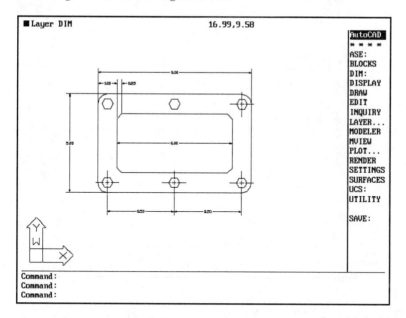

Step 12.0: Issue the VERtical subcommand again and dimension the height of the gasket's interior hole:

`Dim: VER ↵`	Starts the VERtical subcommand
`First extension line origin or RETURN to select:` *Pick the left end of the top inner horizontal line*	Specifies the dimension's origin
`Second extension line origin:` *Pick the left end of the bottom inner horizontal line*	Specifies the second extension line's location
`Dimension line location (Text/Angle):` *Pick a point to the left of the gasket*	Selects a point for the dimension line to pass through
`Dimension text <3.00>: ↵`	Accepts the default text for the dimension

Your drawing now resembles figure 4.19.

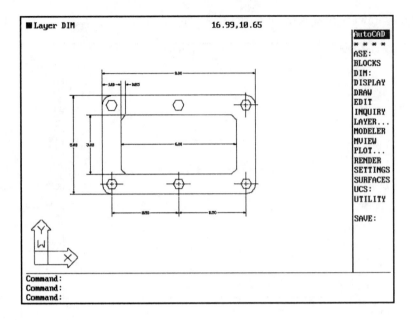

EXERCISE 7: DIMENSIONING A POLYGON

You now need to add the dimension to the polygon in the upper right corner.

TASK TO BE COMPLETED IN THIS EXERCISE

- Add an aligned dimension to one of the drawing's polygons

To add this dimension, use the ALIgned dimension subcommand. ALIgned creates a dimension line that is parallel to the extension line's origins.

Step 10.0: Issue the ALIgned subcommand and create a dimension showing the width of the polygon in the drawing's upper right corner:

Dim: **ALI** ↵	Starts the ALIgned subcommand
First extension line origin or RETURN to select: *Pick the 9 o'clock corner of the polygon*	Specifies the origin of the first extension line

`Second extension line origin:` *Pick the polygon's 1 o'clock corner*	Specifies the second extension line's location
`Dimension line location (Text/Angle):` *Pick a point above the gasket*	Specifies the dimension line's location
`Dimension text <0.50>:` ⏎	Accepts the default text for the dimension line

The drawing is now complete. Your drawing resembles figure 4.20.

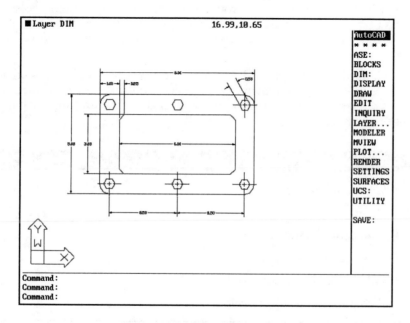

Figure 4.20:
The completed drawing.

Step 11.0: Exit from dimensioning mode by pressing Ctrl-C at the `Dim:` prompt.

ENDING THE DRAWING SESSION

As you learned in previous lessons, after you are finished working on a drawing, you should save the drawing to disk, then exit from the Drawing Editor.

Step 1.0: Issue the SAVE command to save the LESSON4 drawing to disk:

`Command:` *Choose* File, *then choose* Save   Saves the drawing to disk

Step 2.0: Exit AutoCAD:

Command: *Choose* File, *then* Exit AutoCAD   Saves the drawing to disk and exits AutoCAD

SUMMARY

AutoCAD features many drawing and editing commands that enable you to quickly create accurate drawings. The program offers so many tools, in fact, that you often must learn to use several of them to determine which ones work best for you. Generally, a combination of tools works best. As you learned in this lesson, for example, you can draw accurately and easily by using a combination of absolute and relative coordinates.

AutoCAD also enables you to dimension drawings in many ways, so that when people read your drawings, they understand them better. Dimensions help the reader see critical information about the drawing, such as lengths, widths, and angles.

IN THIS LESSON, YOU LEARNED TO DO THE FOLLOWING:

- Create a drawing of a gasket
- Create an array
- Add center marks to the drawing's arcs
- Change the display and copy an object
- Add linear dimensions to the drawing
- Add dimensions to a polygon

By using editing commands in this lesson, you learned that you can create a drawing more quickly by using a combination of drawing and editing commands than by using drawing commands alone. In the next lesson, you expand upon this concept by creating almost all of the drawing by using AutoCAD's editing commands.

REVIEW

1. Set up a new drawing that uses decimal units with three decimal places, a limits setting of X=75 Y=50, and two layers named 700 and 310.

2. In the new drawing, select a starting point in the lower left corner of the screen, and then draw a 3-unit-by-4-unit rectangle using relative coordinates on layer 700.

3. Use ZOOM Window to zoom in on the object you drew in question 2.

4. Use the **FILLET** command to set a fillet radius of .25 units. Then fillet the upper left and lower right corners of the rectangle you created in question 2.

5. Use the **CHAMFER** command to set a chamfer distance of .25 units. Then chamfer the rectangle's lower left and upper right corners.

6. Make a copy of the rectangle you have just modified. Place the copy 60 units to the right of the original.

7. Use ZOOM All to zoom to the outer limits of the drawing, so that you can see both the original object and the copy. Erase the copy. Then use ZOOM Previous to return to the last zoom magnification and area.

8. Prepare to dimension the drawing you created in question 2. Set the dimension variable DIMTXT to **.125** and set the DIMASZ variable to **.125**.

9. Dimension the object using at least two horizontal and one vertical dimensions. Place the dimensions on layer 310.

10. Use **ARRAY** to create four rows and three columns of the entire geometry, including the dimensions. Make the distance between the rows 15 units and the distance between the columns 10 units.

Drawing a Spindle

Overview

No matter how carefully you plan and create your initial drawing, changes are inevitable. In light of this fact, the true power of AutoCAD lies in the program's editing commands and their capabilities. These commands enable you to modify entities you have just drawn, create new entities from existing ones, copy or move objects, and erase entities from a drawing. You can even use editing commands to change a completed drawing into a new and different one. AutoCAD's editing commands give you dozens of options that you can use to refine your drawings in thousands of ways, down to the very finest details.

This lesson introduces two of AutoCAD's most powerful and commonly used editing commands: OFFSET and TRIM. OFFSET and TRIM were added to AutoCAD several years ago, and remain as two of the program's most significant 2D drafting tools. These commands are second only to the LINE and CIRCLE commands as aids to productivity.

Experienced AutoCAD users take advantage of both drawing and editing commands when they need to create complicated objects or shapes that are too exact to be drawn freehand. One type of entity that might look simple but requires great precision is symmetrical geometry. Eggs and gears are good examples of symmetrical objects. If you draw a line down the center of such an object, dividing it exactly in half, you see that the halves are identical in shape and size. CAD users call the center line a *mirror line* because the two halves seem to "mirror" each other. AutoCAD lets you take advantage of this phenomenon when you create symmetrical geometry. You can use drawing and editing commands to create half of a symmetrical entity, and then use the MIRROR command to create a mirror image of the first half. This lesson shows you how to create symmetrical objects with the help of MIRROR and other drawing and editing commands.

This lesson also teaches you how to adapt two manual drawing techniques—construction lines and linetypes—to AutoCAD. *Construction lines* (sometimes called construction entities) help you complete drawings with less effort. *Construction entities* are temporary objects that help you position or develop the drawing's permanent geometry. Although this practice also is common to manual drawing, AutoCAD makes the application of construction lines much easier than is possible in manual drafting.

Manual drafters often use different types of lines (called *linetypes* in AutoCAD) to convey special meaning in a drawing. AutoCAD provides many built-in linetypes, and lets you create your own customized linetypes. Each kind of line can have a specific purpose in the drawing. Hidden line types, for example, show that you can find an edge behind another object, while a center line identifies the center of a part. In this lesson, you learn to use different linetypes, and to assign linetypes (and colors) to different layers in a drawing.

TOPICS COVERED IN THIS LESSON

In this lesson, you learn to perform the following operations:

- Create construction lines
- Use the OFFSET command to copy entities
- Trim entities
- Use the MIRROR command to create symmetrical objects
- Draw an end view of the spindle
- Add detail to the drawing
- Dimension the drawing

This lesson teaches you how to use the following AutoCAD commands:

- **DIM** DIAmeter. Dimensions circles and arcs
- **EXTEND.** Lengthens an entity to a boundary
- **MIRROR.** Creates a mirrored replica of a selected group of entities
- **OFFSET.** Creates a new entity parallel to the original
- **TRIM.** Removes portions of entities that cross another entity, which you specify as a cutting edge

SETTING UP THE DRAWING

Before you actually begin drawing, you need to set up the drawing environment as you did in Lesson 4.

Step 1.0: Start AutoCAD and save the new drawing as **LESSON5**.

Step 2.0: Use the **UNITS** command or Units Control dialog box and set up the drawing with decimal units at two decimal places. Leave all the remaining settings at their default.

The limits in this drawing remain at the default of 12.00,9.00—you do not need to change them or issue the ZOOM command with the All option.

Step 3.0: Use the **LAYER** command or the Layer Control dialog box to create two new layers named 100 and 700. Then use the Color option to assign the color red to the layer named 700. Finally, make 100 the current layer.

Now that your drawing environment is set up, you can begin to create the LESSON5 drawing. After you have completed this lesson, you should have a drawing of a spindle shown in figure 5.1.

Figure 5.1:

The drawing you create in this lesson.

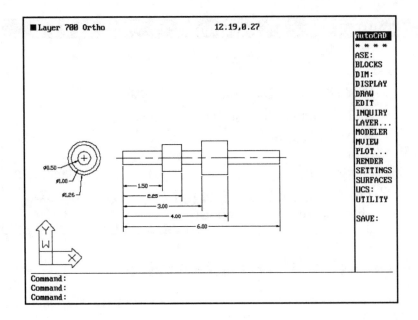

EXERCISE 1: CREATING WITH CONSTRUCTION LINES

You now are ready to create the drawing shown in figure 5.1. You begin this drawing using construction lines, which are temporary lines that you can use to develop or position a part of a drawing. You can modify or erase construction lines when you are finished.

TASKS TO BE COMPLETED IN THIS EXERCISE

- Turn on Ortho
- Create construction lines

TURNING ON ORTHO

You often find that you need to draw lines that are perfectly horizontal (parallel to the X axis) or perfectly vertical (parallel to the Y axis). As you have seen in other lessons, you can draw horizontal and vertical lines by turning on the grid or by specifying certain absolute coordinates. AutoCAD offers an easier way, however, to draw horizontal or vertical lines. When AutoCAD is in Orthographic (Ortho) mode, the program draws only horizontal or vertical lines. You do not have to use a grid (your lines might not always fall on grid points) or use absolute coordinates (you might not be sure which coordinates to use, or you might want to draw using a pointing device). You can switch AutoCAD into Ortho mode to draw the construction lines. You can switch Ortho on and off by pressing F8 at the `Command:` prompt.

Step 1.0: Turn Ortho on:

`Command:` *Press F8*

AutoCAD informs you that Ortho is on by displaying the `<Ortho on>` message after the `Command:` prompt. Notice, also, that `Ortho` appears in the status line to remind you that Ortho is on.

You now can create the horizontal line by using the input device and the LINE command.

Step 2.0: Issue the LINE command and draw the horizontal line in figure 5.2:

`Command:` `<Ortho on>` **LINE** ↵	Starts the LINE command
`From point:` *Pick point at 2.50,4.30* (Ⓐ *in fig. 5.2)*	Begins the line at point Ⓐ
`To point:` *Pick point at* Ⓑ *(move the cursor right until the coordinate display reads 10.50,4.30—see fig. 5.2)*	Ends the line at point Ⓑ
`To point:` ↵	Ends the LINE command

You now can create the vertical line.

Step 3: Issue the LINE command and draw the vertical line as shown in figure 5.2:

`Command:` **LINE** ↵	Starts the LINE command
`From point:` *Pick point at 3.60,8.10* (Ⓒ *in fig. 5.2)*	Begins the line at point Ⓒ
`To point:` *Pick point at 3.60,3.40* (Ⓓ *in fig. 5.2)*	Ends the line at point Ⓓ
`To point:` ↵	Ends the LINE command

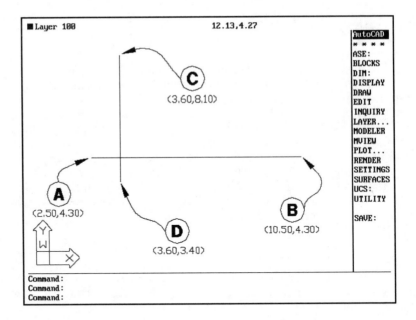

Exercise 2: Using the Offset Command to Copy Entities

OFFSET is one of AutoCAD's most powerful commands. The OFFSET command creates a copy of an existing line and places the copy parallel to the original line. You specify the distance between the copy and the original. You use the OFFSET command in this exercise to create the lines shown in figure 5.3. After they are drawn, you can use portions of these lines to create half of the finished geometry.

TASKS TO BE COMPLETED IN THIS EXERCISE

- Offset horizontal construction lines
- Offset vertical construction lines

Offsetting Horizontal Construction Lines

Before you begin using OFFSET to copy the original construction lines, you need to set an offset distance. The *offset distance* is the distance you want to put between the copy and the original entity.

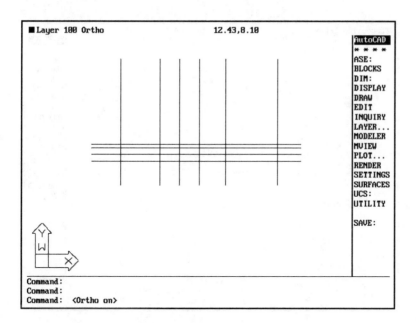

Step 1.0: Issue the OFFSET command or choose Construction then Offset:

Command: **OFFSET** ⏎

Step 1.1: Specify the distance between the original line and the offset line:

Offset distance or Through <Through>: **.25** ⏎	Specifies a distance of .25 units between the existing entity and the offset line

Step 1.2: Begin offsetting by selecting the horizontal construction line you created in the last exercise as the original line (line AB in figure 5.2) to create the horizontal line B in figure 5.4:

Select object to offset: *Pick line* Ⓐ *(see fig. 5.2)*	Selects the line to duplicate

Step 1.3: Specify on which side the offset line should be created in relation to the original line:

Side to offset? *Pick a point above* line Ⓐ *(see fig. 5.2)*

Select object to offset: ⏎	Creates a new line and ends the OFFSET command

Your drawing should now resemble figure 5.4.

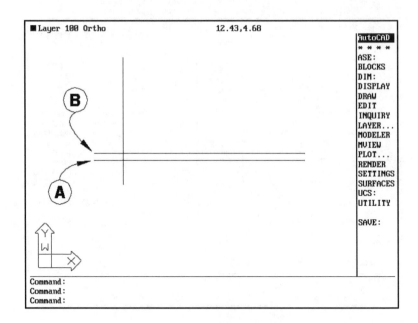

Figure 5.4:

The original horizontal line and the first offset line.

You now can create line C, which is the second horizontal line shown in figure 5.5.

Step 2.0: Issue the OFFSET command, set a new offset distance, and create line C:

Command: **OFFSET** ↵	Starts the OFFSET command
Offset distance or Through <0.25>: **.5** ↵	Specifies the distance between lines (A) and (C)
Select object to offset: *Pick line (A) (see fig. 5.5)*	Selects the line to duplicate
Side to offset? *Pick a point above line (A) (see fig. 5.5)*	Selects the side on which to place the new line and creates the new line
Select object to offset: ↵	Ends the OFFSET command

You now have three horizontal lines and are ready to create the fourth line.

Step 3.0: Issue the OFFSET command, set a new offset distance, and create line (D):

Command: **OFFSET** ↵	Starts the OFFSET command

```
Offset distance or Through          Specifies the
<0.5>: .63 ↵                        distance between
                                    lines Ⓐ and Ⓒ

Select object to offset: Pick line  Selects the line to
Ⓐ (see fig. 5.5)                    duplicate

Side to offset? Pick a point above  Selects the side on
line Ⓐ (see fig. 5.5)               which to place the
                                    new line and creates
                                    the new line

Select object to offset: ↵          Ends the OFFSET command
```

Your drawing now should resemble figure 5.5.

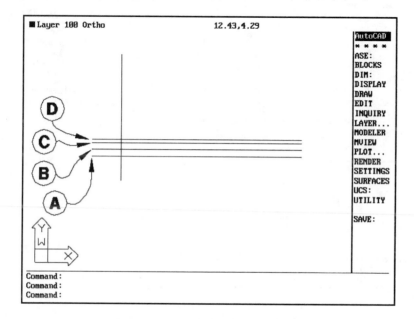

Figure 5.5:

The horizontal lines created by offsetting.

OFFSETTING VERTICAL CONSTRUCTION LINES

Now you can add the new vertical construction lines as shown in figure 5.3. In the following steps, the original vertical line is called line E.

Step 4.0: Issue the OFFSET command, set a new offset distance, and create the vertical line F (see fig. 5.6):

```
Command: OFFSET ↵                   Starts the OFFSET command

Offset distance or Through          Specifies the
<0.63>: 1.5 ↵                       distance between
                                    lines Ⓔ and Ⓕ
```

`Select object to offset:` *Pick line* (E) *(the vertical line in fig. 5.6)*	Selects the line to duplicate
`Side to offset?` *Pick a point to the right of line* (E)	Specifies the side on which to place the new line and creates the new line
`Select object to offset:` ↵	Creates the new line and ends the OFFSET command

Your drawing should now resemble figure 5.6.

Figure 5.6:

The original vertical line (line E) and the first vertical offset line (line F).

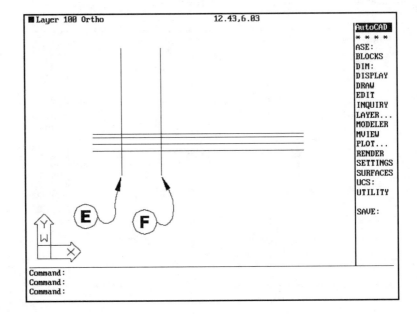

Now continue creating new vertical lines by offsetting.

Step 5.0: Issue the OFFSET command, set a new offset distance, and create the vertical line G (see fig. 5.7):

`Command:` **OFFSET** ↵	Starts the OFFSET command
`Offset distance or Through <1.5>:` **2.25** ↵	Specifies the distance between lines (E) and (F)

`Select object to offset:` *Pick line* Ⓔ *(the vertical line in fig. 5.7)*	Selects the line to duplicate
`Side to offset?` *Pick a point to the right of line line* Ⓔ	Specifies the side on which to place the new line and creates the new line
`Select object to offset:` ↵	Creates the new line and ends the OFFSET command

Step 6.0: Issue the OFFSET command, set a new offset distance, and create the vertical line H:

`Command: OFFSET` ↵	Starts the OFFSET command
`Offset distance or Through <2.25>: 3` ↵	Specifies the distance between lines Ⓔ and Ⓕ
`Select object to offset:` *Pick line* Ⓔ *(the vertical line in fig. 5.7)*	Selects the line to duplicate
`Side to offset?` *Pick a point to the right of line line* Ⓔ	Specifies the side on which to place the new line and creates the new line
`Select object to offset:` ↵	Creates the new line and ends the OFFSET command

Step 7.0: Issue the OFFSET command, set a new offset distance, and create the vertical line I:

`Command: OFFSET` ↵	Starts the OFFSET command
`Offset distance or Through <3>: 4` ↵	Specifies the distance between lines Ⓔ and Ⓕ
`Select object to offset:` *Pick line* Ⓔ	Selects the line to duplicate
`Side to offset?` *Pick a point to the right of line* Ⓔ	Specifies the side on which to place the new line and creates the new line
`Select object to offset:` ↵	Creates the new line and ends the OFFSET command

Step 8.0: Issue the OFFSET command, set a new offset distance, and create the vertical line J:

Command: **OFFSET** ↵	Starts the OFFSET command
Offset distance or Through <4>: **6** ↵	Specifies the distance between lines Ⓔ and Ⓕ
Select object to offset: *Pick line* Ⓔ	Selects the line to duplicate
Side to offset? *Pick a point to the right of line* Ⓔ	Specifies the side on which to place the new line and creates the new line
Select object to offset: ↵	Creates the new line and ends the OFFSET command

Your screen should now resemble figure 5.7.

Figure 5.7:

The vertical lines created by offsetting.

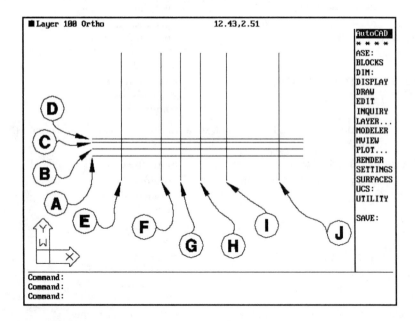

Now that the construction lines are in place, you can edit them to create the spindle.

EXERCISE 3: TRIMMING ENTITIES

The next step in the drawing process is to develop the geometry that makes up the spindle. For this step, you must use the TRIM command to remove portions of the construction lines. After you are finished trimming, the remaining entities form the spindle's base. The TRIM command enables you to remove part of an entity by erasing from one end of the entity back to the point at which it intersects with another entity.

Like the OFFSET command, the TRIM command is another powerful AutoCAD editing command. Unlike OFFSET, however, TRIM takes a little getting used to. Its sequence of selections and returns can confuse the new user. After you issue the TRIM command, AutoCAD replaces the crosshair cursor with a pickbox, then asks you to select a cutting edge or edges. A *cutting edge* is an existing entity that intersects the object you want to trim. After you pick the cutting edge, select the object or objects you want to trim. AutoCAD erases the object up to the point at which it intersects the cutting edge, but leaves the portion that lies past the cutting edge. The program then prompts you to select another object to trim. After you have trimmed all the desired objects, press Enter to end the TRIM command.

TASKS TO BE COMPLETED IN THIS EXERCISE

- Trim the construction lines
- Use TRIM to shape half of the spindle profile

TRIMMING THE CONSTRUCTION LINES

Begin by removing the excess line segments shown on the right side of vertical line E, as shown in figure 5.7.

Step 1.0: Issue the TRIM command, or choose Modify then Trim:

`Command: TRIM ↵`   Starts the TRIM command

Step 1.1: Use the pickbox to select vertical line J as the cutting edge:

`Select cutting edge(s)...`   Specifies the line
`Select objects:` *Pick line* Ⓙ   as the cutting edge
(see fig. 5.8)

Figure 5.8:

Select line J as the cutting edge for the TRIM command.

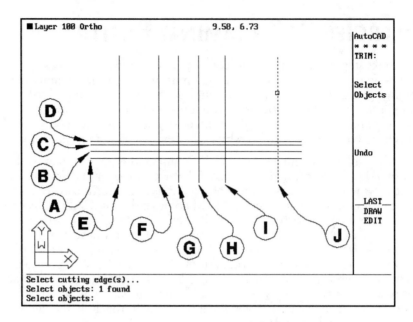

Step 1.2: AutoCAD enables you to pick more than one cutting edge. To stop selecting cutting edges, you must press Enter at the next `Select Objects:` prompt.

Step 1.3: Pick the objects you want to trim:

`<Select object to trim>/Undo:` *Pick line* Ⓐ *to the right of line* Ⓙ *(see fig. 5.9)*	Trims line Ⓐ from its end to its intersection with line Ⓙ
`<Select object to trim>/Undo:` *Pick line* Ⓑ *to the right of line* Ⓙ *(see fig. 5.9)*	Trims line Ⓑ from its end to its intersection with line Ⓙ
`<Select object to trim>/Undo:` *Pick line* Ⓒ *to the right of line* Ⓙ *(see fig. 5.9)*	Trims line Ⓒ from its end to its intersection with line Ⓙ
`<Select object to trim>/Undo:` *Pick line* Ⓓ *to the right of line* Ⓙ *(see fig. 5.9)*	Trims line Ⓓ from its end to its intersection with line Ⓙ

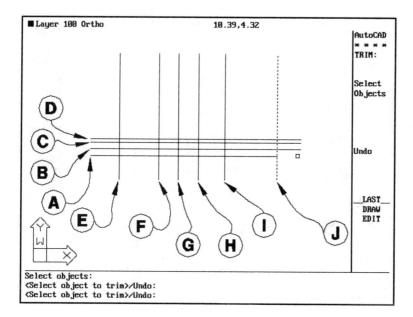

Figure 5.9:
Trimming line A
*from its right end
to its intersection
with line* J.

Step 1.4: Now that all the line segments are trimmed, you can end the TRIM command:

```
<Select object to trim>/Undo: ↵
```

Step 2.0: Now trim the excess line segments on the left side of line E. Issue the **TRIM** command and select line E as the cutting edge (see fig. 5.10) at the `Select cutting edge(s)... Select objects:` prompt. Press Enter to end object selection.

Step 2.1: As you did earlier, pick lines A, B, C, and D, this time to the left of line E. AutoCAD trims the lines from their left end, back to their intersection with vertical line E (see fig. 5.10). After you trim the lines, press Enter at the `<Select object to trim>/Undo:` prompt to end the command.

USING TRIM TO SHAPE HALF THE SPINDLE PROFILE

By trimming the ends from the horizontal lines, you have begun to shape the top half of the spindle's horizontal profile. In the following steps, you continue to carve away the construction lines until the half-profile is complete. Because you now know how to use TRIM, the following steps do not show prompts, options, or your input. You should be able to complete the required trimming on your own.

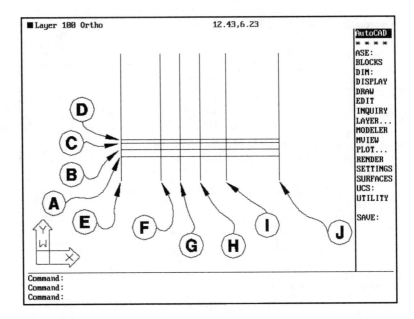

After you are finished, your half-profile should resemble the one in figure 5.11. Later in this lesson, you use the MIRROR command to complete the spindle's profile.

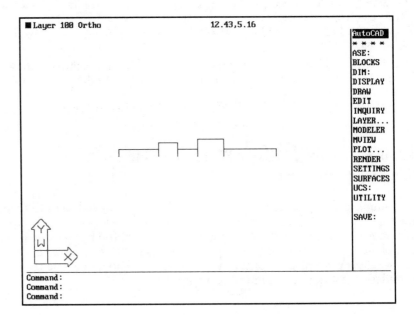

Resume trimming the construction lines.

Step 3.0: Issue the **TRIM** command and pick horizontal line B as the cutting edge. Trim lines E and J above line B (see fig. 5.12), and press Enter to end the TRIM command. This step defines the segments of lines E and J that lie between lines A and B as the half-profile's ends.

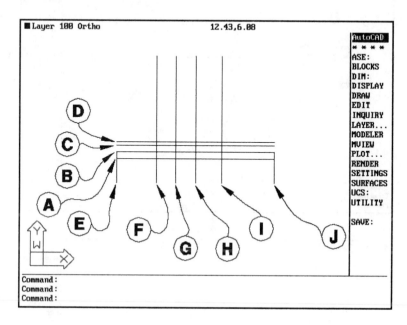

Figure 5.12:

Lines E and J after trimming.

Step 4.0: You now can define the small rise on the spindle's left side, as shown in figure 5.11. Reissue the **TRIM** command and pick line C as the cutting edge. Then trim lines F and G above line C. End the TRIM command.

Step 5.0: Continue by trimming the lines to define the large rise on the drawing's right side, as shown in figure 5.11. Reissue **TRIM** and pick line D as the cutting edge. Then trim lines H and I above line D. End the command. Your drawing now should resemble figure 5.13.

Step 6.0: Clean up the profile's bottom by trimming the vertical lines below line A. Invoke **TRIM**, select line A as the cutting edge, and then trim lines E, F, G, H, I, and J below line A. End the TRIM command.

Step 7.0: Now you can eliminate line A entirely because it is not part of the final profile. Issue the **ERASE** command, pick line A, and then end the ERASE command. Your drawing should resemble figure 5.14.

Figure 5.13:
Lines F, G, H, and I after their tops have been trimmed.

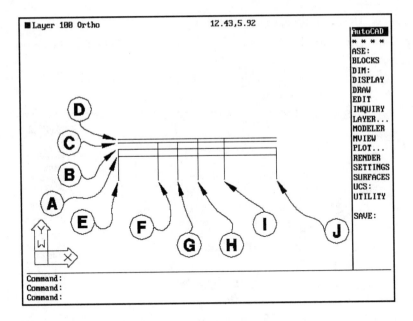

Figure 5.14:
The half-profile with excess lines removed from the bottom.

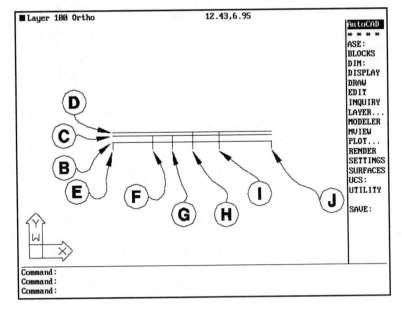

As stated earlier, the TRIM command also enables you to remove line segments that pass between two cutting edges. You can remove the horizontal lines that intersect the large raised section.

Step 8.0: Issue **TRIM** and select line H as the first cutting edge, then select line I as the second cutting edge. Press Enter at the next `Select objects:` prompt to stop the selection of cutting edges. Trim lines C and D to the right of line I, and then trim line D to the left of line H (see fig. 5.14). Your drawing now should resemble figure 5.15.

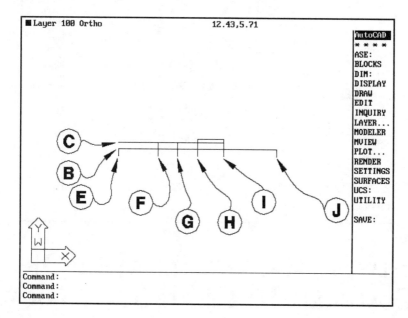

Figure 5.15:
The half-profile with the large raised section nearly defined.

Step 9.0: Define the top of the small raised section by trimming line C from either side of it. Issue **TRIM** and pick lines F and G as the cutting edges. Press Enter to stop the selection of cutting edges. Trim line C to the left of line F, then to the right of line G. End the **TRIM** command. Your drawing should resemble figure 5.16.

The half-profile is nearly finished. You only need to trim out the short line segments that lie within the two raised sections.

Step 10.0: Issue **TRIM** and select lines H and I as the cutting edges. Then trim out the section of line B that remains inside the section, and end the command.

Step 11.0: Finally, trim out the section of line B that lies inside the small raised section. Issue **TRIM** and select lines F and G as the cutting edges. Then select the segment of line B that lies between the cutting edges. End the TRIM command.

Your drawing now should look like the half-profile in figure 5.11.

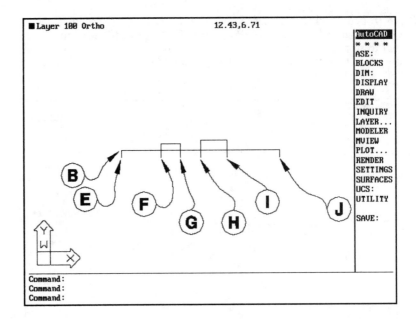

EXERCISE 4: USING THE **MIRROR** COMMAND TO CREATE SYMMETRICAL OBJECTS

You now have half of the drawing's front view. As you learned earlier in this lesson, AutoCAD enables you to duplicate, or *mirror*, an image across a center line, called a *mirror line*. This exercise shows you how to complete the spindle's horizontal profile using the MIRROR command to make a mirror image of the half-profile you just completed.

TASK TO BE COMPLETED IN THIS EXERCISE

• Mirror the spindle's half-profile

After you are finished with this exercise, your spindle should resemble figure 5.17.

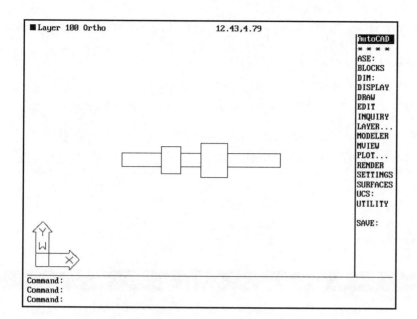

MIRRORING THE SPINDLE'S HALF-PROFILE

Before you can create the duplicate image, you need to specify the entity or entities you want to mirror. You select entities to mirror in much the same way you select them to erase or trim. After you invoke the MIRROR command, the cursor changes to a pickbox so that you can select entities one at a time. Because the spindle profile is made of many entities, however, you can use a window to select them all at once.

You can issue a window by entering a **W** at a `Select Objects:` prompt or by picking a point on the screen away from the object and dragging the crosshairs from left to right. This action selects only those objects fully inside the window. After the objects are selected, you press Enter to stop selecting objects.

You then select the mirror line at the end points of the spindle. Use the object snap Endpoint option. As you learned in Lesson 3, when you do not know the exact coordinate of a point, you can use an object snap to find the exact point.

After the mirror line is defined, AutoCAD then asks you if you want to delete the original objects. For this drawing, you want to keep both entities to create the complete object.

Step 1.0: Issue the MIRROR command or choose Construct then Mirror:

`Command: MIRROR ↵`

Step 1.1: Specify the Window selection option, so that only the entities inside the window are chosen:

```
Select objects: W ↵
```

Step 1.2: Pick the window's first point:

`First corner:` *Pick a point below and to the left of the geometry*	Places the window's first corner

Step 1.3: Pick the window's second point:

`Other corner:` *Pick a point above and to the right of the geometry*	Places the window's second corner, enclosing all the entities in the half-profile (see fig. 5.18)

```
11 found
```

NOTE

After you pick the window's second corner, AutoCAD highlights all the entities in the window, preparing them for mirroring. AutoCAD displays a message that tells you how many entities were selected in the window.

Figure 5.18:

Using a window to select objects for mirroring.

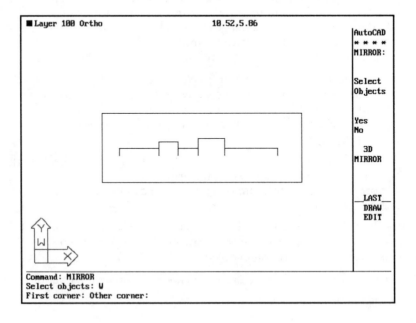

Step 1.4: Now that the half-profile has been selected, you need to end the object-selection process:

`Select objects: ↵`

Step 1.5: Continue with the **MIRROR** command's next prompt by issuing the Endpoint option to indicate the object's end point and define the center line. Use points A and B (see fig. 5.19) to create the line. The line that lies between these two points is the horizontal center of the completed profile. AutoCAD uses the center line to mirror the drawing:

`First point of mirror line: **End** ↵`   Starts the ENDpoint object snap override

`of *Pick point* (A)`
`(see fig. 5.19)`   Specifies the mirror line's first point

`Second point: **END** ↵`   Starts the object snap ENDpoint

`of *Use the pickbox to select point* (B)`
`(see fig. 5.19)`   Specifies the mirror line's second point

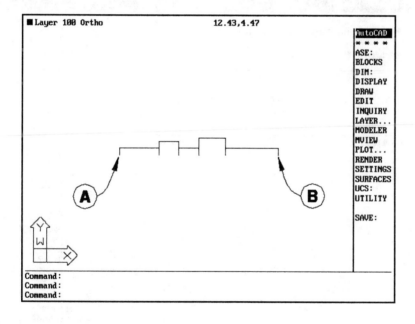

Figure 5.19:
Endpoints to select for creating the mirror line.

Step 1.6: Press Enter at the following prompt to keep the original entity:

`Delete old objects? <N> ↵`   Tells AutoCAD not to delete the original entities after creating the mirror image

In the previous lessons, you learned that blips are left on-screen after you use AutoCAD's editing commands.

Step 2.0: Use the **REDRAW** command now to clean the screen.

Your drawing now should resemble figure 5.17.

EXERCISE 5: DRAWING THE END VIEW OF THE SPINDLE

You now are ready to add an end view of the spindle. You use the CIRCLE command to develop this view. To locate the circle directly to the left of the geometry at a specific distance, you use a construction line.

TASKS TO BE COMPLETED IN THIS EXERCISE

- Create a new construction line
- Draw the spindle's end view

Figure 5.20 shows the two views of the spindle.

Figure 5.20:

End and front views of the spindle.

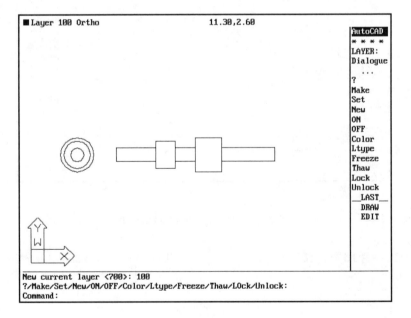

CREATING A CONSTRUCTION LINE

To align the end view with the spindle's profile, you need to create a new construction line. This line is a part of the final drawing, but it helps you position the end view and find the center of the circles that make up the end view. You use AutoCAD's object snap modes to construct the temporary line and the circles.

Step 1.0: Issue the LINE command:

Command: **LINE** ↵

Step 1.1: The construction line must begin at the vertical line's center (point A in figure 5.21) that forms the left end of the spindle's profile. By using the Endpoint object snap and picking the short line, you can snap to point A:

From point: **END** ↵   Activates the Endpoint object snap

of *Pick point* Ⓐ *(see fig. 5.21)*   Specifies the construction line's
                                          starting point

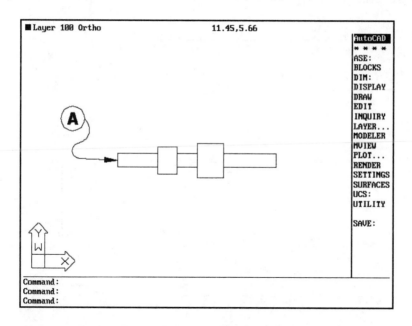

Figure 5.21:

The point to select (using Endpoint) as the construction line's starting point.

Step 1.2: Use relative coordinates to draw a construction line to the left of point A. The 1.5-unit construction line is used to locate the circle's center:

To point: **@-1.5,0** ↵   Draws a line 1.5 units long to the
                                          left from point Ⓐ

To point: ↵   Ends the LINE command

DRAWING THE SPINDLE'S END VIEW

You now can create the end view using the construction line's left end as the center point for the three circles that make up the end view. You use the CIRCLE command with the Diameter option to create this part of the drawing.

Step 2.0: Issue the CIRCLE command, and use the Endpoint object snap to specify the construction line's end as the circle's center:

Command: **CIRCLE** ↵	Starts the CIRCLE command
3P/2P/TTR/<Center point>: **END** ↵	Activates the Endpoint object snap
Of *Use the aperture box to pick the left end of the construction line*	

Step 2.1: Specify the Diameter option and enter the circle diameter:

Diameter/<Radius>: **D** ↵	Selects the Diameter option
Diameter: **1.26** ↵	Defines a circle with a diameter of 1.26 units (see fig. 5.22)

Figure 5.22:

The construction line and the first circle.

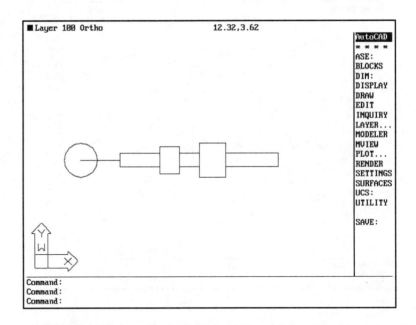

Step 3.0: Now add the second concentric circle. To create this circle, you use the Center object snap. Center lets you snap to the center of an existing circle or arc:

Command: **CIRCLE** ↵	Starts the CIRCLE command

```
3P/2P/TTR/<Center point>: CEN ↵        Activates the Center object snap
of Pick on the circumference of the existing
circle
Diameter/<Radius> <0.63>: D ↵         Selects the Diameter option
Diameter <1.26>: 1 ↵                  Defines a circle with a diameter of
                                      1 unit
```

Step 4.0: Now add the final circle. This time choose the CIRCLE command from the menu. Again, use the Center object snap to position the circle's center:

```
Command: Choose Draw, then Circle,     Starts the CIRCLE
then Center, Diameter                  command with the
                                       Diameter option

3P/2P/TTR/<Center point>: CEN ↵        Activates the Center object snap
of Pick the circumference of the outermost
circle
Diameter/<Radius> <0.50>:              Creates a circle with a
Diameter                               diameter of .5 units
Diameter <1.00>: .5 ↵
```

You no longer need the short construction line used to locate the center of the first circle.

Step 5.0: Use the **ERASE** command to eliminate the construction line. Your drawing now should resemble figure 5.20.

EXERCISE 6: ADDING DETAIL TO THE DRAWING

You now are ready to add detail to the drawing, such as a center line for the profile. To complete this step, you need a special linetype to represent the center line. Unlike Lesson 3, you do not use the LAYER command to perform this operation. Instead, you use the LINETYPE command to control the linetype. First, however, you must use LAYER to place the new linetype on its own layer.

TASKS TO BE COMPLETED IN THIS EXERCISE
• Change the current layer
• Add a center line to the drawing
• Extend the center line

Before you can add detail to the drawing, you must make the layer named 700 the current layer. As you did in Lesson 4, you place the center line on a separate layer than the drawing itself.

Step 1.0: Issue the **LAYER** command or use the Layer Control dialog box and make the layer named 700 the current layer.

ADDING A CENTER LINE TO THE DRAWING

Now you can add the center line to the drawing. This line runs horizontally through the center of the spindle's profile drawing, to act as a reference point for anyone who uses the drawing. Remember that in earlier lessons, you used the LAYER command to assign a special linetype to a layer. You also can use the LINETYPE command to specify a new linetype for drawing.

OPTIONS

The LINETYPE command has the following four options:

- **?.** Displays all the layers loaded in the current drawing
- **Create.** Enables the user to define a new linetype and to store it in a file on disk
- **Load.** Loads a linetype from a file on disk into the current drawing
- **Set.** Defines the type of linetype assigned to all new entities regardless of the layer setting

---

AutoCAD features several built-in linetypes, each of which has a special use. So far, you only have used the Continuous linetype. You use this linetype often in AutoCAD drawings because an unbroken line usually works best when you are creating object outlines. AutoCAD also features a special linetype for use as a center line. The Center linetype is a broken line made of long and short segments. You need to use this linetype as the center line so that the reader does not think it is an actual part of the spindle's profile.

After you specify a new linetype as the current linetype, AutoCAD draws every new object using that type of line. When you want to resume using the continuous linetype, you need to specify continuous as the current linetype.

Step 2.0: Issue the LINETYPE command and set the Center linetype as the default linetype in the drawing:

Command: **LINETYPE** ↵ ~~layer~~	Starts the LINETYPE command
?/Create/Load/Set: **Set** ↵	Selects the Set option
New entity linetype (or ?) <BYLAYER>: **Center** ↵	Selects the Center linetype
?/Create/Load/Set: ↵	Exits the LINETYPE command

You now are ready to draw the center line. Use the LINE command to draw the line through the object's center.

Step 3.0: Issue the LINE command to draw the center line:

Command: **LINE** ↵

Step 3.1: Choose the Endpoint option to locate the center line's starting point:

From point: *Use the pickbox to pick point Ⓐ (see fig. 5.23)*	Selects the starting point
To point: *Use the pickbox to pick point Ⓑ (see fig. 5.23)*	Selects the end point
To point: ↵	Ends the LINE command

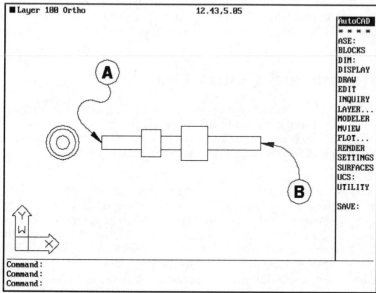

Figure 5.23:

The points to pick (using ENDpoint) to create the center line.

The center line appears in the middle of the spindle profile. Your drawing now should resemble figure 5.24.

Figure 5.24:

The drawing with the center line.

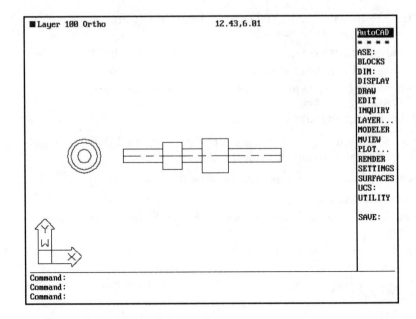

The center line, however, extends only to the profile's end lines. To be correct, the center line should extend past the ends of the object. You use the EXTEND command to fix this problem.

EXTENDING THE CENTER LINE

The EXTEND command enables you to extend an existing entity, which makes it longer. To extend an object, you must designate a boundary to which the object extends. AutoCAD then extends the object until it meets the boundary. You can extend objects as far as you want.

You now want to extend the new center line so that its ends reach beyond the ends of the spindle. To complete this action, you need to set up boundaries near the spindle's ends, and then extend the center line to the new boundaries. To create the boundaries, you can use the OFFSET command to make copies of the existing vertical end lines, and place the copies a short distance from the original end lines. Remember that, because the spindle profile was created by mirroring, it is actually in two parts—top half and a bottom half. Therefore, the end lines are in two segments.

Step 4.0: Issue the OFFSET command and define the amount of offset at .25 units, as follows:

Command: **OFFSET** ↵	Starts the OFFSET command
Offset distance or Through <Through>: **.25** ↵	Defines the distance by which the copied entities are offset from the originals

Step 4.1: Offset the spindle's end lines to create the boundaries for the extended center line:

Select object to offset: *Pick the top segments of the spindle's right vertical end line*	Specifies the object to offset
Side to offset? *Pick a point to the right of the end line*	Places the copied object .25 units to the original's right
Select object to offset: *Pick the top segment of the spindle's left vertical end line*	Selects the object to offset
Side to offset? *Pick a point to the left of the end line*	Places the copied object .25 units to the original's left
Select object to offset: ↵	Ends the OFFSET command

Now that you have the boundary lines (see fig. 5.25), you can extend the center line to these offset lines.

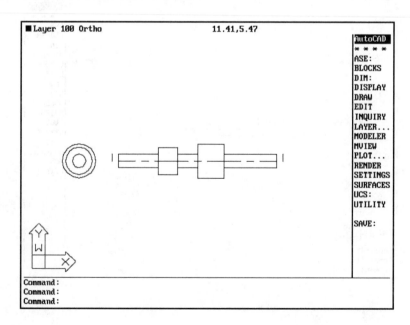

Figure 5.25:

The boundaries for extending the center line.

Step 5.0: Issue the EXTEND command and pick the boundary edges, or use Modify then Extend:

Command: **EXTEND** ↵	Starts the EXTEND command
Select boundary edge(s)	Selects the first
Select objects: *Pick one of the newly offset lines*	boundary edge
Select objects: *Pick the other offset line*	Selects the second boundary edge
Select objects: ↵	Ends object selection

Step 5.1: Pick each end of the center line to extend it to the boundaries:

<Select object to extend>/Undo: *Pick the center line near its right end*	Extends the center line's right end to the right boundary
<Select object to extend>/Undo: *Pick the center line near its left end*	Extends the left end to the left boundary
<Select object to extend>/Undo: ↵	Ends the EXTEND command

You now have the extended center line and can remove the two short construction lines.

Step 6.0: Issue the **ERASE** command and erase the two boundary lines.

Your drawing now should resemble figure 5.26.

Figure 5.26:

The extended center line.

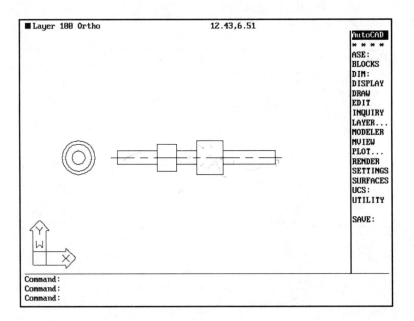

You now are ready to add the dimensions. Before you continue, however, you need to tell AutoCAD to stop using the center linetype, and to resume using the continuous linetype.

Step 7.0: Issue the **LINETYPE** command, then set the linetype back to BYLAYER by entering **S**, then **BYLAYER**. After setting the new linetype, end the LINETYPE command by pressing Enter at the `?/Center/Load/Set:` prompt.

The drawing itself is complete. Now you can add dimensions to the drawing.

EXERCISE 7: DIMENSIONING THE DRAWING

Few AutoCAD drawings are complete without dimensions. In this exercise, you add dimensions to the spindle drawing. You use some of the dimensioning subcommands you learned in Lesson 4, but you also learn some new commands. In this lesson, you not only show the spindle's length, but you also show the combined length of several of its parts. You also learn to apply dimension information to circles.

TASKS TO BE COMPLETED IN THIS EXERCISE
• Set a running object snap
• Set dimension variables
• Add a horizontal linear dimension
• Add baseline dimensions
• Add circular dimensions

...ECT SNAP

..., you need to select several end
...ons, you can set a running object
...points repeatedly. For this exer-
... set a running Endpoint object

use dimscale ✻

Step 1.0: Issue the OSNAP command and set Endpoint as the current snap mode:

Command: **OSNAP** ↵	Starts the OSNAP command
Object snap modes: **END** ↵	Selects the Endpoint option

Now you can use the Endpoint object snap over and over without specifying it each time.

SETTING DIMENSION VARIABLES

As you learned in Lesson 4, AutoCAD's dimension variables determine the appearance of dimensions in your drawings. For this drawing, you need to change the values of three variables: DIMTXT, DIMASZ, and DIMCEN.

Step 2.0: Enter **DIM** to switch AutoCAD into dimensioning mode. The `Dim:` prompt appears.

Step 3.0: Issue the DIMTXT variable and specify a new dimension-text height of .125 units. Issue DIMASZ variable and specify a new dimension-arrow size of .125 units. Finally, issue the DIMCEN variable and specify a value of .10. The DIMCEN setting changes the size of the center marks placed in circles and arcs.

Now that the dimension variables are defined, you can add the dimensions.

ADDING A HORIZONTAL LINEAR DIMENSION

The spindle is made of several segments. In this exercise, you do not dimension each segment individually. Instead, you create a series of dimensions that shows how each segment contributes to the spindle's total length. You begin the process by using the HORizontal command, as you did in Lesson 4. Then you learn a new subcommand that enables you to create progressive dimensions.

The following steps require you to pick lines on the drawing as beginning, ending, and continuing points for the dimensions. Figure 5.27 identifies these key lines.

Use the HORizontal dimensioning subcommand to dimension the profile's first segment, working from left to right. Then use the BASeline subcommand to show how each segment contributes to the profile's overall length.

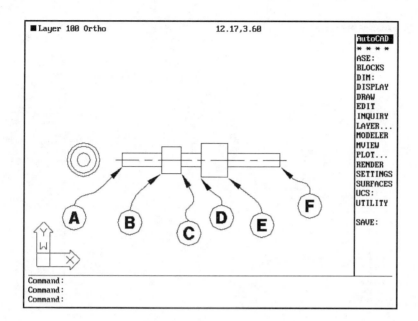

Step 4.0: Issue the HORizontal subcommand and dimension the first segment:

`Dim:` **`HOR`** ↵	Starts the HORizontal dimension command
`First extension line origin or` `RETURN to select:` *Pick line* Ⓐ *(see fig. 5.27)*	Selects the dimension's starting point
`Second extension line origin:` *Pick line* Ⓑ *(see fig. 5.27)*	Selects the dimension's end point
`Dimension line location` `<Text/Angle>:` *Pick a point below the profile*	Selects the side of the drawing where the dimension line should appear
`Dimension text <1.50>:` ↵	Accepts the default value for the dimension text

The first segment should be dimensioned as shown in figure 5.28. You can continue dimensioning by using a new subcommand: BASeline.

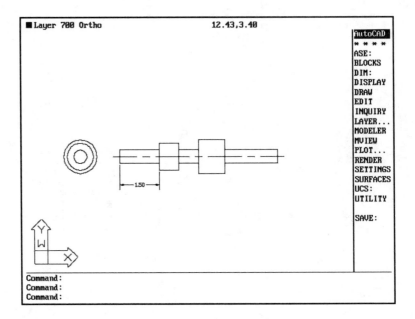

ADDING BASELINE DIMENSIONS

The BASeline subcommand lets you create a series of progressive dimensions that all begin at the same origin. In this case, AutoCAD automatically uses line A (see fig. 5.27) as the origin for all the profile's horizontal dimensions. Each subsequent dimension shows how a new segment adds to the spindle's total length.

Step 5.0: Issue the BASeline subcommand and select the first baseline dimension:

Dim: **BASE** ↵	Starts the BASeline subcommand
Second extension line origin or RETURN to select: *Pick line* Ⓒ *(see fig. 5.27)*	Selects the point to which the dimension should extend
Dimension text <2.25>: ↵	Accepts the default setting and ends the BASeline subcommand

Step 6.0: Reissue the BASeline subcommand and select line D (see fig. 5.27) to create the second baseline dimension. Press Enter to accept the dimension text of 3.00 and end the subcommand.

Step 7.0: Reissue the BASeline subcommand and select line E to create the third baseline dimension. Press Enter to accept the dimension text of 4.00 and end the subcommand.

Step 8.0: Reissue the BASeline subcommand and select line F to create the final baseline dimension. Press Enter to accept the dimension text of 6.00 and end the subcommand.

Your drawing now should resemble figure 5.29.

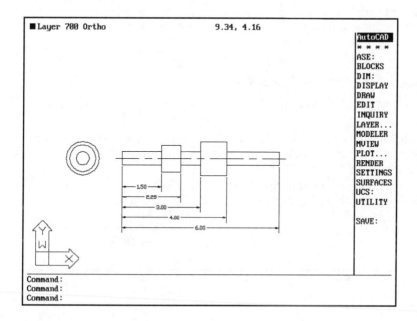

ADDING CIRCULAR DIMENSIONS

You now need to add dimensions to the circles that make up the end view of the spindle. AutoCAD uses the DIAmeter dimensioning subcommand to place circular dimensions in drawings. Circular dimensions specify the diameter of circles.

NOTE

To dimension a circular object, you must select the circle or arc on the circumference. In this and in later lessons, the location on the circumference to select the object will be specified in relation to the hour hands on a clock. For example, three o'clock is to the right, six o'clock is straight down, nine o'clock is to the left, and twelve o'clock is straight up. Additional locations can be determined by imagining where the hour hand would be at the specified time. For example, 6:30 would be just past 6:00, and so forth.

Step 9.0: Issue the DIAmeter subcommand:

Dim: **DIA** ↵   Starts the DIAmeter subcommand

Step 9.1: Select the object to dimension as the largest circle, which has a diameter of 1.26 units:

Select arc or circle: *Pick the*   Selects the circle
outermost circle at the 6:30 position   to be dimensioned
                                                  and specifies
                                                  the position for the
                                                  leader line (arrow)

Step 9.2: Accept the default dimension text:

Dimension text <1.26>:↵   Accepts the default text for the
                                                  dimension

Step 9.3: Show AutoCAD where to place the dimension. Use the pointing device to drag the dimension text downward and away from the circle, so that it is positioned as shown in figure 5.30:

Enter leader length for text: Positions the
Pick a point to define the leader (see fig. 5.30) dimension text in
                                                  relation to the
                                                  circle, and ends
                                                  the subcommand

Figure 5.30:

The first circle dimension.

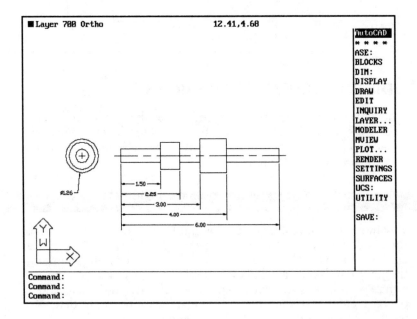

Step 10.0: Reissue the **DIAmeter** subcommand and pick the second-largest circle, which has a diameter of one unit. Pick the circle at the seven o'clock position, and then drag the dimension so that it lies just above the dimension you just created.

Step 11.0: Reissue the **DIAmeter** subcommand and pick the innermost circle, which has a diameter of .5 units. Pick the circle at the eight o'clock position, and then drag the dimension so that it lies just above the dimension you just created.

Your drawing now should resemble the one shown in figure 5.31.

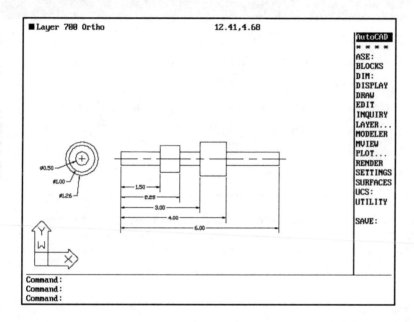

Figure 5.31:
The complete spindle with dimensions.

Step 12.0: Press Ctrl-C at the `Dim:` prompt to switch AutoCAD back into normal drawing mode.

ENDING THE DRAWING SESSION

Step 13.0: Save the drawing to disk and end the current drawing session.

SUMMARY

AutoCAD's edit commands often are the fastest and most productive tools to use to create geometry. When you develop a drawing, for example, you can use construction lines to help position or start entities. Other available editing tools enable you to mirror or extend your drawings.

IN THIS LESSON, YOU LEARNED TO DO THE FOLLOWING:

- Create construction lines
- Use the OFFSET command to copy entities
- Trim entities
- Use the MIRROR command to create symmetrical objects
- Draw an end view of the spindle
- Add detail to the drawing
- Dimension the drawing

In this drawing, you concentrated on using construction lines and editing commands to develop the drawing. In the next lesson, you are introduced to more commands, and you learn how to add cross-hatching to a section view.

REVIEW

1. Draw a 3-unit vertical line and a 2-unit horizontal line. Using offset, develop a 3-unit-by-2-unit rectangle from these lines.

2. Using a diagonal construction line, place a circle in the rectangle's center with a diameter of 1.1731 units.

3. Place a circle in the drawing using the same center of the existing circle. Make the diameter 1.345 units and give it a hidden linetype.

4. Dimension the drawing, placing a center line on the circle using the dimension variable DIMCEN.

5. From the *AutoCAD Tutor Disk*, retrieve the drawing OFFICE. Offset the missing wall lines at a distance of 6 units.

6. Using the **TRIM** command, make a woven star out of the geometry in file REV5-1. (The completed drawing is seen in the lower right corner at a smaller scale.)

7. From the *AutoCAD Tutor Disk*, retrieve the drawing named REV5-2. Mirror the object across the bottom of the vertical lines.

8. Place a center line in the preceding drawing and extend it .25 units beyond the object's ends.

9. Dimension the drawing named REV5-2.

10. Stretch the drawing named REV5-2 by 1.25 units to the right.

Drawing a Gear

Overview

Aside from a knowledge of AutoCAD's tools (commands, use of construction lines, and drawing conventions), a user's biggest asset is his or her ability to solve drawing problems. An efficient AutoCAD user can look at a drawing and understand the best way to create it. This process, of course, differs from traditional drawing on paper. In AutoCAD, you can create tangent lines, trim away construction lines to develop objects, and make multiple copies of one or many objects. As you work through the exercises in this lesson, look at the logic used to develop the geometry. As you become aware of the problem-solving techniques of CAD, you become a productive AutoCAD user.

As you have seen, there are many methods available to develop geometry. One indispensable mode of geometry development is polar coordinates. Polar coordinate input is an option similar to absolute and relative coordinate input. Polar coordinates are measured from the last point, which is the same as relative coordinates. Polar coordinates, however, are specified in distance and angle from the last point. In AutoCAD, as with most CAD and CAM systems, 0 degrees is to the right, 90 degrees is straight up, 180 is to the left, and 270 is straight down. AutoCAD's three coordinate input options enable you to develop any type of geometry.

You already have learned that after an object is drawn, AutoCAD enables you to use the object as many times as necessary in a variety of applications. This is one of AutoCAD's most powerful features. Similar geometry that is equally spaced around a center point, such as spokes on a wheel, is common in many drawings. The ARRAY command enables you to make multiple copies of a single object and rotate them around a center point, greatly reducing the time required to complete a drawing.

As you learned in previous lessons, the modification of existing geometry is a powerful tool in CAD. A new command that enables the user to perform this function is CHANGE. By applying this command, you can alter the properties or physical characteristics of individual objects. Linetype and layer are two examples of properties; physical characteristics include the end point of a line or radius of a circle. These editing capabilities add flexibility and speed to your drawing development and modification, and enable you to correct errors, such as drawing an object on the wrong layer.

Remember that drafting is a form of communication. One of its conventions is crosshatching. *Crosshatching* is used to enhance a drawing's appearance or to specify a specific material, such as copper or plastic. Because the development of such patterns are common (and difficult to accomplish using standard drawing tools), AutoCAD enables you to create hatch patterns or use predefined patterns. These patterns are created inside a boundary defined by geometry. As you will see, existing geometry can be used to develop the boundary, or you can create a single-entity boundary.

TOPICS COVERED IN THIS LESSON

In this lesson, you learn to do the following:

- Define gear teeth using polar coordinates
- Array gear teeth around a circle
- Add a keyway to the gear
- Draw a section view
- Define and add crosshatching
- Add detail to the drawing
- Dimension the drawing

This lesson teaches you how to use the following AutoCAD commands:

- **BHATCH.** Crosshatches an area using a dialog box for input
- **CHANGE.** Modifies existing entities and their properties
- **DIM ANGular.** Dimensions angles
- **HATCH.** Crosshatches an area enclosed by existing entities
- **PLINE.** Draws polylines
- **ARRAY (Polar).** Makes multiple copies of entities in a circular pattern
- **SETVAR.** Modifies system variables
- **DIM Leader.** Draws a dimension leader line with user-specified text

SETTING UP THE DRAWING

Before you actually begin drawing, you need to set up the drawing environment. Set up the drawing environment just as you did in Lesson 3, with minor variations.

Step 1.0: Start AutoCAD and save the new drawing as LESSON6.

In previous lessons you used the UNITS command to set up the drawing's units. In this drawing, however, the only unit setting that needs to be changed is the number of decimal places. As you may recall from earlier lessons, AutoCAD starts with four places to the right of the decimal. This drawing requires only two decimal places. Instead of going through every step in the UNITS command, you can change the variable that controls decimal place precision by using the SETVAR command.

USING THE SETVAR COMMAND

In AutoCAD, all information about the drawing and command settings are stored as system variables. Examples of these system variables include the drawing limits, last radius used in fillet, and type of linear unit. These settings often are displayed as defaults in brackets (<>) when using a command. You can set each of these variables within the command in which they reside by using the SETVAR command. This command also enables you to change individual system variables directly without going through the command. This capability speeds up the drawing process by changing only the single desired variable.

A common example of this application is when you need to change only the number of places to the right of the decimal place and no other unit setting. To do this, you can use the SETVAR command with the LUPREC (Linear Unit PRECision) variable, which changes the number of places beyond the decimal point.

Step 2.0: Issue the SETVAR command:

```
Command: SETVAR ↵
```
Starts the SETVAR command

Step 2.1: Issue the LUPREC system variable:

```
Variable name or ?: LUPREC ↵
```
Specifies the LUPREC system variable as the variable value to modify

Step 2.2: AutoCAD displays the current setting as 4. You can type a new value from 0 to 8. For this lesson, change the value to 2.

```
New value for LUPREC <4>: 2 ↵
```
Defines the number of places beyond the decimal point as 2

In Release 12, you can access any system variable directly by typing the name of the variable to change. In this example, you simply type **LUPREC** at the Command: prompt and then modify its value. If you do not know the name of the variable, you can start the SETVAR command and type *?* at the Variable name or ?: prompt to see a list of all the variable names. After you type a *?*, you will be prompted with Variables to list <*>. If you press Enter here, you will get a complete list of the system variables.

Step 3.0: Issue the **LIMITS** command. Set the lower left corner at 0,0 and the upper right corner at 17.00,11.00.

Step 4.0: Issue the **ZOOM** command with the All option to see the entire drawing to the new limits.

Step 5.0: Use the **LAYER** command or the Layer Control dialog box to create three new layers named **DIM**, **OBJECT**, and **HATCH**. Then use the Color option to assign the color red to the layer named HATCH. Finally, make OBJECT the current layer.

Now that your drawing environment is set up, you can begin creating the LESSON6 drawing. When you have completed this lesson, you should have a drawing like the one shown in figure 6.1.

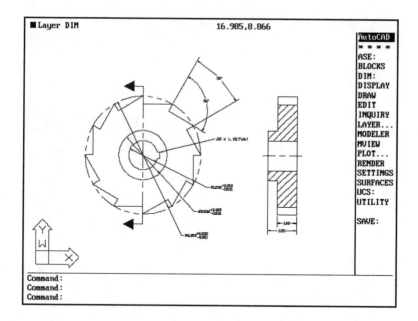

AutoCAD
* * * *
ASE:
BLOCKS
DIM:
DISPLAY
DRAW
EDIT
INQUIRY
LAYER...
MODELER
MVIEW
PLOT...
RENDER
SETTINGS
SURFACES
UCS:
UTILITY

SAVE:

Command:
Command:
Command:

Figure 6.1:
The fully drawn object that you will create in this lesson.

Exercise 1: Defining the Gear's Teeth with Polar Coordinates

You begin the geometry portion of this lesson by creating the single gear tooth shown in figure 6.2. You create this geometry using construction lines and then by trimming and erasing the unneeded geometry.

Tasks To Be Completed in this Exercise

- Create the outline of the gear
- Add construction lines
- Calculate polar angles
- Trim the excess lines

Figure 6.2:

The first gear tooth.

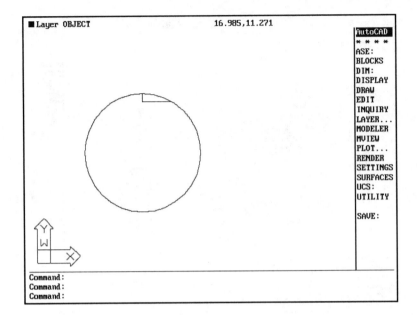

CREATING THE OUTLINE OF THE GEAR

You will develop the gear tooth in figure 6.2 by creating the entities shown in figure 6.3. The angular line B and the vertical line A are construction lines; the horizontal line C and the circle are part of the drawing. After they are developed, you can trim and erase the needed sections to define one tooth of the gear. You start by creating the circle.

To create the gear's outline, use the CIRCLE command to draw a circle. As you learned in previous lessons, you must define the circle's center point, as well as the radius or diameter.

Step 1.0: To create the circle, choose the Draw pull-down menu, then Circle, then Center,Diameter. Enter the absolute coordinate **6,6** as the center point and enter **6** as the diameter.

ADDING CONSTRUCTION LINES

You now have the circle drawn and are ready to add the two construction lines. You define these lines using polar coordinates, which serve as a third option for selecting points in the drawing. Polar coordinates are calculated from the last point defined and are specified as a distance and angle from that point. Angle specification in AutoCAD is seen in figure 6.4.

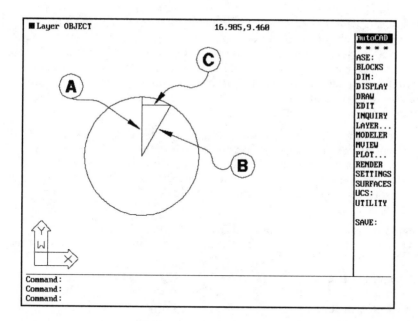

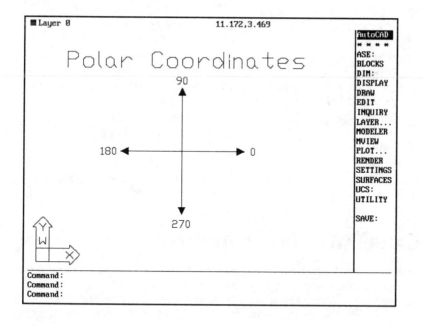

In this coordinate system, AutoCAD places 0 degrees to the right, 90 degrees straight up, 180 degrees to the left, 270 degrees straight down, and 360 degrees to the right. All other angles are available among these angles. The format for typing polar coordinates is *@distance<angle*, in which you specify values for the *distance* and *angle*. To draw a three-unit horizontal line that travels to the right of the point you specify, for example, you type **@3<0**.

To create the construction lines in figure 6.3, begin by drawing the vertical line A. You will use the circle's center point as the construction line's starting point and then use polar coordinates to specify the line's end point. To find the circle's exact center, use the CENter object snap override. This option tells AutoCAD to locate the circle's center automatically.

Step 2.0: Issue the LINE command and invoke the CENter object snap override to locate the starting point of the first construction line at the center of the existing circle:

Command: **LINE** ↵	Starts the LINE command
From point: **CEN** ↵	Invokes the CENter object snap override
Of *Pick the circle on the circumference*	Specifies which entity to find the center of

Step 2.1: You now have specified the starting point of the line and need to specify the end point. You need to draw a construction line straight up from the center of the circle. In polar coordinates, this is a line three units long (the circle's radius) lying at a 90-degree angle.

To point: **@3<90** ↵	Draws a line from the center point, three units long and straight up
To point: ↵	Ends the LINE command

CALCULATING POLAR ANGLES

You now can draw the angular construction line B shown in figure 6.3. Note that in figure 6.1 you can see that the lines defining a tooth are dimensioned 30 degrees apart from each other. Because the line you just drew is at 90 degrees in AutoCAD's system of angles, a line 30 degrees to its right will be at 60 degrees.

As you define geometry using the polar coordinate system, you need to determine the relationship of the new geometry to existing geometry, as well as the angle of the geometry in AutoCAD.

Step 3.0: To add the new angular line, reissue the LINE command and invoke the CENter option. As a starting point, pick a point on the circle and instruct AutoCAD to find the center of the circle you just drew:

Command: **LINE** ↵	Starts the LINE command
From point: **CEN** ↵	Invokes the CENter object snap override
Of *Pick the circle on the circumference*	Specifies which entity to find the center of

Step 3.1: Draw a three-unit line, 60 degrees from the center point to the circumference, as follows:

To point: **@3<60** ↵	Draws a line from the center point, three units long and at an angle of 60 degrees
To point: ↵	Ends the LINE command

You now can draw the horizontal line C shown in figure 6.3. Refer to figure 6.1 to see that line C begins at the end of line B and is at a 90 degree angle, or perpendicular to, line A. You can again use an object snap override to define this line, which finishes the gear tooth. The construction line can then be removed.

Begin line C by starting at the upper end point of line B. You need to define the starting point of the line by using the ENDpoint object snap override. As you learned earlier, ENDpoint enables you to find the exact end point of a line. You need to find the exact end point to finish line B and to construct the gear tooth properly.

Step 4.0: Begin by entering **LINE** at the command prompt.

Step 4.1: To locate the starting point, use the ENDpoint object snap. Pick a point on line B near the circumference of the circle. This picks the end point of the line at the circumference. If you pick the line near the center of the circle, AutoCAD assumes that you want to use the end point near the center of the circle as the starting point for the new line.

Step 4.2: Finish creating the horizontal line by using the PERpendicular object snap override and picking a point on line A. PERpendicular draws a line perpendicular to an existing line. Enter **PER** at the To point: prompt and then pick line A.

Step 4.3: End the LINE command by pressing Enter.

You now can remove line B, which was used as a construction line for positioning the end point of the horizontal line.

Step 5.0: Issue the **ERASE** command, select line B as the entity to erase, and press Enter.

TRIMMING THE EXCESS LINES

You now are ready to remove the section of line A that is not part of the gear tooth. This is the line segment that starts at the center of the circle and extends to the bottom of the tooth (the horizontal line.)

Step 6.0: Issue the TRIM command:

Command: **TRIM** ↵   Starts the TRIM
                                                  command

Step 6.1: As you learned in previous lessons, you must select a cutting edge to trim to. In this drawing, line C, the horizontal line, is used as the cutting edge:

Select cutting edge(s)...   Selects line C
                                                  as the cutting edge

Select objects: *Pick line* Ⓒ
(see fig. 6.3)

Step 6.2: Now that the cutting edge is defined, you can tell AutoCAD to stop selecting edges. You do this by pressing Enter.

Select objects: ↵   Stops the selection
                                                  of cutting edges

Step 15: You now need to tell AutoCAD which entity you want to trim. For this drawing, trim off the vertical segment of line A below its intersection with horizontal line C.

<Select object to trim>/Undo:

Pick line Ⓐ *below line* Ⓒ   Trims away the line
(see fig. 6.3)   segment

<Select object to trim>/Undo: ↵   Ends the TRIM
                                                  command

EXERCISE 2: ARRAYING THE GEAR TEETH AROUND THE CIRCLE

You now are ready to create the 12 gear teeth shown in figure 6.5. The total number of teeth that you need to create is 12. These 12 teeth rotate around the center point of the circle—just like spokes on a bicycle wheel. Because these objects rotate around a common center point, you can use the ARRAY command's Polar option to create the geometry. The Polar option arranges multiple copies of an entity so that they are rotated around a center point.

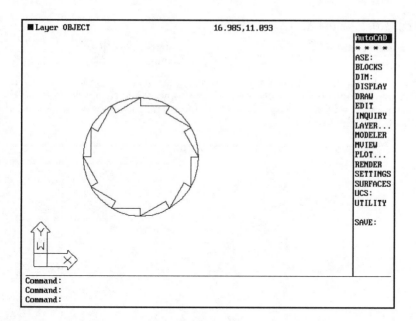

The ARRAY command's Polar option is used any time you have similar objects that rotate around a central axis point. This can range from bolt holes in an automobile rim to seats on a Ferris wheel. The polar array is a time-saving tool that often is applicable in drawings that have circular features.

TASKS TO BE COMPLETED IN THIS EXERCISE

- Array gear teeth around the circle
- Create two inner circles

ARRAYING GEAR TEETH AROUND THE CIRCLE

Now that you have the first gear tooth drawn, you can array it around the inside of the circle to create the rest of the gear teeth. To do this, use the ARRAY command and the center of the circle as the point of rotation around which the teeth are arrayed.

Issue the ARRAY command, then enclose it in a window to copy it 12 times. AutoCAD asks you if you want to create a rectangular array or a polar array. For this exercise, you need to use the Polar array option. This option enables you to copy entities in a circular pattern.

Step 1.0: Issue the ARRAY command:

Command: **ARRAY** ↵   Starts the ARRAY
                                        command

Step 1.1: You now need to enclose the gear tooth inside a window, as seen in figure 6.6. The window selects the entity to copy around the circle. Because the two lines are fully enclosed within the window, and the circle is not, AutoCAD selects only the lines:

Figure 6.6:

*Using a window to
select the tooth for
a polar array.*

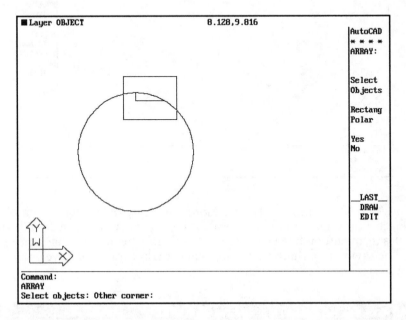

```
■ Layer OBJECT                          8.128,9.816           AutoCAD
                                                              * * *
                                                              ARRAY:

                                                              Select
                                                              Objects

                                                              Rectang
                                                              Polar

                                                              Yes
                                                              No


                                                              _LAST_
                                                              DRAW
                                                              EDIT




Command:
ARRAY
Select objects: Other corner:
```

Select objects: *Pick a point below and to*   Starts the window
the left of the tooth (see fig. 6.6)   selection option and
                                                   defines the window's
                                                   first corner

Other corner: *Pick a point above and to*   Defines the window's
the right of the tooth (see fig. 6.6)   second corner

Step 1.2: End the selection process:

Select objects: ↵   Stops object selection

Step 1.3: Now that you have selected the entity you want to array, use the Polar option to copy it around the inside of the circle:

Rectangular or Polar array   Selects the Polar
(R/P) <R>: **P** ↵   option

Step 1.4: You now need to define the point around which you want to rotate and copy the tooth. Use the CENter object snap override to find the circle's center point. This selects the center as the point around which to rotate the copied teeth:

```
Center point of array: CEN ↵        Selects the CENter
                                    object snap override
```

Step 1.5: AutoCAD then asks you to select the object whose center point you want to find. Use the pick box and pick any point on the circumference of the circle. This tells AutoCAD to use the center of the selected circle as the point to copy and rotate the new geometry:

```
Of Pick a point on the circumference    Selects the circle's
of the circle                           center point as the
                                        point around which
                                        to rotate
```

Step 1.6: AutoCAD prompts you for the number of times to array the selected object. The number you specify is the total number of objects copied around the circle. The number always includes the original object. For this drawing, you need to copy the gear tooth a total of 12 times, including the tooth that already is drawn:

```
Number of items: 12 ↵        Tells AutoCAD to
                             create 12 teeth
                             around the circle
```

TIP

To calculate the number of teeth, remember that the original tooth includes a 30 degree angle and that all the teeth are copied around the full circle. Divide the number of degrees in a circle (360) by the angle in the first tooth you drew (30). The equation 360\30 equals 12 teeth that need to be copied, including the original tooth. Another easier way is simply to count the total number of teeth in figure 6.1.

Before the entities are copied, AutoCAD asks you for the angle to fill. This is the total amount to copy the object around the 360 degree circle. Entering 90 would place the geometry along 1/4 of the circle, 180 around half the circle, and so forth. For this drawing, you want to use the default value of 360 degrees. This spaces the entities equally around 360 degrees, which is the entire circle.

Step 1.7: Tell AutoCAD to space the entities around the entire circle by pressing Enter and accepting the default, as follows:

```
Angle to fill (+=ccw, -=cw) <360>: ↵      Spaces the entities
                                          equally around the
                                          circle
```

AutoCAD then asks if you want to rotate the objects as they are copied. If you look at figure 6.5, you see that as a tooth is duplicated it rotates to maintain its edges with the outer circle. The objects in this drawing are rotated. Objects that are not rotated are like seats on a Ferris wheel; that is, the objects remain at the same angle, regardless of their position around the axis.

Step 1.8: The teeth in this drawing need to be rotated. If the teeth are not rotated, they will be arrayed around the circle in the same direction as the first tooth, producing the wrong results for the drawing:

```
Rotate objects as they are          Rotates the objects
copied? <Y>: ↵                      as they array around
                                    the circle
```

You now should have all the teeth as shown in figure 6.5.

CREATING THE INNER CIRCLES

You now are ready to add the two circles shown in figure 6.7. These are *concentric circles* to the original large circle. This means that the circles all share the same center point. After the circles are added, you can zoom in on the center and edit the geometry.

Figure 6.7:

The object with inner circles.

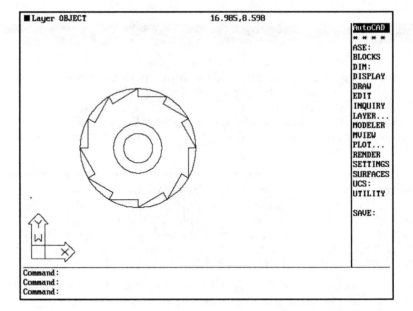

You need to create two circles within the one you already have drawn. Use the CIRCLE command's Diameter option and the center point of the original circle to create two circles with diameters of 2.5 units and 1.5 units.

Step 2.0: Issue the **CIRCLE** command or choose Circle then Center,Diameter.

Step 2.1: When prompted for the center point, specify the CENter object snap override and pick a point on the circumference of the large circle. This gives the new circle the same center as the original circle.

Step 2.2: After the center point is located, invoke the Diameter option and specify a value of **2.5** for the circle size.

Step 3.0: You now can create the last circle using the same method as you did for the preceding circle. Select the center of either existing circle and make the last circle's diameter **1.5** units.

You now are ready to work on the innermost circle to add the keyway seen in figure 6.1. First, however, you should enlarge that area to make it easier to pick points on the circle. To do this, use the ZOOM command with the Window option. The Window option enables you to enlarge a portion of the drawing by enclosing it in a window.

Step 4.0: Issue the ZOOM command:

```
Command: ZOOM ↵
```
Starts the ZOOM command

Step 4.1: Enclose the area you want to enlarge, as follows:

```
All/Center/Dynamic/Extents/Left/
Previous/Vmax/Window/
<Scale(X/XP)>:Pick a point just below
and to the left of the smallest circle
```
Specifies the window's first corner

```
Other corner: Pick a point just above
and to the right of the smallest circle
```
Specifies the window's second corner

NOTE

After zooming in, your circles may not appear round because AutoCAD's default settings determined that the change in zoom was not enough to merit a drawing regeneration.

You can work on this drawing as it appears on-screen, or you can use the REGEN command to clean up the drawing. The REGEN command regenerates the drawing on-screen and eliminates the "edges" on the circle, which makes the drawing easier to see.

Exercise 3: Adding the Keyway

You now are ready to add the keyway shown in figure 6.8. To create this entity, you develop a construction line from the center of the circle, offset it the width of the keyway, and trim away the unnecessary portions. This process resembles the last lesson in which you drew construction lines to create a spindle.

Figure 6.8:

The keyway with labels.

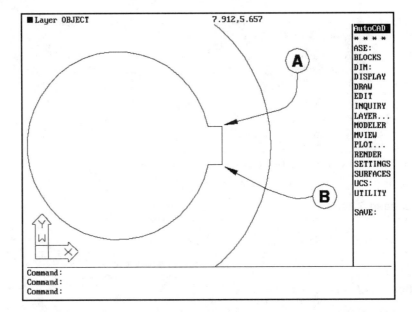

Tasks To Be Completed in this Exercise

- Create construction lines
- Trim away the unneeded geometry to develop the keyway

Creating a Construction Line

To create the keyway, begin by drawing a horizontal construction line from the center of the circle. The length of this line is the radius of the circle (.75 units) plus the depth of the keyway (.10 units). After you draw this line, offset a line above the first line and one below it. Then erase the first line to end up with two construction lines. These two lines define the outer sides of the keyway.

Step 1.0: Issue the LINE command:

`Command: LINE ↵`	Starts the LINE command

Step 1.1: Enter CENter and use the object snap override to select a point on the circle's circumference. This makes the circle's center point the starting point for the first construction line:

`From Point:` *Use object snap Center* *and pick a point on the circumference*	Defines the starting point

Step 1.2: Now draw a horizontal line to the right that is the radius of the circle (.75) plus the keyway depth (.10). Use polar coordinates to specify the line:

`To point: @.85<0 ↵`	Enters the Polar coordinates for a horizontal line

Step 1.3: Press Enter to end the LINE command:

`To point: ↵`	Stops the LINE command

This first line is used to create the two construction lines that make up the sides of the keyway. To make these lines, offset the first line half the size of the keyway width on both sides. The keyway width is .30 units, so offset one line .15 units above the first construction line, and offset the other line .15 units below the first line. The distance between these two lines is .30 units, or the total width of the keyway.

Step 2.0: Enter the **OFFSET** command.

Step 2.1: Enter **.15** as the offset distance for the new lines.

Step 2.2: Select the first line as the object to offset and select a point above the line as the side to offset.

Step 2.3: To create the next line, pick the original construction line and select a point below that line, offsetting the line .15 units.

Step 2.4: Press Enter to exit the OFFSET command.

You now are finished using the original construction line, which is now the middle line. You need to erase it to finish the shape of the keyway.

Step 3.0: Issue the **ERASE** command and pick the middle line as the object to erase, then end the ERASE command by pressing Enter.

As you can see in figure 6.8, the keyway needs a line from point A to point B to close it off. The LINE command and the ENDpoint object snap are used to create this line.

Step 4.0: Issue the **LINE** command.

Step 4.1: Invoke ENDpoint and then pick the right end point on the top horizontal construction lines.

Step 4.2: Invoke ENDpoint and then pick the right end point on the bottom horizontal construction lines.

Step 4.3: Press Enter to exit the LINE command.

TRIMMING THE CONSTRUCTION LINES

The basic outline of the keyway is now constructed. You now need to remove unnecessary construction lines and the circle segment to finish the keyway. The TRIM command removes these entities.

Step 5.0: Issue the TRIM command:

`Command: `**`TRIM`**` ↵`	Starts the TRIM command

Step 5.1: As you learned in previous lessons, the TRIM command enables you to pick objects as the cutting edges until you press Enter. In this drawing, three entities need to be trimmed—pick all three cutting edges:

`Select cutting edge(s)...`	Selects the top
`Select objects: ` *Pick line* Ⓑ	horizontal line as
(see fig. 6.9)	one cutting edge
`Select objects: ` *Pick line* Ⓒ	Selects the bottom
(see fig. 6.9)	horizontal line as a
	second cutting edge
`Select objects: ` *Pick circle* Ⓐ	Selects the small
(see fig. 6.9)	circle as the third
	cutting edge

Step 5.1: The two horizontal lines and the small circle are selected as cutting edges. You now can end the selection process and trim away the unneeded entities:

`Select objects: ↵`	Ends the selection process

Step 5.2: You also need to trim off the line segments that are inside the small circle, as well as the segment of the circle between the line segments. Again, the TRIM command enables you to trim entities until you press Enter. Pick the section of the entities you want trimmed away, as follows:

`<Select object to trim>/Undo: ` *Pick line* Ⓒ *inside the circle*	Trims this line segment to the
(see fig. 6.9)	circle
`<Select object to trim>/Undo: ` *Pick line* Ⓑ *inside the circle*	Trims this line segment to the
see fig. 6.9)	circle

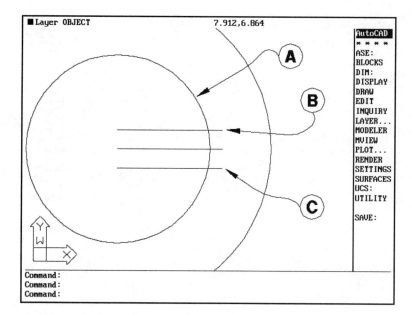

`<Select object to trim>/Undo:` *Pick circle* Ⓐ *between horizontal lines* Ⓐ *and* Ⓑ *(see fig. 6.9)*	Trims this section of the circle between the two lines
`<Select object to trim>/Undo:` ↵	Ends the TRIM command

The center hole now has a keyway. You can return to a full view of the drawing.

Step 6.0: Use the **ZOOM** command with the All option to enlarge the drawing to its full size.

Exercise 4: Drawing a Section View

You now are ready to add the section view to the right of the present object (the front view), as shown in figure 6.10. A *section view* is a drawing of what the part looks like if it is cut along a line. The section line is seen in figure 6.1 as the vertical line with the arrows pointing to the left cutting through the middle of the front view. The arrows define the direction of the view you see after the object is cut along that line.

Figure 6.10:

The completed section view and front views.

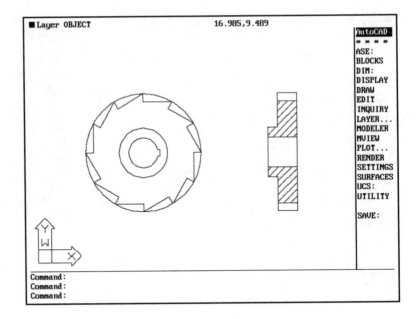

To create the top half of the section view, you will use a standard drafting procedure of projecting lines across the drawing. To project lines in this drawing, you first need to develop a horizontal center line and three vertical lines that start forming the section view. After these lines are created, you draw horizontal lines across from the features in the front view perpendicular to the vertical lines of the section view. You finish the top half of the section view by trimming away the excess lines. After half of the view is defined, you then mirror the view over to complete the full section view.

TASKS TO BE COMPLETED IN THIS EXERCISE

- Draw the right-side view
- Project lines across the screen
- Create the top half of the section view
- Create the bottom half of the section view

DRAWING THE RIGHT-SIDE VIEW

The first step in defining the section view is creating the center line and the three vertical lines that define the sides of the section view (fig. 6.11).

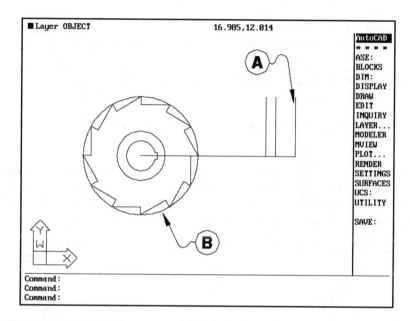

The LINE command is used to draw a construction line from the center point of the circle to the right side of the screen. This line eventually is removed, but first is used to find the center of the section view. After the top half of the section view is drawn, you mirror the entity across this construction line. This construction line also is used as a reference for drawing the three vertical construction lines.

After the three vertical lines are constructed, you draw four horizontal construction lines. Most of these lines also are removed to create the final object.

Step 1.0: Issue the **LINE** command.

Step 1.1: Use the OSNAP command's CENter option to pick the center of circle B (see fig. 6.11). This point is the start of the line.

Step 1.2: Draw a horizontal line eight units to the right by typing @8<0 at the To point: prompt.

Step 1.3: The vertical line A (see fig. 6.11) defines the right side of the section view and is drawn using the end point of the line you have just drawn. Draw a three-unit line straight up (90 degrees) that rubberbands from the last point by typing the polar coordinates @3<90 at the To point: prompt.

Step 1.4: Press Enter to exit the LINE command.

You now can create the other two vertical construction lines for the section view by offsetting line A (see fig. 6.11). These lines correspond to the vertical lines dimensioned 1.00 and 1.50 in the section view of figure 6.1.

Step 2.0: Issue the **OFFSET** command and set the offset value to **1.0**. Select line A and pick a point to the left to create the first vertical line.

Step 3.0: Issue the **OFFSET** command and set the offset value to **1.5**. Select line A and pick a point to the left to create the second vertical line.

PROJECTING LINES ACROSS THE SCREEN

You now are ready to project the lines across from the front view to the section view, as seen in figure 6.12. These lines are construction lines that define all the line segments needed in the top half of the section view. After the lines are projected across, use the TRIM command to remove all line segments except those that are needed to define the view.

Figure 6.12:

The projected construction lines for creating half the section view.

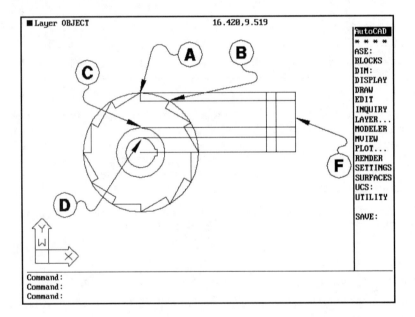

To create these construction lines, you will use two new object snap overrides—QUAdrant and PERpendicular. The QUAdrant option lets you pick a point on a circle or arc that is closest to the 0, 90, 180, or 270 degrees point. PERpendicular enables you to form a line that is perpendicular (at a 90-degree angle) to the last point entered.

Because you will be using these object snaps many times, set a running object snap and set Quadrant and Perpendicular as active.

Step 1.0: Use the Object Snap Settings dialog box to make Quadrant and Perpendicular active:

Command: *Select* Settings, *then* Object Snap	Opens the Object Snap Settings dialog box

Step 1.1: Set the desired running object snaps and exit the dialog box:

Choose Quadrant *and* Perpendicular	Sets the object snaps as running object snaps
Choose OK	Closes the dialog box

You now have a running object snap and are ready to project the lines.

Step 2.0: Issue the LINE command:

Command: **LINE** ⏎	Starts the LINE command

Step 2.1: You now need to tell AutoCAD the point on the circle you want to use as the starting point of the horizontal line. This line will be at the top (or quadrant of the large circle):

To point: *Pick point* Ⓐ *(see fig. 6.12)*	Starts the line at the top of the large circle

Step 2.2: Invoke the PERpendicular option and pick a point on line F to draw the horizontal line from point A to line F:

To point: *Pick line* Ⓕ *(see fig. 6.12)*	Draws a line perpendicular to line F

Step 2.3: End the LINE command:

To point: ⏎	Ends the LINE command

You now need to construct the remaining three construction lines. To construct the next line, you need to use the Perpendicular object snap, as well as the ENDpoint object snap. The line denotes the end of a tooth in the front view, so the starting point must be the end point of the tooth. This line also is perpendicular to line F. Even though a running object snap is set, you can still use the ENDpoint object snap override to issue a different object snap.

Step 3.3: Issue the LINE command and invoke the ENDpoint object snap override:

Command: **LINE** ↵	Starts the LINE command
From point: **END** ↵	Invokes the ENDpoint object snap override
Of *Pick point* (B) *(see fig. 6.12)*	Starts the line at the end of the gear tooth

Step 3.4: Use the default running object snap Perpendicular to draw the line perpendicular to line F:

To point: *Pick line* (F)	Draws a line perpendicular to line F

Step 3.5: Exit the LINE command:

To point: ↵	Exits the LINE command

Finish drawing the construction lines by drawing two lines perpendicular to line F at the top of each of the inner circles.

Step 4.0: Issue the **LINE** command at the From point: prompt. Pick point C (see fig. 6.12) as the starting point of the new line.

Step 4.1: At the To point: prompt, pick line F (see fig. 6.12), which will be perpendicular to the new line.

Step 4.2: End the LINE command by pressing Enter.

Step 5.0: Reissue the **LINE** command at the From point: prompt. Pick point D (see fig. 6.12) as the starting point of the new line.

Step 5.1: At the To point: prompt, pick line F (see fig. 6.12) as the line to draw perpendicular to.

Step 5.2: End the LINE command by pressing Enter.

This completes the construction lines for the drawing. Your drawing should resemble the one shown in figure 6.12.

Step 5.3: Now that you are finished with the Quadrant and Perpendicular running object snap, turn them off:

Command: *Choose* Settings, *then* Object Snap	Opens the Object Snap Settings dialog box

Step 6.0: Set the desired running object snaps and exit the dialog box:

Click on the Quadrant *and* Perpendicular *fields to clear their boxes*	Turns off the running object snaps
Choose OK	Closes the dialog box

You now have a running object snap and are ready to project the lines.

Creating the Top Half of the Section View

You are ready to remove the construction lines and create the top half of the section view. When you finish removing lines, you should be left with an object that looks like the highlighted area in figure 6.13.

To remove the unneeded construction lines, use the ERASE and TRIM commands.

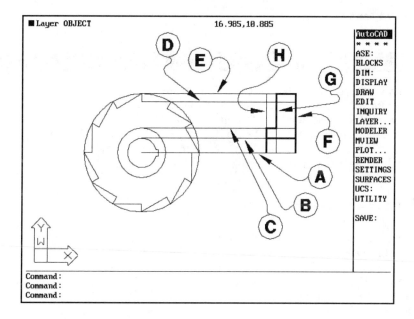

Figure 6.13:

The projected construction lines with the desired geometry shown in bold.

Step 7.0: Issue the **ERASE** command and erase line A (the original horizontal construction line extending from the center of the circle).

TIP

Your screen may be cluttered with blips after you erase and trim lines. Any time you need to clean up the screen, simply issue the REDRAW command at the Command: prompt.

You now can remove the unneeded line segments to create the desired geometry shown as bold in figure 6.13. You do this by using the TRIM command. The sequence may seem repetitious at times, but the object will become clearer as each line is trimmed.

Step 8.0: Issue the TRIM command:

```
Command: TRIM ↵
```
Starts the TRIM command

Step 8.1: When the TRIM command asks you for the cutting edges, invoke the Crossing selection set option. This option works in much the same fashion as the Window object selection option. The Crossing option, however, selects not only any object within the window, but also any object that touches the window's borders:

```
Select cutting edge(s)...
Select objects: C ↵
```
Selects the Crossing selection set option

NOTE

By creating a crossing window, you can select lines B through F in figure 6.13 in a single operation. You do not need to select the front view. You need to trim off a number of line segments to finish the section view object. To do this, select all the lines that make up the section view, including the projected construction lines. By selecting these lines, you make all of them cutting edges.

Step 8.2: To select the cutting edges, pick two points that surround or cross all the construction lines:

```
First corner: Pick a point below and
```
*to the left of the vertical construction
lines (see fig. 6.14)*
Selects the crossing window's first corner

```
Other corner: Pick a point above and to
```
*the right of the vertical construction
lines (see fig. 6.14)*
Selects the crossing window's second corner and cutting edges

Step 8.3: End the selection process:

```
Select objects: ↵
```
Stops the cutting edge selection process

Step 8.4: Select the objects to trim:

```
<Select object to trim>/Undo:
```
Pick lines Ⓑ, Ⓒ, Ⓓ, *and* Ⓔ
(see fig 6.13)
Removes a section of each of these lines to the nearest cutting edge (line H)

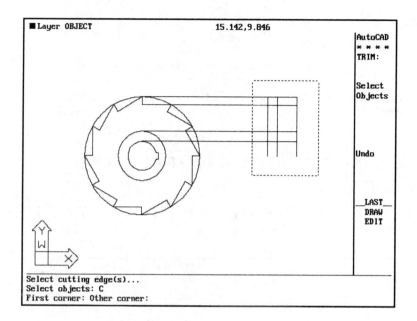

```
AutoCAD
* * * *
TRIM:

Select
Objects


Undo



_LAST_
DRAW
EDIT
```

```
Select cutting edge(s)...
Select objects: C
First corner: Other corner:
```

Figure 6.14:
A crossing window selects cutting edges for trimming.

Step 8.5: Select additional objects to trim:

`<Select object to trim>/Undo:` *Pick lines Ⓓ and Ⓔ (see fig 6.13) between lines Ⓖ and Ⓗ*	Removes these line segments to the next cutting edge
`<Select object to trim>/Undo:` *Pick line Ⓗ (see fig 6.13) near the top end point*	Trims line H down to its intersection with line D
`<Select object to trim>/Undo:` *To complete line Ⓗ (see fig 6.13), again select it near its new top*	Trims it down to its intersection with line C
`<Select object to trim>/Undo:` *Remove an unneeded section of line Ⓖ (see fig 6.13) by picking it near the bottom*	Trims it up to its intersection with line B
`<Select object to trim>/Undo:` *Pick line Ⓖ (see fig 6.13) between lines Ⓑ and Ⓒ*	Trims line G up to its intersection with line C

`<Select object to trim>/Undo:` *Finish the trimming process by picking line* Ⓒ *between lines* Ⓕ *and* Ⓖ	Removes the last line segment
`<Select object to trim>/Undo:` ↵ command	Exits from the TRIM

You now have the top half of the section view, as seen in bold in figure 6.13.

CREATING THE BOTTOM HALF OF THE SECTION VIEW

To create the full view seen in figure 6.15, you can mirror the top half of the section view across its center.

Figure 6.15:

The full section view.

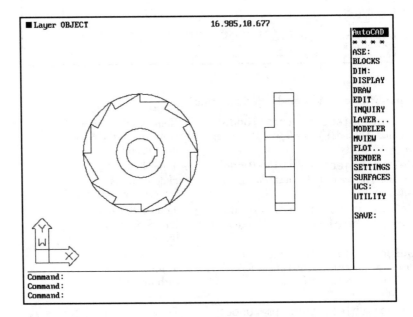

As you learned in Lesson 4, you can create one-half of an object, then duplicate it across a mirror line. The section view in this drawing can be completed by enclosing the top half of the section view in a window, then mirroring it to create the bottom half. This reduces your drawing time by one half.

Step 9.0: Issue the MIRROR command:

`Command: ` **`MIRROR`** `⏎`	Starts the Mirror command

Step 9.1: Enclose the top half of the section view inside a window:

`Select objects:` *Pick a point below and to the left of the section view geometry*	Selects the window's first corner
`Other corner:` *Pick a point above and to the right of the section view geometry*	Selects the window's second corner
`Select objects:` `⏎`	Ends the selection process

Step 9.2: You now need to define the mirror line by picking the lower end points of the selected geometry. Use the ENDpoint object snap override to pick points A and B (see fig 6.16):

`First point of mirror line:` **`ENDP`** `⏎`	Selects the ENDpoint object snap override
`Of` *Pick point* Ⓐ *(see fig. 6.16)*	Selects point A as the first point of the mirror line
`Second point of mirror line:` **`ENDP`** `⏎`	Selects the ENDpoint object snap override
`Of` *Pick point* Ⓑ *(see fig. 6.16)*	Selects point B as the second point of the mirror line

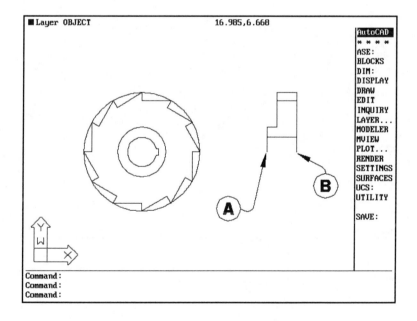

Figure 6.16:

The section view with mirror points labeled.

Step 9.3: AutoCAD asks you if want to delete the old objects. Specify that you do not want to delete the original object because it makes up the top part of the section view:

```
Delete old objects? <N>  ⏎
```
Creates the mirror object and keeps the original

When you finish, your drawing should resemble the one shown in figure 6.15.

EXERCISE 5: DEFINING AND ADDING CROSSHATCHING

You now are ready to add the crosshatching to the section view as shown in figure 6.17. In a section view, crosshatching defines the type of material used to build the part. Different patterns specify different materials, such as plastic, steel, wood, and concrete. AutoCAD comes with several predefined hatch patterns. In addition, you can create hatch patterns and specify your own parameters.

Figure 6.17:

The section view with crosshatching.

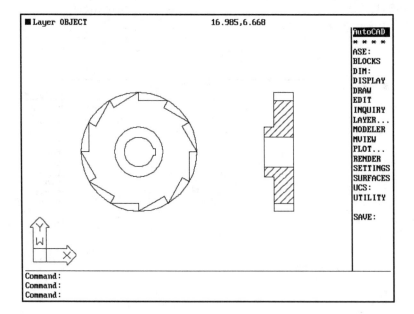

The HATCH and BHATCH command in AutoCAD places crosshatching inside a boundary defined by entities. If the area to be hatched is a simple box composed of four lines, the lines can be selected as the hatch boundary. AutoCAD then places the hatch pattern inside the box. In more complex geometry, such as the section view in this drawing, the existing geometry does not sufficiently define the area.

You can break the existing lines to isolate the hatch area. This option, however, is both time-consuming and alters the original geometry. A more practical approach is to surround the area with a single entity, such as a polyline. This can be done by drawing a polyline or by using the BHATCH command to define the boundary. The command that is used to create a polyline is PLINE. After the polyline is placed around the area you want to hatch, you can place a hatch pattern in the section view. If you use the BHATCH command, you can choose to have the polyline (or boundary) remain after the crosshatch is added or automatically removed.

Tasks To Be Completed in this Exercise

- Change the drawing layer
- Define a boundary for hatching
- Add hatch patterns with HATCH and BHATCH
- Erase the boundary

Changing the Drawing Layer

Before you add the crosshatching, you must change the drawing layers. The crosshatching will be placed on a different drawing layer than the objects. This enables you to remove the hatch layer and edit or view the drawing without the crosshatching. This makes editing the drawing easier because you do not have to work around the hatching.

For the hatch pattern on the top of the section view, you will place the polyline boundary geometry on this layer. After the hatch pattern is added, you will erase the polyline so that only the hatch pattern remains on the drawing layer.

The hatch pattern on the bottom of the section view will be drawn using BHATCH. This will place the crosshatch on this layer but will not leave a polyline boundary that needs to be erased.

Step 1.0: Issue the **LAYER** command and use its **Set** option to make the HATCH layer the current layer.

After you change the layer, you can add the crosshatching as shown in figure 6.17.

Defining a Boundary for Hatching

You now can add the crosshatching to the top of the section view using the HATCH command. Because the area to be hatched in this drawing has several lines that cross over each other, you need to isolate the area before cross hatching can be added. You can do this either by breaking each line that extends outside of the area at the intersecting line, or by using a single entity to define a boundary around the area.

The easier option is to create a single boundary. To do this, use the PLINE command (called Polyline on the Draw pull-down menu). The PLINE command creates a connected series of line or arc segments, which AutoCAD considers to be one object. The PLINE command has several options.

OPTIONS

- **Arc.** Develops arcs rather than polylines
- **Close.** Closes a polyline from the last point to the starting point
- **Endpoint of line.** The default option; prompts for the end point of a line segment
- **Halfwidth.** Enables you to specify the width of a polyline from the center to the outer edge
- **Length.** Draws a polyline at a defined length tangent to the last polyline segment drawn
- **Undo.** Removes the last polyline segment drawn
- **Width.** Enables you to specify the overall width of a polyline

---

The polyline you are going to create is a series of connected lines that share the same end points. Because you need to select several end points during the PLINE command, you can decrease your drawing time by setting a running ENDpoint object snap.

Use the OSNAP command's ENDpoint option to set the running object snap (you can also use the Object Snap Settings dialog box). After the running object snap is set, you can use PLINE to create the boundary for the crosshatching.

Step 2.0: Enter the OSNAP command and invoke the ENDpoint object snap override:

Command: **OSNAP** ↵   Starts the OSNAP
                                               command

Object snap modes: **END** ↵   Defines ENDpoint as
                                               the running object
                                               snap

Now when you issue the PLINE command, the crosshairs turn into an aperture box. This enables you to pick the end point of any line.

You now can create the boundary by tracing over part of the section view with polylines. These lines will be removed after the crosshatching is created.

The boundary lines are created by picking points on the object as outlined in the following steps. You need to trace only those areas that are to be crosshatched.

Step 3.0: Issue the PLINE command:

Command: **PLINE** ↵   Starts the
                                               development of
                                               connected line
                                               segments

Step 3.1: Create the starting point of the boundary by picking point A on the section view, as follows:

From point: *Pick point* Ⓐ   Selects point A
(see fig. 6.18)   as the starting
                                               point for the
                                               polyline

NOTE

AutoCAD tells you the current line-width. One of the options in the PLINE command is to create a line with width. When the line width is set to 0, the PLINE command draws standard lines and arcs.

Current line-width is 0.00   States the current
                                               polyline width

Step 3.2: Continue to pick points for the boundary using the aperture box and the points indicated in the following steps:

Arc/Close/Halfwidth/Length/   Selects point B
Undo/Width/<Endpoint of line>:   as an end point of a
Pick point Ⓑ *(see fig. 6.18)*   polyline segment

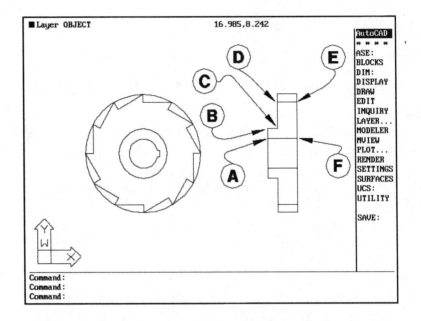

NOTE

If you have a color monitor, you can tell where the new polyline is created because of its different color. If you do not have a color monitor, you have to trust that the new line is being created.

`Arc/Close/Halfwidth/Length/`
`Undo/Width/<Endpoint of line>:`
Pick point Ⓒ *(see fig. 6.18)*
	Selects point C as an end point of a polyline segment

`Arc/Close/Halfwidth/Length/`
`Undo/Width/<Endpoint of line>:`
Pick point Ⓓ *(see fig. 6.18)*
	Selects point D as an end point of a polyline segment

`Arc/Close/Halfwidth/Length/`
`Undo/Width/<Endpoint of line>:`
Pick point Ⓔ *(see fig. 6.18)*
	Selects point E as an end point of a polyline segment

`Arc/Close/Halfwidth/Length/`
`Undo/Width/<Endpoint of line>:`
Pick point Ⓕ *(see fig. 6.18)*
	Selects point F as an end point of a polyline segment

`Arc/Close/Halfwidth/Length/`
`Undo/Width/<Endpoint of line>:`
`C ↵`
	Closes the polygon and ends the PLINE command

You are finished locating end points for the boundary lines; you can remove the running ENDpoint object snap.

Step 4.0: Issue the OSNAP command and cancel the running ENDpoint object snap:

Command: **OSNAP** ↵	Starts the OSNAP command
Object snap modes: **NON** ↵	Cancels the running ENDpoint object snap

ADDING HATCH PATTERNS

You now are ready to add the hatch pattern to the drawing. This is done by issuing the HATCH command and defining your own hatch pattern. The HATCH command enables you to select predefined patterns or create a user-defined pattern. By using the BHATCH command, you can view the 52 hatch patterns that AutoCAD supplies. These patterns range from concrete and brick to steel and swampy material.

AutoCAD also enables you to create your own hatch patterns. The HATCH command's U (for User-defined) option enables you to define a pattern on the fly. In this definition, you can determine the angle of lines, distance between lines, and whether the pattern includes a single or crossing set of lines.

After the pattern is selected or defined, you pick the boundary area. AutoCAD then places the hatch pattern inside the selected area.

Step 5.0: Issue the HATCH command:

Command: **HATCH** ↵	Starts the HATCH command

Step 5.1: Invoke the User option to create your own hatch pattern:

Pattern (? or name/U,style): **U** ↵	Selects the user-defined pattern option

Step 5.2: The hatch pattern enables you to create crosshatch patterns at any angle you desire. For this drawing, you need to make the pattern at a 45-degree angle, as shown in figure 6.17. Specify that you want the cross hatch pattern to be set at a 45-degree angle, as follows:

Angle for crosshatch lines <0>: **45** ↵	Specifies the angle at which to make the hatch pattern

Step 5.3: AutoCAD also lets you define the space between the lines in your pattern. The lines in this drawing are spaced .25 units away from each other. Specify that you want the pattern lines to have spaces of .25 units between each other, as follows:

```
Spacing between lines <1.0000>:    Specifies a spacing
.25 ↵                              for the crosshatch
                                  pattern
```

Step 5.4: You have the option of having a single set of lines, as seen in figure 6.17, or adding a second set of lines that cross over the first set at a 90-degree angle. Specify not to crosshatch the area, as follows:

```
Double hatch area? <N>: ↵         Accepts the default
                                  to not create a
                                  second set of
                                  crosshatch lines
                                  perpendicular to
                                  the first
```

Step 5.5: You now need to tell AutoCAD the boundaries for the hatch pattern. The polyline that you created for the boundary "sits" on top of the original lines you drew for the drawing. This lets you pick the polylines without picking the original drawing. To do this, select the polyline when the pick box appears.

```
Select objects: Pick the polyline   Selects the polyline
Select objects: ↵                   Places the hatch
                                   pattern in the
                                   drawing and exits
                                   from the HATCH
                                   command
```

ERASING THE BOUNDARY

Now that the top hatch pattern is complete, you need to erase the polyline. You may find it difficult to select the polyline and not the hatch pattern with the pickbox. To get around this problem, zoom in on the polylines.

Step 6.0: Issue the **ZOOM** command and select the Window option. Place the window around the middle of the section view so that the window includes only a small portion of the polyline, as shown in figure 6.19.

You now should be able to pick the polyline without erasing any part of the hatch pattern.

Step 7.0: Issue the **ERASE** command. The polylines need to be erased without erasing any part of the hatch pattern. Use the pickbox and pick any line on the top and bottom entity that is not at an angle (the angled lines that make up the hatch patterns). Press Enter to end the ERASE command.

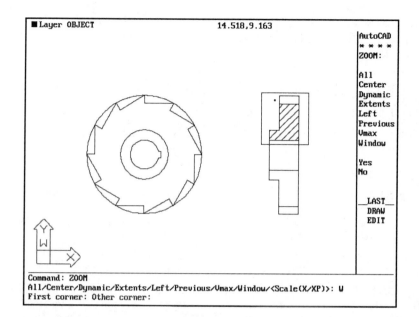

Figure 6.19

A zoom window for erasing the polyline boundary.

When you erase lines that sit on top of other lines, the objects on the bottom also disappear from the screen. AutoCAD only knows that the geometry in this area of the screen has been removed and blanks out this part of the screen. You can bring back the original geometry by issuing the REDRAW command.

Step 8.0: Issue the **REDRAW** command. The original geometry should appear on-screen.

Step 9.0: Now return to the original zoom factor by issuing the **ZOOM** command and selecting the Previous option.

USING **BHATCH** TO ADD CROSSHATCH

As introduced at the beginning of this exercise, both the top and bottom of the section view require a hatch pattern. Now use the BHATCH command to create the crosshatching at the bottom.

The BHATCH command uses a dialog box to perform the same functions as the HATCH command. Three primary advantages of the BHATCH command over the HATCH command is that it will display all of the available hatch patterns on screen. You simply choose the desired pattern. The second advantage is that it allows you to preview a pattern before it is permanently added to the drawing. This enables you to make certain that the pattern is perfectly placed before continuing. The final advantage is that it will create a boundary line around an area by picking a point inside the object where the hatch pattern is to be placed.

The BHATCH command can be typed or chosen from the menu.

Step 10.0: Start the BHATCH command:

`Command:` *Choose* Draw, *then* Hatch	Starts the BHATCH command and displays the Boundary Hatch dialog box

Step 10.1: The Boundary Hatch dialog box enables you to select a hatch pattern from several additional dialog boxes. In addition, you can use input boxes to create a user-defined hatch pattern. Use the Hatch Options dialog box to choose the hatch pattern:

Choose Hatch **O**ptions	Displays the Hatch Options dialog box

Step 10.2: To keep the bottom of the section view the same as the top, use a U (user-defined) hatch pattern. The default should be the same as the last pattern. Confirm that U is the pattern name, 45 is the angle, .25 is the spacing between lines, and double hatch is not active. After this has been confirmed, close the dialog box:

Choose OK	Closes the Hatch Options dialog box

Step 10.3: BHATCH will create a boundary for hatching by picking a point inside the area to hatch:

Choose **P**ick points	Changes the prompt so that you can specify a point within the hatch boundary

Step 10.4: Pick a point inside the enclosed area that you want to hatch. AutoCAD will create a temporary boundary area for hatching:

`Select internal point:` *Pick a point inside the bottom area of the cross section where the crosshatch is to be added*	Defines the boundary area

Step 10.5: Exit the Pick Point option:

`Select internal point:` ↵	Returns to the BHATCH dialog box

The temporary boundary area is now defined.

Step 10.6: Use the Apply button to add the hatch pattern to the drawing:

Choose the Apply button

Adds the hatch
pattern to the
drawing and closes
the dialog box

There should now be a hatch pattern on the top and bottom of the cross section. Because the boundary area in BHATCH is set to be temporary, you do not need to zoom in and erase the polyline as with the top hatch pattern.

As you learned in previous lessons, you should save your drawing every 15 minutes or so. Now is a good time to save your drawing if you have not done so.

Step 11: Issue the **QSAVE** command to save your drawing to disk.

Your drawing now should look like figure 6.17.

EXERCISE 5: ADDING DETAIL

You now are ready to add linetypes and dimensions to the drawing. First, however, you must create the center line and section line with arrowheads, as shown in figure 6.20. You used a process similar to that in Lesson 5 to develop the geometry, except that here you create the construction lines to position the new lines, add the lines, and then change them to their respective linetypes. The arrows on the section lines are created by drawing a polyline with different starting and ending widths.

This exercise shows you how to add the different linetypes and dimensions to the drawing.

TASKS TO BE COMPLETED IN THIS EXERCISE

- Change the drawing layer
- Add a horizontal center line
- Add a vertical section line
- Add arrowheads to the section line

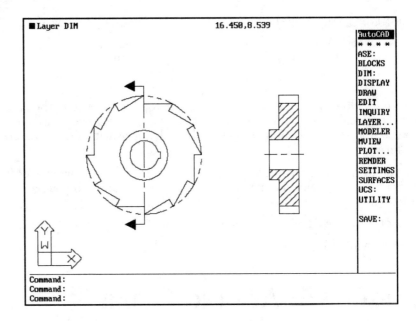

Figure 6.20:
The drawing with different linetypes.

CHANGING THE DRAWING LAYER

Again, you must change the layer so that the linetypes, and eventually the dimensions, are placed on a separate layer. If the dimensions and linetypes are on a separate layer, you can view the drawing with or without them on-screen.

Step 1.0: Enter the **LAYER** command or use the Layer Control dialog box and make the layer named DIM the current layer.

ADDING A HORIZONTAL CENTER LINE

You begin adding the detail to the drawing by first creating the horizontal center line of the section view. The center lines are created by first drawing two construction lines as guides. These construction lines are labeled as lines C and D in figure 6.21. The construction lines are created by offsetting the two vertical lines that make up the top half of the section view (labeled as lines A and B in fig. 6.21), and by drawing a line between the construction lines. After the line is drawn, you will erase the two construction lines from the drawing.

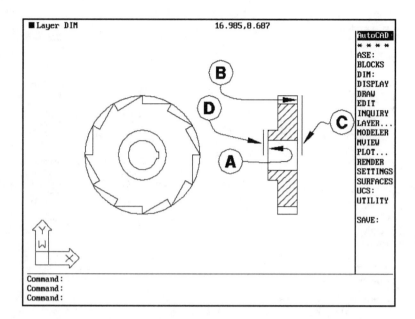

Step 2.0: Invoke the **OFFSET** command and set the offset value to .25.

Step 2.1: Offset line A to the left of the section view. Then offset line B to the right of the section view.

Step 2.2: Press Enter to exit the OFFSET command.

Remember that lines A and B are only part of the top half of the section view that was mirrored earlier in this lesson. Although these line segments are only part of the drawing, they are enough to develop the center line.

Step 3.0: Issue the **LINE** command.

Step 3.1: Use the ENDpoint object snap and draw a line between the bottom end points of lines C and D. This line passes through the center of the section view.

Step 3.2: Press Enter to exit the LINE command.

Step 4.0: After the center line is created, enter the **ERASE** command and erase the two construction lines. Your drawing should resemble the one shown in figure 6.22.

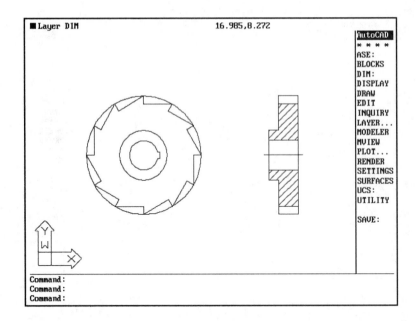

```
■ Layer DIM                    16.985,8.272
                                                          AutoCAD
                                                          * * * *
                                                          ASE:
                                                          BLOCKS
                                                          DIM:
                                                          DISPLAY
                                                          DRAW
                                                          EDIT
                                                          INQUIRY
                                                          LAYER...
                                                          MODELER
                                                          MVIEW
                                                          PLOT...
                                                          RENDER
                                                          SETTINGS
                                                          SURFACES
                                                          UCS:
                                                          UTILITY

                                                          SAVE:


  Command:
  Command:
  Command:
```

ADDING A VERTICAL SECTION LINE

You now are ready to add the vertical section line that runs through the middle of the front view. Use the same process as you did to create the horizontal construction line on the section view. That is, create a construction entity to help you create the vertical line. In this case, however, you will use a circle as the construction entity.

The construction entity is created by offsetting the original front-view circle (circle A in figure 6.23). You will use the construction circle to create the vertical line so that the end points are between the upper and lower quadrants in circle B, also shown in figure 6.23. After you draw this line, you will erase the construction circle and add arrowheads to the line.

Step 5.0: Issue the **OFFSET** command and set the offset value to .5 units.

Step 5.1: Pick circle A (see fig. 6.23) and offset it to the outside, creating circle B.

Now draw the center section line. The section line is drawn from the top of the construction circle to the bottom by picking a point near the top and bottom of the circle. The QUAdrant object snap enables AutoCAD to know which quadrant you want to snap to.

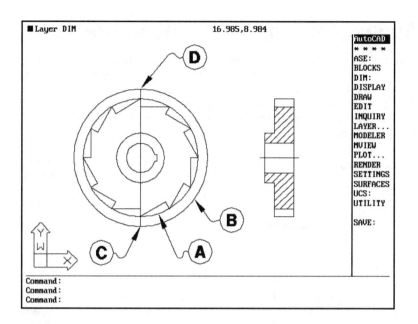

The construction circle and vertical section line.

Step 6.0: Issue the LINE command and invoke the QUAdrant object snap override:

Command: **LINE** ↵	Starts the LINE command
From point: **QUA** ↵	Selects the QUAdrant object snap override

Step 6.1: Specify the starting point of the center line:

Of *Pick point* Ⓒ *(see fig. 6.23)*	Selects the center line's starting point

Step 6.2: Issue QUAdrant and specify the end point of the center line:

To point: **QUA** ↵	Invokes the QUAdrant object snap override
Of *Pick point* Ⓑ *(see fig. 6.23)*	Selects the center line's end point

Step 6.3: Exit the LINE command:

To point: ↵	Exits the LINE command

You now are finished with the construction circle.

Step 7.0: Issue the **ERASE** command and remove the construction circle (circle B) from the drawing.

The AutoCAD Tutor   191

ADDING ARROWHEADS TO THE SECTION LINE

You now need to draw the arrowhead and leader line at both ends of the section line, as shown in figure 6.24. These arrows define the direction from which the section view is seen. You can add these lines by using the LINE command and drawing a one-unit line on each end of the section line. Then create the arrowhead by using the PLINE command's Width option.

Figure 6.24:

The drawing with arrows on section lines.

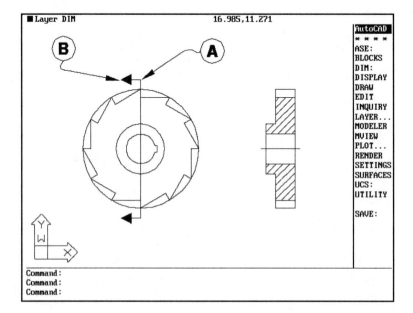

To draw the leader line, use the LINE command's ENDpoint option to draw a one-unit line off the top of the section line. The one-unit line is created to the left of the section line by telling AutoCAD to draw it 180 degrees from point A (see fig. 6.24).

After the line is drawn, use the Width option to add an arrow to its end.

Step 8.0: Issue the **LINE** command and invoke the ENDpoint object snap override. Pick point A (see fig. 6.24).

Step 8.1: Specify a one-unit line to the left of the section line by typing the polar coordinates **@1<180** at the To point: prompt. Press Enter to end the LINE command. This creates the first leader line.

Now add the arrowhead to the leader line. You can use the PLINE command to create lines that have different beginning and ending widths. To do so, you first select a starting point and then the Width option, which creates lines with a specified width. The ending widths can be equal or of different values. After the width is set, select an end point for the polyline.

Step 9.0: Issue the PLINE command and invoke the ENDpoint object snap override to start the arrowhead:

`Command: `**`PLINE`**` ↵`	Starts the PLINE command
`From point: `**`END`**` ↵`	Invokes the ENDpoint object snap override

Step 9.1: Pick the starting point of the polyline:

`Of ` *Pick point* Ⓑ *(see fig. 6.24)*	Selects the starting point of the arrowhead

Step 9.2: Now that the starting point has been defined, all the PLINE options are displayed. For this drawing, you need to change the overall line width of 0 to a starting width of 0 and an ending width of .5. This creates an arrowhead after you select the end point. Invoke the Width option and define the starting and ending widths of the arrowhead, as follows:

`Current line-width is 0.00`	
`Arc/Close/Halfwidth/Length/` `Undo/Width/<Endpoint of line>: `**`W`**` ↵`	Selects the PLINE Width option
`Starting width <0.00>: `**`0`**` ↵`	Defines the starting width as 0
`Ending width <0.00>: `**`.5`**` ↵`	Defines the ending width as .5

Step 9.3: Specify the end point of the polyline:

`Arc/Close/Halfwidth/Length/Undo/` `Width/<Endpoint of line>: `**`@.5<0`**` ↵`	Draws a tapered polyline .5 units to the right

Step 9.4: End the PLINE command:

`Arc/Close/Halfwidth/Length/Undo/` `Width/<Endpoint of line>: ↵`	Ends the PLINE command

You now have the leader line and arrowhead on top of the section line. You need to create the same thing for the bottom of the sect-ion line. You can do this by drawing it as you did the top one, but to decrease your drawing time, use the MIRROR command. You can create a mirror image of the arrowhead and leader line by telling AutoCAD to duplicate the entities across the midpoint of the vertical section line.

Step 10.0: Issue the MIRROR command and pick the arrowhead and leader line:

Command: **MIRROR** ↵	Starts the MIRROR command
Select objects: *Pick the arrowhead*	Selects the arrowhead as one object to mirror
Select objects: *Pick the short horizontal leader line*	Selects the leader line as the other object to mirror

Step 10.1: End the mirror selection process:

Select objects: ↵	Ends object selection

Step 10.2: You now need to instruct AutoCAD to mirror the image across the midpoint of the section line. This is done by using the MIDpoint object snap override. This option enables you to snap to the middle of an entity. In this case, you need to find the starting point to create a horizontal mirror line:

First point of mirror line: **MID** ↵	Invokes the MIDpoint object snap override
Of *Pick the middle of the section line*	Makes the middle of the section line the starting point of the mirror line

Step 10.2: Specify a horizontal mirror line three units long. The length does not matter because the angle of the line from the first point defines the mirror line:

Second point: **@3<0** ↵	Defines a three-unit mirror line

Step 10.3: Just as did in earlier exercises, you want to duplicate the object across the mirror line. First, keep the original object and then make a mirror image of it:

Delete old objects? <N> ↵	Keeps the original object and mirrors it across the mirror line

This finishes the geometry for the drawing. Your drawing should resemble the one shown in figure 6.24, but without the labels.

Exercise 6: Changing Linetypes and Dimensioning the Drawing

Now that you have the desired geometry, you need to give it the correct linetypes. In the previous lesson, you defined the linetype before drawing the object. In this lesson, you created the geometry and now will change the linetype. To do this, use the CHANGE command. The CHANGE command enables you to redefine the properties or geometric definition of an object.

The CHANGE command is helpful in changing geometry that is drawn correctly, but which needs some revisions. CHANGE also is useful when mistakes are made in drawings, such as when you place geometry on the wrong layer or if you need to make quick corrections.

You will finish the drawing by adding the dimensions seen in figure 6.1. The dimensioning tolerances are placed automatically in the drawing using dimension variable settings.

Tasks To Be Completed in this Exercise

- Change the linetype
- Add dimensions

Changing the Linetype

In drafting, linetypes convey specific kinds of information. AutoCAD uses the following kinds of linetypes:

- **Center.** Specifies the center of a part
- **Phantom.** Defines a section line or outer part definition
- **Hidden.** Identifies a hidden edge
- **Continuous.** Specifies a visible drawing feature

For this drawing, you need to use the Phantom and Center linetypes. The Phantom linetype is used to define the section line and the circle that outlines the gear; the center linetype is used to redefine the linetype of line C (see fig. 6.25) in the section view.

Step 1.0: Issue the CHANGE command:

Command: **CHANGE** ↵   Starts the Change
                                         command

Step 1.1: Select line A and circle B in figure 6.25:

`Select objects:` *Pick line* Ⓐ *(see fig. 6.25)*	Selects line A as one object to change
`Select objects:` *Pick circle* Ⓑ *(see fig. 6.25)*	Selects circle B as another object to change
`Select objects:` ↵	Stops object selection

Figure 6.25:

The correct linetypes.

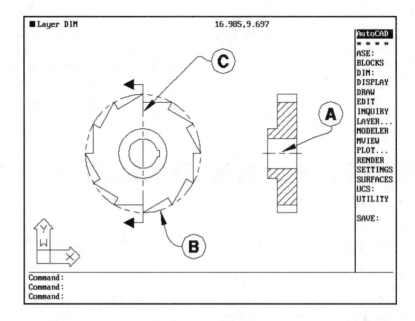

Step 1.2: You now want to change the property of the entities you just picked. Properties include color, layer, linetype, and thickness on the Z axis. Specify that you want to change the property of the linetype, as follows:

`Properties/<Change point>: P` ↵   Tells AutoCAD to change a property of the selected entities

Step 1.3: For this drawing, you need to change the linetype of the line and circle:

`Change what property`
`(Color/LAyer/LType/Thickness) ?`   Tells AutoCAD to change the linetype
`LT` ↵

Step 1.4: Assign the phantom linetype to the line and circle:

```
New linetype <BYLAYER>: Phantom ↵
```
Assigns the phantom linetype to the line and circle

Step 1.5: End the CHANGE command:

```
Change what property
(Color/LAyer/LType/Thickness) ? ↵
```
Ends the CHANGE command

You now can change the linetype of line C in figure 6.25 as you did line A and circle B in the preceding command lines. Rather than change the linetype to Phantom, make it a center linetype:

Step 2.0: Issue the **CHANGE** command and pick line C (see fig. 6.25) as the object you want to change.

Step 2.1: Specify that you want to change the Property, then select the ~~LType~~ *layer* option.

Step 2.2: When AutoCAD prompts you for the new linetype, type **Center** and press Enter.

Step 2.3: Press Enter again to end the command.

ADDING DIMENSIONS

You now are ready to add the dimensions to create the final dawing, as shown in figure 6.26.

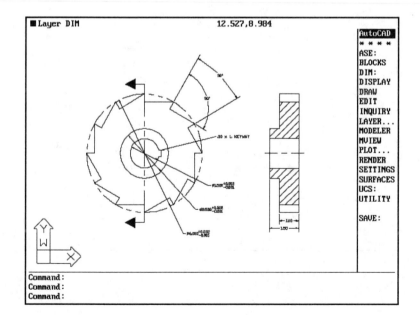

Figure 6.26:
The final drawing with dimensioning.

You will complete the drawing by adding horizontal dimensions across the bottom of the section view. You also will dimension the front view's circles and add tolerance specifications to the drawing.

You can add the angle between the lines that define the teeth by using the ANGular dimensioning subcommand. This subcommand places angular dimensions between two non-parallel lines. Complete the drawing by using the LEAder dimensioning subcommand to add information to the keyway.

Begin the dimensioning process by setting up the dimensioning variables as you did in previous lessons. Begin by setting the DIMTXT and DIMASZ variables. Additional dimensioning variables are changed throughout the dimensioning process as needed.

Step 3.0: Issue the **DIM** command to switch AutoCAD to dimensioning mode.

Step 4.0: Issue the **DIMTXT** variable and set the dimension text size to **.125** units. Then issue the **DIMASZ** variable and set the size of the arrowheads to **.125** units.

You now are ready to add the horizontal and baseline dimensions to the bottom of the section view, as shown in figure 6.27. Use the HORizontal dimensioning subcommand and pick the end points by using the ENDpoint object snap override.

Figure 6.27:

Horizontal and baseline dimensions on the section view.

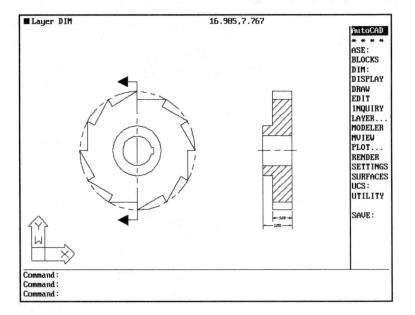

Step 5.0: Issue the HORizontal dimensioning subcommand by entering **HOR**.

Step 5.1: Use the object snap **ENDpoint** to pick the lower right corner of the section view (see fig. 6.27) for the first extension line origin. For the second point, pick the lower left corner of the section view.

Step 5.2: Pick a point below the object to position the dimension line. Accept the dimension text by pressing Enter.

Step 6.0: Issue the **BASeline** dimensioning subcommand.

Step 6.1: Use **ENDpoint** to select the left corner that extends out on the section view (see fig. 6.27) as the extension line origin.

Step 6.2: Press Enter to accept the dimension text.

You now are ready to add the angular dimensions. The ANGular dimensioning subcommand specifies the angle between two non-parallel lines. When using this command, you select the two entities whose angles you want to dimension. Unlike most dimensioning subcommands, you do not need to use object snap overrides because you are selecting entities.

Step 7.0: Issue the ANGular dimensioning subcommand:

`Dim: ANG ↵`	Starts the ANGular subcommand

Step 7.1: Pick the lines that define the area you want to dimension:

`Select arc, circle, line,` `or RETURN:` *Pick line* (A) *(see fig. 6.28)*	Selects line A as one dimensioning boundary
`Second line:` *Pick line* (B) *(see fig. 6.28)*	Selects line B as the second dimensioning boundary

Step 7.2: Specify the location of the dimension line arc:

`Enter dimension line arc location` `<Text/Angle>:` *Pick point* (C) *(see fig. 6.28)*	Specifies the placement of the dimension line arc

Step 7.3: Accept the default dimensioning text:

`Dimension text <90>: ↵`	Accepts the default dimension text

Step 7.4: Center the text between dimensioning lines:

`Enter text location` `(or Return): ↵`	Centers the text between the dimension lines

You now can add the second angular dimension.

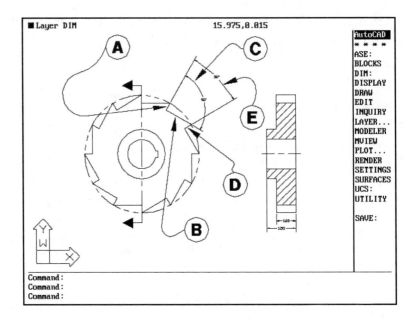

Figure 6.28:

Adding angular dimensions.

Step 8.0: Enter the **ANGular** dimensioning subcommand.

Step 8.1: Select lines A and D (see fig. 6.28) as the objects you want to dimension.

Step 8.2: Position the dimension line arc by selecting point E.

Step 8.3: Accept the default text of 30 by pressing Enter.

Step 8.4: Position the text in the center of the extension lines by pressing Enter.

You now are ready to add the circular dimensions. As shown in figure 6.29, these dimensions have an upper and lower tolerance applied to them. These tolerances are specifications used in the manufacture of the part. You use dimensioning variables to set dimension tolerances in the same manner as dimension text height and arrowhead size.

Notice that the dimension tolerances have three places to the right of the decimal. At the beginning of this lesson, you set the decimal places to two to create this drawing. Now you must change the decimal place value to three. To change the number of decimal places for these dimensions, you can exit from dimensioning mode, issue the UNITS command, and then change the decimal place value. A faster way is to use the LUPREC system variable, which you used in the beginning of this lesson.

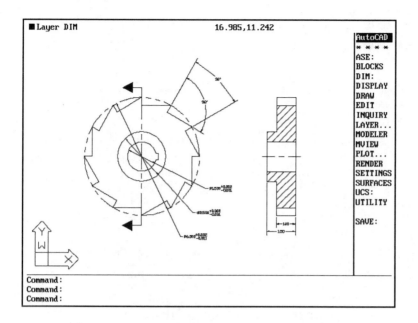

Step 9.0: Enter the LUPREC system variable:

`Dim:` **`LUPREC`** ↵   Starts the LUPREC system variable

Step 9.1: Set the number of decimal places to three:

`>>New value for LUPREC<2>:` **`3`** ↵   Changes the linear unit precision to 3

You now are ready to change the dimension variables that add tolerances to a dimension.

OPTIONS

The following dimensioning variables are used to add tolerances to this drawing:

- **DIMTP.** Specifies positive (+) tolerances
- **DIMTM.** Specifies negative (−) tolerances
- **DIMTOFL.** Causes the dimension line to appear between the extension lines, even if the text is placed outside the extension lines
- **DIMTOL.** Generates tolerances using the settings defined in DIMTP and DIMTM

Step 10.0: Set the upper tolerance value (positive):

Dim: **DIMTP** ↵	Starts the DIMTP dimensioning variable
Current value <0.000> New value:**.002** ↵	Defines a value of .002 for upper tolerance

Step 11.0: Set the lower tolerance value (negative):

Dim: **DIMTM** ↵	Starts the DIMTM dimensioning variable
Current value <0.000> New value: **.001** ↵	Sets the lower tolerance value at .001

Step 12.0: Issue the DIMTOL system variable and set it to On:

Dim: **DIMTOL** ↵	Starts the DIMTOL dimensioning variable
Current value <Off> New value: **On** ↵	Turns on DIMTOL to place tolerance dimensions in the drawing

Step 13.0: Issue the DIMTOFL system variable to make AutoCAD place a leader line through the center of the circle during dimensioning. This helps in identifying the diameter dimension:

Dim: **DIMTOFL** ↵	Starts the DIMTOFL dimensioning variable
Current value <Off> New value: **On** ↵	Turns on DIMTOFL to place a line through the circle

Step 14.0: Issue the DIAmeter subcommand and pick the largest circle. Then show AutoCAD where to place the dimension:

Dim: **DIA** ↵	Starts the DIAmeter subcommand
Select arc or circle: *Pick the large circle at the 5 o'clock position (see fig. 6.29)*	Selects the circle to be dimensioned and specifies the position for the leader line
Dimension text <6.000> ↵	Accepts the default for the dimension

`Enter leader length for text:` *Use the pointing device to drag the dimension* *text downward and away from the circle* *so that it is positioned as shown in* *figure 6.29*	Positions the dimension text in relation to the circle and ends the subcommand

Step 15.0: Reissue the **DIAmeter** subcommand and pick the second-largest circle. Pick the circle at the 4:30 position, press Enter, and then drag the dimension so that it is positioned as shown in figure 6.29.

Step 16.0: Reissue the **DIAmeter** subcommand and pick the smallest circle. Pick the circle at the 4 o'clock position, press Enter, and then drag the dimension so that it is positioned as shown in figure 6.29.

You now can finish the drawing by placing the dimension that details the keyway. You can use the LEAder dimensioning subcommand to create this dimension. The LEAder subcommand creates an arrow, extension line, and text. You manually specify the number and length of the extension lines and type in the desired dimension text.

When you use the LEAder dimension subcommand, you first must select the point at which the arrow on the end of the leader will point. You then select the end points of leader lines. After you finish selecting leader lines, press Enter. The previous dimension text is shown as the default. You then type the text to be placed at the end of the last leader line.

Step 17.0: Issue the LEAder subcommand:

`Dim: LEA ⏎`	Starts the LEAder subcommand

Step 17.1: Invoke the ENDpoint object snap override and specify where you want the leader line to begin and the direction of the arrow:

`Leader start: END ⏎`	Invokes the ENDpoint object snap override
`Of` *Pick the upper right corner* *of the keyway (see fig. 6.30)*	Selects the position at which the arrow points
`To point:` *Pick a point above the* *starting point and outside the largest* *circle (see fig. 6.30)*	Selects the point that the leader line extends to

Step 17.2: End the selection process:

`To point: ⏎`	Stops the leader line end point selection

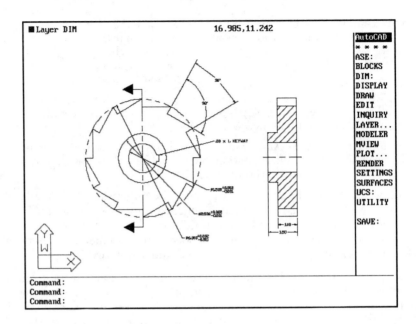

Step 17.4: Enter the text that you want placed at the end of the leader line:

Dimension text <2.500>:
.30 x .1 KEYWAY ↵

Specifies the text
string you want to
add to the drawing

You now are finished with the dimensioning commands and this drawing. Your drawing should look like the one shown in figure 6.30.

Step 18.0: End the dimensioning commands:

Dim: *Press Ctrl-C*

Exits from the
dimensioning area

Step 19.0: Save the drawing to disk and end the current drawing session.

SUMMARY

In this drawing, you learned to apply polar coordinates to define geometry by distance and angle. You then used editing commands to duplicate the entities around an axis. You also learned how to project lines to create a section view, and how to create a crosshatch pattern inside a boundary. After the drawing was completed, you added detail by creating lines with different linetypes, drew arrowheads, and added dimensions with tolerances.

By creating the drawing in this lesson, you expanded on your drawing, editing, and detailing tools. You can use these tools to create geometry quickly. In the next lesson, you will learn to create symbols that can be used as many times as needed. After you draw the symbols, you can use them over and over again, greatly decreasing the time required to complete a drawing.

REVIEW

1. Draw a line that is 3.75 units long and is at a 37-degree angle.

2. From the top end point of the line in question one, draw another line off the first line, with a length of 4.125 units and at an angle of 135 degrees.

3. Define dimension variables that add tolerance to a drawing of +.003 and –.002.

4. Place an angular dimension between the two lines in questions one and two with tolerance settings used in question three.

5. On the end of both lines in questions one and two, use the **PLINE** command to draw an arrow head with a starting width of zero, an ending width of .4, and a length of .5. When you draw the polyline length or end point, remember that the two lines are at an angle.

6. Change the linetype of both lines in questions one and two to hidden lines.

7. Load the drawing REV6-1 from *The AutoCAD Tutor Disk*, and use the **PLINE** command to place a boundary around the inner rectangle.

8. In the drawing REV6-1 on *The AutoCAD Tutor Disk*, hatch the inner rectangle. Create a user-defined hatch that has a crosshatch, an angle of 33, and a distance of .125.

9. Load the drawing REV6-2 from *The AutoCAD Tutor Disk*, and array the small hole at the top around the center of the two large circles. When finished, you should have a total of eight small holes.

10. Create a section view from the front view in drawing REV6-2.

CREATING AN ELECTRICAL SCHEMATIC DIAGRAM

OVERVIEW

No single technique is more powerful in CAD than the development and sharing of symbols. The BLOCK command enables you to take existing geometric shapes or *symbols*, group them by name, and insert them into drawings as often as needed. The availability of the BLOCK command means once you have created a symbol, it does not need to be drawn again. After you insert a symbol into a drawing, the symbol can be scaled and rotated, adding to its functionality.

This lesson shows you how to create electrical symbols, create a block for each symbol, then place the block in a finished drawing. When you create blocks and reuse them in many drawings, you save drawing time. All drafting disciplines use blocks, ranging from electricians who create resistors and ground symbols, to architects designing doors and windows.

As you develop geometry for a block, give special thought to the block's use in future drawings. Think about how the block will be inserted into a drawing, as well as the relationship the block has to a drawing's existing geometry. If a symbol is created without considering how it will relate in various drawing situations, that symbol may be useless and difficult to manipulate in other drawings. This lesson shows you how to create basic electrical symbols that can be inserted in any electrical schematic diagram.

In previous lessons you learned how AutoCAD's drawing aids help you create geometry. In this lesson, you will create electrical symbols using the Snap, Grid, and Ortho drawing aids you are familiar with, as well as learn to use the DONUT command. The DONUT command enables you to develop solid-filled circles, such as a dot, or circles that have width, such as a washer.

In CAD, you usually need to develop a hard copy of your finished drawing. AutoCAD's PLOT command directs your finished drawing to either a printer or a plotter, and gives you a variety of options from which to choose when you are ready to plot or print your drawing. These options include specifying which size paper you want to print on, as well as the scale of the printed drawing. In Lesson 2 you learned that one of AutoCAD's main features is its capability to draw at full scale. You also learned a drawing is scaled in AutoCAD only when plotted or printed. This lesson shows you how to fit a finished drawing on a specified piece of paper, as well as rotate a drawing before printing.

TOPICS COVERED IN THIS LESSON

In this lesson, you learn to do the following:

- Draw a transistor symbol
- Draw an electrical ground symbol
- Draw a resistor symbol
- Draw a terminal and connector symbol
- Insert symbols in a drawing
- Add text to the drawing
- Print the drawing
- End the drawing session

This lesson teaches you how to use the following AutoCAD commands:

- **BLOCK.** Defines a group of entities as a single object (symbol), which can be inserted into drawings

- **DDINSERT.** Invokes a dialog box for the insertion of symbols

- **DONUT.** Creates circles with varying widths

- **INSERT.** Places a previously created symbol in a drawing

- **PLOT.** Creates a hard copy output from a printer or plotter

SETTING UP THE DRAWING

Before you begin drawing, set up the drawing environment as you have in previous lessons.

Step 1.0: Start AutoCAD; save the new drawing as **LESSON7**.

Unlike previous lessons, you do not need to set the limits or units for this drawing. Schematic diagrams do not need to be scaled or dimensioned. When you create a schematic diagram, you only need to make sure the symbols are large enough to be read easily on a hard copy output.

As in previous lessons, however, you need to create drawing layers for this lesson.

Step 2.0: Use the **LAYER** command or the Layer Control dialog box to create two new layers named **500** and **510**. Make 500 the current layer.

Now that your environment is set up, start this lesson by establishing the drawing aids. After you complete this lesson, you should have an electrical schematic diagram like the one shown in figure 7.1.

SETTING UP DRAWING AIDS

You learned in previous lessons how AutoCAD's drawing aids help you decrease the time you spend on a drawing. This lesson also uses these aids. The two drawing aids are SNAP and GRID. Remember that SNAP defines a physical grid for point selection; GRID displays a visual series of dots in the drawing editor.

Figure 7.1:

The completed electrical schematic diagram.

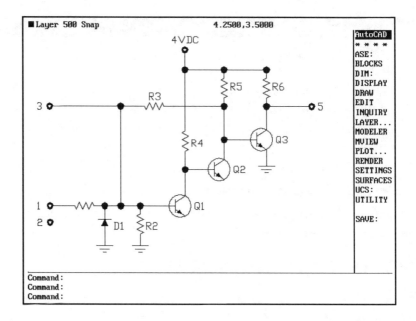

For this lesson, you will set the SNAP increment, turn on the grid, and enlarge the drawing area. The SNAP command defines the smallest increment recognized by AutoCAD when you move the crosshairs. This enables you to select exact points easily in the Drawing Editor. Set the Snap Increment to .125 units for this lesson. This helps you keep the size and spacing of the symbols consistent.

SETTING THE SNAP INCREMENT AND TURNING ON THE GRID

The SNAP command also helps when you insert the blocks to finalize the schematic drawing. When you insert the symbols, each symbol must be a multiple of .125 units away from each other. The ground symbol, for example, may be 1.000 units away from the transistor symbol, whereas the terminal symbol may be 0.625 units away from the resistor symbol. Yet each of these symbols is a multiple of .125 units away from each other. By setting the snap increment to .125 units, you ensure that each symbol is correctly spaced.

You have learned how the SNAP command assists you in physically positioning the crosshairs. AutoCAD's GRID command, on the other hand, helps you visually place the crosshairs. When you turn on the grid using the GRID command, the Drawing Aids dialog box, or by pressing F7, an array of dots appear on-screen. By default, the *grid size*—the amount of space between the dots—is the same as the snap setting. You may use the GRID command or the Drawing Aids dialog box to set the visual grid at an increment different from the snap setting. Keep the grid size at this value for this drawing. This will assist you when inserting the symbols at the lesson's end.

For this lesson, you only need to turn on the grid. No other settings need to be changed. To set the snap and grid in this lesson, use the Drawing Aids dialog box.

Step 1.0: Open the Drawing Aids dialog box:

Command: *Choose* Settings, *then* Drawing Aids	Displays the Drawing Aids dialog box

Step 1.1: Set the Snap Increment size to .125 units. By entering a Snap X spacing value, by default the Snap Y spacing value will be set to the same value:

Enter **.125** *in the Snap X Spacing input box*	Specifies the Snap X spacing (Y defaults to the same value as X)

Step 1.2: Turn on Snap:

Choose the On *box under Snap*	Turns Snap on

Step 1.3: Turn the grid on:

Choose the On *box under Grid*	Turns the grid on

Step 1.4: Exit the Drawing Aids dialog box:

Choose OK	Closes the dialog box

ENLARGING THE DRAWING AREA

To help you create the electrical symbols, you now need to enlarge the drawing area. When you create each symbol, you need to follow the grid pattern exactly as shown in the accompanying figures. After you enlarge the grid area, which increases the viewing size of each symbol, you will be able to pick the correct grid point. To enlarge the drawing area, use the ZOOM command and Window option.

Step 2.0: Issue the ZOOM command:

Command: ZOOM ⏎	Starts the ZOOM command

Step 2.1: AutoCAD gives you the option of zooming into a specific area of the drawing, which you select by enclosing the area in a window. To specify the zoom, select the ZOOM command's Window option; then instruct AutoCAD to define the drawing area at the coordinates 0,0 and 2,2:

```
All/Center/Dynamic/Extents/        Selects the
Left/Previous/                     Window option
Vmax/Window/<Scale(X/XP)>: W ↵

First point: 0,0 ↵                 Defines the lower
                                   left corner of the
                                   zoom window

Second point: 2,2 ↵               Defines the upper
                                   right corner of the
                                   zoom window
```

When you type in the second coordinates, AutoCAD zooms into the area defined by the window.

EXERCISE 1: DRAWING A TRANSISTOR SYMBOL

Now that your drawing area is set up, you are ready to create the drawing LESSON7. In this exercise, you create the transistor as shown in figure 7.2, using the same drawing commands you used in previous lessons. After you draw the transistor, you use the BLOCK command to create a transistor symbol. When you use the BLOCK command, name the block, pick the insertion point, and pick the entities you want to store as a block. After you create all of the electrical symbols in this drawing, you can insert them into the final drawing at the end of the lesson.

Figure 7.2:

The transistor.

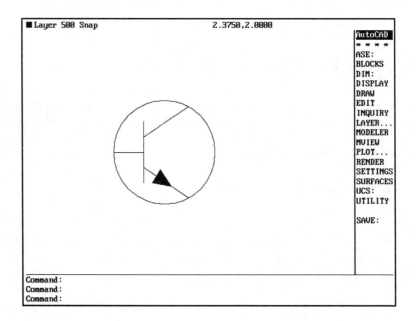

TASKS TO BE COMPLETED IN THE EXERCISE

- Draw the lines for the transistor
- Add the circle to the transistor
- Draw the arrowhead
- Create a transistor symbol

DRAWING THE LINES FOR THE TRANSISTOR

When you create a symbol such as a transistor, you first use the drawing and editing commands to draw the geometry. As you draw the object that you are going to use as a symbol, pay careful attention to the way it is drawn. A symbol should be both accurate and drawn to industry standards. A symbol created in one drawing may be shared with other drawings and should function now and into the future. The transistor, for example, will be used as part of schematic diagrams. In later lessons, you will create architectural symbols to be used in an architectural drawing.

When drawing an object, you also must decide on the drawing's insertion point. The *insertion point* is the point at which the block is inserted in other drawings. In this lesson, for example, the electrical symbols that are inserted into the final drawing are connected to each other by flowlines. *Flowlines* are lines in a schematic diagram that represent connecting paths. When you insert the symbol in the drawing, the symbol's insertion point connects to the flowline.

As you saw in figure 7.1, the flowlines that connect to the transistor intersect the circumference of the transistor's circle. The best way to create the transistor for use as a block is to make sure the lines' end points that touch the circumference fall on grid points. This will help you define the easiest insertion point for use in future drawings.

To create the transistor, first draw the four lines located within the transistor's circle. Then use the CIRCLE and PLINE commands to finish the drawing.

To draw all the lines for the symbols in this lesson, including the transistor, you need to follow the grid pattern *exactly* as shown in the accompanying figures. For this exercise, count each line's number of grid points as they appear in figure 7.3.

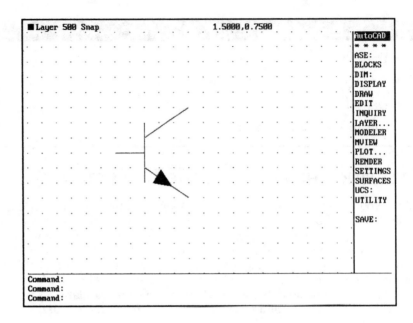

Step 1.0: Issue the LINE command:

Command: **LINE** ↵   Starts the LINE
                                        command

Step 1.1: Follow the grid pattern to locate the starting point of the first line:

From point: *Pick point* Ⓐ   Starts the first line
(see fig. 7.4)

Step 1.2: You now need to continue the angular line to point B (see fig. 7.4). Follow the grid pattern to duplicate the exact size of the line, ensuring that your transistor is the same as the one shown in figure 7.2:

To point: *Pick point* Ⓑ *(see fig. 7.4)*   Selects the end
                                        point of the first
                                        line

Step 1.3: End the LINE command:

To point: ↵   Ends the LINE
                                        command

Step 2.0: Reissue the **LINE** command and draw the second angular line that begins at point B (see fig. 7.5). Use the grid pattern as you did for the first line to make sure the second line is identical to the one shown in figure 7,5

Step 3.0: Reissue the **LINE** command and draw the vertical line that begins at point C, as shown in the previous figure. Again, follow the grid pattern.

Step 4.0: Reissue the **LINE** command and create the horizontal line that

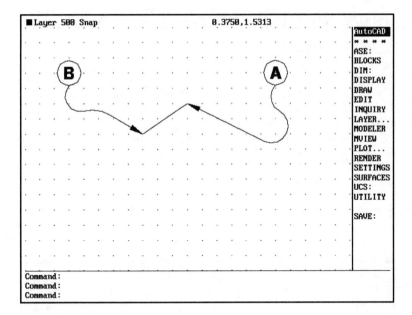

Figure 7.4:
Creating the transistor's first line.

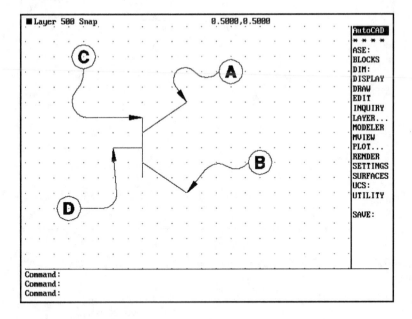

Figure 7.5:
Lines used to create the transistor, with labels.

begins at point D, as shown in the previous figure, using the grid pattern. This line should end at the vertical line you just created.

ADDING THE CIRCLE TO THE TRANSISTOR

You now can add the circle to the transistor as shown in figure 7.6. The circumference of the circle touches at three points: the end points of the two vertical lines, and the horizontal line that projects from the transistor. To create the circle, use the 3P (three-point) option under the CIRCLE command. For this option, you need to specify three points through which the circle's circumference passes. You can use points A, B, and C (see fig. 7.6) to create the circle's circumference.

Step 5.0: Issue the CIRCLE command and invoke the 3P option:

Command: **CIRCLE** ↵	Starts the CIRCLE command
3P/2P/TTR/<Center point>: **3P** ↵	Selects the three-point option

Figure 7.6:

The transistor with circle added.

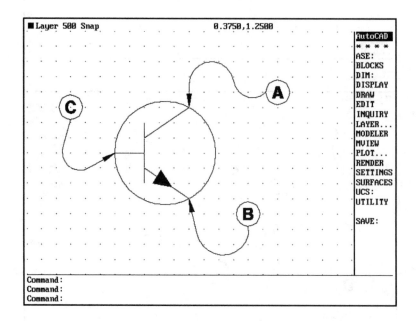

Step 5.1: Instruct AutoCAD to draw a circle that passes through points A, B, and C (see fig. 7.6), by picking the following points:

First point: *Pick point* (A)	Specifies the first point through which the circle passes

| `Second point:` *Pick point* (B) | Specifies the second point through which the circle passes |
| `Third point:` *Pick point* (C) | Specifies the third point through which the circle passes |

Your drawing now should look like the one shown in the previous figure.

DRAWING THE ARROWHEAD

You now are ready to add an arrowhead to the transistor, as shown in figure 7.7, using the PLINE command you learned in Lesson 6. After you issue the PLINE command, select a starting point for the arrowhead. You then select the Width option and create a starting width of 0 units, with an ending width of .125 units. Then finish the arrowhead by selecting an end point.

Because the arrowhead does not fall on the snap locations, you can turn

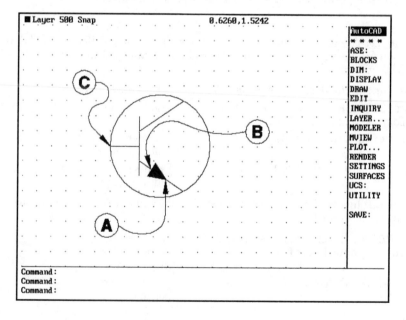

Figure 7.7:

The completed transistor with arrowhead.

off the SNAP command using F9. (The exact location of the arrowhead is not critical to the quality of the symbol.) Find the starting point of the arrowhead by estimating the midpoint (point A in figure 7.7) of the lower angular line. To assist in aligning the arrowhead to the line, use the NEArest object snap override. NEArest places the polyline exactly on the line nearest the point you select using the crosshair cursor.

Step 6.0: Turn off Snap by pressing F9 at the `Command:` prompt.

You learned in Lesson 6 that you can create polylines with varying thicknesses using the PLINE command. To create the arrowhead shown in the previous figure, you first start the PLINE command and then find the starting point of the arrow.

Step 7.0: Issue the PLINE command:

`Command: PLINE ⏎`	Starts the PLINE command

Step 7.1: Invoke the NEArest object snap override and pick the starting point of the arrowhead at point A:

`From point: NEA ⏎`	Activates the NEArest object snap override
to *Pick point* Ⓐ *(see fig. 7.7)*	Selects the starting point of the polyline

Step 7.2: You now need to change the line width of the polyline as you did in Lesson 6. The arrowhead has a starting width of 0 units and an ending width of .125 units:

`Current LINE-width is 0.0000`	Selects the PLINE
`Arc/Close/Halfwidth/Length/Undo/` `Width/<Endpoint of LINE>: W ⏎`	Width option
`Starting width <0.0000>: 0 ⏎`	Defines the starting width as 0 units
`Ending width <0.0000>: .125 ⏎`	Defines the ending width as .125 units

Step 7.3: Invoke the NEArest object snap mode and tell AutoCAD to draw the polyline, as in the following:

`Arc/Close/Halfwidth/Length/Undo/` `Width/<Endpoint of LINE>: NEA ⏎`	Activates the nearest object snap override
to *Pick point* Ⓑ *(see fig. 7.7)*	Draws a tapered polyline

Step 7.4: End the PLINE command:

```
Arc/Close/Halfwidth/Length/Undo/      Ends the PLINE
Width/<Endpoint of LINE>: ↵           command
```

Your drawing now should resemble the one shown in figure 7.7.

CREATING A TRANSISTOR SYMBOL

You now are finished drawing the transistor and are ready to make it into a symbol. The command that stores a group of entities as a symbol is the BLOCK command. The BLOCK command requires that you specify an insertion point and the name of the new block. You then select the objects that comprise the symbol. After you select the objects, the objects disappear from the screen to confirm that they have been made into a block.

One of the most important choices you have to make when you use the BLOCK command is selecting the insertion point. The *insertion point* is the point at which the symbol is inserted, scaled, and rotated in future drawings. When you create the geometry, take the time to analyze how the symbol will be used, and then select the most productive insertion point. For a circular object, such as a wheel or gear, the center of the object probably is the most productive insertion point. When you create rectangular objects, a corner or midpoint of the object usually is chosen as the insertion point.

For this drawing, pick point C in figure 7.7 as the insertion point. Because this point falls on a grid point, you can insert this symbol easily into a drawing, which makes this a good choice for an insertion point.

When you name a block, you should define it using a name that is easily recognized and remembered. (You can view the list of block names by entering a *?* at the first prompt after you issue the BLOCK command.) Block names can be up to 31 characters long. For best results, however, you should keep the name as short as possible, without losing its meaning.

You end the BLOCK command by selecting the entities that comprise the symbol. The entities can be as simple as a line or as complex as a drawing of a two-story house. In this lesson, you select the entities you want included in the drawing using the Window selection set option. After you select the objects and press Enter, the geometry selected as the block disappears. This enables you to confirm that the correct geometry is made into a block. If all the objects are not selected (do not disappear from the screen), issue the U command. The U command brings back the geometry and undoes the BLOCK command. You then can redefine the block correctly. If, however, you want the new block to remain as you created it, but you want the geometry to reappear on-screen, use the OOPS command. This enables you to edit or add to that geometry.

Step 8.0: Before you use the BLOCK command, turn on Snap by pressing F9. Snap helps you select the insertion point for the symbol.

Step 9.0: Issue the BLOCK command:

Command: **BLOCK** ↵	Starts the BLOCK command

Step 9.1: You now need to name the new block. For this drawing, name it TRAN, for transistor. This name will help you remember what the object is when you insert the block into drawings:

BLOCK name (or ?): **TRAN** ↵	Names the new block

Step 9.2: Pick the insertion point for the BLOCK:

Insertion base point: *Pick point* Ⓒ *(see fig. 7.7)*	Picks the insertion point

Step 9.3: You now need to select the entities you want to include as the TRAN block. For this drawing, the entire transistor is included as the block. To select the transistor, use the Window selection set option:

Select objects: *Pick a point just below and to the left of the transistor*	Selects the Window option and specifies the window's first corner
Other corner: *Pick a point just above and to the right of the transistor*	Specifies the window's second corner

6 found

Step 9.4: To create a block of the transistor, end the selection process:

Select objects: ↵	Stops the object selection and creates a block of the geometry

All of the on-screen geometry that you selected now should disappear. This indicates the symbol is created. You will notice the grid points have disappeared also. Each time you use the BLOCK command, the grid points are removed when the geometry disappears from the screen. This can be returned by using the REDRAW command.

Step 10.0: Use the **REDRAW** command to bring the grid back on-screen.

EXERCISE 2: DRAWING AN ELECTRICAL GROUND SYMBOL

You now are ready to create an electrical ground symbol as shown in figure 7.8. Use the same process you used in creating the transistor symbol. First create the geometry for the ground using the grid pattern, then use the BLOCK command to create a ground symbol. Name this block GROUND.

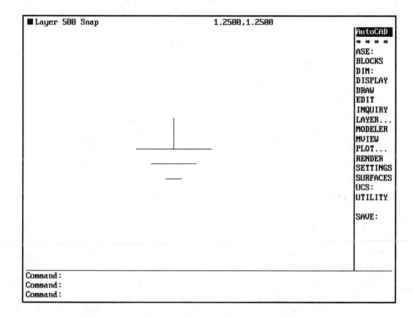

Figure 7.8:

The electrical ground symbol.

TASKS TO BE COMPLETED IN THIS EXERCISE

- Draw the ground geometry
- Create a ground symbol

DRAWING THE GROUND GEOMETRY

The ground geometry is created using only the LINE command. To draw the ground, issue the LINE command and follow grid pattern as shown in figure 7.9.

Figure 7.9:

The ground with end points labeled.

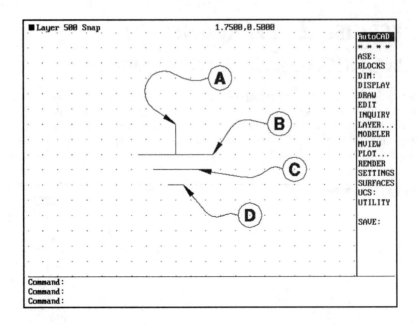

Step 1.0: Issue the LINE command:

`Command: LINE ↵`   Starts the LINE
                                            command

Step 1.1: Start the first line by following the grid pattern shown in figure 7.9:

`From point:` *Pick point* Ⓑ *(see fig. 7.9)*   Starts the first
                                            line

Step 1.2: Draw the first line by picking the end point shown in figure 7.9:

`To point:` *Pick the end point of*   Selects the
the first line   end point of the
                                            first line

Step 1.3: End the LINE command:

`To point:` ↵   Ends the LINE
                                            command

You now need to draw the other two horizontal lines that make up the ground geometry, using the grid pattern and the LINE command.

Step 2.0: Reissue the **LINE** command and draw the second line that begins at point C, as shown in figure 7.9. Use the grid pattern as you did for the first line to make sure your line is identical to the one shown in this figure.

Step 3.0: Reissue the **LINE** command and draw the third line that begins at point D (see fig. 7.9). Use the grid pattern as you did for the first line to ensure your line is identical to the one shown in this figure.

The last line, which begins at point A (see fig. 7.9), is created from the middle of the top horizontal line using polar coordinates. Because this line does not fall on a grid point, you need to turn off Snap.

Step 4.0: Press F9 to turn off Snap.

Step 5.0: Issue the **LINE** command and invoke the MIDpoint object snap override to find the starting point. Pick the top horizontal line as the object to find the midpoint of. Enter the polar coordinates **@.25<90** to draw a vertical line straight up from the horizontal line. Press Enter to exit the **LINE** command.

Your drawing now should look like the one previously shown in figure 7.8.

CREATING A GROUND SYMBOL

You now are ready to take the geometry you just created and make it into a symbol using the BLOCK command. For this drawing, select point A, as was indicated in figure 7.9, using the Endpoint object snap override as the insertion point. If you refer back to figure 7.1, you can see that the ground symbol connects to the other symbols at this point. Although this point is not a grid point now, you still can place the insertion point on a grid point when you insert the symbol into a drawing.

Step 6.0: Issue the **BLOCK** command and name the new block **GROUND**.

Step 6.1: Invoke the Endpoint object snap override and pick point A (see fig. 7.9) as the object to find the end point of. This is the insertion point of the object.

Step 6.2: To specify the objects you want to include as the block, invoke the Window option and enclose the geometry inside the window. Press Enter to select the objects and to create a block of the ground.

Again, all of the selected objects should disappear from your screen.

EXERCISE 3: DRAWING A RESISTOR SYMBOL

You now need to create the next symbol—the resistor symbol seen in figure 7.10. To develop this object, first draw the angular lines using the LINE command. Then add the two vertical lines at the top and bottom of the angular lines. To complete the drawing, trim away the excess lines that cross over at the ends of the geometry. You then can use the BLOCK command to create a block named RESISTOR.

Figure 7.10:

The resistor symbol.

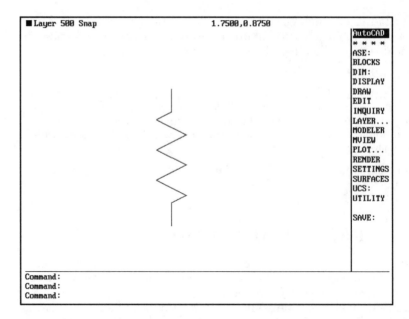

TASKS TO BE COMPLETED IN THIS EXERCISE

- Draw the resistor geometry
- Create a resistor symbol

DRAWING THE RESISTOR GEOMETRY

Begin this symbol by drawing the lines seen in figure 7.11. The end points of the first and last angular line extend beyond the eventual intersection of the vertical lines, which are drawn later in this exercise. By creating the resistor's first and last lines this way, the angle between these lines remains consistent with the other lines. After all the lines are drawn, use the TRIM command to remove the excess line segments.

Step 1.0: Before you start drawing the resistor geometry, you need to turn Snap back on by pressing F9.

To draw the angular lines for the resistor, use the LINE command. Follow the grid pattern shown in figure 7.11 to locate the starting point of the first line.

Step 2.0: Issue the **LINE** command and draw the seven angular lines. Use the grid pattern as you did for the ground symbol to ensure that your lines are identical to the sample shown in the previous figure.

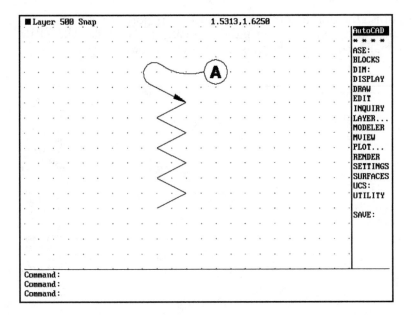

Step 3.0: Reissue the **LINE** command and draw the two vertical lines at the top and bottom of the resistor, as shown in figure 7.12. Again, follow the grid pattern to locate the starting points and end points of the lines.

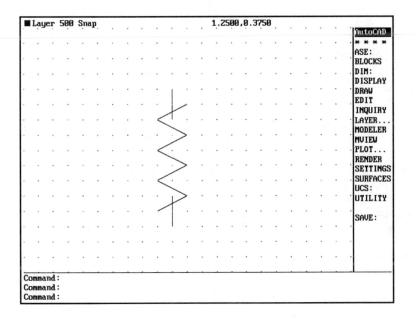

To finish the drawing, trim away unnecessary portions of the two vertical lines and of the top and bottom angular lines. Use the TRIM command to do this. The finished resistor is shown in figure 7.13.

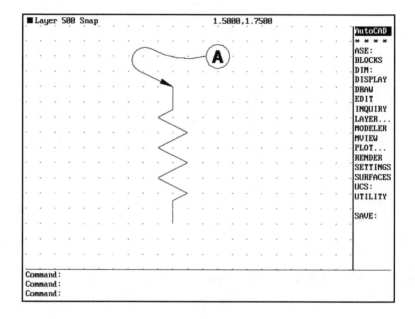

Step 4.0: Issue the TRIM command:

```
Command: TRIM ↵
```
Starts the TRIM command

Step 4.1: Pick both vertical lines and the top and bottom angular lines as cutting edges:

```
Select cutting edge(s)...
```
Selects the top vertical line as one cutting edge

```
Select objects: Pick the top vertical line
```
(see fig. 7.13)

```
Select objects: Pick the bottom vertical
```
line (see fig. 7.13)
Selects the bottom vertical line as the second cutting edge

```
Select objects: Pick the top angular line
```
(see fig. 7.13)
Selects the top angular line as the third cutting edge

```
Select objects: Pick the bottom angular
```
line (see fig. 7.13)
Selects the bottom angular line as the fourth cutting edge

Step 4.2: The two vertical lines and the top and bottom angular lines are selected as cutting edges. You now can end the selection process and trim away the unneeded entities.

```
Select objects: ⏎               Ends the selection
                                process
```

Step 4.3: You need to trim off the line segments of the vertical lines that intersect the angular lines. You also need to trim off the top angular line's segment that is to the right of the top vertical line, as well as trim off the bottom angular line's segment that is to the left of the bottom vertical line:

```
<Select object to trim>/Undo: Pick      Trims this line
the top vertical line below the top angular line    segment to the top
                                         angular line

<Select object to trim>/Undo:            Trims this line
Pick the top angular line to the right of the    segment to the top
top vertical line                        vertical line

<Select object to trim>/Undo:            Trims this line
Pick the bottom vertical line above the bottom    segment to the
angular line                             bottom angular line

<Select object to trim>/Undo:            Trims this line
Pick the bottom angular line to the left of the    segment to the
bottom vertical line                     bottom vertical line
```

Step 4.4: End the TRIM command:

```
<Select object to trim>/Undo: ⏎          Ends the TRIM
                                         command
```

CREATING A RESISTOR SYMBOL

You now need to create a resistor symbol using the BLOCK command. You learned in the last two exercises that AutoCAD enables you to name the block. Name this symbol RESISTOR. You again will use the Endpoint object snap override to specify the insertion point, as well as use the Window selection option to select the entities to be included in the block.

Step 5.0: Issue the **BLOCK** command and name the new block RESISTOR.

Step 5.1: Invoke the ENDpoint object snap override and pick point A, as was shown in figure 7.13, as the object to find the end point of. This is the insertion point of the object.

Step 5.2: To specify the objects you want to include as the block, invoke the Window option and enclose the resistor inside the window. Press Enter to select the objects and to create a block from the geometry.

Again, all of the objects within the window should disappear from your screen.

EXERCISE 4: DRAWING A DIODE SYMBOL

Continue creating the electrical symbols by drawing the diode seen in figure 7.14. In this exercise, you create the object using the LINE and PLINE commands. Use the PLINE command with the Width option to create the arrowhead in the middle of the diode.

Figure 7.14:

The diode symbol.

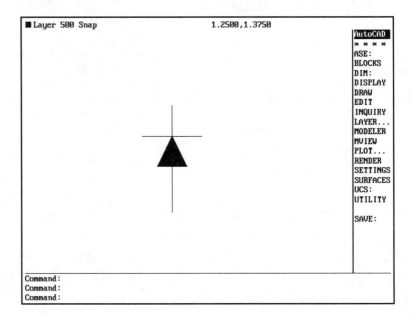

TASKS TO BE COMPLETED IN THIS EXERCISE

- Draw the diode geometry
- Create a diode symbol

DRAWING THE DIODE GEOMETRY

You begin the diode symbol by creating the lines labeled in figure 7.15. To finish the symbol, use the PLINE command with the Width option to add the arrowhead.

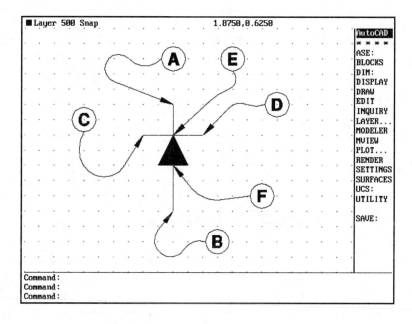

Figure 7.15:

The diode with labeled points.

Step 1.0: Issue the **LINE** command; draw a vertical line that begins at point A and ends at point B, following the grid pattern as you draw (see fig. 7.15).

Step 2.0: Reissue the **LINE** command; draw a horizontal line that begins at point C and ends at point D, following the grid pattern as you draw.

You now need to create the arrowhead by using the PLINE command. In a previous exercise, you learned that you can draw a polyline that has different starting and ending widths. For this object, the starting width is 0 units and the ending width is .25 units.

Step 3.0: Issue the PLINE command:

Command: **PLINE** ↵   Starts the PLINE
                                        command

Step 3.1: Pick the starting point of the arrowhead, following the grid pattern:

From point: *Pick point* Ⓔ   Defines the starting
(see fig. 7.15)   point of the
                                        arrowhead

Step 3.2: Invoke the Width option and define the starting and ending widths of the arrowhead, as shown in the following:

```
Current Line-width is 0.1250
Arc/Close/Halfwidth/Length/Undo/          Selects the PLINE
Width/<Endpoint of Line>: W ↵            Width option
Starting width <0.1250>: 0 ↵             Defines the starting
                                         width of 0
Ending width <0.0000>: .25 ↵             Defines the ending
                                         width of .25
```

Step 3.3: Tell AutoCAD the length you want to draw the polyline, as follows:

```
Arc/Close/Halfwidth/Length/Undo/          Draws a tapered
Width/<Endpoint of Line>:                 polyline to point F
Pick point Ⓕ (see fig. 7.15)
```

Step 3.4: End the PLINE command:

```
Arc/Close/Halfwidth/Length/Undo/          Ends the PLINE
Width/<Endpoint of Line>: ↵              command
```

CREATING A DIODE SYMBOL

Next, create a diode symbol using the BLOCK command and name it DIODE. Use the Endpoint object snap override to specify the insertion point and the Window selection set option to select the object that you want to block as a symbol.

Step 4.0: Issue the **BLOCK** command and name the new block **DIODE**.

Step 4.1: Invoke the ENDpoint object snap override and pick point A (see fig. 7.15) as the object to find the end point of. This is the insertion point of the object.

Step 4.2: To specify the objects you want to include as the symbol, invoke the Window option and enclose the diode inside the window. Press Enter to select the objects and to create a block of the geometry.

Again, all of the selected objects should disappear from your screen.

EXERCISE 5: CREATING A TERMINAL AND CONNECTOR SYMBOL

The last two symbols you create for this lesson are the terminal and connector symbols shown in figure 7.16. These two symbols are drawn using the DONUT command. The DONUT command creates circles that have circumferences of specified widths. After you create each object you will use the BLOCK command to create a symbol of each.

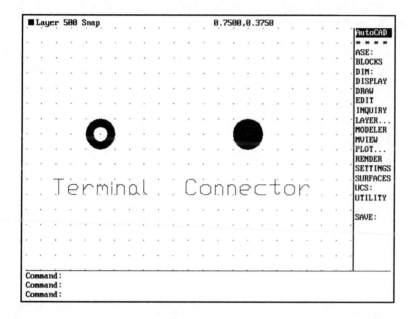

Figure 7.16:
The terminal and connector symbols.

TASKS TO BE COMPLETED IN THIS EXERCISE

- Draw the terminal geometry
- Create a terminal symbol
- Draw the connector geometry
- Create a connector symbol

DRAWING THE TERMINAL GEOMETRY

Begin this exercise by drawing the terminal shown in figure 7.17. You will use the DONUT command to create the object. The DONUT command works similar to the CIRCLE command, except you also must specify the width of the circumference. You specify the circle's circumference by telling AutoCAD the outer and inner diameters of the doughnuts. The outer diameter is the overall size of the doughnut; the inner diameter is the size of the hole. The difference between the two values is the width of the circumference. By specifying an inner diameter of 0, you create a doughnut that has no hole. You will do this when you create the connector geometry.

Figure 7.17:

The terminal geometry.

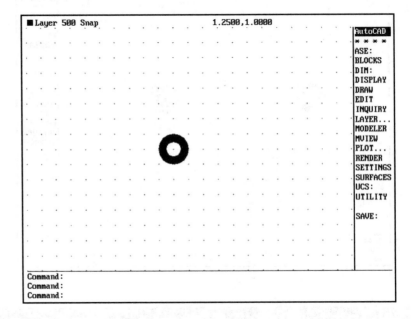

After you specify the diameters of the doughnut, select the center point of the doughnut. This places the object in the drawing. Like the LINE command, DONUT enables you to create multiple copies of the same doughnut until you press Enter or Ctrl-C to end the command. For this exercise, you need to create only one doughnut at a time.

Step 1.0: Issue the DONUT command:

Command: **DONUT** ⏎   Starts the DONUT
                                                  command

Step 1.1: Tell AutoCAD the inside and outside diameters of the doughnut you want to draw, as in the following:

```
Inside diameter <0.5000>: .125 ↵
```
Defines the inside diameter of the doughnut

```
Outside diameter <1.0000>: .25 ↵
```
Defines the outside diameter of the doughnut

Step 1.2: You now need to pick the center of the doughnut. For this drawing, pick any point on-screen:

```
Center of doughnut: Pick any point
in the drawing
```
Specifies the center of the doughnut and draws the doughnut on-screen

Step 1.3: The DONUT command enables you to create doughnuts until you press Enter or Ctrl-C. Because the terminal is created, you can end the DONUT command for now:

```
Center of doughnut: ↵
```
Ends the DONUT command

CREATING A TERMINAL SYMBOL

You now need to create a terminal symbol using the BLOCK command. For this object, you need to pick the center grid point as the insertion point of the block.

Step 2.0: Issue the **BLOCK** command and name the new block **TERMINAL**.

Step 2.1: Pick the center grid point as the insertion point of the object.

Step 2.2: To specify the objects you want to include as the symbol, invoke the Window selection set option and enclose the terminal inside the window. Press Enter to select the objects and to create a block of the geometry.

The selected object should disappear from your screen.

DRAWING THE CONNECTOR GEOMETRY

You now need to draw a connector using the DONUT command. Figure 7.18 shows that the connector is a solid-filled entity. You already learned that to create a solid-filled doughnut you must tell AutoCAD to make the inside diameter of the doughnut 0. For this drawing, the outside diameter of the doughnut is the same as the terminal symbol, which is .25 units.

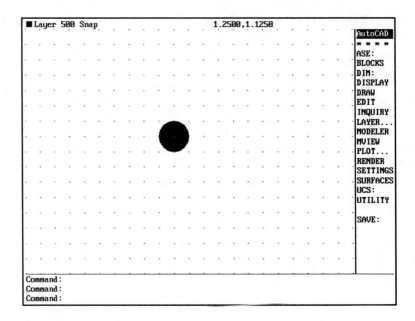

Step 3.0: Issue the DONUT command:

Command: **DONUT** ↵   Starts the DONUT
                                         command

Step 3.1: Tell AutoCAD the inside and outside diameters of the doughnut, as in the following:

Inside diameter <0.1250>: **0** ↵   Defines the inside
                                         diameter of the
                                         doughnut

Outside diameter <0.2500>: **.25** ↵   Defines the outside
                                         diameter of the
                                         doughnut

Step 3.2: Pick the center of the doughnut, as follows:

Center of doughnut: *Pick a point*   Specifies the center
on-screen   of the doughnut and
                                         draws the doughnut
                                         on-screen

Step 3.3: End the DONUT command:

Center of doughnut: ↵   Ends the DONUT
                                         command

Your completed connector should look like the one shown in the previous figure.

CREATING A CONNECTOR SYMBOL

You now need to create a connector symbol using the BLOCK command.

Step 4.0: Issue the **BLOCK** command and name the new block **CONNECT**.

Step 4.1: Pick the middle point of the connector, or the center, as the object's insertion point. To find the center, move your pointing device into the center of the connector. The pointing device will snap to the connector's middle point if Snap is on.

Step 4.2: To specify the objects you want to include in the block, invoke the Window selection set option and enclose the connector inside the window. Press Enter to select the objects and to create a block of the geometry.

The selected objects should disappear from your screen.

EXERCISE 6: INSERTING SYMBOLS IN A DRAWING

You now have created all of the symbols needed for the electrical schematic diagram, and can finish the lesson by placing the symbols in the drawing as seen in figure 7.19. Begin creating the schematic by zooming back to see the entire drawing area. Then turn off the UCS icon in the lower left corner of the screen. This makes that portion of the screen easier to see.

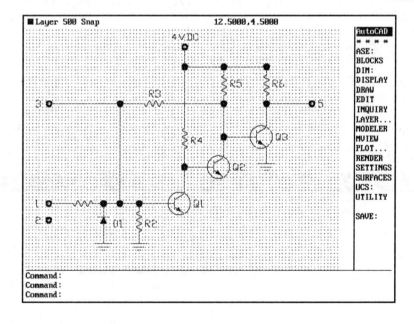

Figure 7.19:

The completed electrical schematic diagram.

Use the INSERT and DDINSERT commands to insert the symbols, followed by the LINE command to create the flow lines. To assist in creating the flowlines, select the ortho mode. With Ortho active, you can draw only straight lines. After you insert the symbols, add the text to the schematic diagram, as seen in figure 7.1.

To place the symbols in the drawing, use the INSERT and DDINSERT commands. To use the INSERT command, specify the block's name, as well as the point of insertion, scale, and rotation angle. When you are using the INSERT command, the insertion point is the point in the drawing at which the block (symbol) is placed. The block "attaches" to the drawing at the insertion point you defined when you created the symbol.

When using INSERT, you can change the scale of a block on both the X- and Y-axis. For example, you can change the overall size of a symbol. If you want to double the size of a symbol, change the scale to 2. Or you can reduce the symbol to half its size by changing the scale by .5. You also can change the shape of symbols as you insert them by scaling them at different points on the object. You can scale one axis of a circle, for example, to create an ellipse. For this lesson, however, the symbols you created for the final drawing were drawn at full scale, meaning they do not need to be rescaled or reshaped. To keep an object's original scale, accept the default value of 1 when AutoCAD prompts you for the scale value.

Finally, when you use the INSERT command, you can rotate the object as it is inserted. As figure 7.19 illustrated, the angle (horizontal) that some resistor symbols are placed at is different from the angle (vertical) at which the original block was drawn. This enables you to use one symbol for multiple resistor positions, adding to your drawing productivity and eliminating unnecessary blocks.

The DDINSERT command performs the same function as the INSERT command. However, this command uses a dialog box to define the symbols settings. When you select Insert from the menu the DDINSERT command is invoked. You may also enter DDINSERT at the command prompt.

TASKS TO BE COMPLETED IN THIS EXERCISE

- Insert symbols in the upper left corner of the drawing
- Insert symbols in the lower left corner of the drawing
- Complete the schematic diagram

Now insert the electrical symbols you just created into a drawing. First, however, enlarge the drawing to its full size using the ZOOM command with the All option.

Step 1.0: Issue the **ZOOM** command and invoke the All option to see the entire drawing.

Turn off the UCS icon that is in the lower left corner of your screen. By turning off the icon, you can insert the symbols into the drawing.

Step 2.0: Issue the UCSICON command and turn off the UCS icon:

Command: **UCSICON** ↵	Starts the UCSICON command
ON/OFF/All/Noorigin/ORigin <ON>: **OFF** ↵	Turns off the UCS icon

USING THE **INSERT** COMMAND

You now are ready to insert the symbols and complete this lesson's drawing. Begin the schematic diagram by inserting the terminal in the drawing's upper left corner, as seen in figure 7.20. Use the INSERT command to place the symbol in the drawing. When prompted for the insertion point of the block, refer back to figure 7.19 to see the symbol's relationship to the entire drawing. Continue to use the grid pattern to help you insert the rest of the symbols in the schematic diagram.

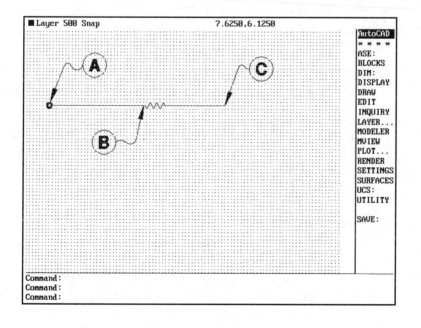

Figure 7.20:
The upper left portion of the schematic diagram, with labels.

Step 3.0: Issue the INSERT command:

```
Command: INSERT ↵
```
Starts the INSERT command

Step 3.1: Now tell AutoCAD which block you want to insert in the drawing. The first symbol you need to insert is the TERMINAL block:

```
BLOCK name (or ?): TERMINAL ↵
```
Specifies the name of the block to insert

Step 3.2: Insert the TERMINAL block at point A (see fig. 7.20), following the grid pattern for guidance:

```
Insertion point: Pick point Ⓐ
(see fig. 7.20)
```
Selects the point at which to insert the block

NOTE

You can rescale an object after insertion. The INSERT command gives you two different scale factors—the X-scale and Y-scale factors—when drawing a two-dimensional object. The default value, 1, inserts the block at a 1:1 scale; that is, the scale at which the block was drawn is maintained. For this lesson, all of the inserted symbols remain at their original scale.

Step 3.3: Keep the scale factor at 1, as follows:

```
X scale factor <1> / Corner /
XYZ: ↵
```
Keeps the X-scale factor at which the block was drawn

```
Y scale factor (default=X): ↵
```
Keeps the Y-scale factor at which the block was drawn

Step 3.4: The INSERT command also enables you to rotate the block around its insertion point before inserting it into a drawing. If you do not want to rotate the object, accept the default angle of 0:

```
Rotation angle <0>: ↵
```
Keeps the angle of rotation at 0 degrees

You now see the terminal symbol, which was stored as a block in a previous exercise.

DRAWING FLOWLINES

To connect symbols together in a drawing, you need to create flowlines. *Flowlines* are lines in a drawing that represent connecting paths. For this drawing, the flowlines are straight horizontal and vertical lines that connect electrical symbols to each other. To help you create the flowlines, turn on the ORTHO mode, which enables you to draw only straight lines.

Step 4.0: Turn on Ortho by pressing F8.

Step 5.0: Issue the **LINE** command. Draw a line from the right side of the TERMINAL symbol to point B (see fig. 7.20). This creates the first flowline.

Now insert the resistor symbol in the drawing. This time use the DDINSERT command. Before you insert the resistor symbol, rotate it 90 degrees so that it aligns as in figure 7.20. Using DDINSERT, you can specify the rotation value before the block is placed in the drawing or you can enter the value in the same way as the INSERT command. In this exercise you will enter the value in the same way as the INSERT command.

Step 6.0: Issue the DDINSERT command by choosing it from the menu:

`Command:` *Choose* Draw, *then* Insert	Starts the DDINSERT command

Step 6.1: Use the block button to display and choose the RESISTOR block:

Choose Block, *then* RESISTOR, *then* OK	Selects the block to insert

Step 6.2: Close the dialog box and specify the options for block insertion:

Choose OK	Closes the dialog box

Step 6.3: You now need to specify the insertion point of the resistor symbol, which is the end point of the flowline. Use the Endpoint object snap override to locate the end point of the flowline:

`Insertion point: END` ↵	Activates the Endpoint object override snap
`Of` *Pick point* Ⓑ *(see fig. 7.20)*	Selects the point to insert the block

Step 6.4: Specify to keep the scale factor at 1, as follows:

`X scale factor <1> / Corner / XYZ:` ↵	Keeps the X-scale factor at which the block was drawn
`Y scale factor (default=X):` ↵	Keeps the Y-scale factor at which the block was drawn

Step 6.5: Specify to rotate the resistor symbol 90 degrees before inserting the block:

```
Rotation angle <0>: 90 ↵
```
                                                 Rotates the block 90 degrees before it is inserted

Step 7.0: Finish this part of the drawing by issuing the **LINE** command and drawing a line from the right end of the resistor to point C (see fig. 7.20).

INSERTING SYMBOLS IN THE LOWER LEFT CORNER OF THE DRAWING

Move your pointing device until the crosshair cursor is at the lower left corner of the screen.

You can finish developing the drawing in any order you want. For this exercise, however, use the same process to develop this part of the drawing as you just did in the upper left corner of the drawing.

Figure 7.21:

The lower left corner of the schematic diagram.

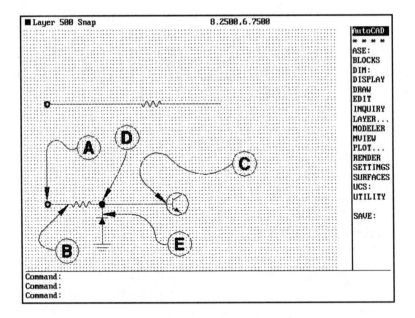

Step 8.0: Issue the **INSERT** or **DDINSERT** command. Instruct AutoCAD to insert the TERMINAL block in the lower left corner of the drawing. Follow the grid pattern to locate point A (see fig. 7.21), and tell AutoCAD to keep the scale factor at 1.

Step 9.0: Issue the **LINE** command and draw a flowline from the right side of the terminal to point B (see fig. 7.21).

Step 10.0: Issue the **INSERT** or **DDINSERT** command and insert the symbol RESISTOR at the right end of the new flowline (point B). Tell AutoCAD to keep the scale factor at 1. Again, the resistor needs to be rotated 90 degrees to duplicate figure 7.21.

Step 11.0: Issue the **LINE** command and draw a flowline from the right end of the resistor to point C (see fig. 7.21).

Step 12.0: Issue the **INSERT** or **DDINSERT** command. Insert the symbol TRAN at point C (see fig. 7. 21). Tell AutoCAD to keep the scale factor at 1, and not to rotate the object.

Step 13.0: Reissue the **INSERT** or **DDINSERT** command and place the symbol CONNECT at point D (see fig. 7.21). Accept the default scale and rotation values for the object.

Step 14.0: Issue the **LINE** command and draw the small vertical flowline that starts at the bottom of the connector and moves down to point E (see fig. 7.21).

Step 15.0: Issue the **INSERT** or **DDINSERT** command and place the symbol DIODE at point E. Use the Endpoint object snap override to locate the end point of the small vertical line. This point is the insertion point for the diode symbol. Accept the default scale and rotation values for the object.

Step 16.0: Complete figure 7.21 by issuing the **INSERT** or **DDINSERT** command. Use the Endpoint object snap override to find the bottom end point of the diode symbol. Use this point as the insertion point for the ground symbol. Accept the scale and rotation values for the object.

COMPLETING THE SCHEMATIC DIAGRAM

Step 17.0: To complete the schematic diagram, follow the grid pattern as shown in figure 7.22. When you insert the symbols, make sure that you keep the scale value set to 1 (the default value). For the remainder of this drawing, do not rotate the resistor symbol or any other symbol. If you have trouble using the INSERT or DDINSERT command, as well as following the different on-screen prompts for the command, refer back to the beginning of this exercise and follow the steps. This will ensure that the drawing you create is similar to the one shown in figure 7.22.

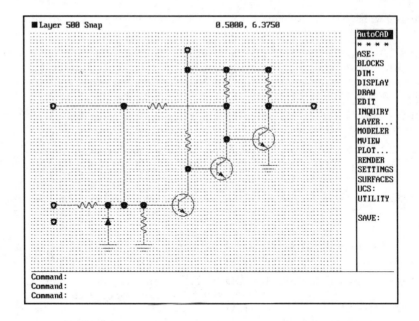

EXERCISE 7: ADDING TEXT TO THE DRAWING

You now have created all of the basic entities in your drawing and are ready to add text to the drawing (see fig. 7.23). Before you add text to the drawing, however, you need to change the drawing layer. After you change the layer, use the TEXT command to place the text in the drawing, following the grid pattern shown.

TASK TO BE COMPLETED IN THIS EXERCISE
• Add text to the drawing

ADDING TEXT TO THE DRAWING

Before adding text to this drawing, you need to change the drawing layer. This enables you to place the text on a layer separate from the objects.

Step 1.0: Using the **LAYER** command or Layer Control dialog box, make layer 510 the current layer.

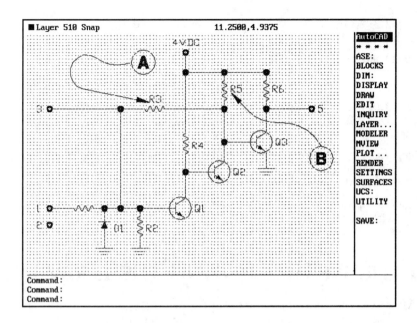

Step 2.0: Issue the TEXT command; tell AutoCAD where you want to place the text string:

Command: **TEXT** ↵	Starts the TEXT command
Justify/Style/<Start point>: *Pick point* (A) *(see fig. 7.23)*	Selects the starting point of the text string

Step 2.1: Now specify the text's appearance. Tell AutoCAD to make the text .25 units tall:

Height <0.2000>: **.25** ↵	Defines the text height of .25 units

Step 2.2: Next, you need to indicate a rotation angle for the text. By default, AutoCAD displays text at a rotation angle of 0, which means that text appears horizontally in the drawing. Accept the default setting of 0 degrees rotation for the new text:

Rotation angle <0>: ↵	Accepts the default rotation angle of 0 degrees, causing text to appear horizontally across the screen

Step 2.3: At the TEXT command's next prompt, type the text you want to add to the drawing:

Text: **R3** ↵   Specifies the text
                                                   string to be added
                                                   to the drawing

Step 3.0: Issue the **TEXT** command and place the text string R5 at point B (see fig. 7.23). Tell AutoCAD to make the text .25 units tall and the rotation angle 0.

Step 4.0: As you did in the preceding exercise, finish adding text to the drawing by following the grid pattern shown in figure 7.23. The text should be .25 units tall, and at a rotation angle of 0.

Your completed drawing should look like the one shown in figure 7.23, but without the labels.

EXERCISE 8: PRINTING THE DRAWING

After you complete a drawing using AutoCAD, you typically need to develop a hard copy of the drawing on a printer or plotter. This gives you a printed drawing that can be shared between individuals or marked for changes, and is increased in size beyond the limitation of the computer screen. Printers, which typically are dot matrix or laser, can print on 8 1/2-by-11-inch or 8 1/2-by-14-inch paper. Plotters are devices that use paper and moving pens to create hard copies of drawings. The size of plotter outputs vary depending on the size of the plotter. Some plotters, for example, are used to plot full-scale drawings of automobiles.

TASK TO BE COMPLETED IN THIS EXERCISE

- Create a hard copy of your drawing

CREATING A HARD COPY OF YOUR DRAWING

In AutoCAD, you can send outputs to a plotter or printer using the PLOT command. The PLOT command displays the Plot Configuration dialog box. From within this dialog box you set the area of the drawing to plot paper size, rotation of paper, scale, and other options.

The PLOT command has the following options:

- **Device and Default Selection.** Selects the default printer or plotter and settings for output.

- **Pen Assignments.** Assigns colors, linetypes, pen widths, and pen speeds to pens. Typically this area is used for color assignment only.

- **Optimization.** Allows for various means of optimizing a drawing while plotting.

- **Display.** Plots the drawing as shown on-screen.

- **Extents.** Plots the drawing to its *extents*, which is its maximum size.

- **Limits.** Plots the drawing within the limits you set up for the drawing.

- **View.** Plots a drawing area that you have preset using the View command.

- **Window.** Plots the area that you have enclosed inside a window.

- **Plot to file.** Enables the user to output a file to disk with a name. This typically is used in a network to queue drawings for later output, or for the development of a graphic file that can be inserted into a different software package, such as a desktop publishing program.

- **Inches, MM.** Enables you to plot the output in inches or millimeters.

- **Rotation and Origin.** *Rotation* enables you to rotate the drawing on the paper as you are printing. You should use this option when you are printing on a piece of paper that is 8 1/2-by-11 inches. This lets you optimize the drawing on the paper.

  Origin enables you to position the paper at a different starting position, or home point. The normal home point is the lower left corner of the paper.

- **Adjust Area Fill.** This option moves the pen location in one-half of a pen width on solid objects during an area fill.

- **Plot area**. This prompt specifies the size of the paper on which to print. The options available are controlled by the type of printer or plotter you use.

- **Hide Lines.** This option is for three-dimensional drawings.
- **Plotted Inches = Drawing Units.** Use this option to specify the scale of the output.
- **Scaled to Fit.** The Fit option plots the drawing to fit the size of the paper.
- **Preview.** Displays the plot on-screen before sending to printer or plotter.
- **FileName.** Allows the specification of a file name when using the Plot to file option.

You now are ready to output a hard copy of your drawing. If you do not have a plotter or printer, perform steps 1.0 - 1.2. At Step 1.3, choose Cancel instead of OK. You will learn how to set up for plotting and will see your output on screen but will not end up with a hard copy of the drawing.

Step 1.0: Issue the PLOT command:

`Command:` *Choose* File, *then* Plot	Starts the PLOT command and displays the Plot Configuration dialog box

Step 1.1: Choose the plot settings for output:

Confirm that Display *is chosen*	Plots what is displayed on screen
Confirm that Inches *is chosen*	Drawing is plotted in inches
Confirm that Scaled to Fit *is chosen*	Drawing is scaled to paper size
Choose Rotation and Origin	Displays the Rotation and Origin dialog box
Choose 90, *then* OK	Rotates the drawing 90 degrees during output

Step 1.2: Preview the entire drawing on screen:

Choose Full	Selects the option to see the entire drawing on-screen during preview

Choose P<u>r</u>eview	Displays the area to plot on screen
Choose **E**nd Preview	Returns to the Plot Configuration dialog box

Step 1.3: Confirm the Plot Configuration and close the dialog box:

Choose OK	Closes the dialog box

Step 1.4: Make sure paper is in the printer or plotter and the hardware is on-line to accept information. Once this has been confirmed, continue with the PLOT command:

`Effective Plotting Area: 8.00` `wide by 11.00 high`	Displays the actual size of the output (yours may be different depending on your output device)

`Position paper in plotter`
`Press RETURN to continue or`
`S to stop for hardware setup:` ↵
	Plots the drawing

You are now finished with this exercise.

Step 2.0: Save the drawing to disk and end the current drawing session.

SUMMARY

In this lesson, you created several electrical symbols using basic drawing and editing commands, including the BLOCK and DONUT commands. After you created the symbols, you inserted them into a drawing and created a schematic diagram. You then printed the drawing using the PRPLOT command.

In the next exercise, you use the PLINE command to draw a spline curve and a cam. You also create a title block that is saved to disk as a block and then inserted into a drawing.

REVIEW

1. Draw a 2-unit-by-3 unit rectangle using **SNAP** and **GRID**.

2. Use the **BLOCK** command and create a symbol using the rectangle from the previous question. Make the lower left corner of the rectangle the insertion point.

3. In the current drawing, draw a doughnut that has no center hole and a diameter of .125 units.

4. Draw a second doughnut in the current drawing that has an inside diameter of .25 units and an outside diameter of .5 units.

5. Insert the block from question two into the current drawing four times. Position the insertion point of the block at the center of the doughnut in question three. Rotate the block 0, 90, 180, and 270 degrees respectively each time you insert a block.

6. Output the drawing to a printer or plotter.

7. From *The AutoCAD Tutor Disk*, retrieve the drawing named **OFFICE** and make each piece of the office furniture a symbol using the **BLOCK** command.

8. From the preceding question, insert the office furniture into each of the rooms.

9. Output the drawing in question eight.

10. Use the completed drawing from the past five lessons and print or plot each one.

DRAWING A CAM

OVERVIEW

You have seen in previous lessons that AutoCAD has a variety of drawing tools. These drawing tools are used to create entities as simple as points, or as complex as spline curves, both of which you create in this lesson. Points typically are used as locators for more sophisticated geometry, not as drawing entities themselves. Spline curves, on the other hand, are used to create advanced features, such as airplane wings and parabolic cams.

In the preceding exercises, you used edit commands to alter the geometry. Each geometry or *entity* contains defining points called grips. *Grips* are small squares that appear when an object is selected and no command is active. You then can perform several editing functions—such as move, copy, stretch, and mirror—to the selected item. This method of selecting and altering without using commands speeds up the editing process because the command sequence is bypassed.

After you develop geometry, you may find that you need specific information about a single entity of the drawing, or of the entire drawing. AutoCAD enables you to query the database; that is, you can tell AutoCAD to list the vital statistics of your drawing, including distances between points and the total area of a drawing. The DIST (Distance) and AREA commands are two of AutoCAD's inquiry commands that enable you to query a drawing's database.

In addition, you can find out everything in the database about a selected object. This includes the parameters used to define that object, such as layer, color, and end points. This information enables you to check your drawing for errors. You also can perform drawing analysis to determine information about the drawing, such as the square footage of a room or the amount of steel needed in a stamping die.

As seen in a previous lesson, blocks created with the BLOCK command can be used only in their drawing of origin. The WBLOCK command enables you to save symbols to disk as a block that can be used in any drawing. A common use of WBLOCK is a title block. Because CAD drawings still are used primarily in drafting environments as hard copy prints, AutoCAD enables you to create title blocks through the WBLOCK command that can be stored on disk and used in any drawing.

Title blocks, which are textual images that are shared with the outside world, need to have a strong visual appearance. AutoCAD's STYLE command enables you to change the text style or font of the text to complement text that is on-screen and in plotted hard copies.

AutoCAD also enables you to insert columns of text using the DTEXT command. When you use the DTEXT command, the text appears on-screen as soon as you type it in. To create text in columns, you simply press Enter to move the cursor to the line under the last entered text line. By using this command when you enter large amounts of text, you can decrease your total drawing time.

TOPICS COVERED IN THIS LESSON

In this lesson, you learn to do the following:

- Draw the outline of the cam
- Shape the cam geometry
- Add detail to the drawing
- Use grips to edit geometry
- Create a title block
- Query the AutoCAD drawing database
- Write a block to disk

This lesson teaches you how to use the following AutoCAD commands:

- **AREA.** Determines the area of an entity or defined boundary
- **DIST.** Specifies the distance between two points
- **DTEXT.** Dynamically places text in the drawing
- **LIST.** Displays database information about an entity
- **PDMODE.** Changes the appearance of points
- **PEDIT.** Edits a polyline
- **POINT.** Inserts a point in the drawing
- **WBLOCK.** Writes a block to disk as a single file

SETTING UP THE DRAWING

Before you actually begin creating the geometry in this lesson, you need to set up the drawing environment.

Step 1.0: Start AutoCAD; save the new drawing as **LESSON8**.

Step 2.0: Use the **UNITS** command or Units Control dialog box to set up the drawing with decimal units at two decimal places. Leave all the remaining settings at their default.

Step 3.0: Issue the **LIMITS** command. Set the lower left corner at 0,0 and the upper right at 11.00,8.50.

Step 4.0: Issue the **ZOOM** command with the All option to see the entire drawing to the new limits.

Step 5.0: Use the **LAYER** command or the Layer Control dialog box to create the following layers:

NODE

CAM

CAM_TXT

CAM_DIM

DIM

TITLE_BLK

TITLE_TXT

Step 5.1: Finally, make NODE the current layer.

Now that your drawing environment is set up, you can begin creating the LESSON8 drawing. When you complete this lesson, you should have a drawing of a cam with a title block, similar to the one shown in figure 8.1.

Figure 8.1:

The drawing you create in this lesson.

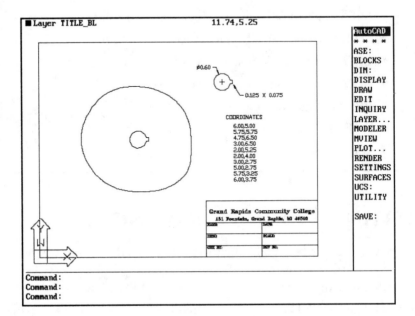

EXERCISE 1: DRAWING THE OUTLINE OF THE CAM

A *cam* is a mechanical object that rotates around its center point, displacing an object that rests on the outer edge. This process is similar to what a bicycle does to its rider if a tire is not round, such as when a flat occurs. The *title block* is a standard drafting element that contains information about a drawing.

To develop a cam, you would typically develop a CAM displacement diagram and transfer the distance from the diagram to the distance from the center of the cam. To save time, this has already been done. The absolute coordinates of the points also have been specified in the drawing. To create the cam, you pick points on-screen and then create a polyline by connecting the points with line segments. The polyline then is reshaped into a smooth curved object, or *spline curve*, using the PEDIT command. To help you pick the points, use the PDMODE system variable to change the visual characteristics of the points. AutoCAD enables you to pick from a wide variety of different point types, depending on their purpose in your drawing.

TASKS TO BE COMPLETED IN THIS EXERCISE

- Change the appearance of points
- Create construction points for the cam
- Draw a polyline

CHANGING THE APPEARANCE OF POINTS

You begin the development of the cam by drawing the points seen in figure 8.2. The POINT command places nodes, or *points*, in drawings at specified coordinates. Points primarily are used as construction geometry. You also might use points, for example, as specific coordinates that you collect when surveying land. Points also can be used to locate the center of an ellipse before and after you draw it. Although AutoCAD's POINT command is not used frequently, you use it when you want to place points in specific coordinates, such as in this exercise to define the cam outline.

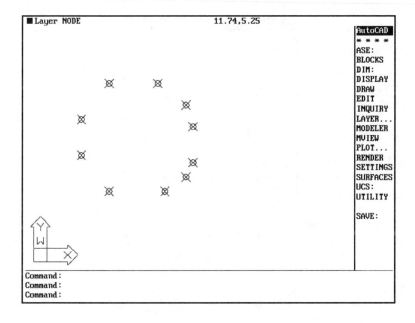

Figure 8.2:

Points in the drawing that help you create the cam.

The points seen in figure 8.2 are not in their default visual mode; that is, usually when you pick a point on-screen using the POINT command, a small dot appears. In this drawing, however, you need to use points as construction entities. To help you see the points when drawing, you need to change their appearance in your drawing. To do this, use the Point Style dialog box. AutoCAD has several different kinds of points from which to choose. For this drawing, change the default point setting to the crossed circle mode, which creates points with boxes around them.

From within this dialog box you can define what points look like on screen, their absolute size and their size in relation to the screen. For this drawing you need only change the appearance of points. When finished with the Point Style dialog box, enter Ctrl-C to exit the POINT command.

Step 1.0: Open the Point Style dialog box to change the appearance of points:

Command: *Choose* Draw, *then* Point	Starts the POINT command
Command: *From the screen menu,* choose Type *and* Size	Opens the Point Style dialog box

Step 1.1: Set the appearance of points:

Choose the circle with an X through it (see fig. 8.3)	Selects this as the way points appear in the drawing
Choose OK	Closes the dialog box

Figure 8.3:

The point styles available in AutoCAD.

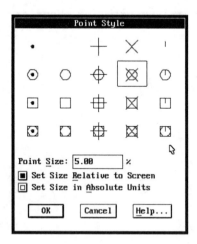

Step 1.2: Press Cancel to exit the current POINT command:

Point: *Press Ctrl-C*   Cancels the POINT
                                         command

CREATING CONSTRUCTION POINTS FOR THE CAM

You now are ready to add the points previously shown in figure 8.2. These points are used later as construction entities to develop the cam geometry. Use the POINT command and type in the absolute coordinates that identify the location of the construction points. Unlike some other AutoCAD commands, the POINT command ends automatically after you pick a point. To place additional points in your drawing, you must reissue the POINT command for each point.

Step 2.0: Issue the POINT command:

Command: **POINT** ↵   Starts the POINT
                                         command

NOTE

If you issue the POINT command by entering **POINT** at the command prompt, the command ends after one point is entered into the drawing. Choosing Point from the pull-down menu issues a POINT command that auto-repeats, enabling the user to specify several points until a cancel or another command is issued.

Step 2.1: The Command: prompt should change to the Point: prompt. Specify where you want the point placed:

Point: **6,5** ↵   Places a point in
                                         the drawing at the
                                         absolute coordin-
                                         ate 6,5

Step 3.0: Issue the POINT command and place the next point, as follows:

Command: **POINT** ↵   Starts the POINT
                                         command

Point: **5.75,5.75** ↵   Places a point in
                                         the drawing at the
                                         absolute coordinate
                                         5.75,5.75

Step 4.0: Use the **POINT** command to complete this part of the drawing by inserting points at the following coordinates. Remember, you must reissue the POINT command after each point is placed:

4.75,6.5

3,6.5

2,5.25

2,4

3,2.75

5,2.75

5.75,3.25

6,3.75

Your drawing now should resemble the one shown in figure 8.2, which is the basic outline of the cam.

DRAWING THE POLYLINE

Now that you have the points that act as the cam's construction entities, you now are ready to add the geometry that eventually becomes the cam, as seen in figure 8.4.

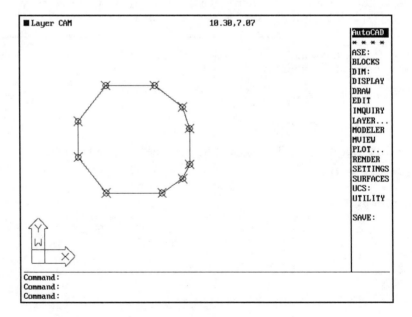

Figure 8.4:

The polyline that defines the cam.

You use the PLINE command to create this geometry. In a previous exercise, the PLINE or POLYLINE command was used to develop a boundary to hatch within. Most often in a drawing, however, the PLINE command is used to create standard polyline geometry that can be viewed as one object, as well as edited into sophisticated objects.

Polylines are single entities on which you can perform single operations, such as placing fillets on all corners at once, or copying the entire polyline using only one command. You also can edit polylines into smooth curves using the end points of the line segments that define the polyline. This is helpful when you need to develop complex geometry, such as the cam in this drawing, the body of an airplane, or the contour of a piece of land.

Now draw a polyline using the points you just placed as the starting and ending points of line segments. These line segments make up the polyline, which is the outline of the cam. Because you need to select several points to define the polyline, you should set a running object snap to locate the entities easily. Use NODe as the running object snap. NODe selects coordinates of the closest point to which you pick on-screen, enabling you to pick the points you just drew more easily.

Step 5.0: Issue the OSNAP command and define NODe as the default selection option:

Command: **OSNAP** ↵	Starts the OSNAP command
Object snap modes: **NOD** ↵	Defines NODe as the default selection option

Because the points are temporary construction geometry, you placed them on their own layer named NODE. Later, when you no longer need the points, you can freeze this layer. When you freeze a layer, AutoCAD ignores that layer's entities, causing the entities to disappear from the screen. You also can freeze a layer when you plot or print a drawing. This omits that layer's entities from the printed or plotted drawing.

Before you draw the polyline, change to the CAM layer.

Step 6.0: Use the **LAYER** command or Layer Control dialog box and make CAM the current layer.

You now are ready to add a polyline through the points labeled in figure 8.5. Because NODe is set as a running object snap, you can select the starting and ending points for the polyline using the aperture box.

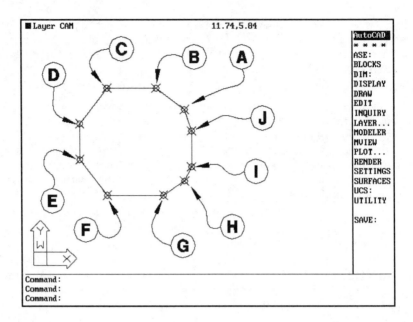

Figure 8.5:

The polyline with points labeled.

Step 7.0: Issue the **PLINE** command.

Step 7.1: Pick point A (see fig. 8.5) as the starting point.

Step 7.2: Pick point B as the end point of the first polyline segment.

Step 7.3: Pick point C as the end point of the next polyline segment.

Step 7.4: Continue with the **PLINE** command and pick points D through J in alphabetical order.

Step 7.5: Enter **C** to issue the Close option. AutoCAD automatically draws a line from point J to point A, finishing the polyline.

Your drawing should resemble figure 8.4.

You now are finished using the running object snap. Anytime you finish using a running object snap, you should set it to none. This eliminates any problems you may encounter trying to pick other points in the drawing. In this drawing, for example, if you keep NODe as the running object snap and try to select a line for editing later in the lesson, AutoCAD automatically picks a point near the line you want.

Step 8.0: Issue the OSNAP command and remove the running object snap:

Command: **OSNAP** ↵   Starts the OSNAP
                                 command

Object snap modes: **NON** ↵   Defines none as the
                                 default selection
                                 option

You also are finished with the construction points. Because the polyline you just created covers most of the points, you may have trouble erasing them individually. If you do erase them, you may need them in the future. When working with points, carefully evaluate their importance before erasing them. Most likely you need them removed from the screen, but not from the drawing. To clear them from the screen, use the LAYER command or Layer Control dialog box and freeze the layer that the points are on, as explained in the following step.

Step 9.0: Issue the LAYER command and use the Freeze option to freeze the layer named NODE:

Command: **LAYER** ↵	Starts the LAYER command
?/Make/Set/New/ON/OFF/ Color/Ltype/Freeze/Thaw/LOck/ Unlock:**F** ↵	Invokes the Freeze option
Layer name(s) to Freeze: **NODE** ↵	Freezes the NODE layer

Step 9.1: End the LAYER command:

?/Make/Set/New/ON/OFF/ Color/ Ltype/Freeze/Thaw/LOck/Unlock: ↵	Ends the LAYER command

EXERCISE 2: SHAPING THE CAM GEOMETRY

You now are ready to complete the cam as seen in figure 8.6. You do this by first changing the polyline into a B-spline curve using the PEDIT command. A *B-spline curve*, or *Bezier curve*, is a curve that is created using a closed polyline as a frame. This frame is then mathematically shaped into a curved object.

After you create the spline curve, add to the part's middle the center hole and keyway. The center hole and keyway, which is similar to the one you drew in Lesson 6, is added by drawing a circle and a construction line. You then offset the construction line to define the keyway. To finish the object, the excess geometry is trimmed away and a line is drawn at the end of the keyway.

TASKS TO BE COMPLETED IN THIS EXERCISE

- Create a B-spline curve
- Add a center hole to the cam geometry
- Add a keyway to the cam geometry

Figure 8.6:

The completed cam.

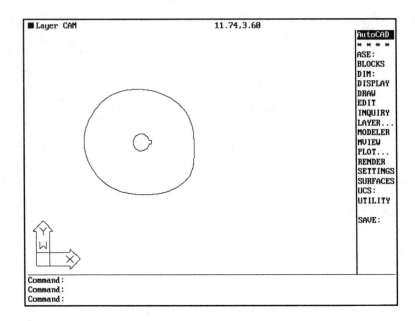

CREATING A B-SPLINE CURVE

The first step in completing the cam is to change the polyline you just created into a spline as illustrated in figure 8.6. A *spline* is a smooth curve that uses the *vertices*, or end points, of the polyline line segments as the control points (the frame). This type of curve, a B-spline, passes through the beginning and ending points of the polyline and pulls the new curve away from the vertices, developing an average fit through the points. This process creates a smooth curve from the polyline line segments. The result of changing the polyline to a spline is seen in figure 8.7.

The command that changes a polyline into a spline is PEDIT. The PEDIT command modifies a polyline in several different ways.

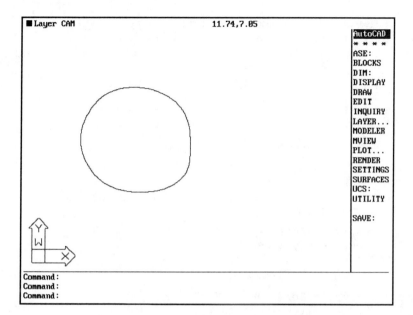

Figure 8.7:
The B-spline curve of the cam geometry.

The PEDIT command has the following options:

- **Open.** Opens a closed polyline

- **Join.** Combines objects that meet at end points into one polyline

- **Width.** Requests a value to change the uniform width of a polyline

- **Edit vertex.** Enables the user to modify the characteristics of the polyline vertices or end points

- **Fit.** Creates a curve that passes through the vertices

- **Spline.** Creates a curve that passes through the average location of the vertices

- **Decurve.** Removes curves created using the Fit curve or Spline curve options

- **Ltype gen.** Controls whether noncontinuous line types are affected by polyline vertices

- **Undo.** Reverses the last PEDIT operation

- **eXit.** Ends the PEDIT command

To use the PEDIT command, you first select a single polyline. Then issue the option or options needed to modify the polyline into the geometry you want. In this drawing, you need to use the Spline option to create a spline curve.

Step 1.0: Issue the PEDIT command:

```
Command: PEDIT ↵
```
Starts the PEDIT command

Step 1.1: Select the polyline you want to modify:

```
Select polyline: Select the polyline
(the cam outline)
```
Specifies the object to be modified

Step 1.2: Now tell AutoCAD to shape the polyline. Use the Spline option to change the polyline into a B-spline curve:

```
Open/Join/Width/Edit vertex/Fit/
Spline/Decurve/Ltype reg/Undo/
eXit <X>: S ↵
```
Changes the polyline into a B-spline curve

Step 1.3: End the PEDIT command:

```
Open/Join/Width/Edit vertex/Fit/
Spline/Decurve/Ltype reg/Undo/
eXit <X>: ↵
```
Ends the PLINE command

Your drawing now should resemble the one previously shown in figure 8.7.

ADDING A CENTER HOLE TO THE CAM GEOMETRY

You now have the spline curve and are ready to add the center hole and keyway in the middle of the cam (see fig. 8.8). You use the same method to do this as you used in Lesson 6. This includes first drawing a circle for the center hole at the center of the cam, and then drawing a construction line from the center hole to create the keyway.

Step 2.0: Issue the **CIRCLE** command. Enter the center point as **4.1,4.6**. Specify the Diameter option and enter **.6**.

To help you create the keyway, you may want to enlarge the circle you just created, as shown in figure 8.9. Use the ZOOM command with the Center option to enlarge the circle.

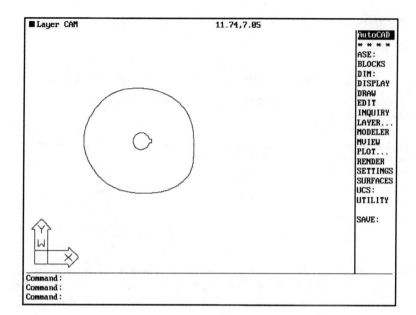

Figure 8.8:
The cam with center hole and keyway.

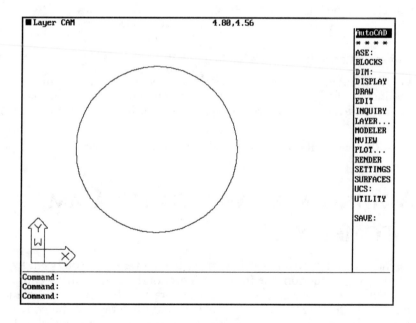

Figure 8.9:
The enlarged center hole.

Step 3.0: Issue the ZOOM command:

```
Command: ZOOM ⏎
```
Starts the ZOOM command

Step 3.1: Select the Center option to specify the center of the zoom area:

```
All/Center/Dynamic/Extents/Left/
Previous/Vmax/Window/
<Scale(X/XP)>: C ⏎
```
Selects the Center option

Step 3.2: Now select the center of the circle as the center of the zoom area. This places the circle in the center of the screen after zooming. Use the Center object snap override to pick the center of the circle:

```
Center point: CEN ⏎
```
Selects the Center object snap override

```
of  Pick the circle
```
Specifies the object that you want to enlarge

Step 3.3: Next, specify a height for zooming. This defines the vertical distance of the zoom area that is centered on the circle. The circle has a diameter of .6 units, so a value of .7 units shows all of the circle, and a small amount of working area above and below the circle:

```
Magnification or Height <8.50>:
.7 ⏎
```
Creates a zoom area with a height of .7 units

Your screen now should look like figure 8.9.

As seen in previous lessons, sometimes when you zoom in a small amount, circular geometry loses its smooth circumference. If this happens, you can recreate the geometry on-screen using the REGEN command.

Step 4.0: Issue the **REGEN** command to regenerate the drawing.

ADDING A KEYWAY TO THE CAM GEOMETRY

You now are ready to add the keyway to the center hole. You begin by creating a construction line from the center of the circle, which ends at the depth of the keyway. As you saw in figure 8.1, the keyway is dimensioned as being 0.125×0.075. This means that the length of the construction line needs to be the depth of the keyway, 0.075 units, plus the radius of the circle, 0.3 units. This makes for a total length of 0.375 units.

Step 5.0: Issue the **LINE** command and start a construction line from the center of the circle. Use the Center object snap override to locate the center of the circle. Specify the ending point of the line as .375 units to the right by entering the polar coordinates **@.375<0**. Press Enter to exit the LINE command.

You now have a construction line (see fig. 8.10) that can be used to develop the width of the keyway. This is done by offsetting the construction line above and below itself at half the keyway width, which is .125 units.

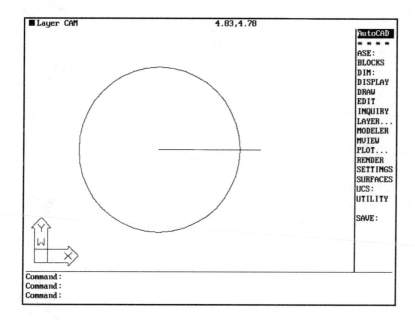

Figure 8.10:

The circle with construction line.

Step 6.0: Issue the **OFFSET** command and specify the offset value as **.0625** units. Select the construction line as the object to offset then pick a point above the line. Select the construction line again and pick a point below the construction line as the sides to offset. Press Enter to exit the command.

Your drawing should resemble the one shown in figure 8.11.

You now can erase the original construction line and then finish developing the keyway.

Step 7.0: Issue the **ERASE** command and remove the middle construction line.

You now need to remove the unneeded segments of the two lines and the circle. You can use the TRIM command to do this.

Step 8.0: Issue the **TRIM** command and select the circle and two lines as the cutting edges. Press Enter to complete the cutting edge selection.

Step 8.1: Select line A (see fig. 8.12) inside the circle as a segment to remove.

Figure 8.11:

The circle with the offset construction line.

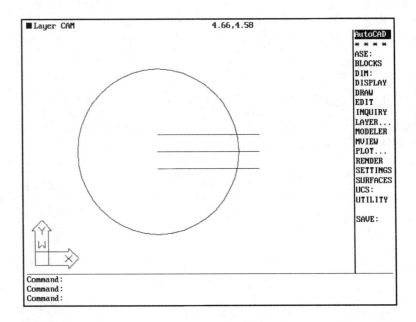

Figure 8.12:

The circle with labeled lines for the keyway.

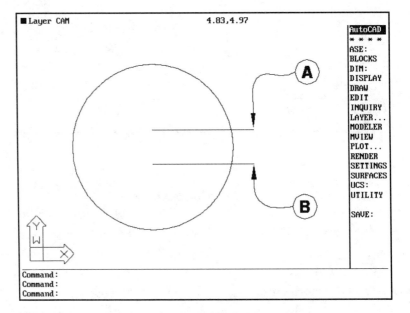

***Step* 8.2:** Select line B (see fig. 8.12) inside the circle as a segment to remove.

***Step* 8.3:** Select the circle between lines A and B. Press Enter to end the TRIM command.

You now are ready to complete the keyway by drawing a vertical line between the end points of the two horizontal lines.

Step 9.0: Issue the **LINE** command and use the ENDpoint object snap override to draw a line between the end points of lines A and B (see fig. 8.12).

Your drawing now should resemble the one shown in figure 8.13.

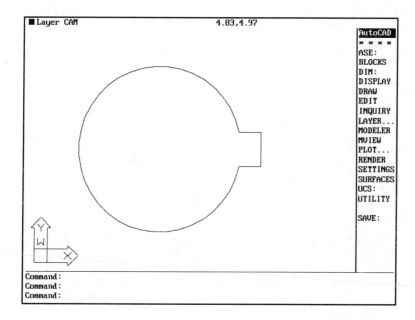

Figure 8.13:

The completed center hole with keyway.

You now are finished with the keyway and can return to the full view of the drawing.

Step 10.0: Issue the **ZOOM** command and select the Previous option to see the entire drawing.

Your drawing should resemble the one previously shown in figure 8.8.

EXERCISE 3: ADDING DETAIL TO THE DRAWING

You now are ready to add the detail to the drawing as shown in figure 8.14. You do this in three phases. First, you duplicate the center hole and keyway to the upper-right corner of the drawing using the COPY command. Once this geometry is copied, use the LEAder and DIAmeter dimensioning subcommands to add the detail.

Figure 8.14:

The drawing with the detail added.

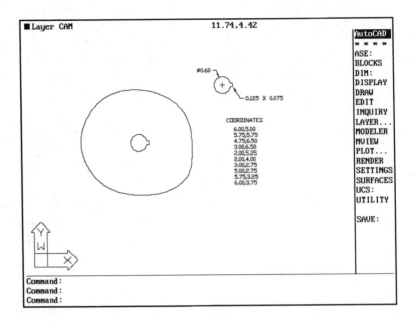

To finish the detailing process, you need to add the text to the drawing using the DTEXT command. The DTEXT, or Dynamic TEXT, command places text in the drawing and displays it in the Drawing Editor as you add it. The DTEXT command also enables you to place text in a drawing in columns, one line directly below another. The lines of coordinate values below the "COORDINATES" title in figure 8.14 are text strings entered in columns.

TASKS TO BE COMPLETED IN THIS EXERCISE

- Duplicate the center hole and keyway
- Dimension the center hole and keyway
- Add dynamic text

DUPLICATING THE CENTER HOLE AND KEYWAY

Before you add the detail to the drawing, duplicate the center hole and keyway. You can use the COPY command to create the duplicate. However, in this exercise use grips to move and copy the geometry. A *grip* is a box that appears at various locations on a selected object when no command is active. Using grips, you can manipulate the object in several different ways. The Grip modes for editing objects are Stretch, Move, Rotate, Scale, and Mirror. Each Grip mode has its own options and performs the same operation as the command with the same name.

To use a grip, first pick the entity or entities to edit. Next, pick one of the grip boxes. This begins the grip operation, displays the Grip modes, and acts as the base point. Stretch is the default Grip mode. By moving the cursor, the selected object is stretched from the selected grip box. When you invoke another Grip mode, the options associated with that mode appear.

USING GRIPS

Use grips to duplicate the hole and keyway. First, select the objects. Then pick one of the grip boxes. When Grip modes appears, choose Move. Because you wish to keep the original, specify Copy. To complete the command, enter the displacement value and a Ctrl-C to exit Grip mode.

Step 1.0: Using a window, select the objects to duplicate:

Command: *Pick a point below and to the left of the circle and keyway*	Defines the first point of the window
Other corner: *Pick a point above and to the right of the circle and keyway*	Defines the second point of the window and displays the grip boxes

Step 1.1: Select a grip base:

Command: *Pick one of the grip boxes*	A box appears in the grip box and the Grip Modes are displayed

Step 1.2: Change the active Grip mode from the default Stretch to Move:

Displays the active grip mode

<Stretch to point>/Base point/ Copy/Undo/eXit: *From the screen menu, choose* Move	Activates the Move Grip mode and displays associated options

Step 1.3: By default, the Move Grip mode moves the original objects selected. To keep the original and move a copy, invoke the Copy option:

<Move to point>/Base point/ Copy /Undo/eXit: *From the screen menu choose* Copy	Creates a duplicate of the original during move

Step 1.4: Specify the displacement value (the distance on the X and Y axis to place the new object from the original). You need to place the center hole and keyway 3 units to the right and 2 units above the original object. Use relative coordinates to specify this point from the last point picked:

```
<Move to point>/Base point/
Copy/Undo/eXit: @3,2 ↵
```
Create a duplicate of the selected object 3,2 units from the selected grip box

Step 1.5: Exit Move Grip mode:

```
<Move to point>/Base point/
Copy/Undo/eXit: ↵
```
Exits Grip mode

Step 1.6: Deactivate grips by entering a cancel:

```
Command: Press Ctrl-C
```
Deactivates grips

Your drawing now should resemble the one shown in figure 8.15.

Figure 8.15:

Cam with dupli-cate center hole and keyway.

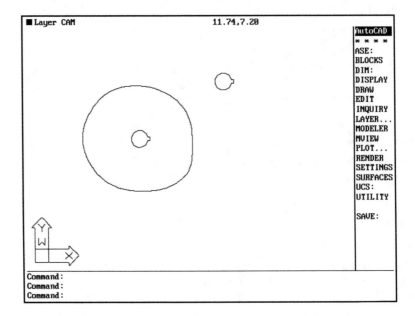

DIMENSIONING THE CENTER HOLE AND KEYWAY

Now that you have duplicated the center hole and keyway, you need to add the dimensions to it. When completed, you should have a drawing like the one shown in figure 8.16. To add the dimensions to the object, use the DIAmeter dimensioning subcommand to detail the circle part of the center hole. For the keyway, use the LEAder subcommand.

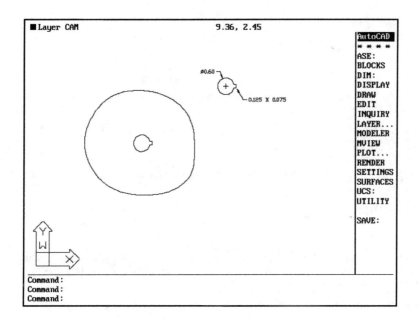

The cam geometry with center hole and keyway dimensioned.

Before you add the dimensions, however, you need to change layers. For this drawing, the dimensions need to be placed on the CAM_DIM layer.

Step 2.0: Use the **LAYER** command or Layer Control dialog box and make CAM_DIM the current layer.

You now are ready to add the dimensions. As with previous lessons, you first need to set the dimension variables. For this drawing, set the height of the dimension text and the size of arrowheads to .125 units.

Step 3.0: Issue the **DIM** command to enter the dimensioning area of AutoCAD.

Step 4.0: Issue the **DIMTXT** variable and set the dimensioning text height to **.125** units.

Step 5.0: Issue the **DIMASZ** variable and set the size of the arrowheads to **.125** units.

Now add the leader seen in figure 8.16. As used in Lesson 6, the LEAder dimensioning subcommand creates a line or lines with an arrowhead at one end, and text at the other end.

Step 6.0: Issue the LEAder subcommand and select the point at which the arrow points:

```
Dim: LEA ↵                          Starts the LEAder
                                    subcommand
```

```
Leader start: Select the keyway at the          Selects the starting
3:30 position                                    point for the leader
                                                 line and the
                                                 location of the
                                                 arrowhead
```

Step 6.1: Select the end point of the leader line. This is the end of the diagonal line in figure 8.16:

```
To point: Pick a point below and to the          Selects the end
right of the starting point                      point of the
(see fig. 8.16)                                  leader line
```

Step 6.2: After you select this point, press Enter to stop selecting end points for the leader line:

```
To point: ↵                                      Tells AutoCAD to
                                                 stop creating leader
                                                 lines
```

Step 6.3: You now need to provide the dimension text for the keyway, which is .125 units by .075 units. AutoCAD adds the small horizontal line next to the text, as was shown in figure 8.16:

```
Dimension text <>: 0.125 x 0.075     Inserts the text
                                     0.125×0.075 at the
                                     end of the leader
                                     line
```

You now have the leader line and are ready to add the diameter dimension to the center hole, using the DIAmeter dimensioning subcommand.

Step 7.0: Issue the DIAmeter subcommand and add the diameter dimension text, as previously shown in figure 8.16:

```
Dim: DIA ↵                                       Starts the DIAmeter
                                                 subcommand

Select arc or circle: Select the center          Selects the circle
hole at the 11 o'clock position                  to dimension and the
                                                 location of the
                                                 leader line

Dimension text <0.60>: ↵                         Accepts the default
                                                 dimension text

Enter leader length for text: ↵                  Accepts the default
                                                 leader length
```

You now are finished using the dimensioning commands and need to exit the dimensioning mode.

Step 8.0: Issue the **EXIT** command or press Ctrl-C to exit the dimensioning mode and return to the `Command:` prompt.

ADDING DYNAMIC TEXT

Now you are ready to add the text below the dimensioned center hole and keyway, as seen in figure 8.17. Because many lines of text are positioned directly below each other in columns, you should use the DTEXT command rather than the TEXT command. The DTEXT (or Dynamic TEXT) command places the text on-screen as you type, as well as enables you to place text in columns.

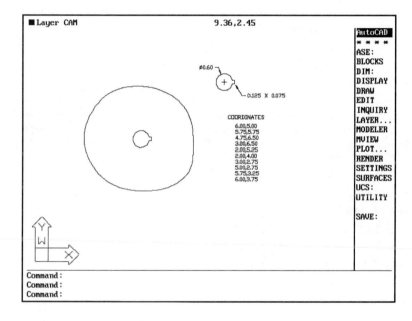

Figure 8.17:

The cam with text added.

Before you add the text, you again must change layers.

Step 9.0: Make CAM_TXT the current layer.

You now are ready to add the text that defines the X,Y coordinates for the previously added points. The DTEXT command begins the same way as the TEXT command. You select a starting point, height, and rotation of the text to be added. The difference between the two commands is the way in which you enter the text. When you enter text using the TEXT command, the text displays at the Command: prompt one line at a time. With DTEXT, the text is displayed both at the Command: prompt *and* in the drawing area. Also, when you use DTEXT you can add several text strings during one command session.

Step 10.0: Issue the DTEXT command:

Command: **DTEXT** ↵   Starts the DTEXT
                                                  command

You now need to tell AutoCAD where you want to start the text.

Step 10.1: Select the starting point for the text by using absolute coordinates, as in the following:

Justify/Style/<Start point>:   Specifies the
7.5,5 ↵   starting point as
                                                  7.5,5 for the text

Step 10.2: Specify the text height and rotation angle:

Height <0.20>: **.125** ↵   Specifies a text
                                                  height of .125

Rotation angle <0>: ↵   Keeps the rotation
                                                  angle at 0 degrees

Step 10.3: You now can enter the text that appears in a column in figure 8.17. To enter the text, you need to type each text line then press Enter to start a new line directly below the last text string. Type the following text strings in sequence to place them in the drawing:

Text: **6.00,5.00** ↵
Text: **5.75,5.75** ↵
Text: **4.75,6.50** ↵
Text: **3.00,6.50** ↵
Text: **2.00,4.00** ↵
Text: **3.00,2.75** ↵
Text: **5.00,2.75** ↵
Text: **5.00,2.75** ↵
Text: **5.75,3.25** ↵
Text: **6.00,3.75** ↵

Step 10.4: End the DTEXT command by pressing Enter after you type the last text string:

Text: ↵   Ends the DTEXT
                                                  command and enters
                                                  the text in the
                                                  drawing database

Finish the drawing by adding the word "COORDINATES" above the text you just entered.

Step 11.0: Issue the DTEXT command:

Command: **DTEXT** ↵   Starts the DTEXT
                                                  command

Step 11.1: To ensure that the word "COORDINATES" is centered over the text, you need to use the Center option:

```
Justify/Style/<Start point>: C ↵      Invokes the Center
                                       option
```

Step 11.2: Specify the point on which the text is to be centered. This point corresponds to the midpoint of the word "COORDINATES":

```
Center point: 7.88,5.3 ↵        Centers the text on
                                 the absolute
                                 coordinate 7.88,5.3
```

Step 11.3: Accept the default height and rotation angles:

```
Height <0.13>: ↵                Accepts the default
                                 text height of .13
                                 units

Rotation angle <0>: ↵           Accepts the default
                                 rotation angle of
                                 0 degrees
```

Step 11.4: Type the text string to be added to the drawing:

```
Text: COORDINATES ↵             Specifies the text
                                 string
```

Step 11.5: End the DTEXT command:

```
Text: ↵                         Ends the DTEXT
                                 command
```

EXERCISE 4: CREATING A TITLE BLOCK

You have learned that drawings are forms of communication that must be shared with many people. Title blocks and borders, as shown in figure 8.18, typically are added to drawings to detail important information about the drawing. You can use the standard drawing and editing commands to create the border and title block. To add the text to the title block, use the STYLE command. The STYLE command enables you to define different fonts to enhance your drawing.

TASKS TO BE COMPLETED IN THIS EXERCISE

- Draw the title block geometry
- Select different text fonts
- Add text to the title block

Figure 8.18:

The drawing with the title block and border.

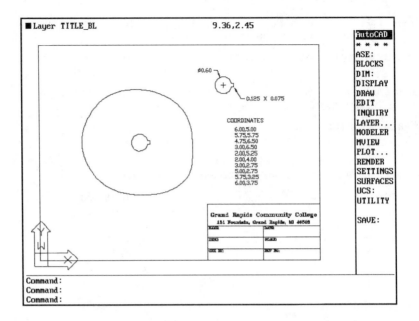

Step 1.0: Before you begin this exercise, you need to change layers. Make TITLE_BLK the current layer.

DRAWING THE TITLE BLOCK GEOMETRY

To create the title block, draw a border around the outside of the drawing. Earlier in this lesson, you set the limits of the drawing size at 8.5 units by 11 units. Typically, the border on a title block is .5 units from the edge of the paper. The border for this drawing needs to start .5 units from the lower left corner, and needs to be 10 units along the horizontal axis and 7.5 units along the vertical axis.

Step 2.0: Issue the **LINE** command and start the first line of the border at the absolute coordinate **.5,.5**. Use the following polar coordinates to specify the end points of the next three lines:

    `@10<0`

    `@7.5<90`

    `@10<180`

Step 2.1: Invoke the Close option to close up the border.

You now are ready to add the title block to the lower right corner of the drawing. Begin by developing the two lines that define the title block area, as shown in figure 8.19. You can see the lines that form the border are parallel to the title block lines. This enables you to use the TRIM and OFFSET commands to create the title block area from the existing border geometry.

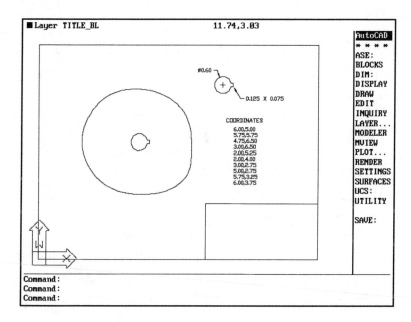

Figure 8.19:

The drawing with lines that form the title block area.

Begin by defining the lines that compose the title block area. The outer dimension of this area is 4 units by 1.95 units.

Step 3.0: Issue the **OFFSET** command and set the offset value to 4 units. Select the right vertical border line and offset it to the left.

Step 4.0: Issue the **OFFSET** command and set the offset value to 1.95 units. Select the bottom horizontal border line and offset it up.

You now need to remove the portion of the lines that you do not need to develop the title block area. In figure 8.20, these are the lines that extend to the left of the vertical line, and above the horizontal line.

Step 5.0: Issue the **TRIM** command and select the new horizontal and vertical lines as the cutting edges. Press Enter to end the cutting edge selection process.

Step 5.1: Select the new vertical line above the horizontal line, and then select the new horizontal line to the left of the vertical line. Press Enter to exit the TRIM command.

Figure 8.20:

Offsetting the border geometry to create the title block area.

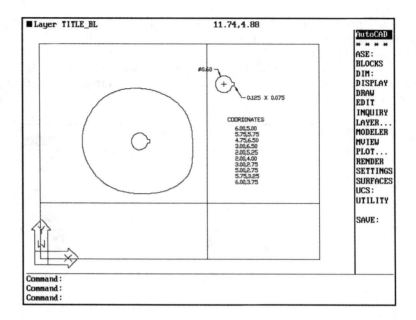

Step 6.0: You now should clean up your screen using the **REDRAW** command.

Your drawing should resemble the one previously shown in figure 8.19.

You now are ready to work inside the two new lines to complete the title block as seen in figure 8.21. To make this process easier, enlarge this area using the ZOOM command. This helps you select the lines and place text in the title block.

Step 7.0: Issue the **ZOOM** command and invoke the Window option. Place a window around the title block outline in the lower right corner of the drawing.

You now are ready to add the inner lines of the title block shown in figure 8.21. A distance of .75 units is between the top line and the line below it. The remaining horizontal lines are .4 units away from each other. The single vertical line is set at the midpoint of the horizontal lines. You again can use the OFFSET and LINE commands to create this geometry.

Step 8.0: Issue the **OFFSET** command and set the offset value to .75 units. Select the top horizontal line and pick a point below it to offset the line .75 units below itself. Press Enter to end the OFFSET command.

Step 9.0: Issue the **OFFSET** command and set the offset value to .4 units. Select the new horizontal line and pick a point below it to offset the line down.

Step 9.1: To create the next line, select the horizontal line you just created and pick a point below it to offset it down. Press Enter to end the OFFSET command.

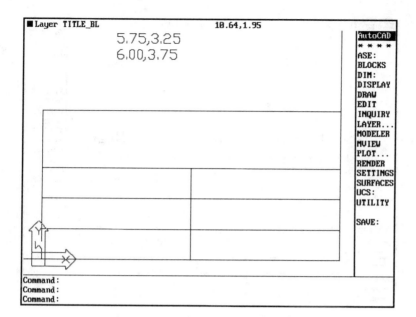

You now should have three horizontal lines inside the title block area. Now you are ready to add the single vertical line through the middle of the title block area. To create this line, use the LINE command and the MIDpoint object snap override to find the midpoint of the second line from the top. Then use the PERpendicular object snap override to draw a line that is perpendicular to the bottom border line.

Step 10.0: Issue the **LINE** command and invoke the MIDpoint object snap override. Select the second horizontal line from the top as the object to find the midpoint of. At the `To point:` prompt, invoke the PERpendicular object snap override and pick the bottom line as the object to draw a line perpendicular to. Press Enter to exit the command.

Your drawing now should resemble the one shown in figure 8.21.

SELECTING DIFFERENT TEXT FONTS

You now can add the title block text as seen in figure 8.22. The text you enter first is standard title block information, such as NAME: and DATE:. Because this information always is part of the title block and never changes, you can place this text on the same layer as the geometry that forms the title block.

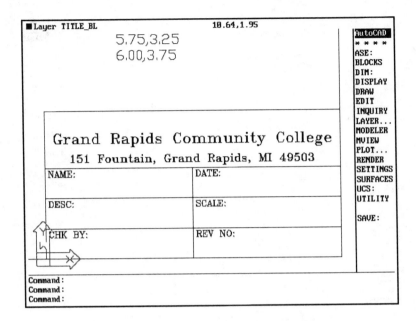

AutoCAD offers several different text styles from which you can choose. These styles help "dress up" the appearance of your finished drawing. To select the text style you want, use the STYLE command or the Select Text Font dialog box. These tools enable you to load new fonts into drawings, and name them for that particular drawing.

In figure 8.22, you can see that the college name at the top of the title block is a different text style than the one you used in previous drawings. This text is called RomanT (Roman Triplex). The other lines in the title block are in RomanC (Roman Complex) font. You can use the STYLE command to load these fonts into your drawing and to make them the default dimension text style when you use the TEXT and DTEXT commands during your drawing sessions.

When you use the STYLE command, the following options appear on-screen:

- **Text style name (or ?).** Names the new font in the current drawing.

- **Font file dialog box.** A dialog box for naming the font to load from the disk into the current drawing.

- **Height <0.00>.** Specifies the height for the text. By speci-fying a height value of 0, you can define the text height each time you use that style.

- **Width factor <1.00>.** Each font is created with a height-to-width ratio. By changing the width factor, you change this ratio. If you change the width factor to a number greater than one, for example, AutoCAD creates tall, skinny text. By speci-fying a width factor of less than one, you can create short, fat text.

- **Obliquing angle <0>.** Specifies the amount that the text slants.

- **Backwards? <N>.** Creates backwards text.

- **Upside-down? <N>.** Creates text that is upside down.

- **Vertical? <N>.** Creates vertical text.

You now can load a new font for this drawing using the STYLE command.

Step 11.0: Issue the STYLE command to load a new text font into the drawing:

Command: **STYLE** ↵	Starts the STYLE command

Step 11.1: Define the name of the font for this drawing:

Text style name (or ?) <STANDARD>: **STYLE1** ↵	Names the new font STYLE1 and displays the Select Font File dialog box

Step 11.2: Specify the name of the font to load from disk into this drawing:

Enter **ROMANT** in the File input box	Specifies RomanT as the new font

Step 11.3: For this drawing, you do not need to change the default settings for the text font characteristics:

`Height <0.00>: ⏎`	Accepts the default of 0 height, enabling you to specify a height each time you use this font in the drawing
`Width factor <1.00>: ⏎`	Accepts the default width-to-height ratio of one
`Obliquing angle <0>: ⏎`	Creates text that is straight up
`Backwards? <N>: ⏎`	Specifies that the text is not entered backward
`Upside-down? <N>: ⏎`	Specifies that the text is entered right-side up
`Vertical? <N>: ⏎`	Specifies that the text is placed left to right, not vertical

STYLE1 now is the current text style for this drawing. When you create text in this drawing, AutoCAD uses this text style as the default style.

ADDING TEXT TO THE TITLE BLOCK

You now are ready to add the text that defines the school name. To position this text, issue the DTEXT command and select the Align option. The Align option enables you to place text between two points.

Step 12.0: Issue the DTEXT command and select the Align option:

`Command: `**`DTEXT`**` ⏎`	Starts the DTEXT command
`Justify/Style/<Start point>: `**`A`**` ⏎`	Invokes the Align option

Step 12.1: Select the points to align the text between:

`First text line point:` *Pick point* Ⓐ *(see fig. 8.23)*	Selects the first point to align the text between

```
Second text line point: Select point     Selects the second
ⒷB (see fig. 8.23)                        point to align the
                                          text between
```

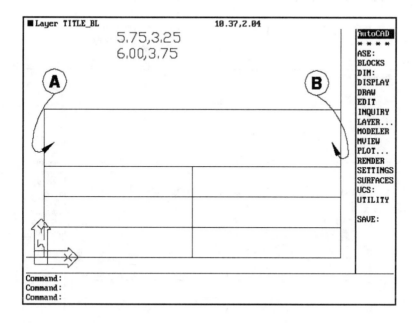

Figure 8.23:

*Labeled points
used to align text
in the title block.*

Step 12.2: Type the text that you want placed between the two points. (You can, of course, type in your own school or company name.):

```
Text: Grand Rapids Community      Specifies the text
College ↵                         to be aligned
                                  between the
                                  two points
```

Step 12.3: End the DTEXT command:

```
Text: ↵                           Ends the DTEXT
                                  command
```

You now need to add the text that falls below this line, which is the address of the school or business (see fig. 8.22). For this text, you need to specify a smaller text height than the text you just entered, as well as center the new text line under the last text line you just created. The font for the new text, however, remains the same—RomanT.

Step 13.0: Issue the DTEXT command:

```
Command: DTEXT ↵                  Starts the DTEXT
                                  command
```

Step 13.1: You now need to tell AutoCAD to center the address text in the title block at point A (see fig. 8.24). To do this, use the Center option:

```
Justify/Style/<Start point>: C ↵        Selects the Center
                                         option

Center point: Pick point Ⓐ               Selects the point to
(see fig. 8.24) ↵                        center the text on
```

Figure 8.24:

The title block with labeled point for address text.

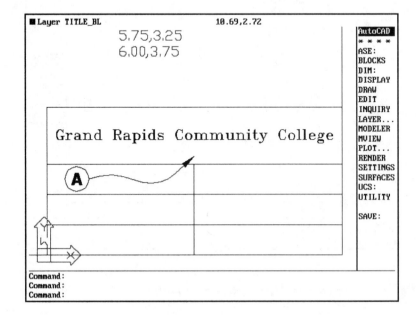

```
■ Layer TITLE_BL                    10.69,2.72
            5.75,3.25                                    AutoCAD
            6.00,3.75                                    * * * *
                                                         ASE:
                                                         BLOCKS
                                                         DIM:
                                                         DISPLAY
                                                         DRAW
                                                         EDIT
                                                         INQUIRY
       Grand  Rapids  Community  College                 LAYER...
                                                         MODELER
                                                         MVIEW
                                                         PLOT...
        Ⓐ                                                RENDER
                                                         SETTINGS
                                                         SURFACES
                                                         UCS:
                                                         UTILITY

                                                         SAVE:



 Command:
 Command:
 Command:
```

Step 13.2: You now need to specify the height of the text, which is shorter than the first line of text you entered:

```
Height <0.20>: .1 ↵                      Defines the text
                                         height
```

Step 13.3: Specify not to rotate the text as it is entered by accepting the default rotation angle:

```
Rotation angle <0>: ↵                    Accepts the rotation
                                         angle of 0 degrees
```

Step 13.4: Type the address text you want entered in the title block, then end the DTEXT command. (Again, if you typed in your own organization in the previous step, type your own address here):

```
Text: 151 Fountain, Grand Rapids,       Specifies the text
MI 49503 ↵                               to place in the
                                         drawing

Text: ↵                                  Ends the DTEXT
                                         command
```

You now need to create a second font for the remainder of the text. This text is the text information shown in figure 8.25. Again, use the STYLE command to load the new font—RomanC (Roman Complex).

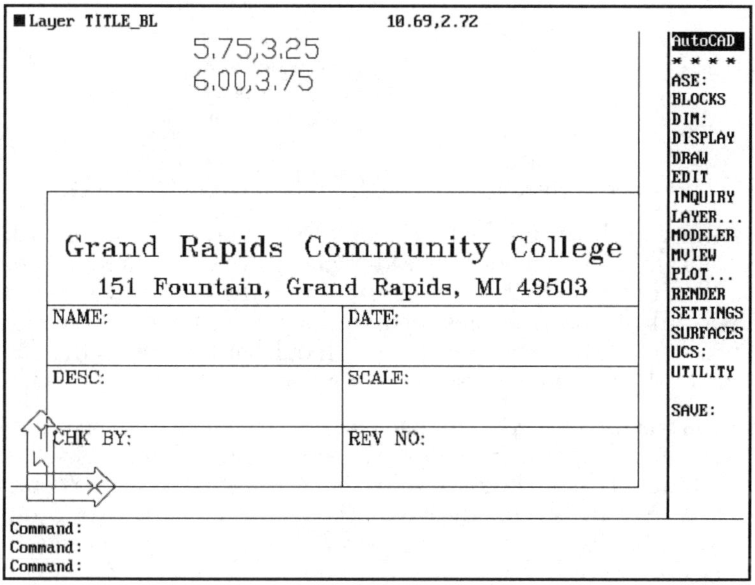

The completed title block.

Step 14.0: Issue the STYLE command and load the second new font for this drawing, as follows:

Command: **STYLE** ↵	Starts the STYLE command
Text style name (or ?) <STYLE1>: **STYLE2** ↵	Names the new font Style2
Enter **ROMANC** *in the* File *input box*	Specifies RomanC as the new font

Step 14.1: As you did for the last font, accept the default settings for the text characteristics, as in the following:

Height <0.00>: ↵	Accepts the default height of 0
Width factor <1.00>: ↵	Accepts the default width-to-height ratio of one
Obliquing angle <0>: ↵	Creates text that is straight up

```
Backwards? <N>: ⏎          Specifies that the
                           text is not entered
                           backwards

Upside-down? <N>:          Specifies that the
                           text is entered
                           right-side up

Vertical? <N>: ⏎           Specifies that the
                           text is placed
                           left to right, not
                           vertical
```

STYLE2 now is the current text style for this drawing.

You now are ready to add the final text information to the title block using the DTEXT command. Instead of placing the text directly below the last line of text, select the starting point of the text strings using the crosshairs. This eliminates pressing Enter numerous times as you enter each text string. This process also is much quicker than using the TEXT command, which you must issue numerous times to complete this task.

When you use the DTEXT command and press Enter after you type in the text string, the cursor box moves to the next line. This method is how you entered the coordinate values earlier in the lesson. To complete this part of the title block, however, you need to enter the text into the title block cells as was shown in figure 8.25. To do this, you need to move the cursor box to each cell, not to the line below the last text string. Do this by simply moving the crosshair cursor to the point at which you want to enter the next text string. Then type in the text string you want.

In this part of the exercise, use left-justified text to duplicate the previous figure. *Left-justified text* is text that starts at a specified point and continues to the right. The advantage of using DTEXT is that when you select a starting point, you see a box that represents the starting point and the text height before you actually enter the text. This enables you to pick a new starting location if the first location is incorrect.

When prompted for a starting point, select the upper left corner of the cell. AutoCAD then places the text above and to the right of the point you select.

Step 15.0: Issue the DTEXT command and pick the starting point of the first text string:

```
Command: DTEXT ⏎          Starts the DTEXT
                          command
```

```
Justify/Style/<Sart point>: Pick the       Specifies the
bottom left corner for the letter           starting point of
"N" in NAME: (see fig. 8.25)                the first text
                                            string
```

Step 15.1: Define the text height and rotation angle:

```
Height <0.10>: .08 ↵                        Defines the text
                                            height

Rotation angle <0>: ↵                       Accepts the rotation
                                            angle of 0 degrees
```

Step 15.2: Type the text string that you want to enter at the selected point, as follows:

```
Text: NAME:                                 Defines the first
                                            text string
```

Step 15.2: Use figure 8.25 as a guide to locate the points for the following text strings. Pick a starting point, enter the text, then pick the next starting point, and continue until the following text is entered into the drawing:

> **DATE:**
>
> **DESC:**
>
> **SCALE:**
>
> **CHK BY:**
>
> **REV. NO.:**

Step 15.3: End the DTEXT command:

```
Text: ↵                                     Ends the DTEXT
                                            command
```

You now are ready to add the information inside each of the cells. For this lesson, fill in the NAME: and DATE: cells using your name and the current date. Before you enter these text strings, however, you need to change layers. This enables you to erase the information in the cells, such as the current date, without altering the title block geometry.

Step 16.0: Make the layer TITLE_TXT the current layer.

Step 17.0: Issue the **STYLE** command and select the text style that you want to use.

Step 18.0: Issue the **DTEXT** command and fill in the NAME: and DATE: cells, using your name and the current date.

Once you finish entering your name and the date, return to a full view of the drawing.

Step 19.0: Issue the **ZOOM** command and select the Previous option.

EXERCISE 5: QUERYING THE AutoCAD DRAWING DATABASE

After developing a drawing, or if you are studying to take the *AutoCAD Certified Operator Examination*, you need to know how to inquire for information about the drawing database. When you take the *AutoCAD Certified Operator Examination*, you are asked to create various drawings and then answer multiple choice questions that are derived from AutoCAD's inquiry commands.

The inquiry commands also help you determine real-world applications for your drawings. You can, for example, use the inquiry commands to find the total area of a house, or list the clearance fit between two parts. You also can determine the length, angle, and layer of an entity using the inquiry commands.

To practice the commands for the *AutoCAD Certified Operator Examination*, you query certain information about your drawing in this exercise. This includes finding the distance between points, listing entities, and finding the area of a single space. In addition, you convert the center hole and keyway in the cam geometry into a single polygon. This helps you find the area of the cam without a hole.

TASKS TO BE COMPLETED IN THIS EXERCISE

- Determine the distance between two points
- List database information
- Determine the area of a single entity
- Convert entities into a single polyline
- Find the area of the cam

DETERMINE THE DISTANCE BETWEEN TWO POINTS

The first command you use to find out information about your drawing is the DIST or DISTance command. The DIST command displays the relationship between two points, including distance, angle, and change on the X, Y, and Z axes. This can help you determine the distance between two walls, the amount of clearance between two parts, or simply to check the accuracy of your drawing.

To use the DIST command, issue the command and then select the two coordinate locations between which you want to measure the distance.

Step 1.0: Issue the DIST command:

Command: **DIST** ↵   Starts the DIST command

Step 1.1: Invoke the Endpoint object snap override and select the points that you want to determine the distance between:

First point: *Using object snap Endpoint*   Specifies the first
pick point Ⓐ *(see fig. 8.26)*   point to determine
          the distance

Second point: *Using object snap Endpoint*   Specifies the second
pick point Ⓑ *(see fig. 8.26)*   point to determine
          the distance

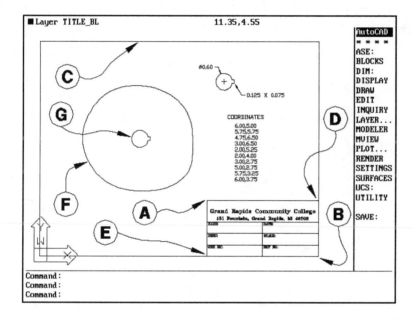

Figure 8.26:

The completed drawing with labeled inquiry points.

Although you used the DIST command to find only the distance between two points, AutoCAD displays the following information about the selected points:

```
Distance = 4.45, Angle in XY Plane = 334, Angle from XY Plane = 0
Delta X = 4.00, Delta Y = -1.95, Delta Z = 0.00
```

As you just learned, the DIST command helps you determine the distance between two points. Often, however, you need to determine specific information about an entity already in the drawing. To do this, use the LIST command.

Listing Database Information

The LIST command displays much of the database information about a single entity. The database information varies with the type of entity, but may include the end points of lines, radii of circles, and center points of arcs. You also may find it useful to know the layer name that the specified geometry is on.

The LIST command is even simpler than the distance command. To use the LIST command, select the geometry that you want to query and the information displays on-screen.

Step 2.0: Issue the LIST command:

Command: **LIST** ↵	Starts the LIST command

Step 2.1: Select the geometry that you want to query:

Select objects: *Select Line* Ⓒ (*see fig. 8.26*)	Selects the object to be queried

Step 2.2: End the LIST command:

Select objects: ↵	Ends the LIST command

AutoCAD displays the following information about the selected entity, including the entity's type, its layer, and 3D information:

```
     LINE    Layer: TITLE_BLK
           Space: Model space
         Handle = 81
    from point, X=  10.50 Y=   8.00 Z=   0.00
      to point, X=   0.50 Y=   8.00 Z=   0.00
   Length =  10.00, Angle in XY Plane =  180
       Delta X =  -10.00, Delta Y =   0.00, Delta Z =
0.00
```

Determining the Area of a Single Entity

The next inquiry command is AREA. The AREA command provides area information defined by coordinates in a drawing or an entity, such as determining the floor space of a room. This is useful in finding the area of geometry in an object that has non-straight sides, such as a circle.

To see how the AREA command selects points, find the area of the title block in your drawing.

Step 3.0: Issue the AREA command:

```
Command: AREA ↵
```
Starts the AREA command

Step 3.1: You now need to select the corners of the object you want to find the area of. Invoke the Endpoint object snap override and select the corners of the title block, as follows:

```
<First point>/Entity/Add/Subtract:
Using object snap Endpoint, pick point
Ⓐ (see fig. 8.26)
```
Selects the first corner of the area to be queried

```
Next point: Using object snap Endpoint,
pick point Ⓓ (see fig. 8.26)
```
Selects the second corner of the area to be queried

```
Next point: Using object snap Endpoint,
pick point Ⓑ (see fig. 8.26)
```
Selects the third corner of the area to be queried

```
Next point: Using object snap Endpoint,
pick point Ⓔ (see fig. 8.26)
```
Selects the fourth corner of the area to be queried

```
Next point: Using object snap Endpoint,
pick point Ⓐ (see fig. 8.26)
```
Selects the last corner of the area to be queried

Step 3.2: End the AREA command:

```
Next point: ↵
```
Ends the AREA command

AutoCAD displays the following to show you the area of the selected object:

```
Area = 7.80, Perimeter = 11.90
```

In addition to finding the area of a polygon, the AREA command determines the area of a single entity. In this drawing, the outer contour of the cam is a polyline. To determine the area of the cam, simply use the AREA command and select the cam using the Entity option.

Step 4.0: Issue the AREA command:

```
Command: AREA ↵
```
Starts the AREA command

Step 4.1: Select the Entity option:

```
<First point>/Entity/Add/
Subtract: E ↵
```
Selects the Entity option

Step 4.2: Next, select the entity of the area that you want to find, as follows:

```
Select circle or polyline: Select
polyline Ⓕ (see fig. 8.26)
```
Selects the cam as the entity of which to find the area

AutoCAD displays the following information about the cam's area:

```
Area = 11.80, Perimeter = 12.23
```

CONVERTING ENTITIES INTO POLYLINES

You also can use the AREA command to combine or subtract areas in the drawing from one another. This is helpful when you have a hole in the drawing, such as the cam, or you want only partial information about a drawing.

In this exercise, the center hole with keyway is an actual hole in the cam. As such, the space occupied by this geometry should be subtracted from the total area of the cam. Because this geometry is not made of straight lines, nor is it a single polyline, the AREA options do not find the true area of the object. You need to convert the multiple entities in this drawing into a single polyline to find the area.

If one of the areas to be queried is a complex shape, such as the hole in the cam, you first must transform it into a polyline using the PEDIT command before you query. The PEDIT command converts single selected objects into polylines. You then can use the Join option to create polylines from entities that are contiguous; that is, the entities' end points must meet at the same coordinates.

You now need to convert the center hole and keyway, which was created as separate entities, into a single polyline.

Step 5.0: Issue the PEDIT command:

```
Command: PEDIT ↵
```
Starts the PEDIT command

Step 5.1: Next, select one of the objects that you want to make into the new polyline. In this case, pick the arc of the center hole and keyway:

```
Select polyline: Select arc Ⓖ
(see fig. 8.26)
```
Selects arc Ⓖ as one entity to convert into a polyline

Step 5.2: Tell AutoCAD to convert the single arc into a polyline:

```
Entity selected is not a polyline
Do you want to turn it into one?
<Y>: ↵
```
Convert the arc into a polyline

Step 5.3: You now need to add the keyway's entities to the polyline you just created, using the Join option:

```
Close/Join/Width/Edit vertex/
Fit curve/Spline curve/Decurve/
LType/Undo/eXit <X>: J ↵
```
Selects the Join option

Step 5.4: To select the geometry that you want to include as a single polyline, use the Window selection set option:

`Select objects:` *Select a point below and to the left of the center hole and keyway*

Selects the Window option, and defines the lower left corner of the window

`Other corner:` *Select a point above and to the right of the center hole and keyway*

Defines the upper right corner of the window

Step 5.5: End object selection:

`Select objects: ⏎`

Ends object selection

`3 segments added to polyline`

Message specifying the number of objects that are added to the polyline

Step 5.6: End the PEDIT command:

`Open/Join/Width/Edit vertex/`
`Fit curve/Spline curve/Decurve/`
`LType/Undo/eXit <X>: ⏎`

Ends the PEDIT command

FINDING THE AREA OF THE CAM

Now that you have converted the center hole and keyway into a single polyline, you can remove ("subtract") the hole from the cam. This action enables you to find the area of the cam without the hole. First issue the AREA command, then use the Add option to keep a running total of the cam area. Next, invoke the Subtract option and remove the center hole and keyway polyline from the cam. When you remove the polyline, AutoCAD recalculates the total area of the cam and displays the area of cam without the hole.

Step 6.0: Issue the AREA command and invoke the Add option:

`Command: AREA ⏎`

Starts the AREA command

`<First point>/Entity/Add/`
`Subtract: A ⏎`

Selects the Add option

Step 6.1: Select the Entity option to add the total area of the cam, as defined by the original polyline (polyline F—see fig. 8.26):

`<First point>/Entity/`
`Subtract: E ⏎`

Selects the Entity option

Step 6.2: Select the polyline that you want to find the area of:

`(ADD mode) Select circle or` `polyline:` *Select polyline* Ⓕ *(see fig. 8.26)*	Selects the cam as the object to find the area of
`Area = 11.80, Perimeter = 12.23` `Total area = 11.80`	Lists the area of the selected polyline (the cam)

Step 6.3: End the Add option, to stop adding areas to the running total:

`(ADD mode) Select circle or` `polyline:` ↵	Ends the Add option

Step 6.4: The area of the cam includes the hole in the total area. To find the area of the cam without the hole, you need to use the Subtract option and remove the center hole and keyway polyline:

`<First point>/Entity/` `Subtract:` **S** ↵	Selects the Subtract option

Step 6.5: Select the Entity option and then select the center hole and keyway polyline. This is the polyline that you need to subtract from the cam:

`<First point>/Entity/Add:` **E** ↵	Selects the Entity option
`(SUBTRACT mode) Select circle` `or polyline:` *Select arc* Ⓖ *(see fig. 8.26)*	Selects the area to subtract from the running total
`Area = 0.29, Perimeter = 2.05` `Total area = 11.51`	

The preceding prompt displays the area of the polyline that you are subtracting. It also shows the new total area of the cam, with the center hole and keyway removed.

Step 6.6: End the Subtract option and the AREA command:

`(SUBTRACT mode) Select circle` `or polyline:` ↵	Ends the Subtract option
`<First point>/Entity/Add:` ↵	Ends the AREA command

Exercise 6: Writing a Block to Disk

In your drawing, you created a title block and border that can be used in other drawings. As you learned in the last lesson, sharing geometry within a drawing is a powerful application of CAD programs. However, title blocks frequently are used in many different drawings. Because of this, you should save the title block and border so that you can use them in any drawing you create.

You learned in the last lesson that a block created using the BLOCK command can be used only in its drawing of origin. The title block and border in this drawing, however, needs to be shared with any drawing. The WBLOCK command enables you to share geometry from one drawing to another. The WBLOCK command saves a new or previously defined block on disk as an individual drawing file. This file can be inserted into existing drawings.

Tasks To Be Completed in this Exercise

- Write the title block to disk
- Add the title block to a drawing

Writing the Title Block to Disk

The WBLOCK command takes an existing block and writes it to disk. It also lets you develop and write a block to disk the same way you create a symbol using the BLOCK command, as you did in the last lesson.

Step 1.0: Issue the WBLOCK command:

Command: **WBLOCK** ↵   Starts the WBLOCK
                                              command and displays
                                              the Create Drawing
                                              File dialog box

Step 1.1: Specify the name of the new block. Because the block is saved as a file on disk, you are limited to only eight characters as a file name:

Enter **TITLEBLK** *in the* File *input box*   Defines the name of
                                              the new block

Step 1.2: You now need to indicate the file name of a previously created block or press Enter. If you specify a previously created block, the block associated with the file name is written to disk using the name you just specified, and the command ends. If you do not specify a name and press Enter, you see the same prompts as if you were creating a standard block. Define the new block by pressing Enter:

```
Block name: ↵                        Enables you to
                                     create a new block
```

Step 1.3: As in the BLOCK command, you need to define the insertion point of the new block. For the title block and border, you need to specify the coordinates 0,0 as the insertion point:

```
Insertion base point: 0,0 ↵          Defines the
                                     insertion point
```

Step 1.4: Now specify the objects that you want saved as a block and saved to disk. Select the lines and text that form the title block and border. You should not, however, select the text that includes variable information, such as your name, date, scale, and so forth:

```
Select objects: Pick the border,     Selects the geometry
the title block geometry, and        that you want to
the title block text                 save as a block
```

Similar to the BLOCK command, the WBLOCK command erases the objects selected as a block from the screen. In this drawing, however, you do not want to lose the geometry you just saved as a block. Use the OOPS command to return the erased geometry to the screen.

Step 2.0: Issue the **OOPS** command to bring back the title block geometry and border.

You now are finished with this drawing.

Step 3.0: Issue **QSAVE** to save the drawing to disk.

ADDING THE TITLE BLOCK TO A DRAWING

Now that you have saved the title block and border to disk, you can call up a previously created drawing and add the title block and border to it. For this exercise, call up the LESSON7 drawing, which is the electrical schematic diagram. Figure 8.27 illustrates LESSON7.

Step 4.0: Under File, choose Open, then **LESSON7**, then OK to display LESSON7 in the drawing editor.

Now that you are in the Drawing Editor, add the title block saved from this lesson's drawing (LESSON8) to the Lesson 7 drawing. Do this by using the INSERT command, just as you did in Lesson 7 to insert the symbols to create the schematic diagram. The insertion point of the title block is 0,0, which is the lower left corner of the drawing.

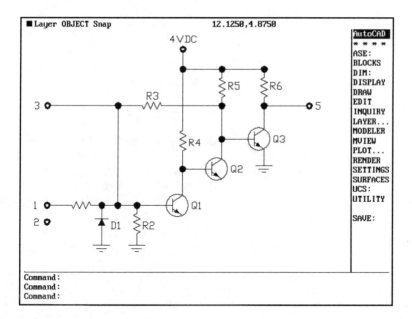

The drawing you created in Lesson 7 is larger than the drawing you created in Lesson 8. Before you insert the title block, you need to scale up the drawing so that the border fits around the schematic diagram. The rotation scale, however, stays the same.

Step 5.0: Issue the INSERT command:

```
Command: INSERT ↵
```
Starts the INSERT command

Step 5.1: Specify the name of the block you want to insert in the drawing:

```
Block name (or ?): TITLEBLK ↵
```
Specifies the name of the block you want to insert

Step 5.2: Specify to insert the block in the lower left corner of the drawing, as follows:

```
Insertion point: 0,0 ↵
```
Defines the insertion point of the block

Step 5.3: Scale the block to fit around the drawing, as in the following:

```
X scale factor <1> / Corner/
XYZ: 1.3 ↵
```
Defines the scale at which to enlarge the block

```
Y scale factor (default=X): ⏎
```
Accepts the default of the Y scale that is the same as the X scale

Step 5.4: Accept the rotation angle of 0 degrees:

```
Rotation angle <0>: ⏎
```
Accepts the rotation angle of 0 degrees

You now should see part of the border and title block. When you drew the schematic diagram in the last lesson, you drew it at the maximum size in the drawing limits. Now, when you insert the title block (which is scaled up by 1.3) in this exercise, the geometry is larger than the current zoom area of the schematic diagram. To see the full viewing area, use the ZOOM command with the All option to change the viewing area. You then should see the title block and border in the Lesson 7 drawing.

Step 6.0: Issue the **ZOOM** command and select the All option.

You now should see the entire drawing. You may need to move the title block to better center it around the schematic. You also should note that now that the viewing area has increased, the grid does not fill the entire screen. When you use the GRID command, AutoCAD only creates a grid that covers the same size area as the drawing limits. To adjust the grid, you can change the limits to fit the new drawing area. Now that you are finished using this drawing, you simply can turn off the grid.

Step 7.0: Press F7 to turn off the grid.

The final drawing should look like the one shown in figure 8.28.

Figure 8.28:

The schematic diagram with the title block and border inserted.

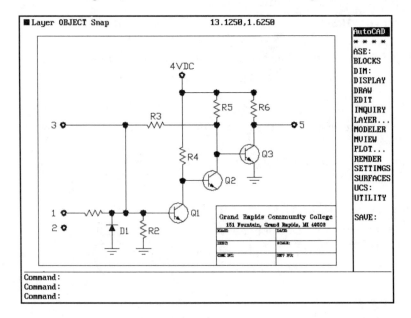

The AutoCAD Tutor

You now can add the text information to the title block using the DTEXT or TEXT command. After you finish entering the text strings, issue the END command and exit this drawing.

Step 8.0: Save the drawing to disk and end the current drawing session.

SUMMARY

Complex geometry development is a key drawing tool in AutoCAD. The PLINE and PEDIT commands enable the user to develop drawings that are difficult, if not impossible to draw by hand. Regardless of your drawing's use, you need to create visually appealing drawings. By changing text fonts, you can "dress up" your drawings. Once you complete a drawing, you can query the database using AutoCAD's inquiry commands.

IN THIS LESSON, YOU LEARNED TO DO THE FOLLOWING:

- Draw the outline of the cam
- Shape the cam geometry
- Add detail to the drawing
- Create a title block
- Query the AutoCAD drawing database
- Write a block to disk

In this drawing, you created a complex object, as well as a title block. After you completed the drawing, you queried the database and shared the title block with another drawing. In the next exercise, you develop a symbol library using drawing and editing commands. You then will use this symbol library to create an architectural drawing of a house.

REVIEW

1. Change the appearance of points as they appear on-screen. Use any value you want.

2. On their own layer, insert points at the following locations: 3,3; 4,4; 5,6; 4,5.25; 3,5; 2,5.25; 1,6; 2,4.

3. On a different layer, draw lines through the points in the preceding question.

4. From the preceding question, convert the lines into one polyline using the **PEDIT** command. When finished, turn the polyline into a spline curve.

5. From the preceding question, make the points invisible using the **LAYER** command.

6. Use the **WBLOCK** command and create a block of the preceding object, with an insertion point of **0,0**.

7. From *The AutoCAD Tutor Disk*, retrieve the drawing named REV8-1.

8. Insert the block you created in question six in the preceding drawing at coordinate 0,0.

9. Use the **DIST** command to determine the distance between the two eyes in the preceding drawing.

10. From the preceding drawing, determine the area of the large circle, minus the two eye circles, the nose circle, and the mouth polyline.

CREATING AN ARCHITECTURAL DRAWING

OVERVIEW

As seen in previous lessons, one of AutoCAD's most powerful tools is its development of symbols. Once you create symbols, you never have to draw them again. This enables you to use them as many times as necessary in other drawings, as well as share them with other AutoCAD drafters. Many drafting disciplines, such as architecture, tool design, and electronics, have their own symbol libraries that drafters can use to help them create drawings in shorter amounts of time.

Symbol libraries store drawings of groups of symbols, rather than individual symbols. This means that although a symbol library may include several hundred drawings, it is comprised of thousands of individual symbols. This method of storage enables drafters to insert the symbol libraries into their drawings, then select the individual symbols needed for that particular part of the drawing.

In this lesson, you create architectural symbols, such as a sink, stove, and bathtub, to be inserted into a cottage. (If you have the *AutoCAD Tutor Disk*, you only need to create the toilet.) You also learn in this lesson to set up the drawing environment to create architectural drawings. To help you create some of the geometry for these symbols, AutoCAD offers an ELLIPSE command. The ELLIPSE command enables you to create oblong circles based on several parameters.

To create drawings as large and complex as a house requires advanced utilization of AutoCAD commands, especially the ZOOM command. A drawing of a house is begun by setting up the drawing in architectural units with limits large enough to fit the building. The Double Line or DLINE command is used to create the parallel lines that define the building walls.

Once the outline is developed, use Offset to position symbols, such as doors and windows. These symbols are stored in a symbol library designed to be shared by many drawings. As symbols are inserted, AutoCAD can insert them as a single entity or as the primitive objects that define the block. Once inserted, you can manipulate blocks just like any entity. They can be copied, mirrored, erased, and so forth.

To add detail to the drawing after boundaries are defined, use predefined hatch patterns to represent real world materials, such as copper, concrete, brick, and brass. This sort of detail assists in the final implementation of the drawing—the actual building of a house.

To accommodate architectural standards, AutoCAD has dimensioning variables that include ticks instead of arrowheads and dimension text that are parallel to the dimension line. In addition, a dimension variable is available that scales all the dimension settings at once. This variable assists in making the drawing's dimensions large enough to be proportionate to the house.

TOPICS COVERED IN THIS LESSON

In this lesson, you learn to do the following:

- Develop a symbol library
- Draw a perimeter wall
- Create interior walls
- Draw a chimney
- Add a countertop to the kitchen
- Insert windows in the drawing
- Insert doors in the drawing
- Dimension the drawing

This lesson teaches you how to use the following AutoCAD commands and options:

- **DIMension Baseline.** Dimensions distances from a single baseline in a linear fashion
- **DIMTAD.** Places dimension text above the dimension line
- **DIMSCALE.** Changes the overall size of all dimension variables
- **ELLIPSE.** Draws an ellipse
- **Double Line (DLINE).** Draws a line with a second parallel line at a specified distance
- **DDHatch.** Enables the selection of a hatch pattern using a dialog box
- **Units, Architectural.** Enables you to measure using feet and inches during coordinate input and dimensioning

You will use architectural units to create the cottage seen in figure 9.1.

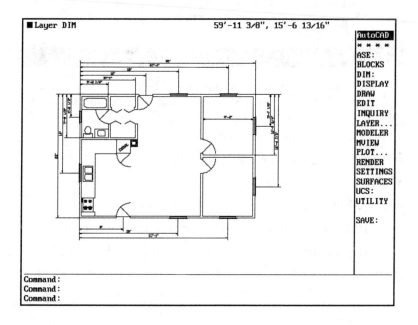

Figure 9.1:

The completed cottage, which you will draw in this lesson.

This book has an optional disk that is available. If you have this disk, you do not have to create the architectural symbol library discussed in the next section. Simply load the SYMBOLS file instead.

You now are ready to develop the architectural symbol library for this lesson. Do this by starting a new drawing and creating all of the blocks within this drawing. These symbols include a stove, sink, refrigerator, lavatory, toilet, doors, and windows. Once each drawing is saved as a block, save the blocks as one drawing. This enables you to use the drawing as a symbol library after you end this lesson.

SETTING UP AN ARCHITECTURAL DRAWING

Before you actually begin creating the geometry in this lesson, you need to set up the drawing environment as you have done in past exercises.

Step 1.0: Start AutoCAD; save the new drawing as **SYMBOLS**.

Step 2.0: Unlike other lessons in this workbook, you need to use architectural units in this lesson. Architectural units are used the same as decimal units, but are displayed in feet and inches. Use the Units Control dialog box and set up the drawing with architectural units. Set the accuracy to **1/16** of an inch. Set the system of angle measures for two fractional places during the display of angles. Leave all the remaining settings at their default.

NOTE

In this lesson, you use architectural units, which measure in feet and inches. The following are some example inputs and the value for each:

- **1.** Defines a value of one inch
- **1".** Defines a value of one inch
- **1'.** Defines a value of one foot
- **1'1".** Defines a value of one foot and one inch
- **1'-3/4".** Defines a value of one foot and three-quarter inches
- **1'1-3/4".** Defines a value of one foot and one and three-quarter inches

---

You now need to set the limits and create this drawing's layers. You learned in previous lessons that AutoCAD draws at full scale. This means that a two-inch line drawn on-screen represents a two-inch line in real life. Because this lesson's drawings are larger than drawings in past lessons, you need to create a drawing area that is large enough to draw the geometry. In this lesson, the largest symbol you create is the bathtub, which is 58 inches long. To accommodate this geometry, you need a drawing area that is set to 8'×6'.

Step 3.0: Issue the **LIMITS** command. Set the lower left corner at 0,0 and the upper right at 8',6'. You must place an apostrophe (') after the number to designate feet.

Step 4.0: Issue the **ZOOM** command with the All option to see the entire drawing to the new limits.

Step 5.0: Use the **LAYER** command or the Layer Control dialog box to create a new layer named **SYMBOLS**. Make SYMBOLS the current layer.

EXERCISE 1: DRAWING THE SYMBOL LIBRARY

Now that your drawing environment is established, begin creating the SYMBOLS drawing. Because this exercise uses commands that you are familiar with, you are prompted only through the last three exercises. When you are referred to a figure, do not add the dimensions to the symbols. The figures show this information only to assist in creating the geometry. If a dimension is not given, estimate and create a symbol that looks like the symbol shown in the figure. Because these symbols represent real objects in a house that can change (such as burners on a stove), they do not need to be dimensionally accurate.

TASKS TO BE COMPLETED IN THE EXERCISE

- Draw architectural symbols
- Save symbols as blocks in the drawing

DRAWING A BATHTUB SYMBOL

The first symbol you create is the bathtub, shown in figure 9.2. To draw the outline of the tub, use the LINE command. You then offset the original lines and use the FILLET command to place a radius on the four corners of the tub. Once you create the geometry, save it as a symbol using the BLOCK command. Make the insertion point of the tub at point A and name the symbol TUB.

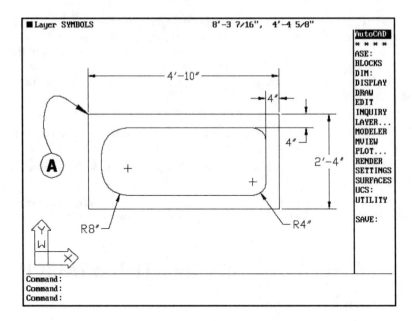

Figure 9.2:

The tub with insertion point.

Drawing a Lavatory

You now are ready to create another bathroom fixture, the lavatory shown in figure 9.3. To create this object, use the same methods you used to create the bathtub. Begin by drawing the outline of the lavatory using the LINE command. The outside dimensions of the lavatory are 2 feet by 6 1/2 inches by 19 inches. Then offset the outer lines to develop the inner lines, which then are contoured using the FILLET command. After you create the lavatory, use the BLOCK command to save the object as a symbol named LAV. In most figures, A indicates the insertion point (see fig. 9.2 and fig. 9.3).

Drawing a Sink Symbol

You now are finished creating bathroom fixtures for your symbol library and are ready to create kitchen symbols. The first symbol you need to create is the sink symbol seen in figure 9.4. You again use the LINE command to draw the outline of the sink. The inner geometry is added using the OFFSET command. You then draw a construction line that extends through the middle of the sink. Offset this line to create the sides of the sink. To finish the geometry, trim away the unneeded line segments and fillet the corners of the inner rectangles as you have done in past exercises. Name the block SINK and place the insertion point at A.

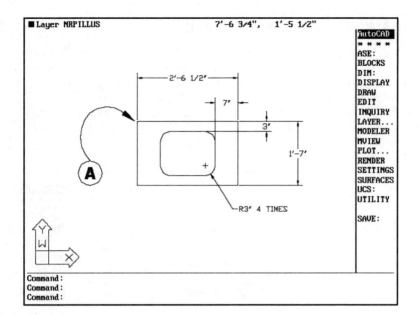

Figure 9.3:
The lavatory geometry.

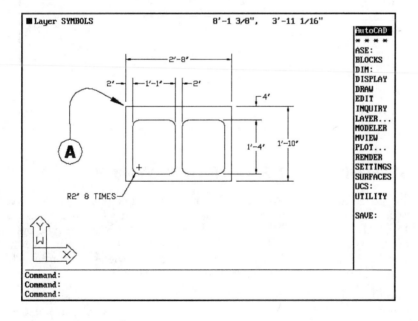

Figure 9.4:
The kitchen sink.

Drawing a Stove Symbol

The second kitchen appliance to create is the stove symbol. (See fig. 9.5.) Again, use the LINE command to draw the outline of the stove. You then offset the top horizontal to create the inner geometry, as well as create construction lines to define the stove knobs and burners. The knobs are drawn as circles, and the burners are developed using the DONUT command. Name the block STOVE and place the insertion point at A.

Figure 9.5:

The stove with insertion point.

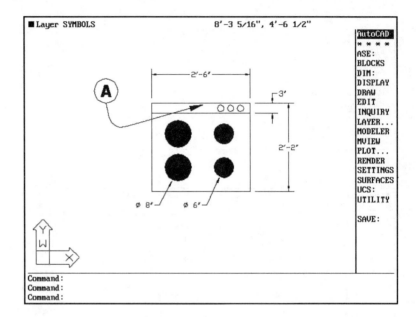

Developing a Refrigerator Symbol

The refrigerator symbol is the last kitchen appliance you create for this lesson. To create the refrigerator as shown in figure 9.6, you use the LINE, ARC, and TEXT commands. Use the Start, Center, Angle option of the ARC command. The starting point is at A, the center point is at B, and the angle is 90. If you need assistance with the ARC command, first perform Exercise five then return to this exercise.

In addition, notice the way in which the text inside the refrigerator geometry is underlined and at an angle. To underline the text, precede the text string with **&&u**. Name the symbol **FRIDGE** and place the insertion point at C.

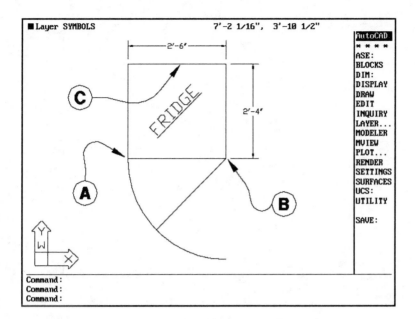

```
                                              AutoCAD
                                              * * * *
                                              ASE:
                                              BLOCKS
                                              DIM:
                                              DISPLAY
                                              DRAW
                                              EDIT
                                              INQUIRY
                                              LAYER...
                                              MODELER
                                              MVIEW
                                              PLOT...
                                              RENDER
                                              SETTINGS
                                              SURFACES
                                              UCS:
                                              UTILITY

                                              SAVE:

Command:
Command:
Command:
```

Figure 9.6:

The refrigerator geometry with text.

DRAWING A DOOR

You now are finished creating the kitchen symbols and are ready to create door and window symbols. In this exercise, you create a door symbol as shown in figure 9.7. The door symbol is created using the LINE, ARC, and OFFSET commands and then saved as a symbol using the BLOCK command.

You first need to draw the door jambs by creating a line then offsetting it to create the second jamb. You then draw the door itself using the LINE command. You finish the door geometry by drawing the arc that represents the door's swing. Before you save the door as a block, you must create a horizontal construction line between the top end points of the two door jambs. You then will use the midpoint of the construction line as the insertion point of the door symbol.

DRAWING THE DOOR GEOMETRY

You begin drawing the door by creating the two door jambs, starting with the left jamb. Use the LINE command to create this jamb, then offset it to create the second jamb. Because the door symbol is used in a 4 1/2-inch wall, the line that defines the jamb also must be this length.

Figure 9.7:

The door geometry.

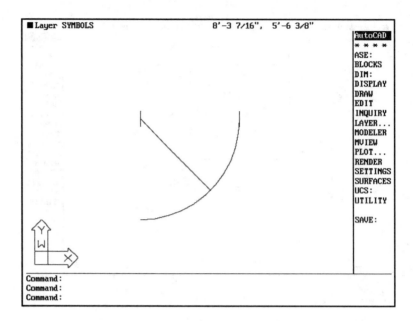

Step 1.0: Issue the **LINE** command and start the first line at the coordinates **3',3'**. Draw the line up 4 1/2 inches by typing **@4-1/2<90** at the To point: prompt.

You now can create the second jamb parallel to the first one. Because the door opening is 2 1/2 feet wide, you need to create the second jamb 2 1/2 feet from the jamb you just drew.

Step 2.0: Issue the **OFFSET** command and set the offset distance to **2'6**. Select the vertical line and offset it to the right.

You now have the door jambs and can add the door.

Step 3.0: Issue the **LINE** command and select the MIDpoint object snap override. Select the left vertical line as the starting point of the line; enter the coordinates **@2'6<315** for the end point of the door. This creates a door that is 2 1/2 feet wide.

You now have the door and can use the ARC command to represent the door's swing. To create this arc for any door symbol, you must decide on three things: the starting and center point of the arc, and the arc's angle. For this geometry, the starting point is the door jamb, located on the drawing's right side. The center point of the arc is the end point of the door, and the arc angle is 90 degrees.

As you create the arc, tell AutoCAD to reverse the angle of the arc by using a negative angle value. This forms an arc that represents the door's clockwise swing.

Step 4.0: Issue the **ARC** command and invoke the MIDpoint object snap override to pick the starting point of the arc:

Command: **ARC** ↵	Starts the ARC command
Center/<Start point>: **MID** ↵	Selects the MIDpoint object snap override
of *Pick the MIDpoint of the right vertical line*	Picks the starting point of the arc

Step 4.1: Select the Center option, then select the center of the arc as the left jamb:

Center/End/<Second point>: **C** ↵	Selects the Center option
Center: *Select the midpoint of the left vertical line*	Specifies the center point of the arc

Step 4.2: Specify the angle of the arc by entering a negative angle value for a reverse arc angle:

Angle/Length of chord/ <End point>: **A** ↵	Selects the Angle option
Included angle: **-90** ↵	Draws an arc in a clockwise manner

You now are finished with the door geometry, as shown in figure 9.7.

CREATING A DOOR SYMBOL

Doors typically are inserted from a door's middle against one wall. To select the insertion point of the block, a construction line must be added. This line is drawn horizontally between the top of the two door jambs. The midpoint of this line then is used as the insertion point of the door symbol.

Step 5.0: Issue the **LINE** command and invoke the ENDpoint object snap override. Select the top end point of one vertical line as the starting point, and then select the top end point of the other vertical line as the ending point.

Step 6.0: Issue the **BLOCK** command and name the block **DOOR**. Use the MIDpoint object snap override to pick the midpoint of the horizontal construction line. This point is the insertion point of the symbol.

You now need to select the geometry that you want to include in the block. You want to include all of the door geometry, excluding the horizontal construction line. Use the pickbox to select the objects you want to include as a symbol, then erase the construction line after the door geometry disappears from your screen.

Step 6.1: Select the objects you want to include as a symbol, including all of the door geometry. The construction line should not be a part of the selected block.

The door geometry should disappear from your screen, which enables you to erase the construction line easily.

Step 7.0: Issue the **ERASE** command and remove the construction line.

DRAWING A WINDOW SYMBOL

You now are ready to draw the window symbol, as shown in figure 9.8. To create this object, you need only use the LINE and OFFSET commands.

Figure 9.8:

The window geometry.

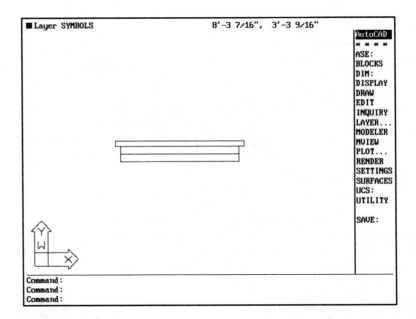

DRAWING THE WINDOW GEOMETRY

Begin by drawing the part of the window that sits inside of the wall, as seen in figure 9.9. To create this part of the window, first draw the middle horizontal line, which is 36 inches wide.

Step 1.0: Issue the **LINE** command and start a line at coordinates **3',3'**. Specify the ending point of the line by entering **@36<0** as the coordinates.

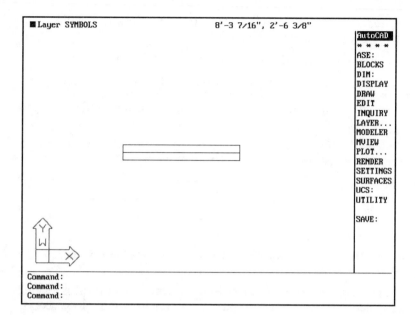

```
                                                    AutoCAD
                                                    * * * *
                                                    ASE:
                                                    BLOCKS
                                                    DIM:
                                                    DISPLAY
                                                    DRAW
                                                    EDIT
                                                    INQUIRY
                                                    LAYER...
                                                    MODELER
                                                    MVIEW
                                                    PLOT...
                                                    RENDER
                                                    SETTINGS
                                                    SURFACES
                                                    UCS:
                                                    UTILITY

                                                    SAVE:


Command:
Command:
Command:
```

Figure 9.9:

The window section that fits inside the wall.

From this line, you can develop the horizontal lines that form the inside and outside window lines (see fig. 9.9.). These lines are drawn so that the distance between each other equals the wall's thickness, which is 4 1/2 inch. Using the OFFSET command, you can offset the existing line half the wall's thickness up and down.

Step 2.0: Issue the **OFFSET** command and set the offset distance at **2-1/4"**. Select the horizontal line and offset it up. Select the same horizontal line and offset it down.

You now need to close the horizontal lines. Use two vertical lines on the ends of the horizontal lines so that your drawing looks like the one in figure 9.9.

Step 3.0: Issue the **LINE** command and invoke the ENDpoint object snap override. Select the right end point of the top horizontal line as the starting point of the first vertical line. Next, invoke ENDpoint again and select the right end point of the bottom horizontal line.

This creates a vertical line on the right side of the horizontal lines. You now need to create a vertical line on the left side of the vertical lines using the same methods.

Step 4.0: Issue the **LINE** command and invoke the ENDpoint object snap override. Select the left end point of the top horizontal line. Next, invoke ENDpoint again and select the left end point of the bottom horizontal line.

This finishes the actual window geometry. Your drawing now should resemble the one shown in figure 9.9.

You now can use the LINE command to add the window trim.

Step 5.0: Issue the **LINE** command and invoke the INTersection object snap override. Select the upper left corner of the window as the starting point of the first line of the window trim. Use the following coordinates as the end points of the remaining lines:

> @1.5<180
>
> @1.5<90
>
> @39<0
>
> @1.5<270
>
> @1.5<180

Step 5.1: After you enter the last end point for the window trim, press Enter to end the LINE command.

You now have completed the last architectural symbol for this lesson and can add it to the symbol library. Your drawing should look like the one shown in figure 9.10.

Figure 9.10:

The finished window with window trim.

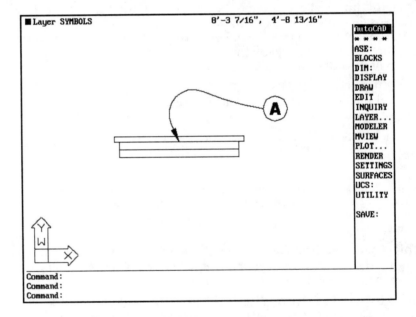

CREATING A WINDOW SYMBOL

You now are ready to add the window geometry to the block library using the BLOCK command. The insertion point for the block is labeled as A in figure 9.10. As with the door symbol, the insertion point on the window corresponds to the symbol's middle on the outside wall.

Step 6.0: Issue the **BLOCK** command and name the block **WINDOW**. Invoke the MIDpoint object snap override and pick point A (see fig. 9.10) as the insertion point. When you are prompted for the objects you want to include in the block, use the Window option and enclose the entire window geometry inside the window.

You are now ready to create another symbol—the toilet, described in the next section.

If you have *The AutoCAD Tutor Disk*, you will begin the exercise at this point. There is a file on disk that contains all of the symbols created up to now. You will need to open this file, create the following symbol, and save the file to disk. You will then be ready to create the cottage seen in figure 9.1.

If you do not have *The AutoCAD Tutor Disk*, skip step 1.0 and begin the exercise that draws a toilet symbol.

Step 1.0: Discard the present drawing and open SYMBOLS.

Follow the next exercise to add a toilet symbol to the drawing.

DRAWING A TOILET SYMBOL

You now are ready to continue creating the symbols for this lesson by drawing the toilet shown in figure 9.11. You first draw the tank using the LINE command. Once this is complete, you project a construction line from the tank to the point at which you want to create the center of the bowl. The bowl is drawn using the ELLIPSE command. The ELLIPSE command enables you to create ellipses, which are oblong circles.

DRAWING THE TOILET GEOMETRY

Begin creating the toilet geometry by drawing the toilet tank using the LINE command.

Figure 9.11:

The toilet geometry with labels for drawing.

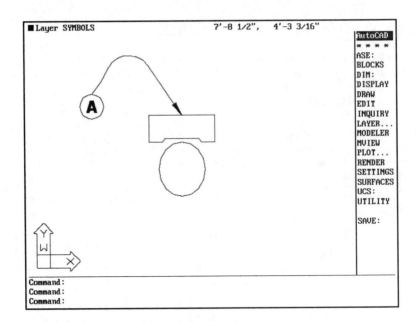

Step 1.0: Issue the **LINE** command and define a starting point of **2',4'**. To finish creating the tank, use the following coordinates:

@1'8<0

@8<270

@4<180

@-1,1

@10<180

@-1,-1

@4<180

Step 1.1: To finish the tank geometry, use the Close option. Type **C** at the next `To point:` prompt and press Enter.

You now can draw the bowl by using the ELLIPSE command. The ELLIPSE command creates ellipses based on center points, axis lengths, or rotation of circles. Before you create the ellipse for this drawing, create a construction line from the tank geometry. This helps position the ellipse in relation to the tank. This construction line starts at the midpoint of the lower horizontal line labeled as A in figure 9.12. The construction line then projects down to locate the center point of the ellipse, which will be the toilet bowl.

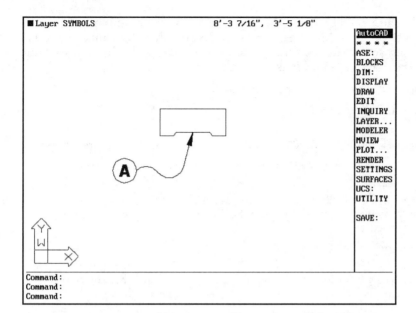

Step 2.0: Issue the **LINE** command and invoke the MIDpoint object snap override. Pick point A (see fig. 9.12) and draw a 9-inch line down by typing **@9<270** at the `To point:` prompt. End the LINE command by pressing Enter.

You now can draw the bowl using the ELLIPSE command. You create ellipses by specifying the major and minor axes of the ellipse, or by defining the amount of rotation of a circle. In this exercise, you will create an ellipse by specifying the major and minor axes of the object. The major axis is defined by a line that passes through the center of the ellipse and whose end points are at the farthest two points on the ellipse's circumference. The minor axis is perpendicular to the major axis, and also passes through the ellipse's center. The minor axis end points are the two closest points on the circumference of the ellipse.

To draw the toilet tank in the current open drawing, center the ellipse on the construction line. Specify the major axis on the Y axis as 16 inches, and specify the minor axis on the X axis as 14 inches.

Now define the minor axis of the ellipse. The minor axis is defined as you do a radius of the circle. That is, you need only define half the total minor axis. In this drawing, the total minor axis is 14 inches. This means that the center of the ellipse is 7 inches from the closest point of the circumference.

You also need to define the direction of the minor axis from the center point. You do this by using relative coordinate values, much as you do when you create lines using relative coordinates. In this drawing, the direction of the minor axis is to the right, or 0 degrees.

Step 3.0: Issue the ELLIPSE command:

`Command: ELLIPSE ⏎`	Starts the ELLIPSE command

Step 3.1: You now need to define the ellipse by using the Center option:

`<Axis endpoint 1>/Center: C ⏎`	Selects the Center option

Step 3.2: The ellipse's center point needs to be placed on the bottom end point of the construction line. To find the end point, use the ENDpoint object snap override:

`Center of ellipse: END ⏎`	Invokes the ENDpoint object snap override
`of` *Pick the bottom end point of the construction line*	Specifies the center point of the ellipse

Step 3.3: Define the axis length and direction of the minor axis:

`Axis endpoint: @7<0 ⏎`	Defines one axis length and direction from the center point

Step 3.4: You now define the major axis of the ellipse. Again, you need only define half the total major axis of 16 from the end point of the construction line:

`<Other axis distance>/ Rotation: 8 ⏎`	Defines the second axis length of the ellipse

Step 4.0: Issue the **ERASE** command and remove the construction line.

Your drawing should resemble the one shown in the previous figure 9.11.

Step 5.0: Issue the **BLOCK** command and name the symbol **TOILET**. Point A in figure 9.11 is the insertion point.

SAVING THE SYMBOL LIBRARY

You are now finished creating or adding to the symbol library. You can now save the drawing to disk and start on the cottage. When needed, the symbols in the SYMBOLS drawing can be used in this or any other drawing, as you will learn later in this lesson.

Step 6.0: Save the drawing to disk.

EXERCISE 2: STARTING A NEW DRAWING

You are now ready to draw the cottage shown in figure 9.1. You first need to start and set-up a new drawing, just as you have done at the beginning of previous lessons.

Step 1.0: Choose File, then New, then name the new drawing **LESSON9**.

Step 2.0: Use the **UNITS** command or Units Control dialog box and set up the drawing with architectural units. Set the accuracy to **1/16 inch**. Set the Precision of angle measures for two decimal places (**0.00**) during the display of angles. Leave all the remaining settings at their default.

Step 3.0: Issue the **LIMITS** command. Set the lower left corner at **0,0** and the upper right at **60',40'**. This will give you an area large enough to draw the cottage.

Step 4.0: Issue the **ZOOM** command with the All option to see the entire drawing to the new limits.

Step 5.0: Use the **LAYER** command or the Layer Control dialog box to create two new layers named WALL,COUNTER and DIM. Finally, make WALL the current layer.

EXERCISE 3: DRAWING A PERIMETER WALL

You begin this drawing by creating the perimeter wall, seen in figure 9.13. This wall represents the overall exterior wall for the cottage. You use the Double Line or DLINE command to create the wall. The DLINE command is one of the AutoLISP extra commands that comes with AutoCAD.

The DLINE command draws continuous double lines, using straight or arc line segments. The width of the lines can be assigned by the user at any time. The end of the lines can be capped (closed) or left open. The key element of this command is that intersecting lines are automatically cleaned up as they are developed.

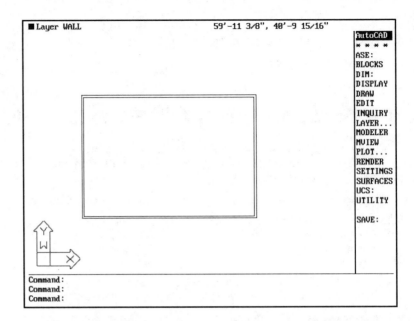

OPTIONS

The following command options can be used with DLINE:

- **Break.** Specifies whether the DLINE command will create a gap between intersecting lines.

- **Caps.** Control caps at the end of double lines. Both will place a cap on both ends, End places one on the last end, None will draw no caps, Start places a cap on the beginning end, and Auto places caps on any open ends.

- **Dragline.** Defines which side the original line will be placed in reference to the offset line.

- **Offset.** Starts a new double line a relative distance from a base point.

- **Snap.** Enables the DLINE command to start or stop by snapping to existing objects. Size determines the area in pixels to search for an object to snap to when a point is selected.

- **Undo.** Reverses the last operation.

- **Width.** Defines the perpendicular distance between the two double lines.

- **Start Point.** Specifies the first point of the double line.

- Draw the outside walls
- Zoom the drawing by factors

DRAWING THE OUTSIDE WALLS

Begin the drawing by creating the perimeter wall, using the double line (DLINE) command. The perimeter of the cottage is 32 feet by 22 feet.

Step 1.0: Perform the initial load of the command by choosing it from the menu:

Command: *Choose* Draw, *then* Line, *then* Double Line	Loads and starts the DLINE command

Step 1.1: Select the Width option to define the width of the **DLINE** command at the width of the walls:

`Dline, Version 1.11, (c) 1990-1992 by Autodesk, Inc. Break/Caps/Dragline/Offset/ Snap/Undo/Width/<start point>:` **W** ↵	Invokes the Width option

Step 1.2: Enter the width of the walls:

`New DLINE width <1/16">:` **4-1/2** ↵	Specifies the wall width as 4 1/2 inches

Step 1.3: Invoke the Dragline option to define on which side the second line will be placed:

`Break/Caps/Dragline/Offset/Snap/ Undo/Width/<start point>:` **D** ↵	Invokes the Dragline option

Step 1.4: Specify on which side the dragline will be placed in relation to the second line's placement. The Dragline is the original line. The side is determined by being on the Left, Center, or Right when looking down the line from starting point to ending point. Because the cottage perimeter is to be drawn counter-clockwise using the exterior dimensions, the dragline will be on the right.

`Set dragline position to Left/ Center/Right/<Offset from center = 0">:` **R** ↵	Places the dragline on the right

Step 1.5: Specify the starting point for the double line:

`Break/Caps/Dragline/Offset/ Snap/Undo/Width/<start point>:` **10',10'** ↵	Defines the starting point

Step 1.6: Using Polar coordinates, define the end points for the next three walls:

```
Arc/Break/CAps/CLose/Dragline/        Draws the first wall
Snap/Undo/Width/<next point>:
@32'<0 ↵
```

```
Arc/Break/CAps/CLose/Dragline/        Draws the second wall
Snap/Undo/Width/<next point>:         and cleans up the corner
@22'<90 ↵
```

```
Arc/Break/CAps/CLose/Dragline/        Draws the third wall
Snap/Undo/Width/<next point>:
@32'<180 ↵
```

Step 1.7: End the command and complete the wall by using the Close option:

```
Arc/Break/CAps/CLose/Dragline/        Closes the object
Snap/Undo/Width/<next point>:         and ends the DLINE
CL ↵                                   command
```

ZOOMING THE DRAWING BY FACTORS

To make it easier to work on the drawing, zoom in on the geometry. Do this by issuing the ZOOM command then selecting the Extents option. The drawing will fill the screen. You then can zoom out by a factor to create a usable working area.

Step 2.0: Issue the **ZOOM** command and select the Extents option to fill the screen with the drawing:

```
Command: ZOOM ↵                       Starts the ZOOM
                                       command
```

```
All/Center/Dynamic/Extents/Left/      Selects the Extents
Previous/Vmax/Window/<Scale           option
(X/XP)>: E ↵
```

Notice that the outside lines of the drawing are on the edge of the screen. To see these lines, you need to reduce the size of the drawing a small amount. ZOOM's Scale option enables you to change the size of the screen drawing by specifying a multiplying factor. A factor of .5, for example, gives you a drawing that is half the size of the drawing, whereas a factor of 2 doubles the size of the drawing. By entering the factor with an X beside it, the scale applies to the current size of the drawing. Without the X, the scale applies to the drawing limits.

Step 3.0: Issue the ZOOM command again and specify to reduce the drawing slightly by setting a scale factor of .9 (1.0 is one times the size of the drawing, which means it stays the same size):

```
Command: ZOOM ↵                       Starts the ZOOM
                                       command
```

```
All/Center/Dynamic/Extents/Left/      Zooms by a factor
Previous/Vmax/Window/<Scale           of .9 from the current
(X/XP)>: .9X ↵                        zoom
```

As in Lesson 7 when you inserted symbols in the electrical schematic diagram, the UCS icon is in the way of your drawing. You can turn it off using the UCSICON command.

Step 4.0: Issue the UCSICON command and turn off the UCS icon:

Command: **UCSICON** ↵	Starts the UCSICON command
ON/OFF/All/Noorigin/ORigin <ON>: **OFF** ↵	Turns off the UCS icon

EXERCISE 4: CREATING INTERIOR WALLS

You now are ready to create the interior walls seen in figure 9.14. You use the DLINE command with the Offset option. This method of creating interior walls is common because interior walls typically are dimensioned from another wall. To develop the doorways, you will use the DLINE command with the Cap option to close the end of the openings.

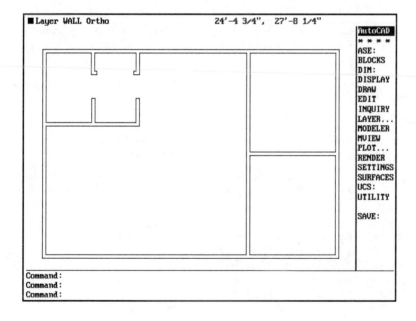

Figure 9.14:

The drawing with interior walls.

TASKS TO BE COMPLETED IN THIS EXERCISE

- Create the bedroom interior walls
- Develop the closet and bathroom walls

CREATING THE BEDROOM INTERIOR WALLS

Step 1.0: The Offset option in the **DLINE** command requires that you specify the direction to offset toward. Because all the walls are either perpendicular or horizontal, this specification of direction will be made easier if ortho is turned on.

Command: *Press* F8 *to turn on ortho*   Turns on ortho

CREATING THE BEDROOM INTERIOR WALLS

Begin by developing the walls that define the two bedrooms on the right. To do this, draw a double line that is offset the distance of the room from an interior intersection. Once this wall is developed, a double line drawn down the middle of the room creates two bedrooms of equal size. To do this correctly, the dragline on the last line must be in the center.

As you draw the double lines, notice the DLINE command automatically removes the intersection between the new wall lines and the existing wall line.

Begin by drawing the vertical wall line offset from the right interior wall, as seen in figure 9.15.

Step 2.0: Invoke the DLINE command:

Command: *Choose* Draw, *then* Line,   Starts the DLINE
then Double Line   command

Step 2.1: Specify the side to position the Dragline. Because this line will be drawn from top to bottom with an interior dimension offset, the dragline will be on the left.

```
Dline, Version 1.11, (c)          Specifies the
1990-1992 by Autodesk, Inc.       Dragline option
Break/Caps/Dragline/Offset/Snap/
Undo/Width/<start point>: D ↵

Set dragline position to Left/    Specifies that the
Center/Right/<Offset from         Dragline will be on
center = 2 1/4">: L ↵             the left
```

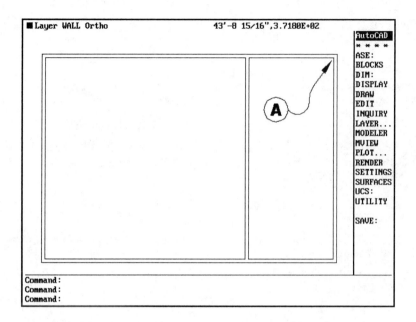

```
AutoCAD
* * * *
ASE:
BLOCKS
DIM:
DISPLAY
DRAW
EDIT
INQUIRY
LAYER...
MODELER
MVIEW
PLOT...
RENDER
SETTINGS
SURFACES
UCS:
UTILITY

SAVE:
```

Command :
Command :
Command :

Figure 9.15:

The first interior wall line.

Step 2.2: Specify the Offset option:

Break/Caps/Dragline/Offset/Snap/   Specifies the Offset
Undo/Width/<start point>: **0** ↵   option

Step 2.3: Pick the point from which the new double line's starting point will be offset. Unlike the OFFSET command, this is a point, not an entity:

Offset from: *Using Object Snap*   Defines the point
INT*ersection pick* Ⓐ *(see previous fig. 9.15)*   from which the
    starting point will
    be offset

Step 2.4: Specify a point that defines the direction from which the starting point will be calculated. Because Ortho is on, you simply pick a point in the direction of the new line:

Offset toward: *Pick a point to the left*   Defines the
of Ⓐ   direction to offset
    the new line

Step 2.5: Define the offset distance as the dimension between the bedroom walls:

Enter the offset distance   Specifies the offset
<7'-9 3/16">: **9'2** ↵   distance and defines
    the starting point
    of the new double
    line

Step 2.6: Define the end point of the double line by using the Object Snap override to pick the opposite wall:

`Arc/Break/CAps/CLose/Dragline/`
`Snap/Undo/Width/<next point>:`
Using Object Snap PERpendicular, pick the
bottom inside wall
	Defines the double
	line end point,
	breaks the
	intersecting line
	segments, and ends
	the DLINE command

Again use the DLINE command and draw the horizontal wall down the middle of the two vertical wall lines to define the two bedrooms.

Step 3.0: Start the DLINE command:

`Command:` *Choose* Draw, *then* Line, *then* Double Line	Starts the DLINE command

Step 3.1: Set the Dragline to be centered. This places the double lines at half the width distance on either side of the Dragline:

`Break/Caps/Dragline/Offset/Snap/` `Undo/Width/<start point>: D`⏎	Specifies the Dragline option

`Set dragline position to Left/`
`Center/Right/<Offset from`
`center = -2 1/4">: C`⏎
	Sets the dragline
	option to Center

Step 3.2: Define the starting and ending points of the wall lines:

`Break/Caps/Dragline/Offset/Snap/` `Undo/Width/<start point>:` *Using* *Object Snap MIDpoint, pick the right line on the* *new interior wall*	Defines the starting point of the line
`Break/Caps/Dragline/Offset/Snap/` `Undo/Width/<start point>:` *Using* *Object Snap MIDpoint, pick the inside line on the* *right exterior wall*	Defines the ending point of the line and ends the DLINE command

DEVELOPING THE CLOSET AND BATHROOM WALLS

You are now ready to develop the interior walls of the closets and bathroom, as seen in figure 9.16. Once again, you will use the DLINE command.

Begin by drawing the wall 10 feet 1 inch across the bottom and 2 feet 6 inches up to the door opening, as seen in figure 9.17.

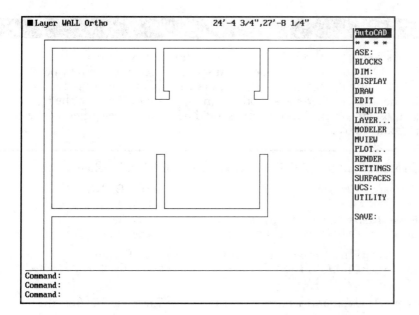

Figure 9.16:
The cottage with closet and bathroom wall added.

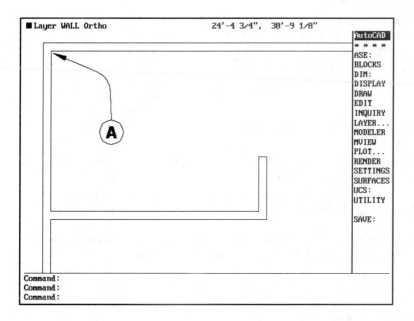

Figure 9.17:
The cottage with one closet wall added.

As you move through this and the following exercise, use the ZOOM command at your own discretion. Because you may be changing the zoom factor of the drawing differently from that of the figures, what you see on screen may vary in size from the figures. However, the geometry should be the same regardless of the zoom factor.

Step 4.0: Start the DLINE command and specify a Left Dragline:

`Command:` *Choose* Draw, *then* Line, *then* Double Line	Starts the DLINE command
`Break/Caps/Dragline/Offset/Snap/` `Undo/Width/<start point>: D ↵`	Specifies the Dragline option

`Set dragline position to Left/`
`Center/Right/<Offset from`
`center = 0">: L ↵`
	Sets the Dragline option at the Left

Step 4.1: Use the Offset option to start the line 7 feet 4 inches from the top inside wall line:

`Break/Caps/Dragline/Offset/Snap/` `Undo/Width/<start point>: O ↵`	Invokes the Offset option
`Offset from:` *Using Object Snap INTersect,* *pick the point at* Ⓐ *(see prior fig. 9.17)*	Defines the point from which to offset
`Offset toward:` *Pick a point below* Ⓐ	Defines the direction to offset the starting point
`Enter the offset distance` `<2'-5 5/16">:7'4 ↵`	Specifies the offset distance

Step 4.2: Enter the end point of the line using polar coordinates. This point is the outside corner of the wall:

`Arc/Break/CAps/CLose/Dragline/`
`Snap/Undo/Width/<next point>:`
`@10'1<0 ↵`
	Defines the end point of the line

Step 4.3: Because the direction of the line changes and the original line goes up the outside line, the dragline needs to be set to Right:

`Arc/Break/CAps/CLose/Dragline/` `Snap/Undo/Width/<next point>: D ↵`	Invokes the Dragline option

`Set dragline position to Left/`
`Center/Right/<Offset from`
`center = -2 1/4">: R ↵`
	Sets the Dragline to Right

Step 4.4: Define the end point of the vertical line at the beginning of the door opening:

```
Arc/Break/CAps/CLose/Dragline/          Defines the double
Snap/Undo/Width/<next point>:           line end point
@2'6<90 ↵
```

Step 4.5: End the DLINE command by pressing Enter. Because the Cap option is set to the default of Auto and the end point does not intersect another line, a line will be placed between the open end points of the two double lines:

```
Arc/Break/CAps/CLose/Dragline/
Snap/Undo/Width/<next point>: ↵
```

Continue with the DLINE command and draw the right vertical wall and door opening as seen in figure 9.18.

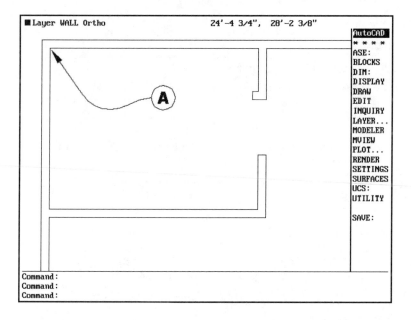

Figure 9.18:
The walls to outline the bathroom.

Step 5.0: Issue the DLINE command and set the dragline to Left:

```
Command: Choose Draw, then Line,          Starts the DLINE command
then Double Line

Break/Caps/Dragline/Offset/               Invokes the Dragline
Snap/UndoWidth/<start point>: D ↵         option

Set dragline position to                  Sets Dragline to left
Left/Center/Right/<Offset
from center = 2 1/4">: L ↵
```

Step 5.1: Use the Offset option to start the line. Use polar coordinates to define the double line end points:

`Break/Caps/Dragline/Offset/Snap/` `Undo/Width/<start point>:` **0** ↵	Invokes the Offset option
`Offset from:` *Using Object Snap INTersect, pick the point at* Ⓐ *(see prior fig. 9.18)*	Defines the point from which to offset
`Offset toward:` *Pick a point to the right of* Ⓐ	Defines the offset direction
`Enter the offset distance` `<2'-8 7/16">:` **10'1** ↵	Defines the offset distance

`Arc/Break/CAps/CLose/Dragline/`
`Snap/Undo/Width/<next point>:`
@2'4<270 ↵
	Defines the first line end point

`Arc/Break/CAps/CLose/Dragline/`
`Snap/Undo/Width/<next point>:`
@7-1/2<180 ↵
	Defines the next line end point

Step 5.2: Exit the DLINE command:

`Arc/Break/CAps/CLose/Dragline/` `Snap/Undo/Width/<next point>:` ↵	Exits the DLINE command and places a cap at the end of the double line

Continue with the DLINE command and add the left side of the closet wall, as seen in figure 9.19.

Step 6.0: Issue the DLINE command by entering it at the command prompt. Set the Dragline to Left. Use the Offset option and polar coordinate to create the double line:

`Command:` **DLINE** ↵	Starts the DLINE command
`Break/Caps/Dragline/Offset/Snap/` `Undo/Width/<start point>:` **D** ↵	Invokes the Dragline option

`Set dragline position to Left/`
`Center/Right/ <Offset from`
`center = -2 1/4">:` **L** ↵
	Sets Dragline to Left

`Break/Caps/Dragline/Offset/Snap/` `Undo/Width/<start point>:` **0** ↵	Invokes the Offset option
`Offset from:` *Using Object Snap INTersect pick the point at* Ⓐ *(see prior fig. 9.19)*	Defines the point to offset from
`Offset toward:` *Pick a point to the left of* Ⓐ	Defines the offset direction
`Enter the offset distance` `<2'-1 1/8">:` **4'6** ↵	Defines the offset distance

`Arc/Break/CAps/CLose/Dragline/`
`Snap/Undo/Width/<next point>:`
@2'4<270 ↵
	Defines the first line end point

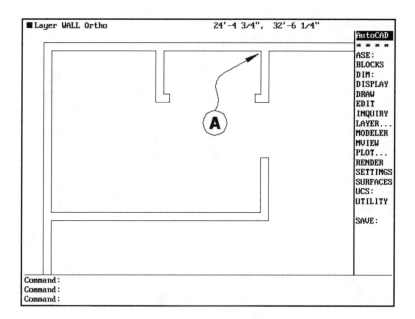

(contents of the AutoCAD drawing screen)

```
■ Layer WALL Ortho                    24'-4 3/4",  32'-6 1/4"
                                                              AutoCAD
                                                              * * * *
                                                              ASE:
                                                              BLOCKS
                                                              DIM:
                                                              DISPLAY
                                                              DRAW
                                                              EDIT
                                                              INQUIRY
                                                              LAYER...
                                                              MODELER
                                                              MVIEW
                                                              PLOT...
                                                              RENDER
                                                              SETTINGS
                                                              SURFACES
                                                              UCS:
                                                              UTILITY

                                                              SAVE:



Command:
Command:
Command:
```

Figure 9.19:

Drawing with one completed closet.

Step 6.1: Change the Dragline setting to Right. Draw the line using polar coordinates and exit the command by pressing Enter:

Arc/Break/CAps/CLose/Dragline/ Snap/Undo/Width/<next point>: **D** ↵	Invokes the Dragline option
Set dragline position to Left/ Center/Right/ <Offset from center = -2 1/4">: **R** ↵	Sets the Dragline to Right
Arc/Break/CAps/CLose/Dragline/ Snap/Undo/Width/<next point>: **@3<0** ↵	Specifies the end point of the line
Arc/Break/CAps/CLose/Dragline/ Snap/Undo/Width/<next point>: ↵	Exit the DLINE command

Complete the interior walls as shown in figure 9.20.

Step 7.0: Issue the DLINE command, set the Dragline to Left, and use the Offset option and polar coordinates to draw the line. Exit the command by pressing Enter:

Command: **DLINE** ↵	Starts the DLINE command
Break/Caps/Dragline/Offset/Snap/ Undo/Width/<start point>: **D** ↵	Invokes the Dragline option
Set dragline position to Left/ Center/Right/<Offset from center = 2 1/4">: **L** ↵	Set the Dragline to Left

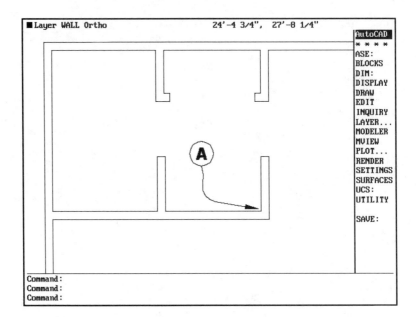

`Break/Caps/Dragline/Offset/Snap/` `Undo/Width/<start point>: O ↵`	Invokes the Offset option
`Offset from:` *Using Object Snap Intersect pick the point at* Ⓐ *(see prior fig. 9.20)*	Specifies the point from which to offset
`Offset toward:` *Pick a point to the left of* Ⓐ	Specifies the offset direction
`Enter the offset distance` `<5'-9">: 4'10 ↵`	Specifies the offset distance

`Arc/Break/CAps/CLose/Dragline/`
`Snap/Undo/Width/<next point>:`
`@2'6<90 ↵`
	Defines the end point of the line

`Arc/Break/CAps/CLose/Dragline/` `Snap/Undo/Width/<next point>: ↵`	Exit the DLINE command

EXERCISE 5: DRAWING A CHIMNEY

You now need to create the chimney seen in figure 9.21. First, draw the lines of the chimney using the DLINE command and polar coordinates. To avoid problems with the DLINE command trimming existing lines, draw the chimney below its final position, away from the wall lines. Use the BHATCH command with a predefined hatch pattern inside the chimney. Once it is complete, use GRIPS to move the chimney in place.

DRAWING THE CHIMNEY GEOMETRY

To create the chimney, use the DLINE command.

Step 1.0: Issue the DLINE command and set the width to 3 1/2 inches:

```
Command: DLINE ⏎                        Starts the DLINE
                                        command

Break/Caps/Dragline/Offset/Snap/        Invokes the Width
Undo/Width/<start point>: W ⏎           option

New DLINE width <4 1/2">: 3-1/2 ⏎       Defines the double
                                        line width
```

Step 1.1: Because the chimney is going to be drawn clockwise from its outside dimensions, set the Dragline to Right:

```
Break/Caps/Dragline/Offset/Snap/        Invokes the Dragline
Undo/Width/<start point>: D ⏎           option

Set dragline position to Left/          Sets the Dragline to
Center/Right/<Offset from               Left
center = -1 3/4">: L ⏎
```

Figure 9.21:

The chimney in its final location.

Step 1.2: Pick a starting point and define the double line end points. End the command using the Close option.

`Break/Caps/Dragline/Offset/Snap/` `Undo/Width/<start point>:` *Pick a point* *below the bathroom walls*	Defines the starting point

`Arc/Break/CAps/CLose/Dragline/`
`Snap/Undo/Width/<next point>:`
`@15<270` ↵
	Defines the first line end point

`Arc/Break/CAps/CLose/Dragline/`
`Snap/Undo/Width/<next point>:`
`@15<180` ↵
	Defines the second line end point

`Arc/Break/CAps/CLose/Dragline/`
`Snap/Undo/Width/<next point>:`
`@15<90` ↵
	Defines the third line end point

`Arc/Break/CAps/CLose/Dragline/` `Snap/Undo/Width/<next point>:` **CL**	Closes the geometry and exits the DLINE command

ADDING A HATCH PATTERN TO THE CHIMNEY

You now are ready to add the hatch pattern to the chimney. The hatch pattern you will use on the chimney defines concrete. As you have learned, AutoCAD comes with several different predefined hatch patterns, from steel to mud material. You can choose any of the predefined patterns, or define your own patterns. To see a list of the pattern names that AutoCAD offers, enter **?** at the first prompt after you issue the HATCH command.

A second method available for viewing the various pattern choices is to use the BHATCH command. This command not only displays all the pattern choices, but also enables you to select the pattern you want visually. Another good source is the back of Autodesk's *AutoCAD User's Guide*, which displays all the hatch patterns.

Step 2.0: Issue the BHATCH command:

`Command:` *Choose* Draw, *then* Hatch	Starts the BHATCH command

Step 2.1: Choose the desired Hatch pattern and define its settings:

Choose Hatch Options	Displays the Hatch Options dialog box
Choose Pattern, *then* next	Displays the predefined hatch patterns and moves to the next icon menu

Choose the pattern AR-CONC	Specifies the hatch pattern
Enter **.5** *in the* Scale *input box*	Reduces the predefined pattern by 1/2
Choose OK	Closes the Hatch Option dialog box
Choose Select Objects	Displays the drawing editor
`Select Objects:` *Select the 8 lines that define the chimney*	Specifies the objects to hatch
`Select Objects:` ↵	Ends the selection process
Choose Apply	Places the hatch pattern in the drawing

To finish the chimney, move the chimney and hatch pattern to the outside corner of the closet using GRIPS.

Step 3.0: Activate the Grips on the chimney and hatch pattern:

`Command:` *Pick two points to place a window around the chimney*	Displays the grip boxes
Pick the grip box at the upper right corner of the chimney	Activates the grip mode

Step 3.1: Change the active grip mode from the default stretch to move:

`** STRETCH **`	Displays the active grip mode
`<Stretch to point>/Base point/ Copy/Undo/eXit:` *From the screen menu, choose* MOve	Activates the move grip mode and displays associated options

Step 3.2: Specify the displacement value by using object snap ENDpoint to pick the point where the active grip should be placed:

`** MOVE **`	
`<Move to point>/Base point/Copy/ Undo/eXit:`	Moves the selected objects to the intersection
Use object snap Intersect *and pick the point at* Ⓐ *in prior figure 9.21*	

Step 3.3: Deactivate Grips by pressing Cancel twice:

`Command:` *Press Ctrl-C twice*	Deactivates Grips

You now are finished with the walls and are ready to add the countertop in the kitchen. Before you create the top, however, you need to see the entire drawing. If you have changed the zoom factor during an exercise, issue the ZOOM command with the All option.

EXERCISE 6: ADDING THE COUNTERTOP TO THE KITCHEN

You now are ready to add the countertop lines, seen on the left side of the drawing in figure 9.22. Offset existing lines A and B (see fig. 9.22) to define these new lines. Although the new lines are too long, leave them as they are for now. You can trim them back once the kitchen appliance symbols are added to the drawing. In addition, when lines are offset, they take the properties of the entity from which they were developed. As you recall, you created a specific layer for the counter at the beginning of this lesson, named COUNTER. Once the lines are developed using Offset, use the CHPROP command to change the layer of the lines to the COUNTER layer.

Figure 9.22:

The open floor plan with countertop lines.

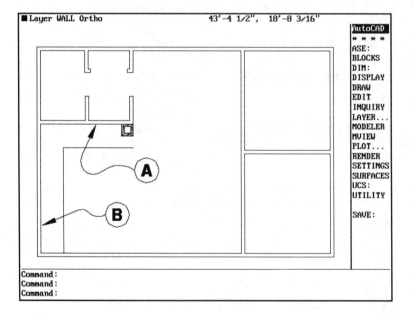

CREATING THE COUNTERTOP

You now can create the lines for the countertop by offsetting the wall lines the width of the countertop, which is 30 inches.

Step 1.0: Issue the **OFFSET** command and set the offset distance to **30**. Select line A (see prior fig. 9.22) and offset it to the right. Next, select line B and offset it down.

In looking at the corners of the counter, you see overlapping lines. These corners need to be cleaned up.

You can use the FILLET command with a radius of 0. This setting trims or extends two nonparallel lines so they meet at a closed corner. Instead of adding an arc between the two lines, FILLET forces the lines to meet at their original angles.

Step 2.0: Issue the FILLET command:

Command: **FILLET** ↵	Starts the FILLET command

Step 2.1: Select the Radius option to set the fillet radius:

Polyline/Radius/<Select first object>: **R** ↵	Selects the Radius option

Step 2.2: Specify a fillet radius of 0:

Enter fillet radius <0'-0">: **0** ↵	Sets the fillet radius value to 0

You now are ready to clean up the corners of the counter using the FILLET command.

Step 3.0: Issue the FILLET command and select the two lines to clean up the corner:

Command: **FILLET** ↵	Starts the FILLET command
Polyline/Radius/<Select first object>: *Pick the new horizontal countertop line*	Selects the first line to place the fillet between
Select second object: *Pick the new vertical countertop line*	Selects the second line to place the fillet between

The FILLET command removes the overlapping lines and cleans up the corner of the counter.

The remaining line segment can be removed after you insert the symbols in the drawing.

CHANGING THE LAYER OF THE COUNTERTOP USING CHPROP

You now need to place the countertop on its own layer using the CHPROP command. As you have learned, the CHPROP (CHange PROPerties) command enables you to modify the properties of an entity—in this case the layer.

Step 4.0: Issue the **CHPROP** command and select both new lines. Press Enter to stop the selection process.

Step 4.1: Select the LAyer option to change the layer of the selected geometry.

Step 4.2: Enter **COUNTER** as the name of the new layer for the geometry. Press Enter to end the command.

EXERCISE 7: INSERT WINDOWS IN THE DRAWING

You now are ready to add the symbols created in the drawing SYM-BOLS. You first need to use OFFSET to define the insertion points for the symbols. Once you have the insertion points, you will insert the entire drawing that includes the architectural symbols (the SYMBOLS drawing). Once you have the architectural symbols inserted, you also will erase the construction lines.

TASKS TO BE COMPLETED IN THIS EXERCISE

- Create construction lines to insert the windows
- Insert a symbol library in the current drawing
- Insert architectural symbols in drawings
- Scale a symbol

You will begin by adding the windows seen in figure 9.23. To find the insertion points for the windows, you need to create construction lines.

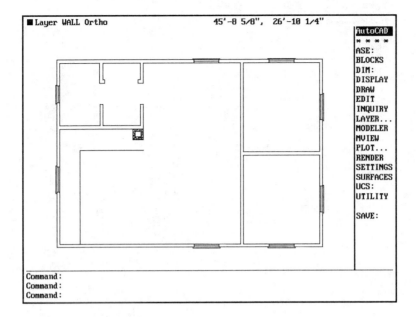

CREATING CONSTRUCTION LINES TO INSERT THE WINDOWS

To insert the window symbols, you first need to define the insertion point for each object. To do this, develop the construction lines (shown in figure 9.24) using the OFFSET command. These lines are used to locate the insertion points of the windows. Then develop the construction line by offsetting the outside left vertical wall and the outside top horizontal wall. If you look at figure 9.1, you will see that the windows are dimensioned from these two lines. By offsetting the walls the same distance as the window dimension, you can use the end point of the new construction lines as insertion points for the windows.

Step 1.0: Issue the **OFFSET** command and set the offset distance to 18'. Select the left outside vertical wall and offset it to the right.

Step 2.0: Reissue the **OFFSET** command and set the offset distance to 27'1. Select the left outside vertical wall and offset it to the right.

Step 3.0: Reissue the **OFFSET** command and set the offset distance to 4'0-1/2. Select the top outside horizontal line and offset it down.

Step 4.0: Reissue the **OFFSET** command and set the offset distance to 5'7-1/8. Select the top outside horizontal line and offset it down.

Figure 9.24:

The cottage with construction lines for windows.

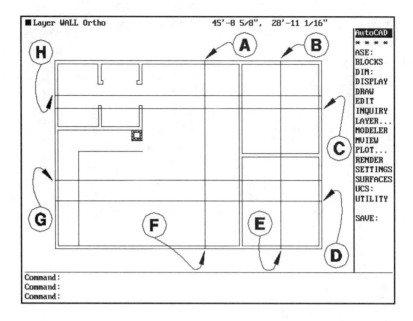

Step 5.0: Reissue the **OFFSET** command and set the offset distance to **14'**. Select the top outside horizontal line and offset it down.

Step 6.0: Reissue the **OFFSET** command and set the offset distance to **16'4-7/8**. Select the top outside horizontal line and offset it down.

INSERTING A SYMBOL LIBRARY IN THE CURRENT DRAWING

You now have your construction lines and are ready to add the symbols. To do this, you first must add the symbol library into the current drawing by inserting the drawing in which the blocks were created. When you first call up the symbol library, you really just want the blocks. You do not want to actually insert the block at a specific insertion point. This means that after you issue the INSERT command and specify the block name you want, simply cancel the command. When you cancel the INSERT command at the `Insertion point:` prompt, you tell AutoCAD to place the block in the current drawing but not in the actual on-screen drawing.

Step 7.0: Issue the INSERT command:

Command: **INSERT** ↵   Starts the INSERT command

Step 7.1: Specify the name of the drawing on disk that has the individual symbols you created for the current drawing, as follows:

```
Block name (or ?): SYMBOLS ↵
```
Calls up the drawing, which stores the architectural symbols for the current drawing

Step 7.2: Cancel the INSERT command. This tells AutoCAD to make the Symbols drawing available to insert in the current drawing:

```
Insertion point: Press Ctrl-C
```
Cancels the INSERT command

You now can insert the individual architectural symbols into the current drawing.

INSERTING ARCHITECTURAL SYMBOLS IN DRAWINGS

You now can insert the individual blocks into the current drawing as required. The first block to insert contains the windows. Because the insertion point of the window is at the middle of the object, you will insert the windows on the end points labeled in the previous figure, figure 9.24. Then rotate the symbol so that it faces in the correct direction, depending on the wall in which it is inserted.

Please note that the following exercises utilize the INSERT command. you may also use the DDINSERT command by selecting the Draw pull-down menu, then selecting Insert.

Step 8.0: Issue the INSERT command and specify the block named WINDOW:

```
Command: INSERT
```
Starts the INSERT command

```
Block name (or ?): WINDOW ↵
```
Specifies the window symbol created as a block in the drawing SYMBOLS

Step 8.1: Invoke the ENDpoint object snap override and pick the insertion point of the window symbol, as follows:

```
Insertion point: Using Object Snap
ENDpoint pick point Ⓐ (see fig. 9.24)
```
Picks the insertion point of the window

Step 8.2: Now scale and rotate the window symbol. For this window, you do not need to scale or rotate the window as it is inserted:

```
X scale factor <1> / Corner /        Accepts the default
XYZ: ↵                                value of an X scale
                                      factor of 1

Y scale factor (default=X): ↵        Accepts the default
                                      value of Y scale to
                                      be equal to X

Rotation angle <0.00>: ↵             Accepts the default
                                      rotation angle and
                                      inserts the window
```

You now can insert the remaining windows.

Step 9.0: Issue the **INSERT** command and specify WINDOW as the block to insert. Invoke the ENDpoint object snap override and pick point B (see prior fig. 9.24) as the insertion point of the window. You do not need to scale or rotate the window.

Step 10.0: Issue the **INSERT** command and specify WINDOW as the block to insert. Invoke the ENDpoint object snap override and pick point C (see prior fig. 9.24) as the insertion point of the window. Accept the scale of the window. At the `Rotation angle <0.00>:` prompt, enter **-90** to rotate the window 90 degrees in a clockwise direction to line up with the wall.

Step 11.0: Issue the **INSERT** command and specify WINDOW as the block to insert. Invoke the ENDpoint object snap override and pick point D (see prior fig. 9.24) as the insertion point of the window. Accept the scale of the window. At the `Rotation angle <0.00>:` prompt, enter **-90** to rotate the window 90 degrees in a clockwise direction to line up with the wall.

Step 12.0: Reissue the **INSERT** command and specify WINDOW as the block to insert. Invoke the ENDpoint object snap override and pick point E (see prior fig. 9.24) as the insertion point of the window. Accept the scale of the window. At the `Rotation angle <0.00>:` prompt, enter **180** to rotate the window 180 degrees.

Step 13.0: Reissue the **INSERT** command and specify WINDOW as the block to insert. Invoke the ENDpoint object snap override and pick point F (see prior fig. 9.24) as the insertion point of the window. Accept the scale of the window. At the `Rotation angle <0.00>:` prompt, enter **180** to rotate the window 180 degrees.

Step 14.0: Issue the **INSERT** command and specify WINDOW as the block to insert. Invoke the ENDpoint object snap override and pick point G (see prior fig. 9.24) as the insertion point of the window. You do not need to scale or rotate the window. Accept the scale of the window. At the `Rotation angle <0.00>:` prompt, enter **90**. This tells AutoCAD to rotate the window 90 degrees in a counterclockwise direction to line up with the wall.

SCALING A SYMBOL

You now need to insert the final window, the one in the bathroom. The bathroom window is a different width from the existing window symbols.

Use the BLOCK command's Scale option to change the width of a symbol during insertion. In this drawing, you need to change the width of the window from 36 inches wide (the X axis) to 24 inches wide. To do this, tell AutoCAD to scale the X width by two-thirds.

Step 15.0: Issue the **INSERT** command and specify the name of the block and the insertion point, using the ENDpoint object snap override:

`Command: INSERT ↵`	Starts the INSERT command
`Block name (or ?) <WINDOW>: ↵`	Accepts the default of WINDOW as the name of the block
`Insertion point:` *Using object snap ENDpoint, pick point* Ⓗ *(see prior fig. 9.24)*	Picks the insertion point of the window

Step 15.1: Scale the window by two-thirds on the X axis, changing the width from 36 inches to 24 inches:

`scale factor <1> / Corner / XYZ: 2/3 ↵`	Scales the window by two-thirds on the X axis

Step 15.2: The Y axis is the same as the wall thickness, which is 4 1/2 inches. Because this value needs to remain the same, specify a scale value of 1 to keep the original value.

`Y scale factor (default=X): 1 ↵`	Keeps the Y factor at 1

Step 15.3: Rotate the window 90 degrees to align it to the wall:

`Rotation angle <0.00>: 90 ↵`	Rotates the symbol 90 degrees

Now that you have inserted the windows, the construction lines are no longer needed.

Step 16.0: Issue the **ERASE** command and remove the six construction lines.

EXERCISE 8: INSERTING DOORS IN THE DRAWING

You now need to insert the doors as shown in figure 9.25. Use the same process to insert the doors as you did the windows. Begin by using Offset to develop construction lines (see fig. 9.26). Once the construction lines are completed, you will insert the doors as an individual geometry that defines the entire symbol. That is, when you create the symbol geometry, such as the door, you draw individual entities, such as lines. When you save the completed symbol as a block, however, AutoCAD considers the individual entities as one. You will need to insert the door as individual entities so that you can use the door as a trimming edge.

Figure 9.25:

The cottage with the doors added.

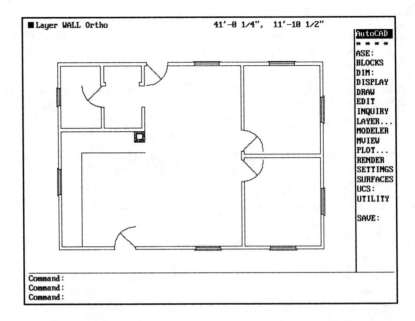

Figure 9.26:

The walls to off-set for the door construction lines.

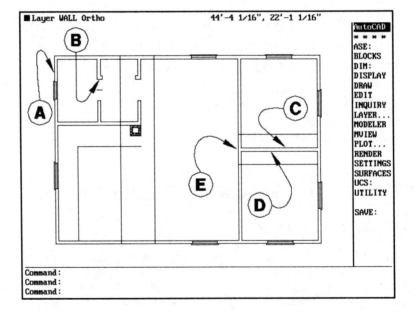

You also will need to change the door swing using the MIRROR command. To finish the doors, trim away the wall lines to the jambs of the doors to create the openings seen in figure 9.25.

TASKS TO BE COMPLETED IN THIS EXERCISE

- Create construction lines for the insertion points
- Insert symbols as individual entities
- Change the swing of a door
- Create the door openings

CREATING CONSTRUCTION LINES FOR THE INSERTION POINTS

To start the exercise, develop the insertion point location for the doors in the living space, such as the front and back doors, and the bedroom doors. Offset the outside vertical line, labeled A in the previous figure, figure 9.26. Begin by developing the construction point for the front and back doors.

Step 1.0: Issue the **OFFSET** command and set the offset distance to **12'**. Select line A (see prior fig. 9.26) and offset it to the right.

Step 2.0: Reissue the **OFFSET** command and set the offset distance to **8'**. Select line A (see prior fig. 9.26) and offset it to the right.

You now are ready to develop the insertion point for the door in the bathroom.

Step 3.0: Reissue the **OFFSET** command and set the offset distance to **1'3**. Select line B (see prior fig. 9.26) and offset it down.

You can finish by adding the construction lines for the doors to the bedroom.

Step 4.0: Reissue the **OFFSET** command and set the offset distance to **1'7**. Select line C and offset it up. Next, select line D and offset it down.

The two new lines need to touch the left interior wall of the bedroom to leave space for properly inserting the doors. Use EXTEND to the left to get to the left side of the left interior wall.

Step 5.0: Issue the **EXTEND** command and select line E (see prior fig. 9.26) as the boundary edge. Press Enter to stop selecting boundary edges. Select both new construction lines near the left end point.

Your drawing should resemble the one shown in figure 9.27, but without the labels.

Figure 9.27:

The floor plan with door insertion points labeled.

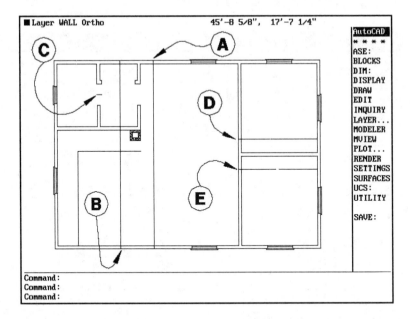

```
■Layer WALL Ortho                45'-8 5/8",  17'-7 1/4"
```

INSERTING SYMBOLS AS INDIVIDUAL ENTITIES

You now are ready to add the door symbols. Because you need to edit the walls that cross over the door's insertion point, use the door as a trimming edge. Although a block cannot be used as a trimming edge, you can insert the block into the drawing as individual entities. This gives access to the lines and arcs that define the door just as if it were not a block. To insert the door in this way, place an asterisk (*) before the block name.

After you have inserted the block in the drawing, use the TRIM command to finalize the door openings. Use the door jambs as cutting edges and remove the unneeded wall line segments.

Begin by placing the door in the living room.

Step 6.0: Issue the INSERT command:

Command: **INSERT** ⏎   Starts the INSERT command

Step 6.1: Specify the block named DOOR as the symbol to insert into the drawing. Precede the name with an asterisk to specify that the symbol needs to be placed in the drawing as the individual lines and arcs that define the door symbol:

```
Block name (or ?) <WINDOW>:        Inserts the block
*DOOR ↵                            DOOR as the
                                   individual entities
                                   that comprise it
```

Step 6.2: Select the insertion point for the door using the ENDpoint object snap override. Because the block name has an asterisk in front of it, it will not be seen in the drawing during insertion.

```
Insertion point: Use object snap    Picks the insertion
ENDpoint and pick end point (A)      point for the door
(see prior fig. 9.27)
```

Step 6.3: Because the block is being inserted with an asterisk, you can scale only the X and Y axes one time in the same aspect ratio. Specify to leave the scale factor at 1.

```
Scale factor <1>: ↵                 Accepts the scale
                                    factor of 1
```

Step 6.4: Accept the rotation angle of 0:

```
Rotation angle <0.00>: ↵            Accepts the rotation
                                    angle of 0
```

The door should now appear in your drawing. Now place the door in the kitchen.

Step 7.0: Issue the **INSERT** command and specify the name ***DOOR** to insert. Invoke the ENDpoint object snap override and pick end point B (see prior fig. 9.27) as the insertion point. Do not scale the door, but rotate it by **180**.

Now insert the door in the bathroom. Because this door opening does not need to be edited as previous ones do, you do not need to insert the symbol with an asterisk. In addition, this door must be moved into place after insertion.

Step 8.0: Reissue the **INSERT** command and specify the block name as **DOOR**. Select point C as the insertion point. Do not scale the door, but rotate it **-90** degrees.

You can now move the door into place.

Step 9.0: Issue the MOVE command and select the last object drawn as the geometry to move. Because the door is a block (without an asterisk before the name), you can select all of it with one selection:

```
Command: MOVE ↵                     Starts the MOVE
                                    command
```

```
Select objects: L ↵              Selects the last
                                 object drawn to edit

Select objects: ↵               Stops the selection
                                 process
```

Step 9.1: Type the displacement to move the door. This will be 4 1/2 inches on the X axis and 0 on the Y axis. Press Enter at the second prompt to enter the value as a displacement.

```
Base point or displacement:      Specifies the
4-1/2,0 ↵                        displacement

Second point of displacement: ↵  Confirms the value,
                                 4-1/2,0 as a
                                 displacement value
```

The next step is to insert the doors in the bedrooms. Begin with the door in the top room (see previous fig. 9.25).

Step 10.0: Issue the **INSERT** command and specify the name as ***DOOR**. Invoke ENDpoint and pick end point D (see prior fig. 9.27) as the insertion point. Do not scale the door, but rotate it by **90** degrees.

You now can insert the door in the bottom bedroom. As with the bathroom, this door needs to be inserted and edited to be positioned correctly in the drawing.

Step 11.0: Issue the **INSERT** command and insert the block ***DOOR**. Invoke ENDpoint and pick end point E (see prior fig. 9.27) as the insertion point. Accept the scale factor of 1 and rotate the symbol **90** degrees.

CHANGING THE SWING OF A DOOR

Notice that the last door you inserted does not swing in the same direction as the one in figure 9.1. To correct this problem, mirror the door across its midpoint and remove the original door.

Step 12.0: Issue the MIRROR command and select the geometry that defines the door:

```
Command: MIRROR ↵               Starts the MIRROR
                                 command

Select objects: Pick the three lines and   Selects the geometry
one arc that define the door                to mirror

Select objects: ↵               Stops the selection
                                 process
```

Step 12.1: Select the two points that define the mirror line. These will be at the middle of the door. You can use the end points of the construction line to locate the middle of the door. Then, using polar coordinates, specify a horizontal second point from the first point for the mirror line:

```
First point of mirror line: Using          Picks the middle of
object snap ENDpoint pick point (E)         the door
(see fig. 9.27)
Second point: @5<0 ↵                        Defines the mirror
                                            line
```

Step 12.2: Because you do not need the original object (the door), tell AutoCAD to delete the old object. This will remove the incorrect swing door and keep the new door with the correct swing:

```
Delete old objects? <N> Y ↵                 Creates a new
                                            mirrored object and
                                            removes the old
```

Now that you are finished inserting doors, the construction lines can be removed.

Step 13.0: Issue the **ERASE** command and select the five construction lines.

CREATING THE DOOR OPENINGS

The next step is to remove the wall lines that pass through the door, as seen in figure 9.28. Do this by using the TRIM command. Because the doors were inserted with an asterisk preceding the name, you can easily trim away the wall line using the short 4 1/2-inch door jambs as the cutting edge.

Step 14.0: Issue the **TRIM** command. Select all of the 4 1/2-inch jambs, located at the end of the doors, as the cutting edges. Press Enter to stop the selection of cutting edges. Then select the wall lines that pass through the middle of the door, between the door jambs.

Your drawing now should resemble the one shown in figure 9.28.

EXERCISE 9: COMPLETING THE DRAWING

You now are ready to complete the cottage shown in figure 9.29. To finish the interior of the cottage, use the INSERT command to place the TUB, TOILET, LAV, SINK, FRIDGE, and STOVE symbols in the drawing. Once the geometry is added, you can clean up the countertop using the LINE and TRIM commands.

Figure 9.28:

The drawing with the wall lines at the doors removed.

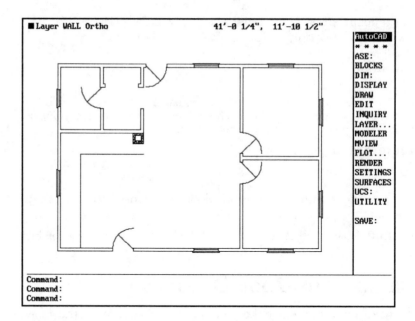

Figure 9.29:

The finished cottage, with the symbols inserted and countertop completed.

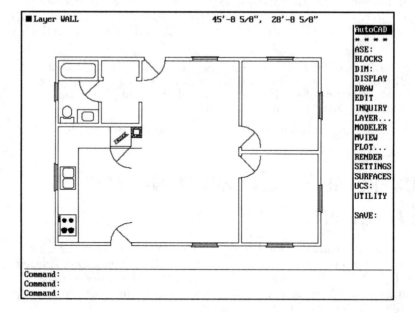

INSERTING THE ARCHITECTURAL SYMBOLS IN THE DRAWING

Step 1.0: Insert the six blocks named TUB, TOILET, LAV, SINK, FRIDGE, and STOVE into the drawing. Because you are not editing the geometry, do not precede the block names with an asterisk. Watch the symbol on-screen to determine the insertion point. Remember that a block can be rotated after the insertion point is selected. (Perform this part of the lesson on your own.) If you make a mistake, you can erase the block or use the U command and repeat the insertion. Use figure 9.1 as a guide for placing each symbol.

FINISHING THE COUNTERTOP

Once you have inserted the blocks, the countertops need to be finished. Begin by placing the short lines that extend from the appliances to the existing countertop line, labeled in figure 9.30.

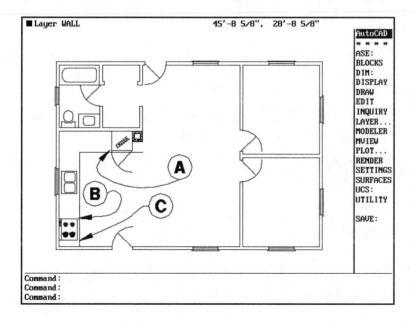

Figure 9.30:
The points labeled for lines to finish the countertop.

First, change to the counter layer.

Step 1.0: Make COUNTER the current layer.

You now can draw the lines needed to finish the countertop.

Step 2.0: Issue the **LINE** command and invoke the ENDpoint object snap override. Pick point A (see previous fig. 9.30) as the end point of the line. Draw the new line perpendicular to the horizontal counter line.

Step 3.0: Reissue the **LINE** command and draw a line from end point B (see previous fig. 9.30), perpendicular to the vertical counter line.

Step 4.0: Reissue the **LINE** command and draw a line from end point C (see previous fig. 9.30), perpendicular to the vertical counter line.

Now finish the countertop by trimming away the unneeded line segments.

Step 5.0: Issue the **TRIM** command and select the three new short lines. Press Enter to stop selecting cutting edges. Select the horizontal countertop line, located to the right of the refrigerator's line, and the vertical countertop line, located between the two short horizontal lines at the stove's end.

DRAWING THE CLOSET DOORS

A few finishing touches are still needed to the drawing's interior. The first of these is the closet doors, shown added in figure 9.31. The LINE command is used to draw these doors. Before drawing the doors, you must be on the correct layer when you create symbols. You did not need to change the layers. Inserted blocks remain on the layer on which they were created.

Step 6.0: Make the layer SYMBOLS current.

The LINE command is used to add the doors to the closet. The starting points for the doors are labeled in figure 9.32.

Step 7.0: Issue the **LINE** command and invoke ENDpoint. Pick point A (see fig. 9.32) as the end point of the first line. To draw the line, type **@12<330;** **@12<30** and press Enter to end the command.

Step 8.0: Reissue the **LINE** command and invoke ENDpoint again. Pick point B (see fig. 9.32) as the starting point of the second line. To draw the line, type **@12<210** and **12<150**. Press Enter to end the command.

Step 9.0: Reissue the **LINE** command and invoke ENDpoint. Pick point C (see fig. 9.32) as the starting point of the third line. Type **@13<30** and **@13<-30** for the ending points of this line. End the command by pressing Enter.

Step 10.0: Reissue the **LINE** command and invoke ENDpoint. Pick point D as the starting point of the last line. For the two end points, type **@13<150** and **@13<210**. Press Enter to end the **LINE** command.

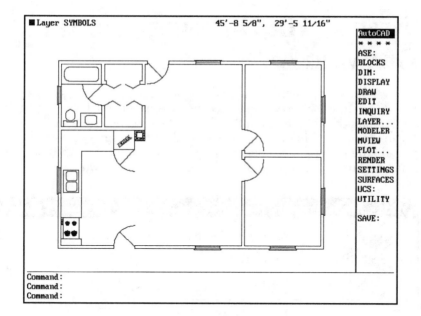

Figure 9.31
The completed drawing with closet doors.

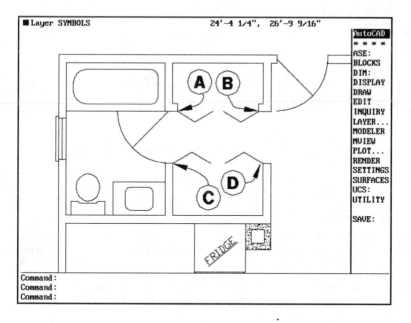

Figure 9.32:
Starting points for the closet doors.

EXERCISE 10: DIMENSIONING THE DRAWING

You now are ready to finish the drawing by adding the dimensions and text that define each room. First, set the dimension variables to architectural standards. To dimension the doors, add a construction line between the jambs. Then, using the standard dimensioning commands, you add the linear dimensions. To finish the drawing, erase the construction lines in the doors and add six-inch text as shown.

TASKS TO BE COMPLETED IN THIS EXERCISE

- Set the dimensioning variables in an architectural drawing
- Scale dimension variables
- Dimension the drawing

To begin, select correct layer.

Step 1.0: Make the DIM layer the current layer.

SETTING THE DIMENSIONING VARIABLES IN AN ARCHITECTURAL DRAWING

You now are ready to dimension the drawing. Because there are some special dimension variables, first set the dimensions for architectural drawings. As illustrated in figure 9.33, the end of lines have ticks rather than arrowheads. In addition, the dimension text is placed above the line and always is aligned to the dimension line, not the horizontal.

Use dimension variables to set the remaining values.

Step 2.0: Enter **DIM** to enter the dimension area. Issue **DIMTAD** and specify to place text above the dimension line, instead of breaking the dimension line as in past lessons.

Step 3.0: Give the dimension variable DIMTSZ a value other than 0. This places ticks, rather than arrowheads, at the end of the dimension lines. The value specified is also the size of the tick.

Step 4.0: Turn off the dimension variable DIMTIH. When on, DIMTIH forces all dimension text that falls inside of the extension line to be horizontal. This allows the text to align itself parallel to the dimension line.

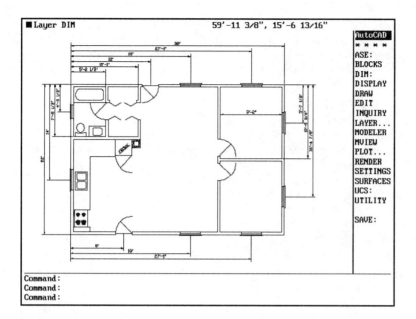

Figure 9.33:

The completed cottage with dimensions.

Step 5.0: Set DIMTOH to off. When on, dimension text that falls outside of the extension lines is always horizontal. When off, the dimension text aligns itself parallel to the dimension line.

SCALING DIMENSION VARIABLES

In this and all past lessons, the dimension variables such as DIMTXT and DIMTSZ are set to the value needed when plotted. Drawings in AutoCAD are drawn at full scale and the DIMVAR values are given at full scale. As a result, these sizes only work in a drawing that is plotted at full scale. If a drawing is going to be plotted at something other than full scale, such as a large architectural drawing, then the dimension variables must be altered in the drawing to appear at the correct size on the plotted paper. The dimension variable that controls this size is DIMSCALE.

DIMSCALE changes the size of all dimension variables by a scale factor. This scale factor is inversely proportional to the plot factor. A drawing that will be plotted at half scale, for example, will be reduced to half its size on paper; a DIMTXT set at .125 would be plotted at .0625. Because of this discrepancy, you need to increase the size of all dimension variables by a factor of two. As set now, the DIMTXT is .250 on the drawing and .125 (the desired value) on the plot. Because it is tedious and time consuming to set each value independently, the DIMSCALE command changes all of the values at once. For a drawing to be plotted at half scale, the DIMSCALE needs to be set to 2. It then adjusts all of the variables in the drawing so that they are correct on the plot.

The rule for determining the value for DIMSCALE is to set it to the plot scale. This value is determined by multiplying the plotting scale. In the preceding example, a drawing plotted at half scale has a plot scale of .5=1. By multiplying these two values together you get an answer of 2. This drawing would be plotted at a standard architectural scale of 1/2"=1'. To convert both sides to inches, you use 2/1=12. By multiplying these two values, you get a result of 24. For this drawing then, the DIMSCALE should be set to 24. This will increase all dimension variable values by 24 in the drawing. When plotted at 1/2"=1', the dimension variables will all be reduced by 24, giving the desired dimension text, ticks, and so forth on the paper.

Step 6.0: Set the DIMSCALE for a drawing to be plotted at 1/2"=1' by typing 24 at the `Current value <1.0000> New value:` prompt.

DIMENSIONING THE DRAWING

After defining the dimension variables, you are ready to add dimensions to complete the drawing as seen in figure 9.33. If you look at the dimension to the doors, you will see that the extension line comes off the center of the door opening. Because there is no geometry at this location, you need to add construction lines between the 4 1/2-inch door jambs for dimensioning. You then can use the midpoint of the construction line as the extension line location.

Step 7.0: Exit DIM mode and issue the **LINE** command and draw two horizontal construction lines between the midpoints of the exterior door jambs.

Step 8.0: Return to DIM mode to continue dimensioning. Using Horizontal, Vertical, and Baseline dimensioning subcommands, add the dimensions to the outside of the drawing. Remember to always use object snaps when making extension line location selections. When dimensioning to the windows, use the INSertion option from the Assist pull-down menu. You also can use the cursor menu (shift-button 2). When you dimension the doors, use the MIDpoint option of the construction lines.

Step 9.0: Once the dimensioning is complete, use **ERASE** to remove the two construction lines.

You now are ready to add the dimensions to the interior of the bedroom. Because the dimensions will begin and end at interior wall lines, you do not need extension lines. The dimension variables DIMSE1 and DIMSE2 suppress the first and second extension lines respectively.

Step 10.0: Set DIMSE1=ON and DIMSE2=ON.

Step 11.0: Issue the Horizontal linear dimension subcommand and place the dimension inside BEDROOM 1. Remember to use an object snap to select exact points.

You now are finished with dimensioning.

Step 12.0: Exit the Dimension area by pressing Ctrl-C.

Step 13.0: Finish the drawing by placing the text in each of the rooms, as shown in figure 9.33. Give the text a height of 6 inches. For the kitchen, rotate the text 90 degrees.

When finished, you can exit AutoCAD.

Step 14.0: Save the drawing to disk and end the current drawing session.

SUMMARY

Development of full-scale drawings also applies to architectural drawings. The UNITS and LIMITS commands helps to define architectural drawing areas. In the development of any drawing, the utilization of a drawing library—with all the symbols stored in one drawing—assists in file maintenance and storage. Once a drawing is completed, detail must be added. Predefined hatch patterns and dimension variables aid in creating an industry-acceptable architectural drawing.

IN THIS LESSON, YOU LEARNED TO DO THE FOLLOWING:

- Develop a symbol library
- Draw a perimeter wall
- Create interior walls
- Draw a chimney
- Add a countertop to the kitchen
- Insert windows in the drawing
- Insert doors in the drawing
- Dimension the drawing

In all of the lessons to this point, you have created two dimensional drawings. The next lesson creates a table that is three dimensional. When using 3D, a drawing can be viewed from any angle. In the first 3D lesson, you will create a wire frame model. A *wire frame* represents the object by the lines at the edges of a geometry contour.

REVIEW

1. From *The AutoCAD Tutor Disk*, retrieve the drawing named REV10-1. Set the units to architectural.

2. Use the preceding drawing and give the uncompleted walls a 4-inch width.

3. Use the preceding drawing and hatch the remaining part of the fireplace. Use the LIST command to determine what the existing pattern is.

4. End the REV10-1 drawing and retrieve SYMBOLS from the *AutoCAD Tutor Disk*. In this drawing, add a furnace and a hot water heater to the library. Draw the furnace so that it is a 37"$tsx29"rectangle that says FURN inside of it. The hot water heater is a 24-inch diameter circle that says HW inside of it.

5. Retrieve REV10-1 from *The AutoCAD Tutor Disk* and insert the architectural library named SYMBOLS.

6. Add doors and windows to the SYMBOLS drawing. Place them anywhere you feel is appropriate.

7. Insert the remaining symbols into the SYMBOLS drawing, including the furnace and hot water heater.

8. Set the dimension variables for an architectural drawing in the SYMBOLS drawing.

9. Dimension the SYMBOLS drawing.

10. Determine the total floor space of the house minus the bathroom using the AREA command.

CREATING A 3D WIREFRAME DRAWING

OVERVIEW

The development and use of three-dimensional drawings is becoming the standard drafting method of the nineties, with Computer Aided Design (CAD) programs leading the way. The preceding lessons gave typical examples of 2D drawings, of which many CAD drawings are today. Yet as CAD becomes more integrated in the workplace, the use of 3D drawings becomes essential. This blend of current technology with traditional knowledge results in projects that vary from a 3D drawing's development of tool paths for building a metal stamping die to creating 3D animation.

Three general categories exist in 3D applications. These include a wireframe model, a surface model, and a solid model. Each category has its own application and variations in complexity, and is introduced in this and the next two lessons. In this lesson, you develop a 3D wireframe.

A dimensional wireframe model shows a 3D object by representing the geometry that defines the edges of its features. In developing this type of drawing, the same tools are used as when creating a two-dimensional drawing. The difference is that you add a third axis—the Z axis. The Z *axis* is perpendicular to the X-Y axis. In AutoCAD, this axis comes out of the screen towards the user.

Although many of the tools used for creating a 3D wireframe are familiar to you, the real key to learning how to draw in 3D comes in understanding how to change the viewpoint and the drawing plane. For many people, particularly those with extensive experience in basic drafting, changing the viewpoint and visualizing in 3D can be difficult.

AutoCAD's 3D drawing environment has a direct relationship to the standard 2D drawing plane. When a new drawing is created, the 2D screen is the top or *plan* view. From here, the right side of the screen is the right side of the drawing, the top of the screen is the back of the drawing, the left side of the screen is the left side of the drawing, and the bottom of the screen is the front of the drawing. By taking the time to begin your drawing correctly within this environment, you can use the VPOINT command to see the desired view of the drawing.

In order to view the drawing in 3D, you must develop the geometry in 3D. Because many drawing tools need a reference drawing plane, such as a circle, fillet, or polyline, AutoCAD provides a command to reposition the coordinate system. The User Coordinate System (UCS) allows the user to change the drawing plane in several flexible ways. By repositioning the X-Y plane, you can easily place traditional 2D geometry in a 3D drawing.

TOPICS COVERED IN THIS LESSON

In this lesson, you learn to do the following:

- Use the Z coordinate
- Create a 3D wireframe geometry
- Change the viewpoint of a drawing
- Reposition the User Coordinate System
- Dimension in 3D

This lesson teaches you how to use the following AutoCAD commands:

- VPOINT
- UCS
- PLAN
- EXPLODE

As with previous chapters, this lesson assumes that you are becoming more proficient as an AutoCAD user. Because of this assumption, areas in the lesson that require zooming are left up to your discretion. Use the ZOOM command any time you feel it is to your advantage. In addition, not all of the details on selecting entities during edit commands are included. Some of the commands that are common to you now, like LAYER and DIMension, do not have explanations. In addition, remember to use object snaps when end points, midpoints, centers, or any exact location of an entity is specified.

SETTING UP A 3D DRAWING

Step 1.0: Start AutoCAD; save the new drawing as **LESSON10**.

In this lesson, you develop the drawing shown in figure 10.1. As you can see, this is a fully dimensioned 3D drawing.

Beginning a 3D drawing is very similar to beginning a 2D drawing. You use the same commands and procedures but applying them to three axes. The units in the drawing are determined just as they were in 2D. Layers are applied in 3D the same as 2D. Limits are a bit different, though. While you don't need to define limits at all for 3D, it can be helpful if you define limits that are large enough for the first geometry you draw. By doing this, the geometry displays on-screen as you create it. Once you begin to change the viewpoint of the drawing, limits become less important.

Step 2.0: Use the **UNITS** command or Units Control dialog box to set up the drawing with fractional units. The precision is **1/16**. Leave all the remaining settings at their default.

Step 3.0: Now define the limits for the drawing. Because you begin by drawing the top of the object, you need limits large enough for this geometry. Issue the **LIMITS** command. Set the lower left corner at **0,0** and the upper right at **48,36**.

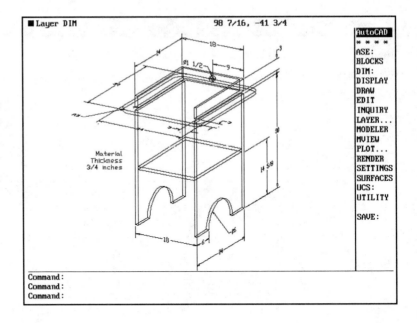

Step 4.0: Issue the **ZOOM** command with the All option to see the entire drawing to the new limits.

Step 5.0: Use the **LAYER** command or the Layer Control dialog box to create the layers OBJECT and DIM. Make the layer OBJECT the current drawing layer.

EXERCISE 1: CREATING THE TABLE TOP IN 3D

You begin this drawing by creating the 3D table top seen in figure 10.2. When developing a 3D drawing, you commonly start from one side (usually the top) and create the two-dimensional geometry. Begin by creating a standard 2D polyline with fillets. Once the 2D outline is completed, copy the object into the Z axis, which creates thickness. Again, a wireframe model displays the 3D geometry by representing the object's significant edges. In this lesson's example—the table top—the object is represented by the contour that defines the top and bottom of the table's edge.

Because this is a 3D wireframe, the entire drawing is created in this manner. As you will see in lesson 12, when using solid modeling it is possible to develop 3D geometry in one operation.

Once the table top is complete, change the screen's view in the next exercise. This gives you the isometric view that is shown in figure 10.2. An *isometric view* is a 2D representation of a 3D drawing. This view assists in visualizing the actual product.

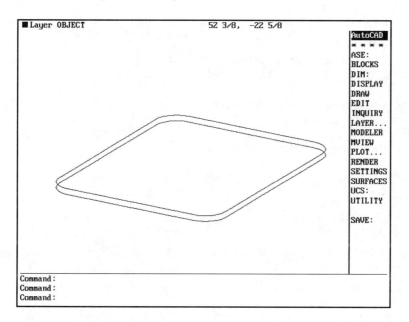

Figure 10.2:
The 3D drawing of the table top, shown in an isometric view.

Now draw the top contour of the table using the polyline (PLINE) command. In a new drawing, you are always looking straight down at an object from above. Because you are currently looking down at the top from the drawing viewpoint, draw the 24 x 30 top outline in the same way as you would in 2D.

Step 1.0: Issue the PLINE command; start the polyline at the absolute coordinate 4,4:

Command: **PLINE** ↵   Starts the
                                        PLINE command

```
From point: 4,4 ↵
```
Starts the polyline at theabsolute coordinate of 4,4

Step 1.1: Use a combination of relative and polar coordinates to create the outline:

```
Current line-width is 0
Arc/Close/Halfwidth/Length/Undo/
Width/<End point of line>: @24,0 ↵
```
Draws a polyline 24 units to the right

```
Arc/Close/Halfwidth/Length/Undo/
Width/<End point of line>:
@30<90 ↵
```
Draws a polyline 30 units straight up

```
Arc/Close/Halfwidth/Length/Undo/
Width/<End point of line>:
@24<180 ↵
```
Draws a polyline 24 units to the left

Step 1.2: Complete the polyline using the Close option:

```
Arc/Close/Halfwidth/Length/Undo/
Width/<End point of line>: C ↵
```
Closes the polyline

Step 2.0: As you saw from the isometric view in figure 10.2, the top of the table has a radius. Use the FILLET command to add the fillet to the corners. You must begin by setting the fillet radius:

```
Command: FILLET ↵
```
Starts the FILLET command

```
Polyline/Radius/
<Select first object>: R ↵
```
Enables input of the fillet radius

```
Enter fillet radius <0>: 3 ↵
```
Defines the radius as 3 units

Step 3.0: You can now place the fillet on the polyline. The FILLET command has a special option for polylines that enables you to place the same radius on all corners in one operation. Begin by invoking the FILLET command:

```
Command: FILLET ↵
```
Starts the FILLET command

Step 3.1: Enter a P to invoke the Polyline option. Once you select the polyline, the defined radius is placed on all corners:

```
Polyline/Radius/
<Select first object>: P ↵
```
Invokes the Polyline option

```
Select 2D polyline: Select the polyline
```
Places a fillet on all four corners

CONVERTING A 2D OBJECT TO 3D

You now are ready to add depth to the drawing's polyline. Use the COPY command to perform this function. The COPY command places an existing entity or entities at a specified distance from the original. To use COPY, you first must select the geometry you want to copy. Then specify the displacement of the object to be copied or a base point and a displacement. The *basepoint* is the point from which the displacement is calculated or measured. The *displacement value* is the amount the object is to be copied on the X, Y, and Z axes. This enables you to place the duplicated object at any point on the drawing.

To add thickness, copy the object into the Z axis. As a coordinate system for 3D drawing, AutoCAD has the standard X axis, which is positive to the right of 0,0,0, and the Y axis, which is positive above 0,0,0. In addition, there is the Z axis, which is perpendicular to the plane defined by these two axes. In this plan view, the positive Z axis comes out of the screen toward you.

To keep track of the relationship between these three axes, use the right-hand rule. Make a fist with your right hand. Stick your thumb out. Your thumb represents positive X. Keeping your thumb out, stick your pointer finger out. Your pointer finger represents positive Y. Now, bring the remaining fingers out so they are pointing away from the finger and thumb. These fingers represent positive Z.

By aligning your thumb and finger with the respective X and Y on the UCS icon in the screen's lower right corner, you are able to calculate the direction of Z. In the default World UCS, this is with your palm facing you.

You now need to copy the polyline 3/4 units into Z. During the specification of displacement, you enter a Z axis as you have an X or a Y. The syntax is X,Y,Z. Coordinate input using the Z axis allows absolute and relative input. (Polar coordinates are only 2D.) There are additional 3D coordinate inputs that combine these options. If you are interested in these, refer to the *AutoCAD Reference Manual*.

Step 4.0: Issue the COPY command and select the object to copy. Because a polyline is a single entity, picking it anywhere selects the entire line:

Command: **COPY**	Starts the COPY command
Select objects: *Pick the polyline*	Selects the object to copy
Select objects: ↵	Stops the selection process

Step 4.1: Enter a displacement value of 0 to copy the polyline on the X and Y, and 3/4 units in the positive Z:

```
<Base point or displacement>/
Multiple: 0,0,3/4 ↵
```
Specifies a displacement of no movement on the X, none on the Y, and 3/4 units in the positive Z direction

Step 4.2: Confirm that the 0,0,3/4 is a displacement and not a base point coordinate:

```
Second point of displacement: ↵
```
Confirms the value as a displacement

Your drawing should not look any different than it did. Because you are looking straight down at the top, you are also looking straight down on the Z axis. Because the object was copied into the Z-axis only, it moved away from you but stayed aligned with the existing geometry, thus making it impossible to see a change from this view.

EXERCISE 2: CHANGING VIEWPOINTS IN 3D

You now need to change the viewpoint of the drawing so it appears isometric. In developing three-dimensional drawings, most of the work you do is performed from some type of isometric view. In an isometric view it is easier to conceptualize what is being drawn and which line is in front of another.

For this exercise, change the viewpoint of the drawing and create the geometry that defines the outside of the leg as seen in figure 10.3. These lines act as object and construction lines for the leg.

To change the viewpoint of a 3D drawing, use the VPOINT command. The VPOINT command changes the user's visual orientation to the object. To understand the VPOINT command, imagine a box hanging from a string in the middle of the room. Changing the viewpoint is like moving around the box, looking at it from any side, above, or below. The view you would see from any one point is the viewpoint. The VPOINT command has three options.

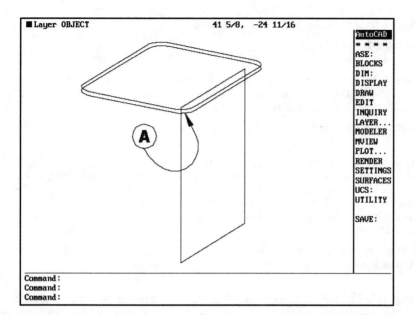

Figure 10.3:
The isometric view with construction lines for the leg.

The VPOINT command has the following options:

- **<viewpoint>(0,0,1).** This coordinate specification option is the default. The viewpoint is defined by specifying the end point of a line that points at 0,0,0. The view is determined by looking down the line at 0,0,0.

- **Rotate.** Defines a viewpoint rotated first around the X-Y plane and then from the X-Y plane. In this plan view, to symbolize rotation around the X-Y plane, use your finger to make a circle parallel to the screen. A circle that rotates from the X-Y plane is perpendicular to the last one.

- **Enter.** Pressing Enter gives you a dynamic world and axis to define the viewpoint by moving the input device and picking a point to specify the viewpoint.

Use the VPOINT command to develop an isometric view. Define a view that displays the object from the front-right side looking at the object from above.

Step 1.0: Invoke the **VPOINT** command:

```
Command: VPOINT ↵
```
Starts the
VPOINT command

Step 1.1: Invoke the Rotate option. This option works in two planes: one that is parallel to the screen, and a second that is perpendicular to the first. Specify angles that rotate around the object in the first, then second plane:

```
Rotate/<Viewpoint> <0,0,1>: R ↵
```
Selects the
rotate option

Step 1.2: In using the rotation object, because you are looking down at the object, the right side of the screen in the right side of the object, the top is the back, the left is the left, and the bottom is the front. To see a front, right side, specify the first angle at 300. Looking at the current plan view, this angle would be the same as if you where drawing a line at 300 degrees using polar coordinates:

```
Enter angle in XY plane from
X axis <270>: 300 ↵
```
Defines the
angle in the
first plane

Step 1.3: The second plane's rotation defines how much the viewpoint is above or below in relation to the last prompt's selected side. An angle of 0 enables you to look straight in at the selected side; with an angle of 90 you are at the top looking down, while a -90 angle enables you to look up from the bottom. Specify a value that places the viewpoint slightly above the object:

```
Enter angle from XY plane
<90>: 20 ↵
```
Displays the
new viewpoint

Notice how the UCS icon also changes. This AutoCAD tool continually changes to remain parallel with X and Y and points in their positive direction.

DRAWING IN THE Z AXIS

Now add the four lines (shown in figure 10.3) that define the outside of one leg. You can draw the four lines using relative and polar coordinates. The use of relative coordinates in 3D only requires adding the X coordinate during input. The polar coordinate across the bottom aligns itself to the 2D drawing plane.

Step 2.0: Start the LINE command:

```
Command: LINE ↵
```
Starts the
LINE command

Step 2.1: Pick the starting point of the line. Because the fillet is 3 units and the legs are 3 units from the edge, this is an easy way to locate the starting point of the line. By using object snap end point, you can locate the starting point of the leg:

`From point:` *Using object snap Center,*   Defines the
pick arc (A) in figure 10.3   starting point
                                             of the line

Step 2.2: To begin the leg, draw a line across the bottom of the table top. Notice the UCS icon: the Y arrow points in the direction of the leg's top. Because the line is parallel to the UCS icon, you do not need a Z coordinate:

`To point: @0,24 ⏎`   Draws a 24-unit
                                             line in the
                                             positive Y
                                             direction

Step 2.3: The line now needs to be drawn down, away from the top in the Z direction. By using the right-hand rule and aligning your thumb with X and pointer finger with Y, you can see that your remaining fingers point up away from the top. Because the table leg goes down, the Z value is a negative number equal to the length of the leg. Because of the zoom factor, the line may go off the screen. After completing the object, you can invoke the ZOOM command to see the entire object:

`To point: @0,0,-30 ⏎`   Draws a line 30
                                             units in the
                                             negative Z
                                             direction

Step 2.4: The bottom of the leg is 24 units in the negative Y direction. Because the end points of the line do not project into the Z axis and the UCS is aligned to the side, you can use a polar direction of 270. Remember, in 3D, polar coordinates remain on the X-Y plane:

`To point: @24<270 ⏎`   Draws a line on
                                             the X-Y plane
                                             24 units long
                                             and straight
                                             down

Step 2.5: Three lines of the leg have been drawn. Just as in 2D, you can complete the polygon using the Close option:

`To point: C ⏎`   Closes the
                                             polygon

Step 3.0: To see the entire drawing, issue the **ZOOM** command with the Extent option. Your finished drawing should look like the illustration shown in the previous figure.

EXERCISE 3: CHANGING THE DRAWING PLANE

In this exercise, you add an arc to the side of the leg. To draw the arc, you must change the UCS or 2D drawing plane. Once the arc is developed, give the leg thickness and connect the end points, as seen in figure 10.4.

Figure 10.4:

Table with one finished leg.

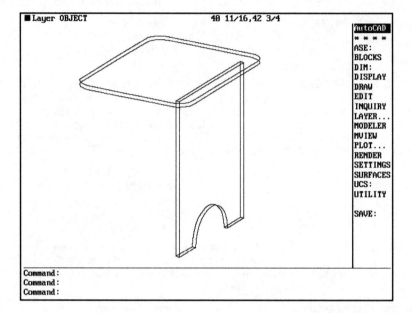

In the previous exercise, you were able to draw a line with specified points into the Z axis, regardless of the orientation of X-Y. The orientation of the X-Y (or 2D) plane is very important to drawing in 3D. Besides polar coordinates, much of the geometry developed is controlled by the X-Y plane. Common commands affected by this plane are ARC, CIRCLE, PLINE, FILLET, and all dimensions. For circular objects, the entity is aligned, or lies flat, on the drawing plane. Because of this relationship, you can define the X-Y plane to be in any desired direction.

The drawing plane is displayed by the UCS icon, and is controlled by the UCS command. The UCS command defines the X-Y or 2D drawing plane for the development and modification of geometry. This command has several options to assist in this function.

OPTIONS

The UCS command has the following options:

- **Origin.** Redefines the location of 0,0,0
- **ZAxis.** Defines the X-Y place by specifying the direction of the Z axis
- **3point.** Defines the UCS base by specifying three points on the X-Y plane
- **Entity.** Aligns the UCS parallel to an existing entity
- **View.** Aligns the UCS parallel to the screen
- **X.** Rotates the current UCS around the X axis
- **Y.** Rotates the current UCS around the Y axis
- **Z.** Rotates the current UCS around the Z axis
- **Prev.** Returns to the previous UCS setting
- **Restore.** Restores a previously saved UCS setting
- **Save.** Saves a UCS setting by name
- **Del.** Deletes a saved UCS setting
- **?.** Lists all saved UCS settings
- **<World>.** Aligns the UCS to the World Coordinate System or original drawing plan view

Because the arc lies on the side of the leg, you first need to change the drawing plane. The most common option is 3point. This option enables you to pick three points on the new plane. You may know from geometry that any plane can be defined by identifying three points on the plane. Because the leg is partially created, you can easily pick three end points to define the new plane.

These points are shown in figure 10.5 with the UCS icon re-aligned.

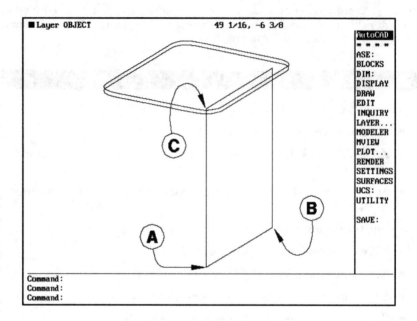

Step 1.0: Invoke the UCS command and select the 3point option:

Command: **UCS** ↵	Starts the UCS command
Origin/ZAxis/3point/Entity/View/ X/Y/Z/ Prev/Restore/Save/Del/?/ <World>: **3** ↵	Enables the selection of three points to define a new UCS setting

Step 1.1: You now need to pick the first point on the new drawing plane. This not only is a point on the plane, but also is the new 0,0,0 or origin. In 2D, this is usually in the lower left corner of the screen. You benefit by placing it in the lower left corner of the object in 3D as well:

`Origin point <0,0,0>:` *Using object snap Endpoint, pick point* Ⓐ *in figure 10.5*

Defines one point on the plane and the new origin, or 0,0,0

Step 1.2: Pick the second point on the plane. This point defines the new positive X, and aligns itself between the point picked and the new origin. Again, because positive X is to the right of 0,0 in 2D, pick a point on the geometry to the right of the new origin:

`Point on positive portion of the X-axis <26,7,-30>:` *Using object snap Endpoint, pick point* Ⓑ *in figure 10.5*

Defines the second point on the plane and defines the direction of the positive X axis

Step 1.3: The final point on the plane also defines the positive Y axis. To remain consistent with 2D, pick a point above the new positive X axis:

`Point on positive-Y portion of the UCS XY plane <24,7,-30>:` *Using object snap Endpoint, pick point* Ⓒ *in figure 10.5*

Defines the third point on the plane and the direction of positive Y

The UCS icon changes to represent to the new orientation of the X-Y drawing plane.

COMPLETING THE TABLE LEG

You are now ready to complete the table leg as seen in figure 10.6. Develop the arc by placing a circle on the bottom line and trimming away the unneeded portions. Once this is completed, copy the object to give it thickness, and connect the corners with lines.

Begin by placing a circle on the line's midpoint that forms the bottom of the table leg.

Step 2.0: Issue the CIRCLE command and position the center of the circle at the bottom line's midpoint. Enter a radius of 6 units to complete the command:

`Command: CIRCLE ⏎`

Starts the CIRCLE command

Figure 10.6:

Drawing with one finished leg.

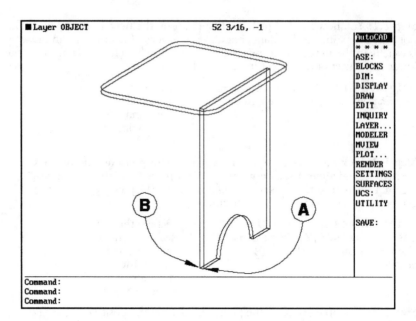

```
AutoCAD
* * * *
ASE:
BLOCKS
DIM:
DISPLAY
DRAW
EDIT
INQUIRY
LAYER...
MODELER
MVIEW
PLOT...
RENDER
SETTINGS
SURFACES
UCS:
UTILITY

SAVE:
```

```
Command:
Command:
Command:
```

`3P/2P/TTR/<Center point>:` *Using object snap Midpoint, pick the bottom line of the leg*	Defines the circle's center point
`Diameter/<Radius>: 6 ↵`	Draws a circle with a radius of 6

Notice how the circle aligns itself parallel to the new UCS.

Now you are ready to turn the circle into an arc and remove the excess line segment. Use the TRIM command. TRIM is another command that is controlled by the UCS. To edit geometry such as circles, the UCS must be parallel to the objects. Because the circle was just drawn on this UCS and was defined by the line to be trimmed away, the UCS does not need to be changed.

Step 3.0: Start the TRIM command:

`Command: TRIM ↵`	Starts the TRIM command

```
View is not plan to UCS.
Command results may not be obvious.
```

Because TRIM is another command that is controlled by the UCS, all entities to be trimmed must be parallel to the current UCS. With the message

```
View is not plan to UCS.
Command results may not be obvious.
```

AutoCAD is informing you that the current viewpoint and UCS are not parallel and some trim results may not be easy to see.

Step 3.1: Select the objects to act as cutting edges. Press Enter when you are finished:

`Select cutting edge(s)...`	Selects one trim cutting edge
`Select objects:` *Pick the circle*	
`Select objects:` *Pick the line that passes through the circle*	Selects another trim cutting edge
`Select objects:` ↵	Stops the cutting edge selection process

Step 3.2: Select the circle and line at the entity location to be removed. When finished, exit the TRIM command:

`<Select object to trim>/Undo:` *Pick the circle below the line*	Removes the bottom half of the circle
`<Select object to trim>/Undo:` *Pick the line between the circle/arc*	Removes the line segment
`<Select object to trim>/Undo:` ↵	Stops the TRIM command

You are now ready to add depth to the leg by copying the geometry. The material width for this drawing is 3/4. Because the geometry you have drawn so far represents the forward edge of the leg, you need to copy into the Z axis to develop the inner edge. In using the right-hand rule and aligning your thumb and pointer finger to the UCS icon, you can see that positive Z is coming toward you. Therefore, to create the correct geometry you need to copy into the negative Z.

Step 4.0: Issue the **COPY** command. Select the objects and copy them 3/4 units into the Z axis:

`Command:` **COPY** ↵	Starts the COPY command

```
Select objects: Pick all the lines and the        Selects the
arc that define the outside of the leg            geometry to
                                                  copy

Select objects: ↵                                 Stops the
                                                  selection
                                                  process

<Base point or displacement>/                     Defines the
Multiple: 0,0,-3/4 ↵                              displacement
                                                  into the
                                                  negative Z axis

Second point of displacement: ↵                   Confirms the
                                                  input as a
                                                  displacement
```

Now complete the leg by using the LINE command to connect the end points, as was shown in the previous figure. Because you are picking all end points, set end point as a running object snap.

Step 5.0: Issue the OSNAP command and set end point as the running object snap:

```
Command: OSNAP ↵                                  Starts the
                                                  OSNAP command

Object snap modes: END ↵                          Sets end point
                                                  as the running
                                                  object snap
```

Step 6.0: Issue the LINE command and connect the end points of the table leg's outside and inside corners:

```
Command: LINE ↵                                   Starts the LINE
                                                  command

From point: Pick point (A) in figure 10.6        Defines the
                                                  line starting
                                                  point

To point: Pick point (B) in figure 10.6          Defines the
                                                  ending point of
                                                  the line

To point: ↵                                       Stops the LINE
                                                  command
```

Step 7.0: Issue the **LINE** command five more times and complete the side as shown in the previous figure. Draw the lines between the inside and outside of the table leg.

Step 8.0: When you are finished selecting end points, remove the running object snap using the **OSNAP** command or Running Object Snap dialog box.

EXERCISE 4: COMPLETING THE LEGS AND MIDDLE SHELF

You are now ready to add the second leg and the shelf in the middle of the table as shown in figure 10.7. Do this using the MIRROR command to develop the second leg. Once drawn, use a filter to locate the starting point of the shelf. The shelf is drawn with a line and copied to create thickness.

TASKS TO BE COMPLETED IN THIS EXERCISE

- Change the UCS to World
- Mirror the table leg
- Change the UCS to Previous
- Draw the shelf using a filter to pick the starting point
- Copy the shelf to create thickness

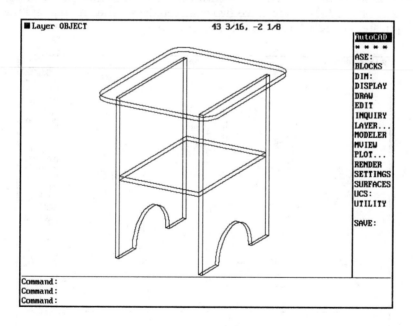

Figure 10.7:

Drawing with both legs and middle shelf.

Using the MIRROR Command

To develop the second leg, you mirror the existing leg across the bottom of the table top. To do this, you must change the UCS.

The MIRROR command is controlled by the UCS. Objects are mirrored across the current X-Y plane and need the UCS to be parallel to the top. Because the top was drawn in the plan view, it is the same as the World drawing plane. The *World drawing plane* is the standard X-Y plane, which is the default in a new drawing.

Step 1.0: Issue the UCS command and set the UCS to World:

Command: **UCS** ↵	Starts the UCS command
Origin/ZAxis/3point/Entity/ View/X/Y/Z/Prev/Restore/Save /Del/?/<World>: ↵	Accepts the default of World and returns the UCS to the World Coordinate System

You can now mirror the leg. To mirror the leg, you must select the entities to mirror and define the mirror line as being through the middle of the top shelf. You now have two complete legs—the original and the duplicate. Figure 10.8 shows this step completed.

Figure 10.8:

Table after mirror with mirror line labels.

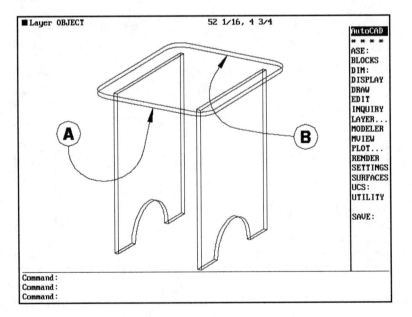

Step 2.0: Issue the **MIRROR** command and select the objects to mirror:

Command: **MIRROR** ↵   Starts the
                                         MIRROR command

Select objects: *Pick all of*   Selects the
the leg's lines and the arc   objects to
                                           mirror

Select objects: ↵   Stops the
                                           selection
                                           process

Step 2.1: Pick the mirror line as the midpoints between the table top:

First point of mirror line: Defines the
Using object snap Midpoint, pick point Ⓐ   first point on
in figure 10.8   the mirror line

Second point: *Using object snap Midpoint,*   Defines the
pick point Ⓑ *in figure 10.8*   second point to
                                         define the
                                         mirror line

Step 2.2: Press Enter to accept the default. This does not delete the old object:

Delete old objects? <N> ↵   Completes the
                                         command without
                                         removing the
                                         original object

Using Filters

Now you can add the shelf as seen in figure 10.9. To do this, you start a line up 14 5/8 units from the inside corner of the front leg. To start a new line an absolute distance from an existing entity, use a filter.

A *filter* is a point selection tool that determines the X, Y, or Z value of a specified point and enables you to add the missing X, Y, or Z. To use a filter, at the prompt asking for a point, type **.X, .Y, .Z, .XY, .XZ,** or **.YZ**. This specifies the coordinate value that AutoCAD calculates when you pick a point. You are then prompted with (need ?). The ? is replaced with the appropriate missing coordinate.

In this drawing, the shelf is positioned 14 5/8 units above the corner at A in figure 10.10.

Because filters work with absolute values, you must reposition the origin (0,0,0) at the filter point. Use the UCS command with the Origin option to perform this operation.

Figure 10.9:
Table with middle shelf.

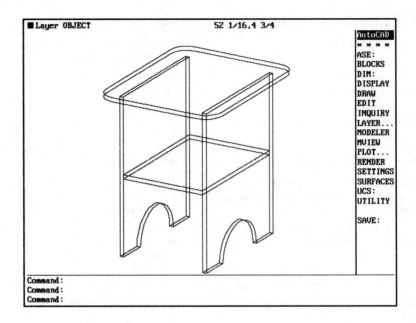

Figure 10.10:
Table with labels for shelf.

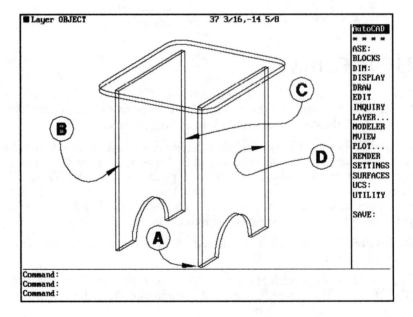

Step 3.0: Issue the UCS command and invoke the Origin option:

`Command: UCS ↵`	Starts the UCS command
`Origin/ZAxis/3point/Entity/View /X/Y/Z/Prev/Restore/Save/Del/?/ <World>: O ↵`	Invokes the Origin option

Step 3.1: Pick the leg's bottom as the new position of 0,0,0:

`Origin point <0,0,0>:` *Using object snap Endpoint, pick point Ⓐ in figure 10.10*	Repositions the origin

Notice how the UCS icon did not change its orientation, but did lose the W inside. The icon is still parallel to the top, but the Z coordinate 0 is no longer in the World Coordinate System. The Origin option moved 0,0,0 to the bottom of the table but did not change the direction of the 2D drawing plane.

Now use the LINE command with a filter to draw the bottom lines of the shelf.

Step 4.0: Start the LINE command:

`Command: LINE ↵`	Starts the LINE command

Step 4.1: You need to start the line up 14 5/8 units from the bottom of the leg. If you look at the UCS icon, you see that this is in the Z direction. Issue the .XY filter to calculate the X,Y location of the end point of the leg:

`From point:` *From the screen menu choose .xy*	Invokes the .XY filter

Step 4.2: Pick the end point to apply the filter:

`of` *Using object snap Endpoint, pick point Ⓐ as shown in figure 10.10*	Calculates the X,Y location of this point as the X,Y starting point of the new line

Step 4.3: Enter the Z value to be added to the calculated X,Y value for the starting point of the new line.

`(need Z): 14-5/8 ↵`	Specifies the Z value of the starting point and starts the line

Step 4.4: Specify the end points of the next three lines by using object snap perpendicular and selecting the inside lines of the table legs.

`To point:` *Using object snap Perpendicular,*   Defines the end
pick line Ⓑ *in figure 10.10*   point of the line

`To point:` *Using object snap Perpendicular,*   Defines the end
pick line Ⓒ *in figure 10.10*   point of the line

`To point:` *Using object snap Perpendicular,*   Defines the end
pick line Ⓒ *in figure 10.10*   point of the line

Step 4.5: Use the Close option to finish the line for the shelf:

`To point:` **C** ↵   Closes the
    polygon

You can now copy the lines to add thickness to the shelf. Again, if you look at the UCS icon, you can see that the lines need to be copied into the positive Z axis.

Step 5.0: Issue the COPY command and select the objects to copy:

`Command:` **COPY** ↵   Starts the COPY
    command

`Select objects:` *Select the four*   Selects the
new shelf lines   objects to copy

`Select objects:` ↵   Stops the
    selection
    process

Step 5.1: Use a displacement value to copy the shelf:

`<Base point or displacement>/`   Specifies to
`Multiple:` **0,0,3/4** ↵   copy the lines
    3/4 units into
    the positive Z
    axis

`Second point of displacement:` ↵   Confirms the
    input as being
    a displacement

EXERCISE 5: ADDING THE TOP EDGE

You are now ready to add the top edge as previously shown in figure 10.6. To create this edge, use offset to develop construction lines on the shelf's top lines. Working from here, offset the lines to define the material thickness. Then clean up the corners using FILLET. Give the object a radius of 0. Finally, copy the lines to create height and complete the geometry with the LINE command.

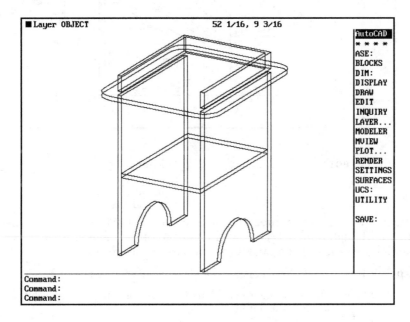

Figure 10.11:
Top Shelf with Edge.

Begin by offsetting the lines that define the top of the table. However, because these lines are polylines, the OFFSET command affects the entire entity. To avoid disturbing the entire geometry, convert the polyline to individual lines and arcs with the EXPLODE command.

Step 1.0: Invoke the EXPLODE command:

Command: **EXPLODE** ↵	Starts the EXPLODE command

Step 1.1: Select the complex object to convert to its individual entities:

Select object: *Select the polyline at* Ⓐ *(see fig. 10.12)*	Select the object to explode

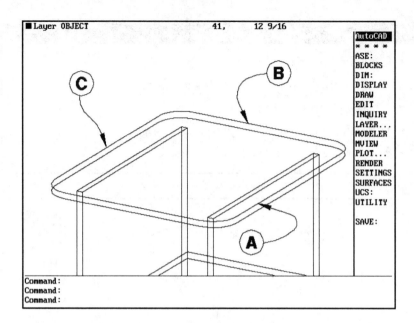

Figure 10.12:

Top of table to add edge.

```
AutoCAD
* * * *
ASE:
BLOCKS
DIM:
DISPLAY
DRAW
EDIT
INQUIRY
LAYER...
MODELER
MVIEW
PLOT...
RENDER
SETTINGS
SURFACES
UCS:
UTILITY

SAVE:
```

```
Command:
Command:
Command:
```

Select object: ↵

Polyline becomes individual lines and arcs

You can now offset the three outside lines to develop the edge's bottom lines. Although the UCS is set at the bottom of the table, it is still parallel with the top and offsets the lines in the desired direction.

Step 2.0: Issue the **OFFSET** command and set the offset distance to **3**.

Step 2.1: Select the line in figure 10.12 at A and pick a point to the far left of the line. This offsets the line 3 units.

NOTE

When using the OFFSET command, the side to pick should be selected at an extreme distance. If you pick too closely to the offset object, the isometric view can adversely effect the direction. If this doesn't work, zoom in or out and try again.

Another option is when selecting the side to offset, invoke Object snap override and pick an object or the side to offset.

If line A in figure 10.12 will not offset correctly after selecting the line to offset (line A), use Object snap endpoint and select Line C (see fig. 10.12) to define the side to offset.

Step 2.2: Select the line in figure 10.12 at B and pick a point to the far left and below the line. This offsets the line 3 units.

Step 2.3: Select the line in figure 10.12 at C and pick a point to the far right of the line. This offsets the line 3 units. Press Enter to exit the OFFSET command.

You now are ready to add the inner lines that define the thickness of the material, as seen in figure 10.13. Again, use the OFFSET command. The existing lines are offset toward the middle of the material's thickness. When finished, use the FILLET command with a radius of 0 to remove the overlapping lines developed by OFFSET.

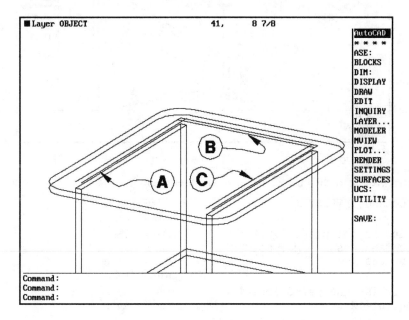

Figure 10.13:
Top shelf with overlapping line for edge.

Step 3.0: Invoke the **OFFSET** command and set the offset distance to 3/4.

Step 3.1: Select each of the three new lines and offset them toward the table top's middle. Press Enter to exit OFFSET when finished.

Now clean up the corners that overlap as seen in figure 10.13. Use FILLET with a 0 radius. (You also could use TRIM.) When finished, draw a line between the open end points of the lines. Figure 10.14 shows what your drawing should look like after completing these steps.

Figure 10.14:

Top shelf with edge bottom complete.

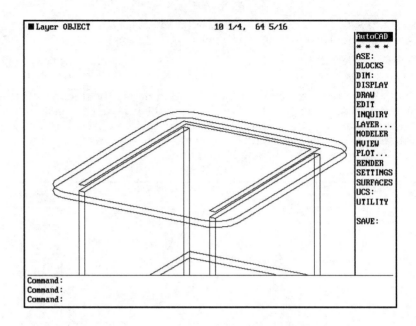

```
■Layer OBJECT                          10 1/4,  64 5/16
                                                          AutoCAD
                                                          * * * *
                                                          ASE:
                                                          BLOCKS
                                                          DIM:
                                                          DISPLAY
                                                          DRAW
                                                          EDIT
                                                          INQUIRY
                                                          LAYER...
                                                          MODELER
                                                          MVIEW
                                                          PLOT...
                                                          RENDER
                                                          SETTINGS
                                                          SURFACES
                                                          UCS:
                                                          UTILITY

                                                          SAVE:


Command:
Command:
Command:
```

Step 4.0: Start the FILLET command and set the radius to 0:

`Command: `**`FILLET`**` ↵`	Starts the FILLET command

`View is not plan to UCS.`
`Command results may not be`
`obvious.`
	Displays the same information as with TRIM

`Polyline/Radius/<Select first` `object>:`**`R`**` ↵`	Selects the radius option
`Enter fillet radius <3>: `**`0`**`↵`	Sets the fillet radius as 0

Step 5.0: Reissue the FILLET command and clean up the corners:

`Command: `**`FILLET`**` ↵`	Starts the FILLET command
`View is not plan to UCS.` `Command results may not be obvious.`	
`Polyline/Radius/<Select first` `object>:` *Pick line* (A) *in figure 10.13*	Selects the first line
`Select second object:` *Pick line* (B) *in figure 10.13*	Selects the second line and cleans up the corner

Step 6.0: Reissue the **FILLET** command and select lines B and C (as was shown in figure 10.13) to remove the overlapping lines.

You now have cleaned up the bottom contour of this edge and are ready to finish the bottom of the edge, as previously shown.

Step 7.0: Issue the **LINE** command and use object snap ENDpoint to draw the two lines between the open ends, as seen in figure 10.14.

You now have finished the bottom contour and can copy the object up to develop the top contour. The object is copied a distance equal to the height of the shelf. Again, by looking at the UCS icon you see that the object must be copied in the positive Z axis.

After you have developed the top of the edge, use the LINE command and connect the end points. When finished, the object should look like figure 10.15.

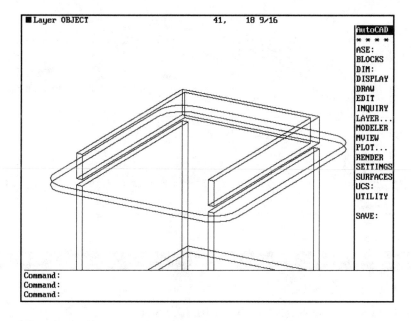

Figure 10.15:
Table with edge.

Step 8.0: Issue the **COPY** command and select all the lines in the shelf's bottom contour. Press Enter to stop selecting objects. Enter **0,0,3** as the displacement. Press Enter to confirm the value as a displacement.

Step 9.0: Because you are selecting several end points, set a running object snap to end point.

Step 10.0: Issue the **LINE** command and connect the top and bottom edge contour, as seen in figure 10.15.

Step 11.0: When finished, set the running object snap back to none.

Exercise 6: Adding the Hole in the Edge

Now that you have completed the edge, add the cord hole shown in figure 10.16. Again set the UCS parallel to the plane that the circle is to be placed in. Using the **OFFSET** command, develop a construction line to position the circle. Once inserted, copy the circle to add depth.

Figure 10.16:

Edge with cord hole.

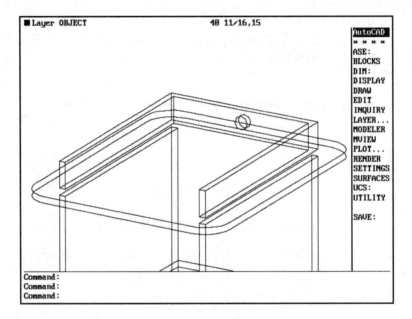

Tasks to be Completed in this Exercise

- Change the UCS
- Develop a construction line with OFFSET
- Add a circle
- Copy the circle to create thickness

As you can see in figure 10.16, the circle is parallel to the back geometry in the edge. Because a circle is drawn parallel to the current UCS position, reposition the UCS to align with the back of the edge.

In addition to the 3point and Origin options, you can align the UCS using the ZAxis option. The ZAxis option defines a new UCS position based on the concept that the Z axis is always perpendicular to the X-Y plane. By defining two points that are on the Z axis, the UCS is defined perpendicular to a line passing through those two points.

To align the UCS parallel to the back edge, use the UCS ZAxis option and pick two points in a line that is perpendicular to the back.

Step 1.0: Start the UCS command and select the ZAxis option:

Command: **UCS** ↵	Starts the UCS command
Origin/ZAxis/3point/Entity/ View/X/Y/Z/Prev/Restore/Save/ Del/?/<World>: **ZA** ↵	Selects the ZAxis option

Step 1.1: Pick the two points on the Z axis that are perpendicular to the desired UCS. The first point is the new origin; the second point is in the positive Z direction:

Origin point <0,0,0>: *Using object* *snap Endpoint, pick point* Ⓐ *in figure 10.17*	Defines the new 0,0,0
Point on positive portion of Z-axis <7 3/4,30 1/4,1 3/4>: *Using object snap Endpoint, pick point* Ⓑ *in figure 10.17*	Defines a point in the positive Z axis direction

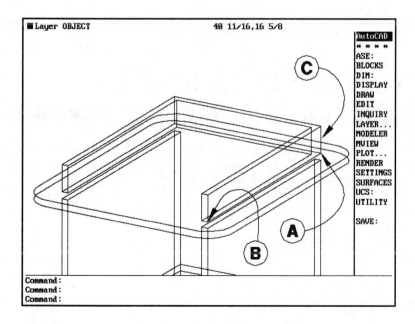

Figure 10.17:
Labels for ZAxis UCS option.

You are now ready to add the construction line for the circle. This line is offset from the outside edge.

Step 2.0: Issue the OFFSET command; create the construction line 9 units over from the outside edge:

Command: **OFFSET** ↵	Starts the OFFSET command
Offset distance or Through <3/4>: **9** ↵	Defines the offset value
Select object to offset: *Pick line Ⓒ in figure 10.17*	Selects the object to offset
Side to offset? *Pick a point above and to the left of the line*	Defines the side to offset
Select object to offset: ↵	Stops the OFFSET command

You can now add the circle. Place the circle on the construction line's midpoint. Once the circle is drawn, use the COPY command and create the inside contour of the hole. Complete the operation by erasing the construction line.

Step 3.0: Issue the **CIRCLE** command. Use the object snap Midpoint and select the new construction line as the center of the circle. Choose the DIAmeter option and enter a diameter value of 1.5.

Step 4.0: Issue the **COPY** command and select the new circle. Press Enter to stop selecting objects. Enter a displacement value of 0,0,3/4. Press Enter again to complete the command.

Step 5.0: Invoke the **ERASE** command and remove the construction line.

EXERCISE 7: LOOKING AT THE OBJECT FROM DIFFERENT VIEWPOINTS

As mentioned earlier, one of the real advantages of 3D is being able to see the object from different views, which makes it easier to conceptualize the geometry. You completed the object lines in the drawing while working in one viewpoint. To see how changing viewpoints works, use the VPOINT command to see the new 3D drawing from several different sides.

Step 1.0: Use the VPOINT command and coordinate specifications to see a right-side view:

Command: **VPOINT** ↵	Starts the VPOINT command
Rotate/<Viewpoint> <13/16, -1/2,5/16>: **1,0,0** ↵	Shows the drawing from the right side

Step 2.0: Use the VPOINT command and look at the back of the object using the Rotate option:

Command: **VPOINT** ↵	Starts the VPOINT command
Rotate/<Viewpoint> <1,0,0>: **R** ↵	Selects the Rotate option
Enter angle in XY plane from X axis <0>: **90** ↵	Selects the back side
Enter angle from XY plane <0>: **0** ↵	Selects an angle looking straight at the back side

Step 3.0: Issue the PLAN command. The PLAN command goes directly to a World plan or a plan of the current UCS. The plan World View is the original top of the drawing:

Command: **PLAN** ↵	Starts the PLAN command
<Current UCS>/Ucs/World: **W** ↵	Selects the World plan view

Next, add the dimensions to the drawing. You can now return to a viewpoint suitable for dimensioning.

Step 4.0: Use the VPOINT command and return to the front, right view used to create the geometry:

Command: **VPOINT** ↵	Starts the VPOINT command
Rotate/<Viewpoint> <0,0,1>: **R** ↵	Selects the Rotate option

```
Enter angle in XY plane from          Selects the
X axis <270>: 300 ↵                   front, right
                                      side

Enter angle from XY plane             Displays the
<90>: 20 ↵                            front, right
                                      side from 20
                                      degrees above
```

EXERCISE 8: DIMENSIONING IN 3D

You now are ready to add the dimensions shown in figure 10.18. When you add dimensions to 3D drawings, you must control the UCS. Dimensions are placed directly on the X-Y drawing plane, which is parallel to the UCS and at a Z depth of 0.

Figure 10.18:

Dimensioned Drawing.

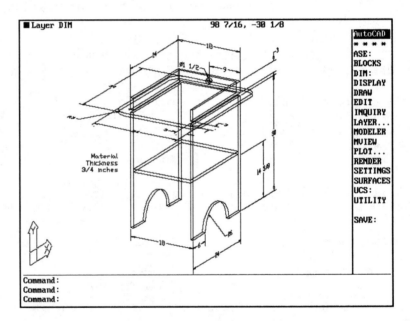

As you dimension the drawing, you need to continually change the UCS so that it not only is parallel to the plane's dimension, but also is located at the geometry's Z zero plane. In addition, you must always be aware of the orientation of the X-Y plane. With dimensioning, X is the horizontal axis and Y is the vertical axis. The dimensioning command works just as if you were in 2D and were aligning the dimensions to the 2D plane.

Before you begin adding dimensions, you must be on the correct layer.

Step 1.0: Make the layer DIM current.

Because you are picking mostly end points, set a running object snap.

Step 2.0: Use the **OSNAP** command or Running Object Snap dialog box and set end point as a running object snap.

In addition to layers, you need to set some dimension variables values. First, enter the dimensioning mode.

Step 3.0: Enter **DIM** to enter dimensioning mode.

Step 4.0: Set Dimscale = **6**. This scales a dimension information by a factor of 6.

Step 5.0: Set Dimdli = **7/8**. This variable defines the amount dimensions lines that are offset during baseline dimensions.

Now you are ready to add dimensions. Begin by placing the 18 unit dimension across the front. To do this, first place the UCS on this plane. Because this is a horizontal dimension, 0,0,0 is in the lower left corner, X is to the left, and Y is straight up along the leg. You must first exit DIM mode.

Step 6.0: Press Ctrl-C to exit DIM mode.

Step 7.0: Issue the UCS command and select the 3point option:

Command: **UCS** ↵	Starts the UCS command
Origin/ZAxis/3point/Entity/ View/X/Y/Z/Prev/Restore/Save/ Del/?/<World>: **3** ↵	Selects the 3point option

Step 7.1: Pick the three points that place the UCS across the front of the table legs:

Origin point <0,0,0>: *Pick point Ⓐ in figure 10.19*	Defines the new 0,0,0
Point on positive portion of the X-axis <1/4,-30 3/4,23 1/4>: *Pick point Ⓑ in figure 10.19*	Defines a point on the plane and the positive X direction

Point on positive-Y portion of the UCS XY plane <-3/4, -29 3/4,23 1/4>: *Using object snap Midpoint, pick point © in figure 10.19*	Defines a point on the plane and the positive Y direction

Figure 10.19:

Points for dimensioning the front of the table.

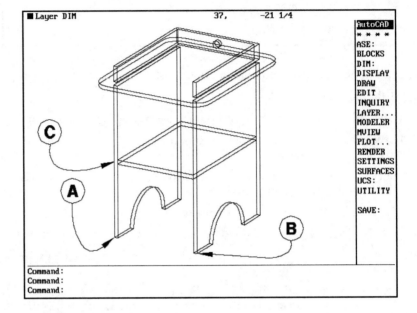

You now are ready to add the dimensions. Because the definition of the X axis is across the bottom of the legs, this dimension is a horizontal dimension.

Step 8.0: Enter **DIM** to return to DIM mode.

Step 9.0: Invoke the HORizontal subcommand:

Dim: **HOR** ↵	Starts the HORizontal subcommand

Step 9.1: Pick the extension line origins:

First extension line origin or RETURN to select: *Pick point Ⓐ in figure 10.19*	Defines the first extension origin
Second extension line origin: *Pick point Ⓑ in figure 10.19*	Defines the second extension origin

Step 9.2: Pick a point to position the dimension line:

Dimension line location   Defines the
(Text/Angle):*Pick a point for the line*   dimension line
below the legs   location

Step 9.3: Accept the default dimension text:

Dimension text <18>: ↵   Places the
                                 dimension in
                                 the drawing

You now can add the dimension to the drawing's top, as seen in figure 10.20. Even though these dimensions are on a parallel plane, the origin needs to be relocated so they are placed properly. If you attempt to dimension the drawings with the plane in its current location, the dimension would be placed out in space in front of the object on the current drawing plane.

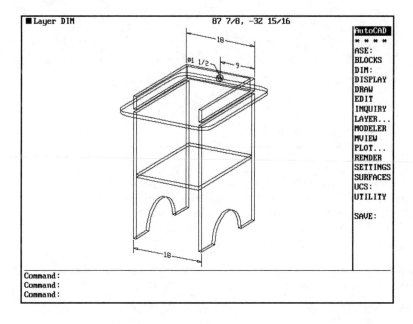

Figure 10.20:
Table with dimension on top.

Step 10.0: First press Ctrl-C to exit DIM mode.

Step 11.0: Use the UCS command's Origin option to move the drawing plane into dimensioning position:

Command: **UCS** ↵   Starts the UCS
                                 command

```
Origin/ZAxis/3point/Entity/        Selects the
View/X/Y/Z/Prev/Restore/Save/      origin option
Del/?/<World>: O ↵
Origin point <0,0,0>:              Positions the
```
Pick point (A) *in figure 10.21*   new origin

Figure 10.21:

Labels for changing the UCS origin and dimensioning.

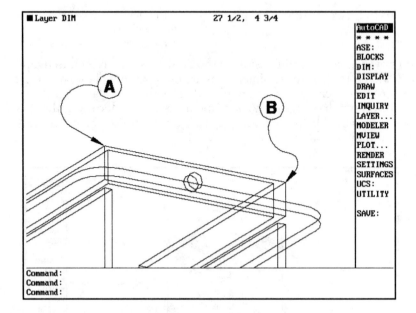

Now add the dimensions to the top. The two linear dimensions have their dimension line parallel to the X axis, so they are horizontal. Use the HORizontal subcommand for these dimensions. The circular dimension is added with the DIAmeter subcommand.

Step 12.0: Enter **DIM** to return to DIM mode.

Step 13.0: Issue the HORizontal subcommand; add the 9 unit dimension between the outer edge and the circle:

```
Dim: HOR ↵                         Starts the
                                   HORizontal
                                   subcommand

First extension line origin        Defines the
or RETURN to select: Pick          first dimension
end point (B) in figure 10.21      point
Second extension line origin:      Defines the
Using object snap Center, pick the circle    second
                                   dimension point
```

```
Dimension line location              Defines the
(Text/Angle): Pick a point above     position of the
for the dimension line               dimension line

Dimension text <9>: ↵                Enters the
                                     dimension
```

You now can add the baseline dimension using the BASE subcommand.

Step 14.0: Issue the **BASE** subcommand and add the 18 unit dimension across the top:

```
Dim: BASE ↵                          Starts the BASE
                                     subcommand

Second extension line origin         Defines the end
or RETURN to select: Pick point Ⓐ    point for the
in figure 10.21                      dimension

Dimension text <18>: ↵               Completes the
                                     command
```

You can complete the dimensions in this area by adding the dimension to the circle between points A and B, as was shown in figure 10.21. Use the DIAmeter subcommand to add this dimension.

Step 15.0: Invoke the DIAmeter subcommand; add the circular dimension to the top of the table:

```
Dim: DIA ↵                           Starts the
                                     DIAmeter
                                     subcommand

Select arc or circle: Pick the circle at    Selects the
the 11 o'clock position              circle and
                                     defines the
                                     leader line
                                     location

Dimension text <1-1/2>: ↵            Accepts the
                                     default
                                     dimension text

Enter leader length for text:        Positions the
Pick a point for the leader          leader and
                                     exits the
                                     command
```

Now add the dimensions to the right side. However, you must first exit the dimension area and change the UCS. Again, the UCS must align itself to the location of the dimensions.

Step 16: Exit dimension mode:

```
Dim: Press Ctrl-C                    Exits the
                                     dimension area
```

You now need to add the dimensions as seen in figure 10.22. To do this you need to align the UCS to the right side. You could easily use the UCS command and 3point option to do this realignment. However, because the new UCS position is perpendicular to the existing UCS, you can rotate the existing UCS around one of its axes.

Figure 10.22:

Table with dimensions on the right side.

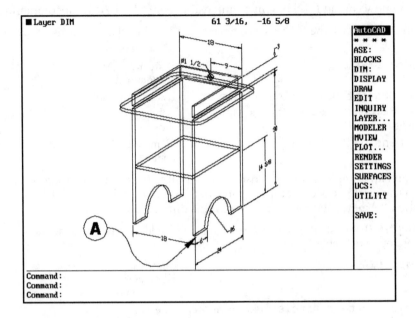

The X, Y, and Z options within the UCS command enable you to rotate around one of these specified axes. If you look at the UCS icon, you see that the Y axis is pointing straight up. You need to rotate the geometry around this axis.

Step 17.0: Invoke the UCS command and select the Y option:

```
Command: UCS ↵                          Starts the UCS
                                        command

Origin/ZAxis/3point/Entity/             Selects the
View/X/Y/Z/Prev/Restore/Save/           option to
Del/?/<World>: Y ↵                      rotate around
                                        the Y axis
```

Step 17.1: To determine what direction to rotate, imagine that you grab the axis and wrap the fingers of your right hand around it, with your thumb pointing in the positive Y direction. Your fingers now are wrapped in a positive rotation angle. To keep the X axis pointing to the right, you need to rotate around the Y axis in a positive direction. Because the new UCS position is perpendicular to the old UCS position, the angle is 90:

```
Rotation angle about Y axis          Rotates the UCS
<0>: 90 ↵                            90 degrees
                                     around the
                                     Y axis
```

The UCS icon now displays the correct UCS plane. However, the origin of the plane still needs to be positioned exactly on the side to dimension. Again, use the Origin option of the UCS command to perform this function.

Step 18.0: Invoke the UCS command and reposition the origin:

```
Command: UCS ↵                       Starts the UCS
                                     command

Origin/ZAxis/3point/Entity/          Selects the
View/X/Y/Z/Prev/Restore/Save/        Origin option
Del/?/<World>: 0 ↵

Origin point <0,0,0>:                Moves the
Pick point Ⓐ in figure 10.22         origin to this
                                     point
```

You now can return to the dimension mode and continue dimensioning, which you can finish on your own. Remember that horizontal dimensions have their numbers at the same angle as the dimension line, and are on the X axis (see the 24-unit dimension on the right side in figure 10.23). Vertical dimensions have their numbers perpendicular to the dimension line and are on the Y axis (see the 14 5/8-unit dimension on the right side in figure 10.23).

Step 19.0: Enter the dimensioning area:

```
Command: DIM ↵                       Starts the
                                     dimension mode
```

Step 20.0: Dimension the rest of the drawing on your own. Change the UCS as needed. Use figure 10.23 as a guide.

When you are finished dimensioning and are ready to complete the drawing, add the text seen in figure 10.24. As you can see, this text is not aligned with the drawing's geometry but lies flat across the screen. The UCS command with the View option defines a UCS that is parallel to the screen or viewpoint.

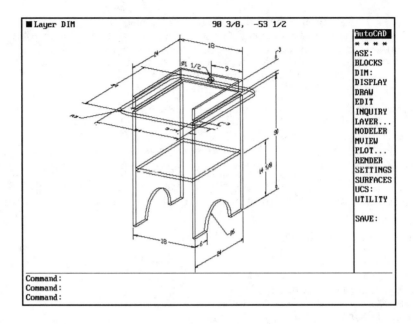

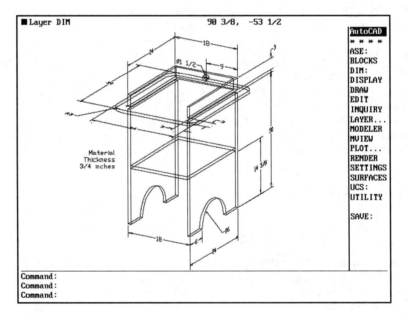

Step 21.0: Issue the UCS command and select the View option:

```
Command: UCS ↵
```
Starts the UCS command

```
Origin/ZAxis/3point/Entity/
View/X/Y/Z/Prev/Restore/Save/
Del/?/<World>: V ↵
```
Aligns the UCS to the screen

The UCS icon now is parallel to the screen. To finish the drawing, use DTEXT and add the text that defines material thickness. As you can see in figure 10.24, this text aligns itself along the right side. Use the Right justified text option to perform this function.

Step 22.0: Issue the DTEXT command; select the Right justified text option:

```
Command: DTEXT ↵
```
Starts the DTEXT command

```
Justify/Style/<Start point>: R ↵
```
Specifies the Right justified text option

Step 22.1: Pick the starting point of the right justified text and enter the text information:

```
Starting point: Pick a point just to the
```
left of the middle shelf of the table

Specifies the starting point for right justified text

```
Height <3/16>: 1 ↵
```
Specifies a text height of 1

```
Rotation angle <0>: ↵
```
Accepts the default of 0 rotation angle

Step 22:2: Enter the text to be placed in the drawing:

```
Text: Material ↵
```
Defines the first line of text

```
Text: thickness ↵
```
Defines the second line of text

```
Text: 3/4 inches ↵
```
Defines the final line of text

```
Text: ↵
```
Exits the DTEXT command

Your drawing is now finished and should look like figure 10.24.

Step 23.0: Save the drawing to disk and end the current drawing session.

SUMMARY

The development of three-dimensional geometry is becoming the standard in CAD drawings. This lesson's drawing used commands learned in previous lessons, such as PLINE, CIRCLE, LINE, COPY, and OFFSET, to develop a 3D wireframe. During the development of this geometry you changed the viewpoint of the drawing. In addition, you also used the UCS command to change the drawing plane. Once finished, you added dimensioning in a 3D environment.

IN THIS LESSON, YOU LEARNED TO DO THE FOLLOWING:

- Use the Z coordinate
- Create 3D wireframe geometry
- Change the viewpoint of a drawing
- Reposition the User Coordinate System
- Dimension in 3D

In this lesson, you developed a 3D wireframe drawing. In the next lesson, you take the 3D wireframe created in this lesson and develop a surface model.

REVIEW

1. Draw a box with an X value of **5**, a Y value of **3**, and a Z value of **2**.

2. Using **VPOINT**, change to an isometric view of the box in question **1**.

3. On one end, the 3×2 side, place a circle with a diameter of **1** directly in the rectangle's middle.

4. Using the **COPY** command, place the circle in question **3** on the opposite parallel end.

5. Change the above drawing to a left side view, plan view, and front view.

6. Place a three-way fillet on all four corners of the above box.

7. From an isometric view, dimension the above drawing. When finished, save the drawing as REV11-2.

8. Recall REV11-1 from the sample disk. Trim away all the lines that extend beyond the geometry.

9. In drawing REV11-1, place a circle with a diameter of **2.5** centered on the points/nodes in the drawing. Make certain the circles are parallel to the side they are placed upon.

10. Dimension drawing REV11-1.

CREATING A 3D SURFACE MODEL

As you learned in Lesson 10, three-dimensional wireframe models are powerful tools for many applications in 3D. Because no geometry lies between the corners of a 3D wireframe object, however, the object is of limited used for the development of advanced contours—such as a car's dash board—or for visualization. If you want an accurate visual depiction of a 3D object, or if your object needs complicated contours, you can create the object as a 3D surface model.

In a three-dimensional surface model, you apply *meshes*—or surfaces—across the wireframe model's edges. From these surfaces you can develop more advanced tool paths or visually represent the geometry as a solid.

AutoCAD provides several types of surface options. Before you can select the right surface option, however, you need to understand the basics of 3D surface modeling in AutoCAD. Further, when you create a surface model, you should know which command is correct for developing the desired type of surface. You also need to understand the characteristics of the solid model itself, such as whether the object's contours are flat or curved, and the number of axes in which the surface moves.

When you consider the type of surface command to apply to your model, you also need to determine the number of polymeshes to use in the surface. A *polymesh* is a single flat polygon that defines a surface. If you do not use enough polymeshes in a surface, and the surface is around a circular contour, the edges appear polygonal in nature, that is, the edges may appear jagged, with sharp corners, rather than smoothly contoured and rounded. On the other hand, when you increase the number of polymeshes in the surface, you also significantly increase the drawing's size, thus decreasing the speed with which AutoCAD can manipulate the drawing. You must always balance your choices between these two considerations.

You should use several layers when you develop a surfaced model. By using multiple layers, you can easily isolate portions of the drawing and more easily apply its surfaces. Further, many times in adding surfaces to a drawing, the original wireframe model does not have the proper contours to accommodate the available surface command. To work around this problem, you may need to expand or modify the wireframe. When you must make such modifications, however, you should never change the wireframe's visual appearance. This is because the wireframe model is an important feature and a drawing in itself that you may need in the future.

TOPICS COVERED IN THIS LESSON

In this lesson, you learn to do the following:

- Apply surfaces to a wireframe model
- Change the number of polymeshes in a surface
- Use layers to optimize the surface function
- Section a drawing for surfacing

COMMANDS COVERED IN THIS LESSON

This lesson teaches you how to use the following AutoCAD commands:

- RULESURF
- EDGESURF
- TABSURF
- SURFTAB(1,2)
- VIEW
- HIDE

SETTING UP TO SURFACE A DRAWING

In this lesson, you add a surface to the table that you created in Lesson 10, as shown in figure 11.1. You start by opening the drawing, freezing the dimension layer, and creating the layers that hold the surfaces.

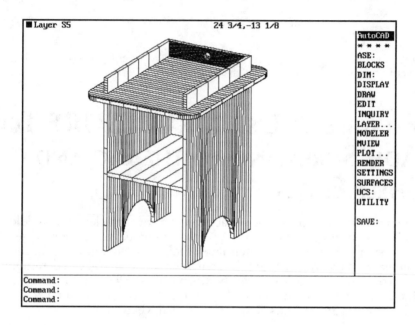

Step 1.0: Choose the Open command from the File menu, and then choose LESSON10 as the drawing to edit. Because you are going to modify the drawing for this lesson, you want to save another version of the drawing file.

Step 2.0: From the File menu, choose Save as, and name the drawing **LESSON11**.

Because you are editing an existing drawing, you do not need to define the units or limits. You do need to add the surfaces that are needed to develop the layers.

When adding surfaces to a 3D wireframe, you can work more productively by using the LAYER command to create several layers and turn them on and off as needed. Also, because you need to section a drawing to add complex surfaces, you should create a special layer to hold temporary geometry. Because you do not need to see or use the drawing's dimensions, you can freeze the layer that contains the dimensions.

Step 3.0: Use the **LAYER** command or Layer Control dialog box to add the following new layers:

S1

S2

S3

S4

S5

TEMP

Step 3.1: Use the Freeze option to suspend the DIM layer (you do not need this layer in this lesson). Finally make layer **S1** current.

EXERCISE 1: USING **RULESURF** TO ADD SURFACING TO THE LEG AND SHELF EDGES

You now are ready to add the surface to the edge of the legs and middle shelf, as seen in figure 11.2. Before you add a surface, you must analyze the existing wireframe and determine which is the appropriate surface command to use. In analyzing the area to be surfaced, you can determine that you will be placing a surface between two entities, which are the lines that form the corner of the legs and shelf. This type of surface is called a *Ruled Surface*—its command is called RULESURF.

The RULESURF command creates a polymesh, or ruled surface, between two entities. You do not need to use object snaps or change the UCS while you create surfaces. You only need to select the defining curves at the same ends when you use RULESURF. If you do not, the surface will twist on you. If this happens, erase the surface or use the UNDO command and redraw the surface.

In this exercise, you use the RULESURF command to place a surface between the corners of the geometry. If you look at figure 11.2, you can see that the polymesh surface is made up of smaller sections on the curves than on the straight surfaces. The number of segments must be increased around curved entities because a surface is made up of several small flat patches. In this exercise, you use the system variable SURFTAB1 to change the number of surface patches that are placed on the curved surfaces.

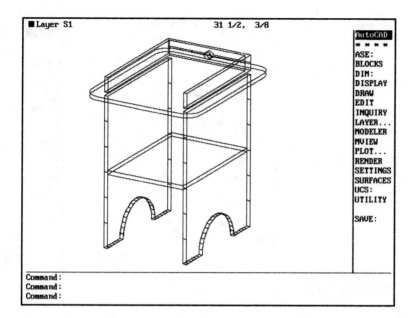

Table with surface on leg and shelf edges.

TASKS TO BE COMPLETED IN THIS EXERCISE

- Place a surface between two entities
- Change the number of polymeshes in a surface

To begin, place a surface between the lines at the bottom of the leg. The number of surface patches can remain at the default setting of six because these lines are straight.

Step 1.0: Start the ruled surfaces command:

| Command: *Choose* Draw, *then* 3D Surfaces *then* Ruled Surface | Starts the RULESURF command |

Step 1.1: Pick one of the lines that is to enclose the surface:

| Select first defining curve: *Pick the line labeled* Ⓐ *in figure 11.3* | Selects the first contour for the surface |

Step 1.2: Pick the second line that is to enclose the surface:

| Select second defining curve: *Pick the line labeled* Ⓑ *in figure 11.3* | Selects the second contour for the surface |

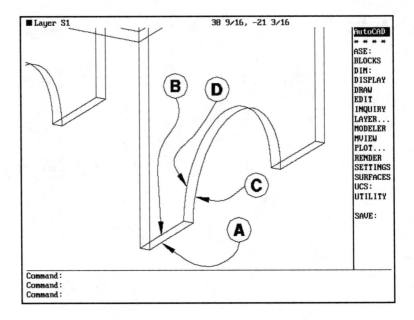

CHANGING THE NUMBER OF POLYMESHES IN A SURFACE

To continue, place a ruled surface between the two arcs at the bottom of the legs. You need to change the number of divisions developed in the ruled surface because this is a circular object. If you do not, the surface is *polygonal* in nature, which means the surface is made up of several angled lines and does not appear circular. The AutoCAD variables that control the number of polygon meshes divided into a surface contour are SURFTAB1 and SURFTAB2. SURFTAB1 controls surfaces that lie between the first two defining contours and SURFTAB2 controls the surfaces that lie between a third and fourth defining contour if the surface command requires it.

You need only SURFTAB1 because the RULESURF command places a surface between two entities.

Step 2.0: Issue the SURFTAB1 system variable:

Command: **SURFTAB1** ↵   Enables you to set
the SURFTAB1
variable

Step 2.1: The default setting is six. Because this is a small, simple arc, a setting of 18 creates a visually smooth curve:

`New value for SURFTAB1 <6>: 18 ↵`   Defines the number of polymeshes between the first and second contour

You now are ready to add a surface to the arc at the bottom of the table leg. Use the RULESURF command again because the surface is to be developed between two simple contours.

Step 3.0: Start the ruled surfaces operation:

`Command:` *Choose* Draw, *then* 3D Surfaces   Starts the RULESURF
then Ruled Surface   command

Step 3.1: Select the two arcs that are to enclose the surface:

`Select first defining curve:`   Selects the first
pick arc Ⓒ *in figure 11.3*   defining entity
`Select second defining curve:`   Places the surface
pick arc Ⓓ *in figure 11.3*   between the two arcs

You are ready to add the surface to the remaining entities. Because these are straight lines, you can set the SURFTAB1 variable back to six. This decreases the number of entities in the drawing but still creates a suitable surface.

Step 4.0: Issue the system variable SURFTAB1 and set its value to six:

`Command: SURFTAB1 ↵`   Starts the SURFTAB1 variable
`New value for SURFTAB1 <18>: 6 ↵`   Sets the variable at six

You now can continue surfacing the table by adding surfaces to the edges on the right leg as seen in figure 11.4.

Step 5.0: Choose Draw, then 3D Surfaces, then Ruled Surface. Pick two opposite lines on the right table leg and add the surface to the drawing. Continue until the drawing has the same surface as figure 11.4. Remember, if you make a mistake, enter the **U** command or erase the surface and perform the operation again.

COPYING SURFACES

At this point, you are finished with the surfaces on the edge of the right leg and now can add the surface to the left leg. Like lines and circles, surfaces are AutoCAD entities that can be copied from one location to another. To speed the process of adding surfaces to the left edge, copy the existing objects to the left side.

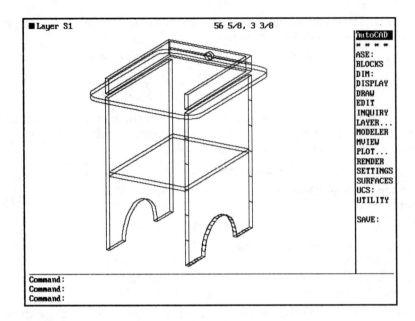

The geometry you are about to copy has definable points between the object to be copied and the position of the copy. For this reason, specify the copy distance by using the base point option. Pick a point on one leg and the same respective point on the opposite leg.

Step 6.0: Start the COPY command:

`Command: COPY ↵`   Starts the COPY command

Step 6.1: Select the objects to copy. Finish the selection process by pressing Enter:

`Select objects:` *Pick all of the newly*   Selects the geometry
created surfaces   to duplicate

`Select objects: ↵`   Stops the selection process

Step 6.2: Pick the base point as one corner on the right leg:

`<Base point or displacement>`   Defines the base
`/Multiple:`*Use object snap Endpoint and*   from which to copy
pick point Ⓐ *in figure 11.5*

Step 6.3: Pick the second point of displacement as the same respective point on the left leg:

`Second point of displacement:`   Copies the surface
Use object snap Endpoint and pick point   to the left leg
Ⓑ *in figure 11.5*

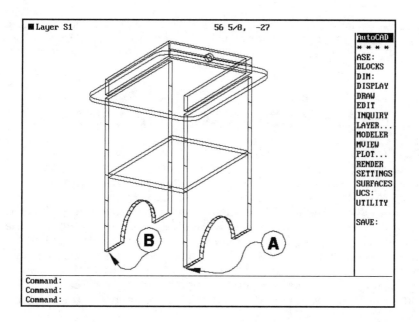

Figure 11.5:
Surfaces on both leg edges.

To complete the exercise, add a ruled surface to the edge of the middle shelf, as shown in figure 11.6. The current SURFTAB1 setting (six) again is sufficient because this is a straight surface.

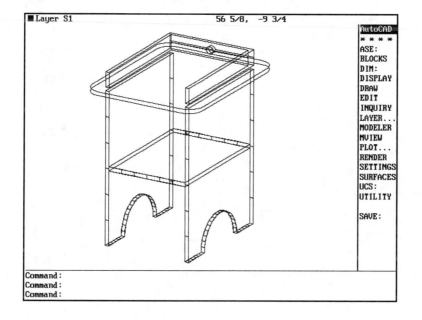

Figure 11.6:
Surfaces appear on the shelf and table edges.

Step 7.0: Choose Draw, then 3D Surfaces, then Ruled Surface. Pick two opposite lines on the front of the middle shelf edge to add the surface to the drawing. Continue by performing the same operation on the back of the middle shelf. Use figure 11.6 as a reference.

EXERCISE 2: SURFACE THE SHELF EDGES

Continue the drawing by adding surfaces to the top shelf edges and vertical edging, as seen in figure 11.7. Use the same process, RULESURF, to surface this geometry. Recall that in Lesson 10 the top shelf was developed with a polyline. To create construction lines for the top edges, the top polyline was exploded. The RULESURF command does not allow you to mix closed and open paths during a ruled surface. In the last exercise you exploded the top polyline so that it now is an open group of arcs and lines and the bottom entity is a closed polyline. Before you can continue adding surfaces, you must change the polyline to an open path.

Figure 11.7:

Surfaces on the top shelf edges and vertical edges.

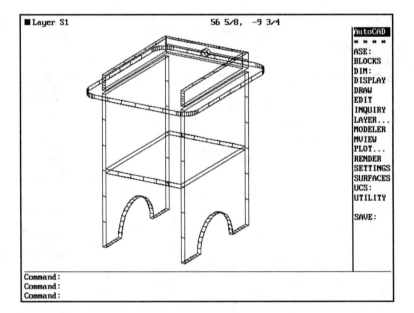

To complete this exercise, you first must explode the bottom polyline. Afterward, you use the RULESURF command to place a surface around the edge of the shelf. Before you place a surface on the curved surfaces, you use the system variable SURFTAB1 to change the number of polymeshes. To complete the exercise, set SURFTAB1 back to six and add the surface to the top vertical edging.

TASKS TO BE COMPLETED IN THIS EXERCISE

- Explode the polyline
- Use RULESURF to add surfaces
- Use SURFTAB1 to change the number of polymeshes

Begin by using the EXPLODE command to change the bottom polyline to its basic entities.

Step 1.0: Enter the EXPLODE command and pick the polyline that forms the bottom edge of the top shelf:

Command: **EXPLODE** ↵	Starts the EXPLODE command
Select object: *Select the bottom polyline at* Ⓐ *on the top shelf (see fig. 11.8)*	Selects the object to explode
Select object: ↵	The polyline becomes individual lines and arcs

You now are ready to add the surfaces. To aid in productivity, use the RULESURF command on all the straight lines first, then change SURFTAB1 and add the surface to the arcs.

Step 2.0: Enter the RULESURF command:

Command: **RULESURF** ↵	Starts the RULESURF command
Select first defining curve: *Select line* Ⓐ *in figure 11.8*	Selects the first entity
Select second defining curve: *Select line* Ⓑ *in figure 11.8*	Place the surface in the drawing

Continue by adding the remaining surfaces to the straight lines on the top shelf.

Step 3.0: Issue the **RULESURF** command and surface the remaining three straight edges on the top shelf.

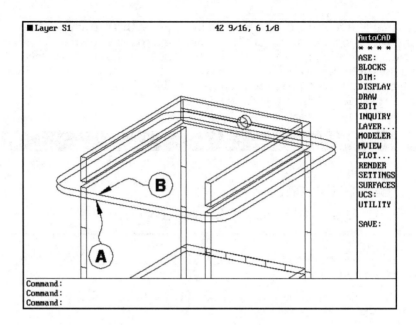

You are finished with the straight edges and now can place the surface on the round corners of the shelf. Before you do this, you must change the number of polymeshes in the surface to create a smooth round contour.

Step 4.0: Issue the variable SURFTAB1 and set its value to 12:

Command: **SURFTAB1** ↵   Starts the SURFTAB1 variable

New value for SURFTAB1 <6>: **12** ↵   Sets the variable to 12

You can now finish this shelf by placing a surface between the fillets that form the rounded corners of the shelf edge.

Step 5.0: Invoke the **RULESURF** command and pick opposite arcs on the top and bottom shelf near the same respective end. Perform this function four times. Your finished drawing should appear as figure 11.9.

You can now use the same process as before to add the surface around the edges of the shelf. Begin by adding a surface to one front edge and work your way around until you have placed all five surfaces in the drawing.

Again, because these are all straight lines, set SURFTAB1 back to the original setting of six. Afterward, use the RULESURF command to apply the surfaces.

Step 6.0: Issue the variable SURFTAB1 and set its value to six.

You are now ready to add the surface. Begin at the front edge and work around the top.

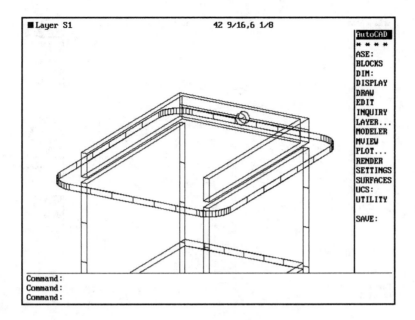

Figure 11.9:
Completed surfaces on top shelf edges.

Step 7.0: Issue the RULESURF command and add the first surface to the edge:

Command: **RULESURF** ↵	Starts the RULESURF command
Select first defining curve: *Pick line Ⓐ in figure 11.10*	Selects the first defining entity
Select second defining curve: *Pick line Ⓑ in figure 11.10*	Selects the second defining entity

You can now add three surfaces to the top. Even though these lines are different lengths, the polymeshes angle themselves to fill in the required area.

Step 8.0: Issue the **RULESURF** command and select opposite lines at the top of the vertical edges to place a surface between the lines.

You can now finish this exercise by placing the surface across the front edge (see fig. 11.11).

Step 9.0: Issue the **RULESURF** command and select opposite lines on the front of the vertical edges to place a surface between the lines.

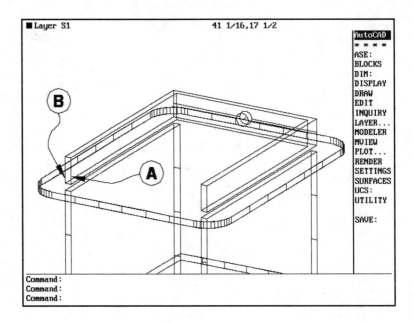

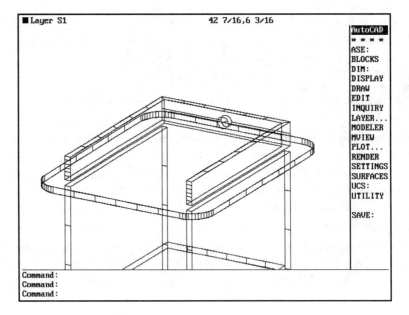

EXERCISE 3: ADDING A SURFACE TO THE SIDES OF THE LEGS

You are now ready to add the surface to the sides of the leg as seen in figure 11.12. You again use the RULESURF command to develop these surfaces. Before you begin, freeze the current layer and make a new layer current. This makes it easier to select the defining contours because you cannot surface between polymeshes. When finished with the entire drawing, you can thaw all the surface layers and see the entire drawing.

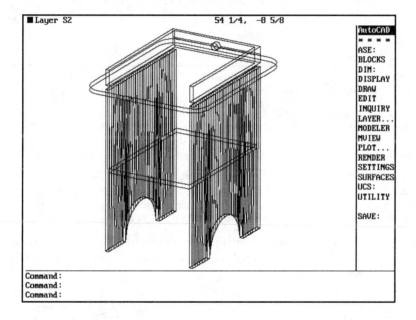

After the S1 layer is frozen and a new layer is the current layer, you can begin to develop the surface. In reviewing the definition of a ruled surface, the command develops a surface between two contours. In this drawing, the bottom of the leg is drawn with two lines and an arc. Because of this, you need to join the bottom geometry into one contour. This type of editing is common during surfacing. You often need to modify a wire frame to create the required defining curves.

You can use the PEDIT command to turn one of these objects into a polyline and then join all three entities into one. Polylines are controlled by the UCS. To edit an entity with the PEDIT command, all the geometry must be parallel to the current UCS. Because of this, the UCS needs to be changed so that it is parallel to the right side. You then can use the RULESURF command to add a surface to the outside of one table leg. Finally, copy the first surface you create to the three other surfaces—the same surface is applied to more than one part of the drawing.

Start the exercise by freezing the layer S1 and making S2 current.

Step 1.0: Issue the **LAYER** command and set S2, then freeze S1. If you want to use the Layer Control dialog box instead, choose S2 and make it current, then choose S1 and click on the Freeze button. Choose OK to complete the command.

To make the bottom of the outside leg into one entity, use the PEDIT command. The PEDIT command is first used to change one of the objects into a polyline. After this is finished, use the Join option to combine the two lines and one arc into a single polyline.

To use the PEDIT command with the Join option, all the objects must be on the same UCS. Use the 3point UCS option to align the 2D plane with the side of the leg.

Step 2.0: Issue the UCS command and select the 3point option:

`Command: UCS ↵`	Starts the UCS command

`Origin/ZAxis/3point/Entity/`
`View/X/Y/Z/Prev/Restore/Save/Del/`
`?/<World>: 3 ↵`
	Selects the three point option

Step 2.1: Pick the three points to align the UCS:

`Origin point <0,0,0>:` *Use object snap Endpoint and pick point* Ⓑ *in figure 11.13*	Defines the new origin
`Point on positive portion of the` `X-axis<1,0,0>:` *Use object snap Endpoint and pick point* Ⓑ *in figure 11.13*	Defines a point on the X-axis

`Point on positive-Y portion of`
`the UCSX-Y plane <-1/2,7/8,.07>:`
Use object snap Midpoint pick point Ⓒ *in figure 11.13*
	Defines a point on the Y-axis

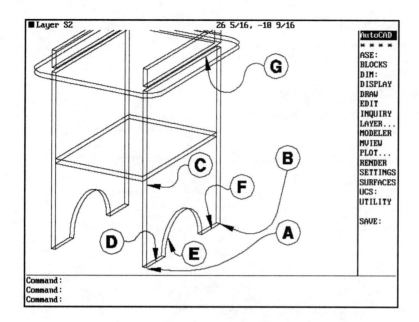

The UCS is now parallel to this side and you can create the polyline. To begin, select one of the entities and then convert it to a polyline. To complete the process, enter the Join option and then select all the objects that are on the same UCS and are connected to points that make up the first polyline segment.

Step 3.0: Issue the PEDIT command:

Command: **PEDIT** ↵   Starts the PEDIT
                                              command

Step 3.1: Select one entity to convert to a polyline:

Select polyline: *select line* Ⓓ   Selects the line to
(see fig. 11.13)   convert to a
                                            polyline

Step 3.2: You are prompted that the entity is not a polyline and asked if you want to turn it into one. Press Enter to accept the default of Yes:

Entity selected is not a polyline Prompts you that the
                                   selected entity is
                                   not a polyline

Do you want to turn it into one?   Accepts the default
<Y> ↵   of turning the line
                                   into a polyline

Step 3.3: Specify the Join option:

```
Close/Join/Width/Edit vertex/        Invokes the Join
Fit/Spline/Decurve/Ltype gen/        option
Undo/eXit <X>: J ↵
```

Step 3.4: Select the entities to add to the new polyline:

```
Select objects: Select arc Ⓔ        Selects one entity
(see fig. 11.13)                      to add to the new
                                      polyline
```

```
Select objects: Select line Ⓕ       Selects another entity to
(see fig. 11.13)                      add to the polyline
```

Step 3.5: Press Enter to stop adding entities to the polyline:

```
Select objects: ↵                    Stops the selection
2 segments added to polyline         process and displays
                                      the number of
                                      segments added to
                                      the polyline
```

Step 3.6: Press Enter to exit the PEDIT command:

```
Close/Join/Width/Edit vertex/        Exits the PEDIT
Fit/Spline/Decurve/Ltype gen/        command
Undo/eXit <X>: ↵
```

Now that you have a single entity at the bottom of the leg, you can use the RULESURF command to add the surface. It is more difficult for the polymeshes to make a smooth edge on this contour because it is a combination of an arc and two lines. For this reason, you need to increase the number of polymeshes divided into the contour.

Step 4.0: Invoke the variable SURFTAB1 and change its value to 36:

```
Command: SURFTAB1 ↵                  Starts the SURFTAB1
                                     variable
```

```
New value for SURFTAB1 <6>: 36 ↵    Defines the number
                                     of polymeshes as 36
```

Now use the RULESURF command to add the surface to the drawing.

Step 5.0: Issue the RULESURF command and select the defining contours:

```
Command: RULESURF ↵                  Starts the RULESURF  command
Select first defining curve:         Selects the first
Select the line at Ⓕ in figure 11.13  defining entity
Select second defining curve:        Adds the surface to
Select the line at Ⓖ in figure 11.13  the side
```

You can now use the COPY command's Multiple option to place the same contour on the inside of the leg and both sides of the opposite leg. Use the same basepoint process as in the earlier exercise.

Step 6.0: Enter the COPY command and select the object you want to copy:

Command: **COPY** ↵	Starts the COPY command
Select objects: *Select the new surface*	Selects the object to be copied
Select objects: ↵	Stops the selection process

Step 6.1: Invoke the Multiple option:

<Base point or displacement> /**Multiple: M** ↵	Invokes the Multiple option

Step 6.2: Select a base point from which all the copies are positioned:

Base point: *Use object snap Endpoint and pick point Ⓐ in figure 11.14*	Defines the base point

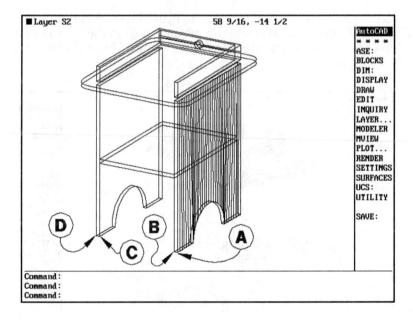

Figure 11.14:
Table with surface on one side.

Step 6.3: Pick the three points of displacement to position the duplicate geometry:

Second point of displacement: *Use object snap Endpoint and pick point Ⓑ in figure 11.14*	Defines the first location to copy the object

`Second point of displacement:` *Use object snap Endpoint and pick point* Ⓒ *in figure 11.14*	Defines the second location to copy the object
`Second point of displacement:` *Use object snap Endpoint and pick point* Ⓓ *in figure 11.14*	Defines the third location to copy the object

Step 6.4: Stop the COPY command:

`Second point of displacement: ↵`	Stops the COPY command

EXERCISE 4: ADDING THE SURFACE TO THE TABLE TOP AND MIDDLE SHELF

You are ready to add the surfaces seen in figure 11.15. Again, use the RULESURF command to create this geometry. As in the last exercise, you need to modify existing geometry into a single object to create the best polymesh.

Figure 11.15:

Surface on top and middle shelf.

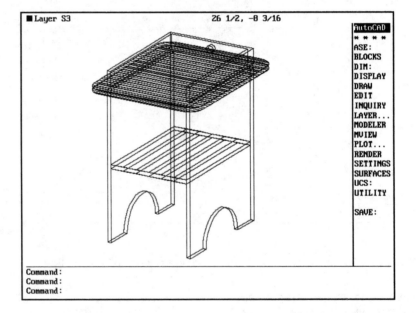

To work on the drawing more easily, first change the current layer. After you do this, change the UCS to World and use PEDIT to develop the contours for the surface. Finish the exercise by adding a Ruled Surface to the top and bottom of the two shelves.

TASKS TO BE COMPLETED IN THIS EXERCISE

- Change the UCS
- Use PEDIT to join geometry
- Add surface with RULESURF

Start the exercise by freezing the layer S2 and making S3 current.

Step 1.0: Issue the **LAYER** command and set S3, then freeze S2. If you want to use the Layer Control dialog box instead, choose S3 and make it current, then choose S2 and click on the Freeze button. Choose OK to complete the command.

Develop the surface across the top of the table by using the outside contours. At this point, these contours are composed of a line and two arcs. You need to combine both ends of the defining contours into single entities before adding the surface.

Use the PEDIT command to perform this operation. As you learned in the last exercise, before you can use PEDIT on a command you need to change the UCS so that it is parallel to the objects you want to modify. As you may recall from the last lesson, the top of the table was drawn in the World coordinate system. You can align the UCS to the geometry by using the World option of the UCS command.

Step 2.0: Issue the **UCS** command and enter **W** to change the UCS to the World option.

You are ready to modify the arcs and lines. Use the PEDIT command to convert one entity to a polyline and then join the remaining objects to the new polyline.

Step 3.0: Issue the PEDIT command and select the first entity:

Command: **PEDIT** ↵	Starts the PEDIT command
Select polyline: *Pick arc* Ⓐ *(see fig. 11.16)*	Selects the first object to be joined into a polyline

Figure 11.16:

Table top with labels for the PEDIT command.

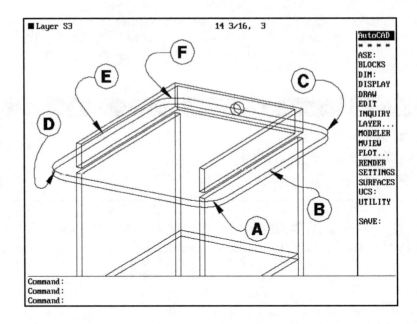

Step 3.1: Convert the arc into a polyline:

```
Entity selected is not a polyline
Do you want to turn it into one?        Turns the arc into a
<Y>↵                                    polyline
```

Step 3.2: Invoke the Join option and select the objects to add to the new polyline:

```
Close/Join/Width/Edit vertex/           Starts the Join
Fit/Spline/Decurve/Ltype gen/           option
Undo/eXit <X>: J↵
```

```
Select objects: Pick line Ⓑ            Selects one entity
in figure 11.16                         to add to the new
                                        polyline
```

```
Select objects: Pick arc Ⓒ             Selects the final
in figure 11.16                         entity to add to the
                                        polyline
```

```
Select objects: ↵                       Stops the selection
                                        process
```

```
2 segments added to polyline
```

Step 3.3: Exit the PEDIT command:

```
Close/Join/Width/Edit vertex/           Stops the PEDIT
Fit/Spline/Decurve/Ltype gen/           command
Undo/eXit<X>: ↵
```

You now need to perform the same operation on the opposite side of the table top. You then have a continuous entity onto which you can apply a surface using the RULESURF command.

Step 4.0: Issue the **PEDIT** command. Select the arc at point D (see fig. 11.16) as the polyline to edit. Press Enter to convert the arc to a polyline.

Step 4.1: Invoke the Join option and select the objects at point E and point F in figure 11.16. Press Enter to stop selecting objects. Press Enter again to exit the PEDIT command.

You now have two continuous contours. Use the PEDIT command to add a surface.

Step 5.0: Issue the **RULESURF** command and select the two new polylines as the first and second defining curves to finish the command.

You now have one surface across the top. To aid in productivity, copy the top surface down to add a surface to the bottom of the shelf. Use the COPY command and pick points to define the displacement.

Step 6.0: Issue the COPY command and select the object you want to copy:

Command: **COPY** ↵	Starts the COPY command
Select objects: *Select the new surface*	Selects the object to copy
Select objects: ↵	Stops the selection process

Step 6.1: Pick the two points that define the copy displacement:

<Base point or displacement> /Multiple:*Use object snap Endpoint and pick point* Ⓐ *in figure 11.17*	Defines the basepoint
Second point of displacement: *Use object snap Endpoint and pick point* Ⓑ *in figure 11.17*	Defines the point to which you want to copy

You now have finished the table top shelf and can surface the middle shelf. You can use the RULESURF command again to add the geometry. You do not need to join the geometry into one object in the middle shelf because continuous lines exist across the ends of it.

Use the RULESURF command and add a surface to the top of the middle shelf.

Step 7.0: Issue the **RULESURF** command. Select the line at point C in figure 11.18 as the first defining curve. Select the line at point D as the second defining curve.

Figure 11.17:

Top shelf with labels for the first copy of the surface.

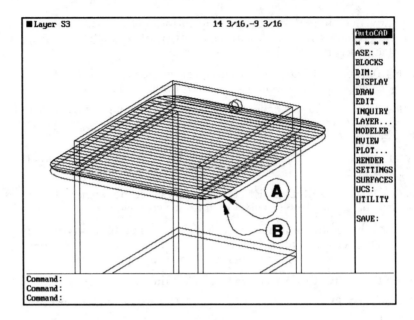

Figure 11.18:

The middle shelf and labels for defining the surface.

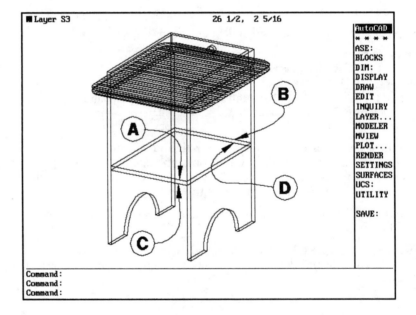

Although you can copy this geometry to add the surface to the bottom of the shelf, it is just as easy to use the RULESURF command again because the geometry is already two straight lines.

Step 8.0: Issue the **RULESURF** command and select the lines at point A and point B as the first and second defining curves.

EXERCISE 5: SURFACE THE HOLE AREA IN THE EDGING

You now are ready to add a surface across the back edge of the table, as seen in figure 11.19. No surface command exists that directly performs this operation. In many drawings, you must section the drawing so that a surface can be added. This is especially true for entities that trace, outline, or pass through the wireframe. They are created on a separate layer that is frozen after the surface has been added.

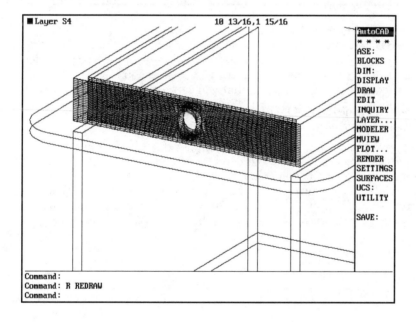

Figure 11.19:

Surface to the hole and the back edge.

To add a surface to the face of the vertical edge that the hole passes through, you first change the viewpoint of the object so that you can see it better. Before you do this, save the current view so that you can return to it easily. After you do this, use the polyline command to draw a line through the middle of the face that traces around the hole.

To complete the sectioning, add two lines from the ends of the middle line to the top contour of the geometry. All three lines are on a temporary layer. A surface can then be added as an Edge Defined Patch. This surface can then be mirrored to complete one face of the vertical edge. To develop the surface on the back face, erase the first surface, add the new surface, and use the OOPS command to retrieve the first surface.

TASKS TO BE COMPLETED IN THIS EXERCISE

- Save a view of the drawing
- Change the UCS
- Draw a surface contour using PLINE
- Add a surface using an Edge Defined Patch
- Mirror the surface
- Erase and retrieve a surface with OOPS

To add the next surface, you must do some additional manipulation of the geometry. To make this easier, turn around the object to see the area more clearly. Later in the exercise you will return to the current view point. As a result, save the current view before you use the VPOINT command. First make certain that you can see the entire drawing.

Step 1.0: Issue the **ZOOM** command with the Extents option to display the entire drawing on-screen.

To save the current display on-screen, use the VIEW command. You can save one or several views that can be restored at any time in the drawing. As a drawing becomes complex, this is a powerful option that enables you to return to zoom factors or viewpoints during the editing process. Saved views also are helpful when you make presentations because the views are saved and can be displayed easily by name.

The VIEW command has the following options:

- **?.** Displays the names of previously saved views
- **Delete.** Enables you to remove from the drawing a previously saved view
- **Restore.** Enables you to retrieve by name a previously named view
- **Save.** Stores the current view on-screen by entering a name
- **Window.** Enables you to place a window around the view to be saved

Use the VIEW command to save the current view on-screen:

Step 2.0: Issue the VIEW command:

`Command: VIEW ⏎`   Starts the VIEW command

Step 2.1: Invoke the SAVE command:

`?/Delete/Restore/Save/Window: S ⏎`   Saves the current view by name

Step 2.2: The view can have any name you want. For your own benefit, name it something meaningful that you can retrieve easily. For simplicity, name this view V1 (for the first view):

`View name to save: V1 ⏎`   Names the new view
                                       V1 and saves it for
                                       future retrieval

You can now change the viewpoint of the drawing. Because you are working on the back side, use the VPOINT command with the rotate option to display a back left view.

Step 3.0: Issue the VPOINT command and invoke the Rotate option:

`Command: VPOINT ⏎`   Starts the VPOINT command
`Rotate/<View point> <0,0,1>: R ⏎`   Selects the Rotate option

Step 3.1: Enter a value to display the back left side:

`Enter angle in XY plane`   Defines a value to
`from X axis <300>: 120 ⏎`   display the back
                                             left side

Step 3.2: Enter a value to view the object slightly from above the selected side:

```
Enter angle from XY plane <20>:        Displays the object from the
20 ↵                                    new viewpoint
```

Now use the PLINE command to add the contour seen in figure 11.20. This contour divides the object into sections onto which you can then apply surfaces.

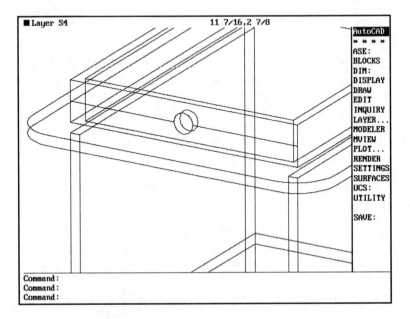

Because this entity will not be part of the drawing, you need to make the TEMP layer the current drawing layer. You then can freeze the layer after you are finished using it.

Step 4.0: Using the **LAYER** command, make the TEMP layer current and freeze layer S3.

The PLINE command is one of the commands controlled by the User Coordinate System (UCS), which means the UCS must be parallel to the polyline. Use the UCS command with the Entity option to set the UCS parallel to the side for the new polyline. A circle also is controlled by the UCS. For this reason, you can specify the Entity option and then select the circle to make the UCS for the polyline parallel to the UCS of the circle.

Step 5.0: Issue the UCS command and invoke the Entity option:

`Command: UCS ↵`	Starts the UCS command

`Origin/ZAxis/3point/Entity/`
`View/X/Y/Z/Prev/Restore/Save/`
`Del/?/<World>: E ↵`
	Invokes the Entity option

Step 5.1: Select the entity to align the UCS with. Where you select the object orients the positive X direction. To add a polyline across the back of the circles, place X near the quadrant or the circle at 9 o'clock. This makes the UCS parallel to the circle:

`Select Entity:` *Select the circle at point* Ⓑ *in figure 11.21*	Aligns the UCS parallel to the circle and places positive X to the left and Y straight up

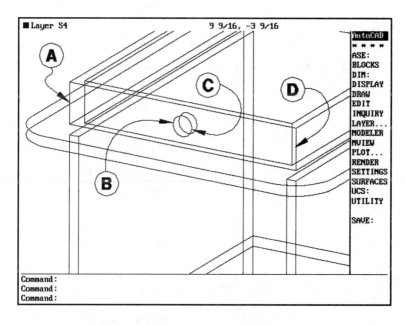

Figure 11.21:

Points for development of polyline contour.

You now can add the polyline that becomes one contour for the new surface. Start the polyline at the midpoint of the left vertical line, draw a line to the left quadrant of the circle, and then use the arc option to trace around the circle. The polyline ends at the midpoint of the right vertical line.

Step 6.0: Issue the PLINE command and select the starting point:

```
Command: PLINE ↵
```
Starts the PLINE command

```
From point: Use object snap midpoint
and pick point Ⓐ in figure 11.21
Current line-width is 0
```
Defines the starting
point of the polyline

Step 6.1: Pick the end point of the straight polyline section:

```
Arc/Close/Halfwidth/Length/
Undo/Width/<Endpoint of line>:
Use object snap Quadrant and pick point
Ⓑ in figure 11.21
```
Defines the end
point of the polyline

Step 6.2: Invoke the Arc option to trace the top half the circle with an arc:

```
Arc/Close/Halfwidth/Length/
Undo/Width/<Endpoint of line>:
A ↵
```
Invokes the Arc
option

Step 6.3: Invoke the CE option to align the center of the polyline arc with the center of the circle. Then select the circle's center as the center of the new arc:

```
Angle/CEnter/CLose/Direction
/Halfwidth/Line/Radius/Second
pt/Undo/Width/<Endpoint of arc>:
CE ↵
```
Invokes the Center
option

```
Center of arc: Use object snap Center
and pick the circle at point Ⓒ
in figure 11.21
```
Defines the center of the
existing circle as the center
of the new arc

Step 6.4: Define the end point of the arc to create a half circle:

```
Angle/Length/<End point>:
Use object snap Quadrant and pick
point Ⓒ in figure 11.21
```
Defines the end
point of the arc

Step 6.5: Invoke the Line option to return to line mode and complete the polyline at the right vertical line midpoint:

```
Angle/CEnter/CLose/Direction/
Halfwidth/Line/Radius/Second pt/
Undo/Width/<Endpoint of arc>: L ↵
```
Invokes the Line
option

```
Arc/Close/Halfwidth/Length/Undo/
Width/<Endpoint of line>: Use object
snap Midpoint and pick point Ⓓ
in figure 11.21
```
Defines the end of
the polyline

```
Arc/Close/Halfwidth/Length/Undo/
Width/<Endpoint of line>: ↵
```
Stops the PLINE
command

Because the back face is shorter than the front face, you cannot copy the polyline or surface that you apply to it. Use the same procedure you used to add the contour to the front side to contour the back side.

Step 7.0: Issue the PLINE command and select the starting point:

Command: **PLINE** ↵   Starts the PLINE command

From point: *Use object snap midpoint*   Defines the starting
and pick point (A) *in figure 11.22*   point of the
                                                polyline

Current line-width is 0

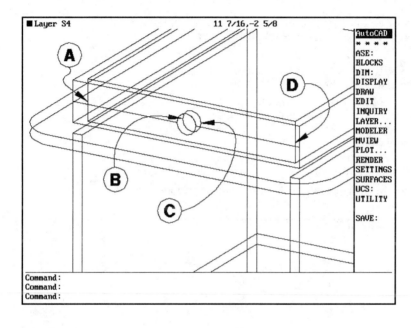

Figure 11.22:
*Labels for adding
polyline across
back circle.*

Step 7.1: Pick the end point of the straight polyline section:

Arc/Close/Halfwidth/Length/   Defines the end
Undo/Width/<Endpoint of line>:   point of the
Use object snap Quadrant and pick point (B)   polyline
in figure 11.22

Step 7.2: Invoke the Arc option to trace the top half of the circle with an arc:

Arc/Close/Halfwidth/Length/   Invokes the Arc
Undo/Width/<Endpoint of line>:   option
A ↵

Step 7.3: Invoke the CE option to align the center of the polyline arc with the center of the circle. Then select the center of the circle as the center of the new arc:

Angle/CEnter/CLose/Direction/   Invokes the Center
Halfwidth/Line/Radius/Second pt/   option
Undo/Width/<Endpoint of arc>:
CE ↵

`Center of arc:` *Use object snap center and pick the circle at point* Ⓒ *in figure 11.22*

Defines the center of the existing circle as the center of the new arc

Step 7.4: Define the end point of the arc to create half a circle:

`Angle/Length/<End point>:` *Use objectsnap Quadrant and pick point* Ⓒ *in figure 11.22*

Defines the end point of the arc

Step 7.5: Invoke the Line option to return to line mode and complete the polyline at the right vertical line midpoint:

`Angle/CEnter/CLose/Direction/`
`Halfwidth/Line/Radius/Second pt/`
`Undo/Width/<Endpoint of arc>: L ⏎`

Invokes the Line option

`Arc/Close/Halfwidth/Length/`
`Undo/Width/<Endpoint of line>:`
Use object snap midpoint and pick point Ⓓ *in figure 11.22*

Defines the end of the polyline

`Arc/Close/Halfwidth/Length/`
`Undo/Width/<Endpoint of line>: ⏎`

Stops the PLINE command

You are almost ready to add the single surface seen in figure 11.23.

Figure 11.23:

Edge defined patch.

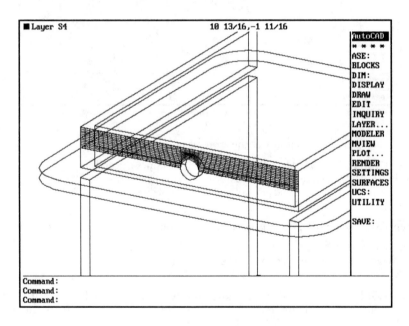

Because this is a complex contour, use the Edge Defined Patch or EDGESURF command to add the surface to this area. The EDGESURF command creates a surface between four connected entities. Currently, the new polyline and the top edge exist. Because the vertical lines extend beyond the defining curve, you need to add short construction lines to create four contours to develop the surface.

Step 8.0: Start the **LINE** command and use object snap Endpoint to draw a line between points A and B in figure 11.24.

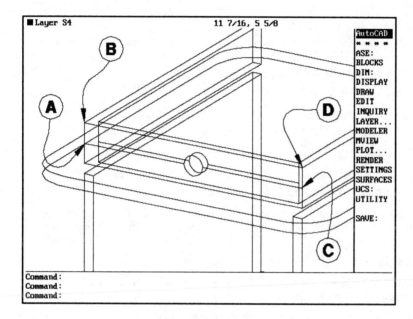

Step 9.0: Start the **LINE** command and use object snap Endpoint to draw a line between the points at point C and D in figure 11.24.

The same operation needs to be performed on the back face connecting the middle polyline with the top line.

Step 10.0: Start the **LINE** command and use object snap Endpoint to draw a line from the left end of the back polyline to the left end of the top line.

Step 11.0: Start the **LINE** command and use object snap Endpoint to draw a line from the right end of the back polyline to the right end of the top line.

ADDING AN EDGE DEFINED PATCH

You are now ready to add the surface by selecting the four connect contours using an Edge Defined Patch. Surface the bottom and mirror the geometry across the middle to finish the top. First, make layer S4 current, but do not freeze the current TEMP layer. You need to see this layer to select the contours that define the surface.

Step 12.0: Use the **LAYER** command or Layer Control dialog box and make S4 current.

Because this contour has curved surfaces, you need to define the variable SURFTAB1 before you use the EDGESURF command. In addition, you need to set SURFTAB2 because EDGESURF surfaces are defined by a third and fourth contour.

Step 13.0: Set the value of SURFTAB1:

Command: **SURFTAB1** ↵	Starts the SURFTAB1 variable
New value for SURFTAB1 <36>: **48** ↵	Sets the variable to 48

Step 14.0: Set the value of SURFTAB2:

Command: **SURFTAB2** ↵	Starts the SURFTAB2 variable
New value for SURFTAB1 <6>: **12** ↵	Sets the variable to 12

You are now ready to add the surface to the front of the face between the polyline and the top corner. Use the Edge Defined Patch or EDGESURF command and select the polyline, top line, and two connecting lines as the defining contour.

Step 15.0: Issue the EDGESURF command:

Command: *Choose* Draw, *then* 3D surface, *then* Edge Defined Patch	Starts the EDGESURF command

Step 15.1: Select the four defining contours or edges:

Select edge 1: *Pick the polyline between* (A) *and* (C) *(see fig. 11.24)*	Selects the first contour
Select edge 2: *Pick the line between* (B) *and* (D) *(see fig. 11.24)*	Selects the second contour
Select edge 3: *Pick the line between* (B) *and* (A) *(see fig. 11.24)*	Selects the third contour
Select edge 4: *Pick the line between* (C) *and* (D) *(see fig. 11.24)*	Selects the last contour and draws the surface

You now have one half of the Edge Defined Patch. Mirror this object over to complete the surfacing of the outside edges. Because the UCS is parallel to the back face of the vertical edge, it does not need to be changed.

Step 16.0: Issue the MIRROR command and select the object to mirror:

Command: **MIRROR** ↵	Starts the MIRROR command
Select objects: *Pick the new surface*	Selects the objects to mirror
Select objects: ↵	Stops the selection process

Step 16.1: Select the mirror lines at the midpoints of the vertical lines. By using midpoint over the end point of the surface, you avoid picking an end point of a polymesh by mistake:

First point of mirror line: *Use object snap Midpoint and pick the vertical line at point Ⓐ (see fig. 11.25)*	Defines one point on the mirror line
Second point: *Use object snap Midpoint and pick the vertical line at point Ⓑ (see fig. 11.25)*	Defines the second point of the mirror line

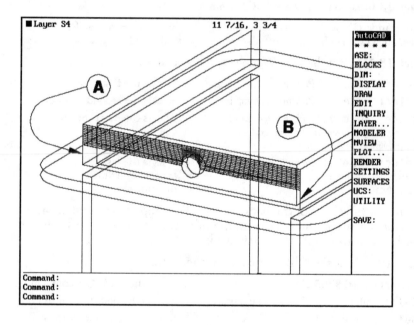

Figure 11.25:
First edge defined patch.

Step 16.2: Accept the default, which does not delete the old object:

Delete old objects? <N> ↵	Keeps the original polyline

You now have the front surface for this area. You can use the same procedure to develop the surface area on the back side. However, as is often the case in surface development, one surface is in front or over the top of the area for the new surface. You can solve this problem in one of several ways, such as changing layers or changing the view point.

In the steps that follow, erase the two surfaces currently in the drawing. Afterward, use the same process to add the surfaces to the back. Once completed, you can use the OOPS command to retrieve the erased surfaces. As long as you select both of them during the same ERASE command and nothing else is erased in between, this is a helpful procedure for developing surfaces around conflicting areas.

Step 17.0: Issue the **ERASE** command and select both of the new surfaces. Press Enter to complete the command.

You can now add the surface to the back face of the vertical edge using the same process as on the front face.

Step 18.0: Issue the EDGESURF command:

`Command:` *Choose* Draw, *then* 3D surface, *then* Edge Defined Patch	Starts the EDGESURF command

Step 18.1: Select the four defining contours or edges:

`Select edge 1:` *Pick the back polyline*	Selects the first contour
`Select edge 2:` *Pick the back top line*	Selects the second contour
`Select edge 3:` *Pick the right short vertical line between the top line and the polyline*	Selects the third contour
`Select edge 4:` *Pick the left short vertical line between the top line and the polyline*	Selects the last contour and draws the surface

You now have half of the back surface. To complete the operation, mirror this surface across the midpoint of the vertical lines as you did with the front face of the vertical edge.

Step 19.0: Issue the MIRROR command and select the object to mirror:

`Command:` **MIRROR** ↵	Starts the MIRROR command
`Select objects:` *Pick the new surface*	Selects the objects to mirror
`Select objects:` ↵	Stops the selection process

Step 19.1: Select the mirror lines at the midpoints of the vertical lines:

`First point of mirror line:` *Use object snap Midpoint and pick the short vertical line on the left*	Defines one point on the mirror line
`Second point:` *Use object snap Midpoint and pick the short vertical line on the right*	Defines the second point of the mirror line

Step 19.2: Accept the default, which does not delete the old object:

`Delete old objects? <N> ⏎`   Keeps the original
                                polyline

You now need to retrieve the erased surface that was removed with the ERASE command.

Step 20.0: Issue the OOPS command:

`Command: OOPS ⏎`   Retrieves the last
                      erased entities

EXERCISE 6: FINISHING THE SURFACES

You are now ready to finish the drawing by adding the surfaces to the circle and the side of the vertical edges as seen in figure 11.26. Before you do this, return to the viewpoint saved earlier before adding the current surfaces. You can use the VIEW command to restore the viewpoint because you saved it as a view.

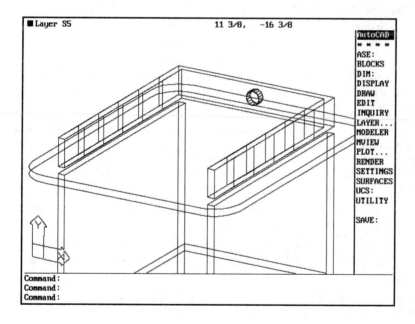

Figure 11.26:

Surface between hole and on sides of vertical edges.

You now could use the RULESURF command to place the surface between the two circles; however, to experience another surface command, use a Tabulated Surface. This surface command projects a surface contour along a vector. The vector is a line drawn between the center of the circles.

To complete the surface, use the RULESURF command to place a surface between the lines that define the corners of the vertical edges.

TASKS TO BE COMPLETED IN THIS EXERCISE

- Restore a saved view
- Add a construction line for a Tabulated Surface
- Create a Tabulated Surface
- Finish surface the drawing with Ruled Surfaces

Begin by restoring the earlier saved view V1.

Step 1.0: Issue the VIEW command:

Command: **VIEW** ↵	Starts the VIEW command

Step 1.1: Invoke the Restore option and specify the view to restore:

?/Delete/Restore/Save/Window: **R** ↵	Invokes the Restore option
View name to restore: **V1** ↵	Restores the previously saved view V1

Now add the surface between the two circles. Although you can use the RULESURF command to place a surface between the circles, use a tabulated surface in this exercise. The TABSURF command creates a surface based on a contour and a vector.

To use the TABSURF command in this area, you need a construction line through the middle of the circle that serves as the vector. Because this line is not intended as part of the finished drawing, place it on the TEMP layer. In addition, freeze the current layer to make it easier to develop the new surfaces.

Step 2.0: Make layer TEMP current and freeze layer S4.

You now need to add the construction line that serves as the directional vector and distance for the tabulated surface. Because this surface intersects the two circles, draw a line between the center point of the circles.

Step 3.0: Issue the LINE command and draw a line between the circle center points:

Command: **LINE** ↵	Starts the LINE command
From point: *Use object snap Center and pick circle* (A) *in figure 11.27*	Defines the starting point of the line

| `To point:` *Use object snap Center and pick circle* Ⓑ *in figure 11.27* | Defines the end point |
| `To point:` ⏎ | Ends the LINE command |

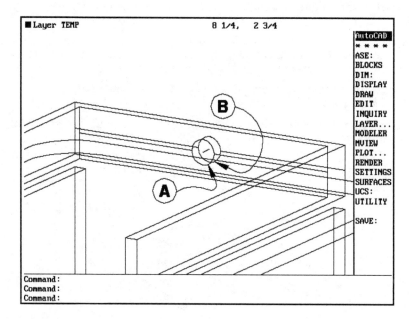

Figure 11.27:
Construction line for the tabulated surface.

You can now add the Tabulated Surface. To optimize the number of polymeshes in the drawing, however, reduce the SURFTAB1 setting to 18.

Step 4.0: Issue the **SURFTAB1** variable and set its value to 18.

To draw the construction line, you made the TEMP layer current. Before you add the surface, you need to make the layer S5 current. Do not freeze layer TEMP because you need to see the construction line to develop the tabulated surface.

Step 5.0: Issue the **LAYER** command and make layer S5 current.

You now are ready to add the Tabulated Surface. Use the TABSURF command, select a contour or curve, and then select a vector. The selected contour is then projected as a surface in the same direction and at the same length as the vector.

Step 6.0: Start the Tabulate Surface option:

| `Command:` *Select Draw, then 3D surfaces, then* Tabulated Surface | Starts the TABSURF command |

Step 6.1: Select the object that is the contour. In selecting the front circle, pick the object at the bottom so that you select the circle and not the polyline that traces over the top:

`Select path curve:` *Select the circle at* — Selects the contour
(A) *(see fig. 11.27)* — of the surface

Step 6.2: Select the vector that the contour is to follow. The end at which you pick the line defines the direction of the surface. The surface is projected away from the picked points in the line's direction:

`Select direction vector:` *Pick the* — Selects the vector
construction line near the front circle — and draws the surface

You can now finish the drawing by adding the surface to the remaining part of the drawing as seen in figure 11.28.

Figure 11.28:

The surface on the vertical edges and the hole.

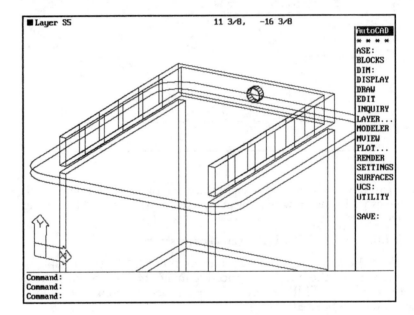

Again, because the area to be surfaced is made up of straight lines, you can reduce the number of polymeshes.

Step 7.0: Issue the variable SURFTAB1 and set its value to 6.

You now are finished with the construction lines and can freeze the TEMP layer.

Step 8.0: Issue the **LAYER** command and freeze TEMP.

You can now use the RULESURF command to finish the drawing.

Step 9.0: Issue the **RULESURF** command and add the six remaining surfaces between the top and bottom lines on the vertical edges. Use figure 11.28 as a guide and remember to select the contours near the same ends.

EXERCISE 7: REMOVING HIDDEN LINES

You have now finished the drawing and are ready to see the drawing with all hidden lines removed, as seen in figure 11.29. To see this geometry, you must first thaw the remaining layer. In addition, to perform a hidden line removal properly, all non-surface geometry such as the object lines and dimensions must be frozen. If you do not freeze the object lines, the circle appears as a solid and is not shown as a hole. After all the layers are correct, use the HIDE command. The HIDE command visually removes all geometry that would not be seen on a real object from the current view point.

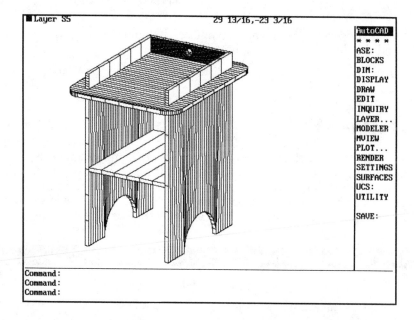

Figure 11.29:

The table with hidden lines removed.

TASKS TO BE COMPLETED IN THIS EXERCISE

- Thaw all Surface layers
- Freeze all object lines
- Perform a hidden line removal

Begin by setting the layers.

Step 1.0: Choose the Layer Control dialog box or issue the **LAYER** command. Thaw all the surface layers: S1, S2, S3, S4 (S5 is thawed and is the current layer). Freeze all the remaining layers in the drawing.

You now are ready to remove the hidden lines. Make sure the entire drawing is on-screen. When you begin the HIDE command, the screen goes blank. After the command finishes performing its hidden line removal, the drawing appears. This image is temporary and cannot be edited. Nevertheless, you can plot it using the hidden line removal option in the PLOT command.

Step 2.0: Issue the HIDE command:

```
Command: HIDE ↵
```
Starts the HIDE command and performs a hidden line removal

After the hidden line removal is complete, the drawing is finished. You can end the drawing and exit AutoCAD.

Step 3.0: Save the drawing to disk and end the current drawing session.

SUMMARY

Development of a surface model requires the use of and usually the modification of a wireframe model. During the application of a surface, care must be taken not to alter the original wireframe. In addition, a balance must be kept between using enough polymeshes in a surface to develop a smooth contour and not to increase the size of the drawing.

IN THIS LESSON, YOU LEARNED TO DO THE FOLLOWING:

- Apply surfaces to a wireframe model
- Change the number of polymeshes in a surface
- Use layers to aid in adding surfaces
- Section a drawing for surfacing

In this drawing you added surfaces to an existing 3D wireframe drawing. In the next drawing you create a solid model three-dimensional drawing. A solid model is the most sophisticated application of 3D.

REVIEW

1. Retrieve the drawing REV11-1. Use the **RULESURF** command to place a surface between the two lines.

2. Retrieve the drawing REV11-2. Use the **RULESURF** command to surface the box.

3. Retrieve the drawing REV11-3. Change SURFTAB1 to 24. Use the **RULESURF** command to surface the object.

4. Retrieve the drawing REV11-4. Use the **PEDIT** command to change the side with two arcs and three lines to a polyline.

5. Use the **EDGESURF** command to place a tabulated surface variable on REV11-4. Change the surftabs as needed.

6. Retrieve the drawing REV11-5. Draw a polyline around the circle to apply a surface across the side with the circle.

7. Use only the **RULESURF** command to place a tabulated surface variable on the drawing REV11-5. Change the surftabs as needed.

8. Retrieve the drawing REV11-5. Draw a line between the center of the two holes.

9. Use the **TABSURF** command to place a tabulated surface variable between the two holes. Change the tabulated surfaces as needed.

10. Recall the drawing REV11-2 from the disk. Surface the drawing without the dimensions visible. Use **RULESURF, EDGESURF,** and **TABSURF** at least once in the drawing.

BUILDING A 3D SOLID MODEL

OVERVIEW

The final and most sophisticated application of three dimensional geometry is a solid model. AutoCAD's optional *Advanced Modeling Extension* (AME) enables the user to create a drawing that is mathematically viewed as a real solid object. The AME also enables users to calculate advanced database queries, such as volume or moments of inertia.

In a solid model, geometry is created through the individual development of primitive entities. These entities, known as *primitives*, are mathematical representations of basic 3D shapes found in the real world. Different types of primitives include a box, sphere, cone, torus, cylinder, and wedge. Primitive entities can be created through the use of circles and polylines with a thickness in the Z axis.

As geometry is developed, it is edited to create the desired shape. This editing includes combining several different primitives into one, subtracting one primitive from another, or finding the intersecting area of multiple primitives.

After geometry is developed, it can be used to develop tool paths or for visualization, the same way a 3D surface model is used. The geometry also can be queried because it is mathematically a solid object. These calculations take into consideration the size, weight, and material used in the part.

Lastly, when the drawing is complete, you can develop multiple views in several viewports on the screen. These viewports can be manipulated individually or together. Finished geometry can be used to develop wire frame models that you later can turn into a full shaded image of the drawing.

TOPICS COVERED IN THIS LESSON

In this lesson, you learn to do the following:

- Develop solid model geometry
- Intersect, union, and subtract solid model geometry
- Divide the screen into viewports
- Profile a solid model
- Mesh a solid model
- Shade a solid model

COMMANDS COVERED IN THIS LESSON

This lesson teaches you how to use the following AutoCAD commands:

- **THICKNESS.** Defines the Z axis thickness of a 2D object
- **SOLIDIFY.** Converts a polyline or a circle with a thickness into a solid model
- **BOX.** Develops a 3D solid-model box
- **CYLINDER.** Develops a solid-model cylinder
- **UNION.** Joins multiple solid primitives into one
- **INTERSECT.** Joins multiple solid primitives into one, defined by the 3D space shared by the original primitives
- **SUBTRACT.** Removes one primitive from another
- **TILEMODE (Tiled viewport mode).** A system variable that controls whether you work in Model Space or Paper Space
- **MVIEW.** Develops multiple viewports when tiled viewport mode is off
- **PSPACE.** Changes the display mode to paper space
- **MESH.** Places a mesh around a solid model
- **SHADE.** Displays a meshed solid or surface model as a shaded image

SETTING UP THE DRAWING

In this lesson you will be creating the fitting shown in figure 12.1. Unlike past exercises, you will create this geometry using AutoCAD's solid modeling extension. This lesson shows you how to use this option to create a solid model. A *solid model* is a mathematically accurate model of three-dimensional geometry. The primitives are created using standard geometric entities called *solid primitives*, which are boxes, spheres, cones, cylinders, and so forth.

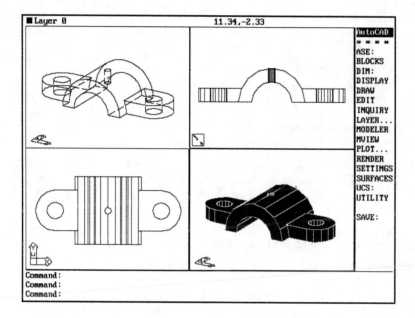

Figure 12.1:

The completed solid model drawing.

Step 1.0: Start AutoCAD and save the new drawing as **LESSON12**.

Step 2.0: Use the **UNITS** command or Units Control dialog box and set up the drawing with decimal units at two decimal places. Leave all the remaining settings at their default.

The limits can remain at the default setting of 12,9.

Step 3.0: Use the **LAYER** command or the Layer Control dialog box to create the layers **SOLID** and **TEMP**. Assign the color Blue to the layer SOLID and make it the current layer.

Setting the Viewpoint and UCS for a New Drawing

You are ready to begin the drawing. In this drawing, as with all 3D drawings, you first need to decide what side of the geometry you want to begin. It is easier to change the viewpoint or create multiple view drawings if you align each part's sides, the top, left, front, and so forth, to AutoCAD's drawing environment. In Lesson 10 you started the table by drawing the top first. You were able to start drawing on the top or plan view of the drawing. In this drawing, you begin by drawing the half cylinders that define the contour of the front. Because of this, you need to change both the viewpoint and UCS to be parallel to the visual front of AutoCAD's drawing environment.

As you learned in Lesson 10, the VPOINT command displays a specific viewpoint by calculating coordinates or rotation angles. These options work only if the top of the object is drawn on the top (or *world plan*) of the AutoCAD drawing environment, and the front of the object is drawn on the front (the VPOINT Rotate 270-0 option) of the AutoCAD drawing environment.

The easiest way to align your 3D model with AutoCAD UCS is to use the VPOINT command to display the view so that it shows the side of the object you want to draw first. Then use the UCS command and align the UCS to the view.

Step 4.0: Issue the VPOINT command and use the Rotate option to change the viewpoint to the front of the AutoCAD drawing environment:

Command: **VPOINT** ↵	Starts the VPOINT command
Rotate/<View point> <0.00,0.00, 1.00>: **R** ↵	Invokes the Rotate option
Enter angle in X-Y plane from X axis <270>: **270** ↵	Selects the front of the drawing
Enter angle from X-Y plane <90>: **0** ↵	Displays the front straight-on view

The drawing environment is now at a front view. Notice how the UCS icon has become a broken pencil. This informs you that the UCS is perpendicular to the viewpoint and is, in effect, not useful. If you were to draw a circle it would appear as a line in the drawing.

Step 5.0: Issue the UCS command and use the View option to align the UCS to the view:

```
Command: UCS ↵                        Starts the UCS command
Origin/ZAxis/3point/Entity/View/      Aligns the UCS to
X/Y/Z/Prev/Restore/Save/Del/?/        the current
<World>:V ↵                           viewpoint
```

EXERCISE 1: CREATING SOLID CYLINDERS

Begin this drawing by creating the concentric cylinders seen in figure 12.2. To develop a solid model, you must analyze the type of geometric figures that define the drawing. Be aware that in the final drawing, these figures may be only partials of a whole. If you look back at the opening figure, for example, you see that the cylinders finally become only half cylinders. The modify commands in the solid modeler enable you to alter the geometry to develop the desired final object.

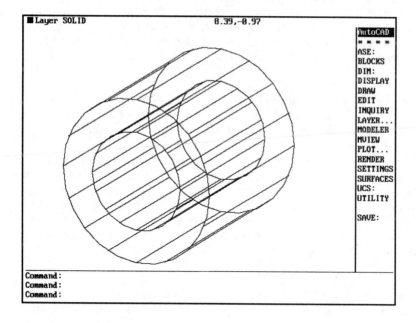

Figure 12.2:
Two concentric cylinders.

To develop the geometry in figure 12.2, create two cylinders, one inside the other. After you create the cylinders, change the viewpoint to see them as isometric. The cylinder inside of the larger one is a hole. The inside cylinder must be removed by using a modify command because cylinders are solid objects (like steel rods). The cylinder with a hole through its middle becomes the foundation for the development of the entire drawing.

TASKS TO BE COMPLETED IN THIS EXERCISE

- Set the wire density
- Draw two concentric cylinders
- Change the viewpoint
- Subtract the smaller cylinder from the larger

Solid model primitives can become massive database files. For this reason, AutoCAD enables you to control the density of the wire frame displayed on the geometry. By default, this is set to the lowest value of one. The drawing you are about to create is small. To help you better visualize the drawing, set the wire density to four.

Step 1.0: Set the wire density to four:

Command: *Choose* Model, *then* Display, *then* Set Wire Dens.	Enables you to set wire density
Wireframe mesh density (1 to 12) <1>: 4 ↵	Sets the wireframe density to four

You now are ready to develop the two concentric cylinders as solid cylinders. *Solid cylinders* are circular columns defined by center point(s), diameter or radius, and height. A cylinder can be circular or elliptical. By default, the circular or elliptical side of the cylinder is aligned with the UCS. You can use the Baseplane option to create a temporary 2D construction plane to align the circular or elliptical side of the cylinder during its development.

The first cylinder has a radius of 1.25" and a height of 2.5".

Step 2.0: Start the solid cylinder (SOLCYL) command. An icon menu appears displaying all of the solid primitives. Pick the icon that displays the cylinder:

Command: *Choose* Model, *then* Primitives, *then* Cylinder, *then* OK	Starts the solid cylinder command

Step 2.1: Pick a center point anywhere near the center of the screen:

`Baseplane/Elliptical/<Center`   Defines the center
`point><0,0,0>`: *Pick a point in the center*   of the solid cylinder
of the screen

Step 2.2: Enter the radius of the cylinder's circle:

`Diameter/<Radius>:` **1.25** ↵   Defines a radius of 1.25

Step 2.3: Enter the height of the cylinder. The height is the amount the cylinder projects into the Z axis:

`Center of other end/<Height>:`   Defines a height of 2.5
2.5 ↵

The solid cylinder is added to the drawing. From this viewpoint it looks like a cylinder because the height is projecting from the screen.

Again, cylinders resemble solid rods, so you need to add a second cylinder that defines the hole in the middle of the object. This cylinder will be concentric (or have the same center) as the first cylinder. You can use object snaps like center on solid primitives the same as two dimensional objects. The radius of the cylinder will be the size of the hole (.75) and will have the same height as the first cylinder. If the height was not the same height or greater, it would leave a hole that does not project through the entire object but one that has a bottom.

Step 3.0: Start the solid cylinder (SOLCYL) command:

`Command:` *Choose* Model, *then* Primitives,   Starts the solid
then Cylinder *then* OK   cylinder command

Step 3.1: Pick the center point of this cylinder as the same center on the existing cylinder:

`Baseplane/Elliptical/<Center`   Defines the center
`point><0,0,0>`: *Using object snap CENter,* of the solid
select the existing solid on the   cylinder
circle circumference

Step 3.2: Enter the radius of the circle of the cylinder:

`Diameter/<Radius>:` **.75** ↵   Defines a radius of 1.25

Step 3.3: Enter the height of the cylinder. The height is the amount the cylinder projects into the Z axis:

`Center of other end/<Height>:`   Defines a height of 2.5
2.5 ↵

You can now change the viewpoint of the object to see the depth of the cylinder. You are currently looking straight at the front of the object. Use the VPOINT command and change the viewpoint to a right front view, looking at the object from above.

Step 4.0: Issue the VPOINT command and invoke the Rotate option:

```
Command: VPOINT ↵
```
Starts the VPOINT command

```
Rotate/<View point>
<0.00,-1.00,0.00>:R ↵
```
Selects the Rotate option

Step 4.1: Enter an angle that displays the front right side:

```
Enter angle in XY plane from
X axis <270>: 300 ↵
```
Selects a front right view

Step 4.2: Enter an angle to see the selected side slightly from above:

```
Enter angle from XY plane
<0>: 20 ↵
```
Shows the view at an angle of 20 degrees

SUBTRACTING SOLID PRIMITIVES

As mentioned earlier, solid cylinders are obviously solid. At this point, you have two solids occupying the same space in the drawing. The inner cylinder was drawn to be the center hole. To make this so, you need to subtract the primitive occupied by the smaller cylinder from the larger cylinder, thus creating a hole.

The command that subtracts one solid from another is SUBTRACT. After you invoke the command, AutoCAD goes through two calculations, which are displayed at the command prompt, and updates the drawing database. Although you do not see a difference on-screen, only one cylinder with a hole exists, not two separate cylinders.

Step 5.0: Issue the SUBTRACT command:

```
Command: Choose Model, then Subtract
```
Starts the SUBTRACT command

Step 5.1: Select the source object. This is the object from which the second object is to be subtracted:

```
Source objects...
Select objects: Select the large cylinder
```
Selects the primitive that will remain

Step 5.2: Press Enter to stop selecting source objects:

```
Select objects: ↵
```
Stops the selection process

Step 5.3: Select the objects to subtract from the source object:

```
Objects to subtract from them...
Select objects: Select the small cylinder
```
Selects the primitive to remove

Step 5.4: Stop the selection process:

```
Select objects: ↵
```
Stops the selection process

EXERCISE 2: INTERSECTING SOLIDS

You now need to create the geometry shown in figure 12.3. As you can see, this object is half of the existing cylinder. You can create this object by placing a solid box around the area you want to keep. After you do this, have AutoCAD calculate and keep the primitive shared by both objects.

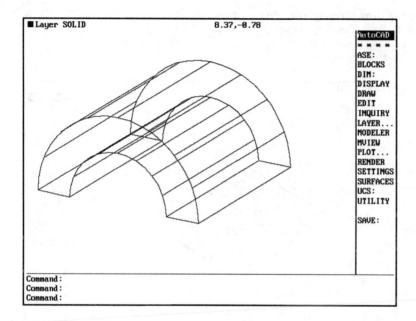

Figure 12.3:
Half cylinders after being modified.

To develop the half cylinders, begin by enclosing the geometry you need to keep with a second primitive. This new primitive is a solid box. When the area to keep is shared by two primitives, use the INTERSECT command to remove the bottom of the cylinder and keep the intersecting primitives.

TASKS TO BE COMPLETED IN THIS EXERCISE

- Place a solid box around the primitive you want to keep
- Intersect the two primitives

Begin by placing a solid box around the top of the cylinder. The BOX command creates a three-dimensional box (a rectangle with depth). The BOX command enables you to select a starting point at a corner or center. The definition of the box can then be specified by an equal-sided cube, the length/width/height, or the 3D opposite corner.

Use the solid BOX command to create a box around the top of the cylinder.

Step 1.0: Start the Solid Box command:

`Command:` *Choose* Model, *then* Box   Starts the Solid Box command

Step 1.1: Select the corner of the box. This will be the lower left corner of the box on the X-Y drawing plane:

`Baseplane/Center/<Corner of box>`   Defines the front,
`<0,0,0>`: *Using object snap QUADrant,*   lower left corner of
pick the large cylinder at point Ⓐ   the box
in figure 12.4

Figure 12.4:

Cylinder with box.

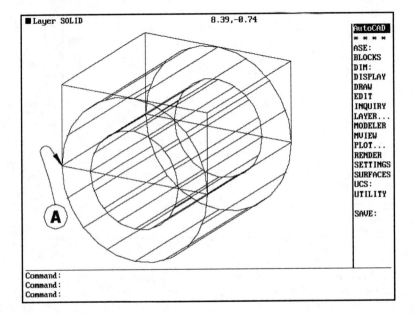

Step 1.2: Invoke the Length option to specify the length, width, and height of the cylinder:

`Cube/Length/<Other corner>: L ↵`   Invokes the length option

Step 1.3: Specify the length. The length is the distance on the X axis. Look at the UCS icon to see that this is across the front of the cylinder. The cylinder has a radius of 1.25" or a diameter of 2.5". To enclose the cylinder, the length will be equal to the diameter:

`Length: 2.5 ↵`   Specifies the length or distance in
                                        the X axis

Step 1.4: Specify the width. The width is the distance on the Y axis. The Y axis is in the up direction. The starting point of the solid box is at the middle quadrant of the cylinder; therefore, to enclose the cylinder, the width must equal the radius:

Width: **1.25** ↵   Specifies the width or distance in
                                           the Y axis

Step 1.5: Specify the height. The height is the distance into the Z axis. The Z axis is equal to the height of the cylinder. The solid box starting point is on the front of the cylinder; therefore, to enclose the cylinder, the height must be in the negative direction:

Height: **-2.5** ↵   Specifies the height or distance in
                                           the Z axis and creates the solid box

Now there is a box around the top half of the cylinder. The space shared by the box and the cylinder is the desired geometry. To isolate this primitive in the drawing, use the Solid INTERSECT command. The Solid INTERSECT command calculates the area shared by multiple primitives, keeps the shared space, and removes the remaining area.

Step 2.0: Issue the INTERSECT command:

Command: *Choose* Model, *then* Intersect   Starts the INTERSECT command

Step 2.1: Select the objects that intersect each other:

Select objects: *Select the box*   Selects one object
Select objects: *Select the cylinder*   Selects another object
Select objects: ↵   Stops the selection process and
                                        removes the area not shared by
                                        both primitives

EXERCISE 3: CREATING SOLIDS FROM 2D ENTITIES

You are ready to add the extension that projects out of the side of the cylinder. Unlike previous exercises, this geometry will be developed in part by a nonsolid object that is changed to a solid. To do this, first develop construction lines to position a polyline with thickness, then convert the polyline into a solid primitive. Solid primitives are then added to complete one extension (see fig. 12.5).

Figure 12.5:

*Drawing with
right extension
developed
with polyline.*

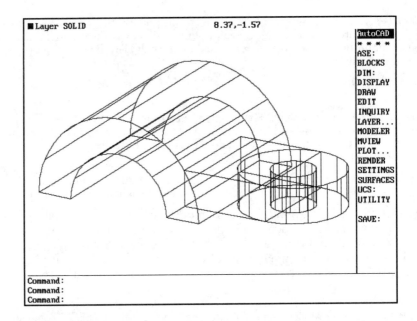

TASKS TO BE COMPLETED IN THIS EXERCISE

- Develop construction line
- Change 2D thickness
- Draw polyline
- Convert polyline to solid primitive
- Add solid primitives

Begin by creating construction lines, which you will use to position the geometry that defines the right extension. Place the construction lines on the TEMP layer so that they will not be part of the solid model drawing.

Step 1.0: Maker layer **TEMP** the current layer.

Begin by drawing a line down the middle of the cylinder. This line serves as the starting point for developing the construction lines. Two dimensional geometry, such as lines, can be added to a solid model drawing using the same process as in 2D.

Step 2.0: Issue the LINE command. Pick the start and end points of the line at the center the cylinders:

Command: **LINE** ↵	Starts the LINE command
From point: *Use object snap CENter and select the solid cylinder at point* Ⓐ *(see fig. 12.6)*	Starts a line at the center of the end of the cylinder
To point: *Use object snap CENter and select the solid cylinder at point* Ⓑ *(see fig. 12.6)*	Ends the line at the center of the end of the cylinder
To point: ↵	Stops the LINE command

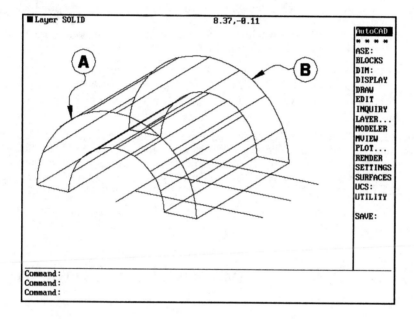

Figure 12.6:

Construction lines for the right extension.

You now are ready to add the remaining three construction lines. You do this by drawing a line from the middle of the current center line and then offsetting the distance of the solid extension.

To offset the lines across the bottom of the object, you need to change the UCS to the bottom. Because the UCS was changed to the front at the beginning of this lesson, the top and bottom of the object are correctly aligned with the UCS World. Use the UCS command with the World option to define the correct user coordinate system.

Step 3.0: Issue the UCS command and invoke the World option:

```
Command: UCS ↵                          Starts the UCS command
Origin/ZAxis/3point/Entity/             Sets the UCS to the
View/X/Y/Z/Prev/Restore/Save/           World Coordinate
Del/?/<World>: W ↵                      System, parallel to
                                        the flat section of
                                        the half cylinder
```

You now can add the line from the midpoint of the existing construction line. This new line defines the center of the hole in the right extension, which is two units to the right of the middle of the half cylinder.

Step 4.0: Enter the **LINE** command. Use the object snap midpoint and pick the construction line as the starting point of the line. At the **To point:** prompt, enter **@2<0** to draw a line perpendicular to the construction line two units to the right. Press Enter to exit the LINE command.

You now use the OFFSET command to create two perpendicular construction lines from the new line. These two lines define the outer sides (or the width) of the extension. The overall width of the two lines is 1.5 units.

Step 5.0: Issue the **OFFSET** command and set the offset distance to **.75**. Select the new perpendicular construction line as the object to offset and then pick a point to the lower left. Select the new perpendicular construction line again and offset the line by picking a point to the upper right. Press Enter to stop the OFFSET command and finish the construction line development.

Your drawing with construction lines should look like the previous figure, figure 12.6.

DRAWING SOLID PRIMITIVES USING GEOMETRY WITH THICKNESS

In addition to using solid primitives to develop geometry, you can also develop primitives using polylines and circles with thickness. *Thickness* is the amount an object projects into the Z axis. In 2D, thickness is always 0. Thickness is a subset of the ELEV or Elevation command that also defines the placement of geometry in relation to the Z axis or X-Y plane. By default, elevation is 0 and objects are placed directly on the X-Y plane. In addition, the THICKNESS system variable can be directly accessed by entering **THICKNESS** at the command prompt.

When solid model geometry is developed, the thickness of an object usually is set equal to the material thickness. After the thickness is set, the outline of the geometry turns into a wire frame model. This model is then converted into a true solid model primitive.

To create the first volume, begin by defining a thickness of .5, then draw the geometry. This geometry is the linear section of the right extension.

Step 6.0: Enter the THICKNESS variable to define the thickness (*thickness* is the distance a two-dimensional object will project into the Z axis):

```
Command: THICKNESS ⏎
```
Starts the THICKNESS variable

Step 6.1: Define the thickness equal to the material thickness:

```
New value for THICKNESS
<0.00>: .5 ⏎
```
Sets the thickness to .5, the same as the thickness of the extension in the drawing

You can now draw the polyline with thickness that defines the extension. Because you are going to be developing actual drawing geometry, return to the solid layer.

Step 7.0: Make the layer **SOLID** current.

You can now add the polyline seen in figure 12.7. The construction lines are used to define the start and end points of the polyline.

Step 8.0: Start the PLINE command and select the starting point:

```
Command: PLINE ⏎
```
Starts the PLINE command

From point: *Use object snap ENDpoint and pick point* Ⓐ *in figure 12.7*
Defines the starting point of the polyline

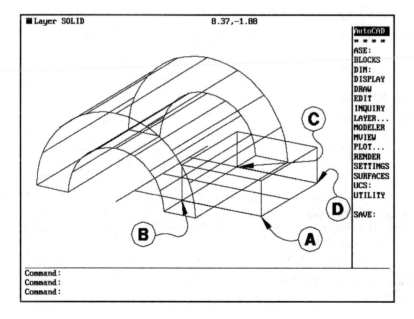

Figure 12.7:
Solid model with polyline extension.

Step 8.1: Select the next three end points of the polyline. The polyline appears in the drawing with a .5-unit thickness:

```
Current line-width is 0.00
```

`Arc/Close/Halfwidth/Length/Undo/` `Width/<Endpoint of line>:` *Use* *object snap INTersection and pick point* Ⓑ	Defines the second point of the polyline
`Arc/Close/Halfwidth/Length/Undo/` `Width/<Endpoint of line>:` *Use* *object snap INTersection and pick point* Ⓒ *in figure 12.7*	Defines the third point of the polyline
`Arc/Close/Halfwidth/Length/Undo/` `Width/<Endpoint of line>:` *Use* *object snap ENDpoint and pick point* Ⓓ *in figure 12.7*	Defines the forth point of the polyline

Step 8.2: Finish the process by using the Close option:

`Arc/Close/Halfwidth/Length/Undo/` `Width/<Endpoint of line>:` **C** ↵	Closes the polyline polygon

You now should have a polyline with thickness. At present, the polygon extends into the cylinder; this will be corrected after all the solid primitives are developed for both extensions in the drawing. You now need to convert the polyline to a solid. The SOLIDIFY command converts a polyline or circle with thickness into a solid primitive.

Step 9.0: Issue the SOLIDIFY command:

`Command:` *Choose* Model, *then* Solidify	Converts a 2D close entity with thickness into a solid

Step 9.1: Specify the object to convert into a solid primitive:

`Select objects:` *Select the polyline*	Selects the object to solidify
`Select objects:` ↵	Stops the SOLIDIFY command and converts the polyline to a solid primitive

You are now ready to add the circular primitives to the extension. These are concentric cylinders the centers of which are at the midpoint of the end of the linear extension. Use the Solid CYLINDER command twice to add these solid primitives.

Use the CYLINDER command to add the round top and hole to this primitive on the right side.

Step 10.0: Issue the Solid CYLINDER command, and specify the center point, radius, and height:

Command: *Choose* Model, *then* Primitives, *then* Box, *then* OK	Starts the CYLINDER command
Baseplane/Elliptical/<Center point> <0,0,0>: *Use object snap MIDpoint and pick point* (A) *in figure 12.8*	Defines the center of the cylinder
Diameter/<Radius>: .75 ↲	Defines the radius
Center of other end/<Height>: .5 ↲	Defines the cylinder height

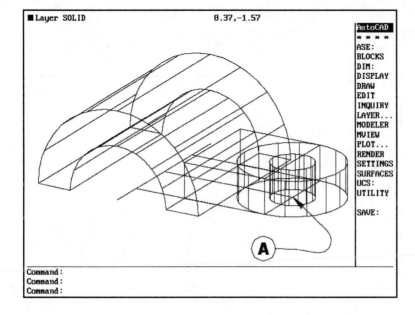

Figure 12.8:
Solid model with solid primitives for right extension.

A cylinder is created, based on the values you entered, that extends into the solid beside it. These intersections will be cleaned up after the extensions are added to both sides.

You now can add the cylinder that defines the hole in this extension.

Step 11.0: Issue the solid cylinder command, specify the center point, diameter, and height:

Command: *Choose* Model, *then* Primitives, *then* Cylinder, *then* OK	Starts the CYLINDER command
Baseplane/Elliptical/<Center point><0,0,0>: *Use object snap CENter and select the new cylinder*	Defines the center of the cylinder at the same center as the existing cylinder

```
Diameter/<Radius>: D ↵          Invokes the Diameter option
Diameter: .625 ↵                Defines the diameter
Center of other end/<Height>: .5 ↵   Defines the cylinder height
```

EXERCISE 4: COMPLETING THE SOLID MODEL

You now have all the solid primitives for one extension. You can mirror these objects across the center of the middle cylinder to add the extension on the other side. Afterward, you can modify the geometry into one solid model as seen in figure 12.9 by using UNION and SUBTRACT.

Figure 12.9:

Drawing with both extensions.

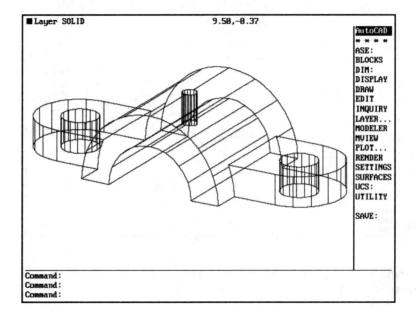

The final part of this modification is to add the hole seen in figure 12.9. You do this by defining a cylinder that extends well beyond both sides of the existing primitive. After you create it, the cylinder is subtracted from the source primitive, which leaves a hole.

TASKS TO BE COMPLETED IN THIS EXERCISE

- Mirror one extension
- Union solid primitives
- Subtract solid primitives
- Add a cylinder

Begin by using the MIRROR command to duplicate the right extension on the left side.

Step 1.0: Issue the MIRROR command and select the objects to mirror:

Command: **MIRROR** ↵	Starts the MIRROR command
Select objects: *Select the linear solid at Ⓐ (see fig. 12.10)*	Selects one object to mirror
Select objects: *Select the large cylinder at Ⓑ (see fig. 12.10)*	Selects a second object to mirror
Select objects: *Select the small cylinder at Ⓒ (see fig. 12.10)*	Selects the final object to mirror
Select objects: ↵	Stops the selection process

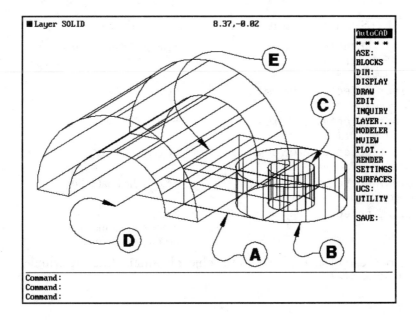

Figure 12.10:
Preparing to mirror solid primitives.

Step 1.1: Select the end points of the mirror line as the center of the half circles. Accept the default to not remove the old objects:

`First point of mirror line:` *Use object snap ENDpoint and pick point* Ⓓ *in figure 12.10*	Defines the first point of the mirror line
`Second point:` *Use object snap ENDpoint and pick point* Ⓔ *in figure 12.10*	Defines the second point of the mirror line
`Delete old objects? <N>` ↵	Specifies to keep the old objects

Now that you have the solid primitives that define both extensions, you are ready to finish the object. To do this, join geometry that should be one entity, and subtract any extra geometry.

You begin by using the UNION command to combine all the geometry that defines a solid entity. Geometry that represents holes is not selected.

The UNION command combines separate primitives into one. Any area occupied by both will be modified to make a proper transition between the two primitives.

Step 2.0: Issue the UNION command:

`Command:` *Choose* Model, *then* Union	Starts the UNION command

Step 2.1: Select the geometry that is one primitive in the model:

`Select objects:` *Select the half cylinder in the middle of the solid geometry*	Selects one solid to join
`Select objects:` *Select the linear solid in the right extension*	Selects another solid
`Select objects:` *Select the large cylinder in the right extension*	Selects another solid
`Select objects:` *Select the linear solid in the left extension*	Selects another solid
`Select objects:` *Select the large cylinder in the left extension*	Selects the final solid
`Select objects:` ↵	Stops the selection process and joins the five primitives into one

You now can place the holes in the object by subtracting the cylinders on both ends.

Step 3.0: Issue the SUBTRACT command. Select the source primitive and the primitive to be removed:

`Command:` *Choose* Model, *then* Subtract	Starts the SUBTRACT command
`Source objects...` `Select objects:` *Select the newly unioned solid primitive anywhere on the geometry*	Selects the object to have the primitive subtracted from
`Select objects:` ↵	Stops the selection process
`Objects to subtract from them...` `Select objects:` *Select the right small cylinder*	Selects one primitive Selects one primitive
`Select objects:` *Select the left small cylinder*	Selects the other primitive to remove
`Select objects:` ↵	Stops the selection process and completes the subtract operation

You can now finish the geometry by adding the hole through the top of the large half cylinder. To do this, you create a cylinder that goes through the half cylinder and extends beyond it. Even though the cylinder is much longer than necessary, its height does not matter because you subtract the primitive that passes through the solid primitive.

First, create the cylinder that projects through the existing primitive. Because this cylinder is directly in the center of the half cylinder, the construction line through the middle of the cylinder can be used as the center point. The diameter of the cylinder will be .25". The height is an arbitrary distance that projects beyond the boundaries of the cylinder.

Step 4.0: Issue the CYLINDER command. Select the starting point, enter a diameter, and a height:

`Command:` *Choose* Model, *then* Primitives, *then* Cylinder, *then* OK	Starts the CYLINDER command
`Baseplane/Elliptical/<Center point> <0,0,0>:` *Use object snap MIDpoint and select the line at* Ⓐ *(see fig 12.11)*	Defines the center of the cylinder at the middle of the half cylinders
`Diameter/<Radius>: D` ↵	Invokes the Diameter option
`Diameter: .25` ↵	Defines the diameter
`Center of other end/<Height>: 4` ↵	Defines the cylinder height beyond the edge of the half cylinder

Figure 12.11:

Solid with hole through top.

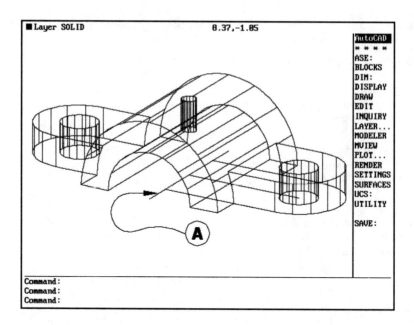

You can now use this new cylinder to create the hole in the large primitive. Again, use the SUBTRACT command to remove the primitive.

Step 5.0: Issue the SUBTRACT command and remove the small cylinder primitive from the large primitive:

`Command:` *Choose* Model, *then* Subtract	Starts the SUBTRACT command
`Source objects...` `Select objects:` *Select the large primitive anywhere on the geometry*	Selects the object from which the object is to be subtracted
`Select objects:` ⏎	Stops the selection process
`Objects to subtract from them...` `Select objects:` *Select the new long cylinder*	Selects the primitive to remove
`Select objects:` ⏎	Stops the selection process and completes the subtract operation

You are now finished with the solid model geometry. To complete the drawing, develop multiple views of the existing geometry. But before you continue, freeze the construction layer.

Step 6.0: Freeze the layer TEMP.

EXERCISE 5: CREATING MULTIPLE VIEWS

One advantage to creating any 3D drawing, whether it is a wire frame, surface model, or solid model, is the capability to view the geometry from any view. You can even create multiple views of a drawing on a single screen or piece of paper, as figure 12.12 illustrates. AutoCAD enables you to split the screen several different ways. From here you can change the viewpoint and geometry independently in the drawing.

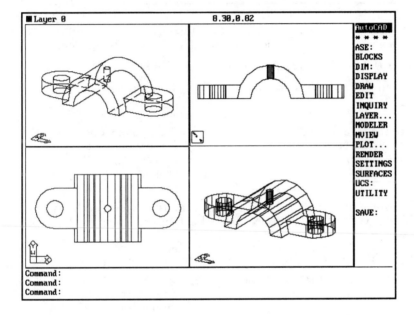

Figure 12.12:
Drawing with four views.

You begin by placing the drawing in paper space. Paper space toggles the drawing area from a three-dimensional world to a flat drawing plane. You will see a paper space icon in the lower left corner of the screen instead of a UCS icon, and the object in the drawing will disappear. To see your object after you change to paper space you must use MVIEW. MVIEW creates multiple viewports inside of paper space. These viewports can be manipulated to change the drawing viewpoints or scale. In addition, a wire frame profile can be developed. You have the option of showing the hidden lines in the profile as appropriate in the current viewpoint.

To begin, toggle tilemode off. This changes the drawing editor to paper space and enables you to develop multiple views of the model.

Step 1.0: Issue the Tilemode variable and toggle it off:

`Command:` *Choose* View, *then* Tilemode, *then* Off	Toggles to a flat paper space environment

`Entering Paper space.`
`Use MVIEW to insert Model`
`space viewports.`
	Places the drawing in paper space and the drawing disappears without viewports

To display the original geometry, insert multiple views in the drawing. Use the MVIEW command and develop four views that fit the entire screen.

Step 2.0: Issue the MVIEW command and define four viewports:

`Command:` *Choose* View, *then* Mview, *then* 4 Viewports	Starts the MVIEW command and defines the number of viewports to create

Step 2.1: Specify to fit the four views to the current screen:

`Fit/<First Point>:` **F** ↵	Fits the viewports to the screen

You will now see the same view in all four viewports. As you can see by the square in the lower left corner of the screen, the UCS icon has been replaced by a paper space icon. In paper space, you cannot modify the geometry. Paper space is similar to holding a piece of glass over the model. You can see the model and you can add geometry to the glass, but you cannot modify the actual model. Nor can you change its viewpoint. To manipulate the views independently, you must change to model space. The MSPACE command places you into a three-dimensional world inside each of the multiple views in paper space.

Step 3.0: Issue the MSPACE command:

Command: *Choose* View, *then* Model space   Toggles to model space

You will now see the UCS icon appear in each of the four views. In one view you will see cross hairs—this is the current view. In the other views you will see an arrow. To change between views, place the arrow in the desired view and press the input device button.

For the first operation in model space, change the view in viewport D (the lower left corner) to a plan view. To do this, first make this the active viewport, then use the PLAN command to display the geometry in a World Plan View:

Step 4.0: Change the active viewport:

Command: *Move the arrow to viewport*   Selects the active
Ⓓ *(see fig. 12.13) and press*   viewport
the input device pick button

Step 5.0: Use the PLAN command to change the view to a World Plan View:

Command: PLAN ↵   Starts the PLAN command

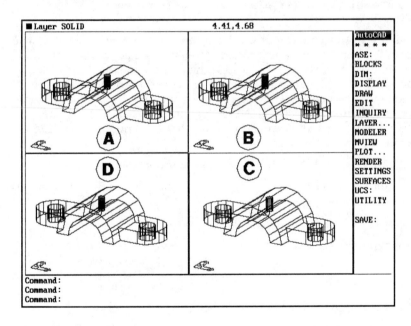

Figure 12.13:
Drawing with four labeled viewports.

```
<Current UCS>/Ucs/World: W ↵          Changes the
                                       viewpoint to a
                                       World Plan View
```

After this is complete, change the viewport in the upper right corner to a front view. You first select the active viewport, then use the VPOINT command to enter the options for the desired view.

Step 6.0: Change the active viewport:

```
Command: Move the arrow to viewport    Selects the active
ⒷB (see fig. 12.13) and press          viewport
the input device pick button
```

Step 7.0: Issue the VPOINT command and select a right side view:

```
Command: VPOINT ↵                      Starts the VPOINT
                                       command

Rotate/<View point>                    Selects the Rotate
<0.47,-0.81,0.34>:R ↵                  option
Enter angle in X-Y plane from X        Selects the front of
axis <300>: 270 ↵                      the object
Enter angle from X-Y plane             Selects a front
<20>: 0 ↵                              looking straight in
```

You now need to use the PROFILE command to take the object in the upper left corner view and convert it to a wire frame. Because this object has hidden lines, you must first load the desired linetype from disk using the LINETYPE command. By default, only the continuous linetype is loaded into a drawing. This has not been apparent in previous lessons because commands such as LAYER load linetypes as needed. The PROFILE command, however, requires that the linetype be loaded before it displays the different linetype.

Step 8.0: Issue the LINETYPE command and invoke the Load option:

```
Command: LINETYPE ↵                    Starts the LINETYPE command
?/Create/Load/Set: L ↵                 Invokes the Load option
```

Step 8.1: Use a wild card to load all the linetypes into the drawing:

```
Linetype(s) to load: * ↵              Specifies a wild card
                                       to load all linetypes
                                       (the Select Linetype File
                                       dialog box appears)
```

Step 8.2: Specify the file from which the linetypes will be loaded:

```
Choose ACAD, then OK                   Specifies the file ACAD
Command: ↵                            Ends LINETYPE
```

You now have all the linetypes loaded. To continue, make the upper left viewport active, then use the PROFILE command and the solid model to develop a wire frame with hidden lines.

Step 9.0: Change the active viewport:

Command: *Move the arrow to viewport* (A) *(see fig. 12.13) and press the input device pick button*	Selects the active viewport

You now are ready to develop a wire frame model from the profile (or edges) of the solid model.

Step 10.0: Issue the PROFILE command:

Command: *Choose* Model, *then* Display, *then* Profile Solids	Starts the PROFILE command

Step 10.1: Select the object to profile:

Select objects: *Select the primitive in the active viewport*	Selects the geometry from which to develop the wire frame
Select objects: ↵	Stops the selection process

Step 10.2: Accept the defaults to develop a wire frame with hidden lines projected against the viewport plane:

Display hidden profile lines on separate layer ? <Y>:↵	Generates hidden lines and places them on their own layer
Project profile lines onto a plane <Y>:↵	Develops the profile as 2D geometry on a plane
Delete tangential edges <Y>: ↵	Does not place lines between tangent objects

The new geometry appears in black and the solid model remains in blue. Next, you need to freeze the solid model in this view and keep only the new profile layers visible. You cannot use the LAYER command to perform this function because freezing the solid layer affects all the viewports. The VPLAYER or Vport Layer command enables you to modify layers independent of other viewports. The Layer Control dialog box also has a button for controlling layers within viewports.

Regardless of your using the VPLAYER command to freeze the solid layer in this viewport, you need to make another layer the current drawing layer before you can freeze the SOLID layer. Use the LAYER command or Layer Control dialog box to perform this function.

Step 11.0: Make layer 0 current.

You can now use the VPLAYER command to freeze the SOLID layer in the current viewport.

Step 12.0: Issue the VPLAYER command:

```
Command: VPLAYER ↵
```
Issues the VPLAYER command

Step 12.1: Invoke the Freeze option:

```
?/Freeze/Thaw/Reset/Newfrz/
Vpvisdflt: F ↵
```
Invokes the Freeze option

Step 12.2: Specify the layer to freeze:

```
Layer(s) to Freeze: SOLID ↵
```
Specifies the layer to freeze

Step 12.3: Specify that the SOLID layer is frozen in the current viewport only:

```
All/Select/<Current>: ↵
```
Accepts the default and freezes the layer in the current viewport only

Step 12.4: Exit the VPLAYER command:

```
?/Freeze/Thaw/Reset/Newfrz/
Vpvisdflt: ↵
```
Exits the VPLAYER command

You should see the profile of the solid model with hidden lines. You now need to scale each of the objects so they are the same size in all the viewports. You can use the MVSETUP command to perform this function. The MVSETUP command is an AutoLISP program that assists you in finalizing the appearance of multiple views.

Step 13.0: Start the MVSETUP command:

```
Command: Choose View, then Layout,
then MV Setup
```
Loads the AutoLISP program MVSETUP

Step 13.1: Invoke the Scale viewports option:

```
Align/Create/Scale viewports/
Options/Title block/Undo: S ↵
```
Invokes the scale viewports option

Step 13.2: Selects the viewports to scale by placing the pick box on the rectangle surrounding the view and pressing the input device button or by using a crossing window in the middle where the views meet:

```
Select the viewports to scale:
```
Select viewport Ⓐ *in figure 12.13*
Selects one viewport

```
Select the viewports to scale:
```
Select viewport Ⓑ *in figure 12.13*
Selects one viewport

```
Select the viewports to scale:        Selects one viewport
Select viewport Ⓒ in figure 12.13
Select the viewports to scale:        Selects one viewport
Select viewport Ⓓ in figure 12.13
Select objects: ↵                     Stops the selection process
```

Step 13.3: Invoke the Uniform option to scale all of the viewports at once and at the same scale:

```
Set zoom scale factors for           Accepts the Uniform option
viewports.Interactively/
<Uniform>: ↵
```

Step 13.4: Accept the default to scale the paper units equal to the model units:

```
Enter the ratio of paper space       Accept the unit of
units to model space units...        one for space units
Number of paper space units.
<1.0>: ↵
Number of model space units.         Leaves the scale at one to one
<1.0>: ↵
```

Step 13.5: Exit the MVSETUP command:

```
Align/Create/Scale viewports/        Exits the command
Options/Title block/Undo: ↵          and scales all
                                     objects in each view
                                     the same size
```

You now need to align your viewports inside each individual port. If this were an orthographic drawing, you could use the horizontal and vertical alignment option in the MVSETUP command. Because this is not, you can do each viewport individually using the PAN command. The PAN command enables you to change the visual position of an object on-screen without changing its zoom factor.

Step 14.0: Use the PAN command and reposition the geometry in the selected viewport. Issue the **PAN** command, pick a point from which to move visually (in the middle of the geometry), and then pick a point to visually move to (in the middle of the viewport). Continue until each view is similar to those previously in figure 12.13.

EXERCISE 6: SHADING A DRAWING

You are ready to shade the drawing, as shown in figure 12.14. You will do this by placing a mesh on the solid model and then using the SHADE command to change the appearance of the geometry.

Figure 12.14:

Final drawing with shaded primitive.

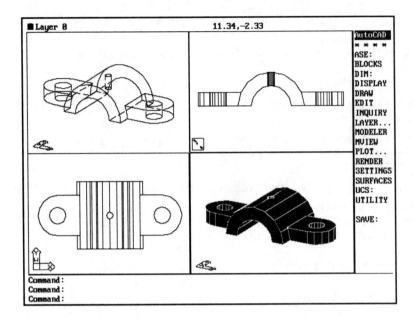

You first select the viewport to shade. Next, you use the MESH command to apply a solid mesh to the geometry. A *mesh* is a series of multi-edged opaque faces. These faces make the solid appear as a solid object. The solid model must have a mesh before a hidden line removal or shade operation can be performed. After a mesh is applied, the SHADE command develops a shaded model.

TASKS TO BE COMPLETED IN THIS EXERCISE

- Change the current viewport
- Mesh a solid primitive
- Shade a solid primitive

Begin by selecting the viewport that displays the primitive to mesh.

Step 1.0: Change the active viewport:

Command: *Move the arrow to viewport* © *(see fig. 12.13) and press the input device pick button*	Selects the active viewport

You can now add multi-edged faces across the solid model by using the MESH command. These are opaque surfaces used for shading or hiding a solid model.

Step 2.0: Start the MESH command:

`Command:` *Choose* Model, *then* Display, *then* Mesh	Starts the MESH command

Step 2.1: Select the object to mesh:

`Select objects:` *Select the object in the current viewport*	Selects the solid model to mesh
`Select objects:` ↵	Stops the selection process and applies a mesh to the primitive

You can now shade the drawing. The SHADE command creates a visually solid rendering of the surfaced drawing.

Step 3.0: Issue the SHADE command:

`Command:` *Choose* Render, *then* Shade	Starts the SHADE command and shades the drawing

You are finished with the drawing. Save the drawing to disk and exit AutoCAD.

Step 4.0: Save the drawing to disk and end the current drawing session.

SUMMARY

Solid model three-dimensional geometry is the most complex of all the 3D drawings. Through the utilization of primitive geometry shapes, you develop a 3D drawing that is mathematically representative of real-world geometry.

IN THIS LESSON, YOU LEARNED TO DO THE FOLLOWING:

- Develop solid model geometry
- Intersect, union, and subtract solid model geometry
- Divide the screen into viewports
- Profile a solid model
- Mesh a solid model
- Shade a solid model

In this lesson you completed the last drawing, which was a 3D solid model. If you want to become a proficient AutoCAD user, you must continue to use and apply the software in a working environment. As AutoCAD changes with each release, it gives you opportunities to enhance your skills on one the most sophisticated drawing packages available.

REVIEW

1. Draw a cylinder with a diameter of 2" and length of 4".

2. Draw a cylinder with the same center point of the cylinder in question one. Give this cylinder a diameter of 1" and a length of 2".

3. Subtract the cylinder in question two from the cylinder in question one.

4. Mesh the primitive in question three.

5. Shade the primitive in question four.

6. Draw a 4-by-4-by-4-inch box.

7. Center a sphere with a diameter of 2 on one corner of the box in question six.

8. Intersect the box and sphere in question seven.

9. Recall drawing REV13-1. Use **UNION** and **SUBTRACT** to make this a single solid primitive.

10. Using **TILEMODE** and **MVIEW**, show the drawing in REV13-1 in four different viewports. Show the primitive in each viewport at a different viewpoint, and make the object in the upper right corner a profile with hidden lines.

Symbols

(Ⓐ ...) (bubble points), 9
(*) asterisk, 348
("computer-specific") aspects, 5
("electronic drafting table"), 17
<viewpoint>(0,0,1) option, 369
<World> option, 373
? (display layers) option, 51, 134
? option, 373, 433
1 Segment option, 56
2P (two-point) option, 36
3D
   changing viewpoints, 368-371
   converting from 2D, 367-368
   dimensioning in, 394-403
   solid models, 451-455
   surface models, 407-408
      adding surfaces, 416-419
      setting up, 409-410
   wireframes
      adding text, 401
      drawing panes, 372-378
      setting up, 363-364
      table top, creating, 364-368
3P (three-point) option, 36
3point option, 373

A

absolute coordinates, drawing, 54-55
activating
   dimensioning mode, 86
   grids, 29
   Orthographic (Ortho) mode, 111
active layer, 52

adding
   arcs, center marks, 87-89
   baseline dimensions, 142-143
   center lines to drawings, 134
   chamfers to rectangles, 80-81
   chimneys, hatch patterns,
      336-338
   circular dimensions, 143-145
   construction lines to gears,
      154-156
   countertops, 353-354
   crosshatching, 178-187
   details to drawings, 133-139
   dimensions, 197-206
      horizontal linear, 140-141
      to spindles, 139
      tolerances, 201-203
   dynamic text to cam, 275-277
   end views to spindles, 130-133
   hatch patterns, 183-184
   keyway
      to cam, 266-269
      to gear drawing, 164-167
   linear dimensions to drawings,
      93-101
   text
      to drawings, 37-39
      to title block, 284-290
   text strings, 39-40
   vertical linear dimensions,
      100-101
Adjust Area Fill option, 245
Advanced Modeling Extension
   (AME), 451
Align option, 284-285
ALIgned dimensioning command,
   102
All option, 50

INDEX

E

Grid command, 15, 29
GRID commands, 209-212
grids, 27
    activating, 29
    size, 29
Grip modes, 271
grips, 251, 270-272

H

Halfwidth option, 180
hardware
    platforms, 16
    requirements, 6
HATCH command, 179-180,
    183-184
hatch patterns, adding to chimneys,
    336-338
Height option, 283
hidden lines, 67
    creating, 68
    removing, 447-448
Hidden linetype, 195
Hide Lines option, 246
horizontal (X) axis, 55
horizontal center lines, adding to
    gear drawings, 188-189
horizontal construction lines,
    112-115
Horizontal dimensioning command,
    358
HORizontal dimensioning
    command, 140
horizontal linear dimensions
    adding, 140-141
    creating, 94-101

I

Inches, MM option, 245
information boxes, 8-9
input, user, 7
input devices, 19
    mouse, 19
    puck, 19
    stylus, 19
inquiry commands, 4
INSERT command, 209, 236-238,
    348, 351
inserting
    architectural symbols into
      drawings, 353
    doors, 345-351
    libraries, symbol, 342-343
    symbols, 235-241, 348-350
      architectural, 343-344
      lower left corner, 240
      upper left corner, 237-239
    windows, 340-345
INSertion option, 64, 358
insertion points, 213, 219
    creating, 347-348
    defining, 340-345
Inside AutoCAD Release 12, 10
interior walls, creating, 325-334
INTERSECT command, 452
intersecting solid primitives,
    459-461
INTersection option, 64
isometric view, 365
Issue term, 9

J

Join option, 263, 294
Justify option, 37

K

keyboard shortcuts
   Ctrl-C (terminate command), 27
   F1 (graphics mode/text mode
     toggle), 49
   F8 (Orthographic mode), 111
keyway
   adding
     to cam, 266-269
     to gear drawing, 164-167
   dimensioning, 272-274
   duplicating, 270-271

L

large rectangles, drawing, 30-32
Last option, 59
lavatory symbol, drawing, 308
LAYER command, 51, 109
   defining, 52-53
   options, 51
Layer Control dialog box, 51, 67,
   109
layers
   active, 52
   countertops, modifying, 340
   creating, 67
   defining, 51-52
   modifying, 67

LEAder dimensioning subcommand,
   198, 203
Left option, 50
Length option, 180
libraries, Symbol
   drawing, 307-321
   saving, 320
   inserting, 342-343
limits
   drawings, 49
   viewing, 50-51
LIMITS command, 49
Limits option, 245
LINE command, 351
Line command, 15, 22
linear dimensions
   adding to drawings, 93-101
   horizontal, creating, 94-101
   vertical, 100-101
lines, 22
   ("ghosted"), 23
   center, extending, 136-139
   construction, 108
     creating, 131
     horizontal, 112-115
     trimming, 119-121
     vertical, 115-118
   constructions, deleting, 119
   creating, 22
   drawing, 23, 111
   hidden, 67
     creating, 68
     removing, 447-448
   mirror, 108
   rubberband, 23
Linetype command, 133, 139
   options, 134
linetypes, changing, 195-197

MIDpoint, 64
Multiple, 91
NEArest, 64
New, 51
NODe, 64
Object Snap, 64
Obliquing angle, 283
OFF, 51
Offset, 322
ON, 51
Oops, 59
Open, 263
Optimization, 245
Origin, 245, 373
Pen Assignments, 245
PERpendicular, 64, 170
Plot area, 245
Plot to file, 245
Plotted Inches = Drawing Units, 246
Prev, 373
Preview, 246
Previous, 50
QUAdrant, 64, 170
Radius, 36
Restore, 373, 433
Rotate, 369
Rotation, 245
Save, 373, 433
Scale, 50
Scale(X/XP), 50
Scaled to Fit, 246
Segments, 56
Select, 59
Set, 51, 134
Single, 59
Sketch, 56
Snap, 322

Spline, 263
Start Point, 322
Start point, 37
Style, 37
TANgent, 64
Text command, 37
Text style name, 283
Thaw, 52
TTR (tangent, tangent, radius), 36
Undo, 180, 263, 322
Unlock, 52
Upside-down?, 283
Vertical?, 283
View, 245, 373
Vmax, 50
Width, 180, 263, 322
Width factor, 283
Window, 50, 245, 433
X, 373
Y, 373
Z, 373
ZAxis, 373, 391
ZOOM command, 50
Origin option, 245, 373
origins of dimensions, 142
Orthographic (Ortho) mode, activating, 111
outside walls, drawing, 323-324

P

PDMODE system variable, 255
PEDIT command, 262-264, 421
Pen Assignments option, 245
perimeters walls, drawing, 321-325
PERpendicular option, 64, 170

tolerances, adding to dimensions,
201-203
training centers, 11
transistor symbols
arrowheads, 217-219
circles, 216-217
creating, 219-220
drawing, 212-220
lines, 213-215
TRIM command, 279, 351
Trim command, 119-125, 348
trimming
construction lines, 119-121
entities, 119-125
TTR (tangent, tangent, radius)
option, 36

U

UCS command, 373
UNDO command, 32, 57
Undo option, 180, 263, 322
UNION command, 452
units, specifying, 47
UNITS command, 47, 109, 321
Units Control dialog box, 109, 321
Unlock option, 52
Upside-down? option, 283
user input, 7
user interface, 13-15

V

values, displacement, 367
variables
dimension
architectural drawings,
356-358
architectural standards, 356
configuring, 86-87
DIMASZ, 140
DIMCEN, 140
DIMTXT, 140
scaling, 357
system, COORDS, 29
vertical construction lines,
offsetting, 115-118
Vertical dimensioning command,
358
vertical
linear dimensions, adding to
drawings, 100-101
section lines, adding to gear
drawings, 190-191
VERtical subcommand, 100
Vertical? option, 283
VIEW command, 433
View option, 245, 373
viewing drawings
limits, 50-51
Zoom command, 89-90
viewpoints
changing in 3D, 368-371
setting, 454-455
views
isometric, 365
multiple, creating, 473-479
plan, 362

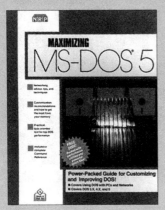

You'll Find All You Need To Know About Graphics with Books from New Riders!

Inside Generic CADD
New Riders Publishing

This is the only book for professional and affordable computer-assisted drafting and design! It's heavily illustrated and referenced—covering every command. Easy-to-follow tutorial exercises make learning fast.

Through Version 5.0

1-56205-001-X, 544 pp., 7³/₈ x 9¹/₄
$29.95 USA

Inside Autodesk Animator
Leah Freiwald & Lee Marrs

Here is your complete guide to Autodesk Animator! With tutorials and powerful user techniques, this book is the perfect resource for anyone who animates. Includes complete reference tables and charts.

Video Paint, Image Processing, & Animation

0-934035-76-8, 480 pp., 7³/₈ x 9¹/₄
$29.95 USA

Inside AutoSketch, 2nd Edition
Frank Lenk

This is the perfect guide to AutoSketch's extensive graphics capabilities! Full of tips, techniques, and examples for drafting and technical drawing, the text provides guidelines for producing industry-standard drawings. Covers mechnical, schematic, architectural, and other standard drawings.

Versions 2 & 3

0-934035-96-2, 384 pp., 7³/₈ x 9¹/₄
$24.95 USA

Inside CorelDRAW!, 3rd Edition
Daniel Gray

Here is the practical introduction to computer-aided graphic design! The text details what users need for excellent results and includes dozens of hands-on examples and tutorials for using CorelDRAW! with Windows programs. The book includes a disk containing fonts, clip art, and Windows utilities programs.

Through Release 2.1

56205-139-7, 700 pp., 7³/₈ x 9¹/₄
$4.95 USA

CorelDRAW! On Command
New Riders Publishing

This book is the graphical approach to using CorelDRAW! The text contains over 100 reference entries organized by task. A special binding allows the book to lie flat for easy referencing.

Through Release 2.1

1-56205-042-7, 140 pp., 6³/₄ x 8¹/₂
$19.95 USA

To Order, Call: (800) 428-5331 OR (317) 573-2500

NRP
NEW RIDERS PUBLISHING

Add to Your New Riders Library Today
with the Best Books for the Best Software

Yes, please send me the productivity-boosting material I have checked below. Make check payable to New Riders Publishing.

❏ **Check enclosed.**

Charge to my credit card:

❏ **VISA**   ❏ **MasterCard**

Card # _____

Expiration date: _____

Signature: _____

Name: _____

Company: _____

Address: _____

City: _____

State: _____ ZIP: _____

Phone: _____

The easiest way to order is to pick up the phone and call 1-800-541-6789 between 9:00 a.m. and 5:00 p.m., EST. Please have your credit card available, and your order can be placed in a snap!

Quantity	Description of Item	Unit Cost	Total Cost
	Inside CorelDRAW!, 2nd Edition	$29.95	
	AutoCAD 3D Design & Presentation*	$29.95	
	Maximizing Windows 3 (Book-and-Disk set)	$39.95	
	Inside AutoCAD, Special Edition (for Releases 10 and 11)*	$34.95	
	Maximizing AutoCAD: Volume I (Book-and-Disk set) Customizing AutoCAD with Macros and Menus	$34.95	
	AutoCAD for Beginners	$19.95	
	Inside Autodesk Animator*	$29.95	
	Maximizing AutoCAD: Volume II (Book-and-Disk set) Inside AutoLISP	$34.95	
	Inside AutoSketch, 2nd Edition*	$24.95	
	AutoCAD Reference Guide, 2nd Edition	$14.95	
	AutoCAD Reference Guide on Disk, 2nd Edition	$14.95	
	Inside CompuServe (Book-and-Disk set)	$29.95	
	Managing and Networking AutoCAD*	$29.95	
	Inside AutoCAD, Release 11, Metric Ed. (Book-and-Disk set)	$34.95	
	Maximizing MS-DOS 5 (Book-and-Disk set)	$34.95	
	Inside Generic CADD*	$29.95	
	Inside Windows	$29.95	
	AutoCAD Bible	$39.95	
	*Companion Disk available for these books	$14.95 ea.	

❏ **3½″ disk**

❏ **5¼″ disk**

Shipping and Handling: See information below.	
TOTAL	

Shipping and Handling: $4.00 for the first book and $1.75 for each additional book. Floppy disk: add $1.75 for shipping and handling. If you need to have it NOW, we can ship product to you in 24 to 48 hours for an additional charge, and you will receive your item overnight or in two days. Add $20.00 per book and $8.00 for up to three disks overseas. Prices subject to change. Call for availability and pricing information on latest editions.

New Riders Publishing • 11711 N. College Avenue • P.O. Box 90 • Carmel, Indiana 46032
1-800-541-6789   1-800-448-3804
Orders/Customer Service   FAX

To order: Fill in the reverse side, fold, and mail